Gertrude Stein's Transmasculinity

Chris Coffman

EDINBURGH
University Press

Edinburgh University Press is one of the leading university presses in the UK. We publish academic books and journals in our selected subject areas across the humanities and social sciences, combining cutting-edge scholarship with high editorial and production values to produce academic works of lasting importance. For more information visit our website: edinburghuniversitypress.com

Edinburgh University Press Ltd
The Tun – Holyrood Road,
12(2f) Jackson's Entry,
Edinburgh EH8 8PJ

First published in hardback by Edinburgh University Press 2018

Typeset in 11/14 Adobe Sabon by
IDSUK (DataConnection) Ltd, and
printed and bound by CPI Group (UK) Ltd,
Croydon, CRO 4YY

A CIP record for this book is available from the British Library

ISBN 978 1 4744 3809 4 (hardback)
ISBN 978 1 4744 3810 0 (paperback)
ISBN 978 1 4744 3811 7 (webready PDF)
ISBN 978 1 4744 3812 4 (epub)

Contents

Illustrations

Figures

Plates

Plate 2 Pablo Picasso, *Les Demoiselles d'Avignon* (1907). Oil on canvas. Acquired through the Lillie P. Bliss Bequest. © 2018 Estate of Pablo Picasso / Artists Rights Society (ARS), New York. Digital Image copyright © The Museum of Modern Art/Licensed by SCALA / Art Resource, NY.

Plate 3 Pablo Picasso, *Homage a Gertrude* (1909, *sic*). Tempera on wood. Gilbert A. Harrison Collection of Material by and Relating to Gertrude Stein (Collection 2108). UCLA Library Special Collections, Charles E. Young Research Library, UCLA. © 2018 Estate of Pablo Picasso / Artists Rights Society (ARS), New York.

Plate 4 Pablo Picasso, *The Architect's Table* (1912). Oil on canvas mounted on panel. The Museum of Modern Art, New York City, The William S. Paley Collection. Digital Image © The Museum of Modern Art/Licensed by SCALA / Art Resource, NY. © 2018 Estate of Pablo Picasso / Artists Rights Society (ARS), New York.

Plate 5 Edouard Manet, *Le déjeuner sur l'herbe* (1863). Oil on canvas. RF 1668. Musée d'Orsay, Paris, donation by Etienne Moreau-Nelaton in 1906. Digital image licensed by SCALA / Art Resource, NY.

Acknowledgements

Although I first sowed the seeds of what would eventually become *Gertrude Stein's Transmasculinity* during a summer 2006 National Endowment for the Humanities seminar on 'Modernist Paris' led by Maria diBattista and Suzanne Nash, sustained work on this book began in earnest during a 2011–12 academic year sabbatical leave awarded by the University of Alaska Fairbanks. Viewing the *Seeing Gertrude Stein* and *The Stein Collects* exhibits along with related cultural events in San Francisco in summer 2011 sparked my thinking about the relationship between Stein's transmasculinity and her work as both a writer and an art collector, prompting me to take *Gertrude Stein's Transmasculinity* in an interdisciplinary direction. Along the way, this project has benefited from conversations with Sine Anahita, Melissa Bradshaw, Lee Callahan, Deborah Cohler, Merrill Cole, Madelyn Detloff, Melina Draper, Jonathan Eburne, Mat Fournier, Octavio González, Jordana Greenblatt, Karen Grossweiner, Len Gutkin, Cindy Hardy, Eileen Harney, Maureen Hogan, Stephanie Hsu, Shayle Hutchison, Alla Ivanchikova, Shawna Lipton, E. L. McCallum, Judith Roof, Patricia Juliana Smith, William Spurlin, Kayt Sunwood, Robert Tobin and Annalisa Zox-Weaver, as well as from responses from peer reviewers and attendees at conferences at which I presented early versions of these materials. Sessions organised by the International Comparative Literature Association's Comparative Gender Studies Committee at ICLA and ACLA conferences have proven particularly generative, and I am grateful for the community I have found there. I have also benefited from travel funding from United Academics AAUP/AFT Local 4996, the University of Alaska Fairbanks College of Liberal Arts, the UAF English Department, and the UAF Women, Gender, and Sexuality Studies Program to present early versions of these materials. Special thanks are due to CLA Dean Todd Sherman for continuing to provide me with time to complete this study. *Gertrude Stein's Transmasculinity* would also not have been possible without the pioneering work of Stein scholars before me, in particular the archival research of Ulla Dydo, Wanda Corn and Tirza True Latimer. Above all, this book and my life would have been far more difficult without the support of my parents: James P. Coffman, who passed away before I saw *Gertrude Stein's Transmasculinity* into print; and Anne W. Coffman, who encouraged me to persist and was my sounding board as I finalised its contents.

The Interlibrary Loan department at UAF has provided vital assistance in obtaining items cited in this book; thanks especially to Brad Krick for his assistance over the years. The staff at Yale University's Beinecke Library and the John F. Kennedy Library's Ernest Hemingway Collection proved equally helpful. Georgia Glover at David Higham Literary, Film and TV Agents facilitated permission to quote from Gertrude Stein's unpublished notebooks held at the Beinecke Library as well as several other works; Yessenia Santos of Simon & Schuster and Kirk Curnutt of the Ernest Hemingway Society arranged permission for excerpts from several of his texts. The two epigraphs from Hemingway at the beginning of Chapter 6 are from ERNEST HEMINGWAY, SELECTED LETTERS 1917–1961 by Carlos Barker, editor, Copyright © 1981 by Carlos Baker and The Ernest Hemingway Foundation, Inc. Reprinted with permission of Scribner, a division of Simon & Schuster, Inc. All rights reserved. For help with obtaining images, I thank Sara Azam and Melissa Barton of Yale University's Beinecke Library; Erin Beasley at the Smithsonian Institution's National Portrait Gallery; Dorran Boyle at Scripps College's Denison Library; Meghan Brown of Art Resource; Conna Clark in the Philadelphia Museum of Art Library and Archives; Andrea Felder at The New York Public Library; Molly Haigh in Library Special Collections at the Charles E. Young Research Library at UCLA; Lynda Kachurek in Rare Books and Special Collections at the University of Richmond's Boatwright Memorial Library; and Etheleen Staley of the Staley-Wise Gallery. For approving my requests for permission to reprint images, I thank Edward Burns of the Carl Van Vechten Trust; Denise Faïfe of the Musée d'Orsay; Todd Leibowitz of the Artists Rights Society; and Joshua Lynes of the Estate of George Platt Lynes. A generous subvention granted by Larry Hinzman in the UAF Office of the Vice Chancellor for Research enabled me to include many of these excerpts and images in *Gertrude Stein's Transmasculinity*; special thanks to Cassie Pinkel in the Office of the Vice Chancellor for Research for her advice and extensive assistance.

Portions of *Gertrude Stein's Transmasculinity* were originally published elsewhere. An early version of Chapter 4 appeared in *Arizona Quarterly* 70:4 (2014), and a different iteration of Chapter 3 was first published as 'Reading Stein's Genders: Transmasculine Signification in the 1910s and 1920s' in *Texas Studies in Literature and Language* 59:1 (2017), pp. 1–27. Copyright © by the University of Texas Press. Thanks to *Arizona Quarterly* and *TSLL* for permission to republish.

Introduction: Gertrude Stein's Transmasculinity

> Rather than looking for literal transsexuals in the modernist past, . . . we might look to modernist literature as offering new narratives of embodiment that enable new configurations of gender and sexual identity.
>
> Pamela Caughie, on Virginia Woolf's *Orlando*

> It takes time to make queer people, and to have others who can know it.
>
> Gertrude Stein, *The Making of Americans*

The Parisian salon hosted by Gertrude Stein and Alice B. Toklas was unique among queer modernist spaces. Unlike Natalie Barney's salon emphasising women, femininity and Sapphic identity or the cosmopolitan Paris of queer outcasts surveyed in 'John' Radclyffe Hall's 1928 *The Well of Loneliness*, Stein's and Toklas's avant-garde salon did not take sexual orientation or gender identity as its organising principle, despite its hosts' queer presence.[1] Their salon was nonetheless a crucial transactional point in the establishment of Stein's queer persona and her development as an experimental writer. I say 'persona' rather than 'identity' not only because of the contemporary significance of 'queer' as an anti-identity marker, and not only because 'queer' as an indicator of sexual orientation was not deployed and politicised in the early twentieth century as it is now, but also because – unlike, for example, Barney's space – Stein's and Toklas's salon did not seek to organise a community defined by a specific sexual orientation or gender identity. Their salon did, however, bring together key avant-garde and modernist innovators, and in so doing, consolidated an aspect of Stein's subjectivity that served as a conduit for her queerness: her sense of herself as a genius among geniuses.

Stein once wrote of Pablo Picasso, Henri Matisse and herself that the two men have 'a maleness that belongs to genius. Moi aussi, perhaps.'[2] Stein's early association of her 'genius' with 'maleness' points to the way the salon allowed her to act out – and organise her social and artistic life around – a form of transmasculinity inscribed through homosociality with other 'geniuses'.[3] However, 'genius' is an unstable concept in her work: as Karen Cope, Jaime Hovey, Aidan Thompson and Barbara Will demonstrate, Stein's writings undercut myths about the autonomy of the 'genius'.[4] The indeterminate play of pronouns in her most experimental texts mirrors the instability of the visual signs through which her masculinity was manifested throughout her lifetime.[5] Rearticulating 'genius' as a form of masculinity that need not be attached to a male body, Stein shakes up its late nineteenth- and early twentieth-century association with both maleness and homosexuality.[6] 'Genius', 'maleness' and 'masculinity' are not words that point to stable ontologies in her life or writings, for – as Judith Roof observes – 'individual genderings are always multiple, changing', and 'idiosyncratic'.[7] But however varied in their implications, signifiers of masculinity did persist throughout Stein's lifetime, cropping up not only in her and others' writing but also in images of her person.

In training my lens on signs of Stein's masculinity, I seek to cast it in a favourable light – as similar to contemporary transmasculinities. By 'transmasculinity', I refer to a broad range of masculine traits in persons assigned female at birth. My choice of terminology encompasses not only those who embody what Halberstam calls 'female masculinity' but also those who consider themselves transgender or transsexual.[8] Moreover, it includes those who understood their masculinity in relation to earlier constructs of gender variance (such as late nineteenth- and early twentieth-century 'inverts') or who fashioned their own style of masculinity outside of any official discourses.

I nonetheless do not situate Stein on a 'continuum' of transmasculinities in order to categorise her.[9] As Halberstam points out, gender 'categories are constantly under construction', subject to revision, and often difficult to distinguish from one another.[10] Moreover, Stein eventually came to reject the early twentieth-century gender ideologies that initially attracted her, such as Otto Weininger's pseudoscientific claims to masculine superiority in *Sex and Character* (1903). She does not fit easily within any dominant gender 'regime', whether early twentieth century or contemporary.[11] I thus use the term 'transgender' in its broadest possible sense: to argue that Stein embodied what Susan Stryker describes as a 'variation from gender norms and expectations', and to assert that she fit Stephen Whittle's expansive definition of transgender by living 'at odds with' the designation '"woman"' assigned by 'formal authorities'.[12] Although I do not assert that Stein had what we would now call a transgender *identity*, I do argue that she lived out – and eventually came to articulate – a unique mode of transmasculine *subjectivity* that enabled her copious literary production as well as her relationships with Toklas and her masculine colleagues.

Theorising Stein's transsubjectivity

In analysing Stein's masculinity and its implications for her varied relationships, *Gertrude Stein's Transmasculinity* operates in the tradition of queer and trans-theory that 'queers historicist imperatives'.[13] As Carla Freccero explains, these theories eschew the 'notion of empirical history' and affirm the role of 'fantasy and ideology . . . in the production of "fantasmatic" historiography as a way to get at how subjects live'.[14] Readers' libidinal investments have always been – and will continue to be – implicated in shifting understandings of Stein's masculinity. As Ellis Hanson argues, 'the historicizing imperative is itself an erotic function, a paradox or conundrum, deeply invested in fantasy and an unconscious drive to represent or even narrate a fundamentally inaccessible Real or historical origin'.[15] Caught up in the delirium Jacques Derrida calls 'archive fever', apparently impartial historiographical approaches are confounded by the 'interminable' compulsion 'never to rest . . . from searching for the archive right where it slips away'.[16] Because this process is unceasing and subtended by 'fantasies', nobody can really 'see gender for what it is', as Roof reminds us.[17] Deploying 'historiography . . . as a mode of fantasy', I do not claim to examine Stein's masculinity objectively.[18] Instead, I embrace the spirit of Stein's own *The Autobiography of Alice B. Toklas* (1932: 1933), which – as Sashi Nair notes – calls 'into question the division between objectivity and subjectivity, and between fiction and autobiography'.[19]

Rather than fall prey to the fantasy of objectivity motivating straight historicism, I engage in the trenchant interrogation of gender and embodiment for which Stryker and Paisley Currah call in the introduction to the 2014 inaugural issue of *TSQ*. They assert that

> While it would be anachronistic to label a previous era's departures from currently normative expressions of gender as 'transgender' in an identitarian sense, there is another sense in which *transgender* as a critical term demarcates a conceptual space within which it becomes possible to (re)name, (dis)articulate, and (re)assemble the constituent elements of contemporary personhood in a manner that facilitates a deeply historical analysis of the utter contingency and fraught conditions of intelligibility of all embodied subjectivity. It can be used to pose new comparative questions about gender difference over geographic space as well as over historical time.[20]

These questions press when they concern Stein, who gradually rejected early twentieth-century discourses of gender that initially attracted her. Although she lived when 'Sapphism' was all the rage and the 'invert' had become 'a species', she never securely attached herself to any culturally legible gender formation.[21] Even her initial attraction to Weininger's claims about masculine superiority – which were behind her tentative assertion of 'a maleness that belongs to genius' – quickly faded during her years as a budding novelist.[22] The mutability of Stein's early identification with hegemonic masculinity bears out Patricia Elliot's and Katrina Roen's observation that 'although a person's gender identity and expression are not separable from socially and historically dominant representations of gender, neither are they reducible to those representations of gender'.[23]

Moreover, in the middle of the 1930s, Stein explicitly rejected the concept of identity, suggesting in texts such as *The Geographical History of America* (1935: 1936), 'Identity A Poem' (1935: 1940), and *Everybody's Autobiography* (1936: 1937) that it is nothing but a 'puppet show'.[24] As Charles Bernstein notes, Stein's 'triple marginalization' from dominant early twentieth-century constructs of 'gender, sexual orientation', and 'ethnicity . . . provided an ontological grounding for her' rejection of available identity categories.[25] *Gertrude Stein's Transmasculinity* is thus not grounded in any of the narrowly identitarian gender classifications characterising late twentieth- and early twentieth-century discourse. I neither use the words 'transgender' and 'transmasculine' to make an ontological claim about Stein's 'gender identity' nor to suggest that she simply moved from one side of the gender binary to the other, as if masculinity were singular and gender could be reduced to only two options. Rather, I do so to unleash what Eve Kosofsky Sedgwick describes as the 'multiply transitive' potential of the word 'queer', a potential also implied by the prefix 'trans-'.[26] Stryker, Paisley Currah and Lisa Jean Moore advocate the use of '[t]rans-' because the dash avoids 'nominalism' and leaves the prefix's meaning 'open-ended'.[27] Like Sedgwick's 'queer', 'trans-'s' future movements are open to difference yet not permanently attached to any position. And like Sara Ahmed's *Queer Phenomenology*, 'trans-' invokes 'the body's orientation in space and time', articulating an unpredictably 'transitive' embodiment.[28] With this understanding of the mobility of 'trans-' in view, I employ the word 'transmasculinity' to call attention to the shifting and anti-identitarian forms of subjectivity Stein articulated in her life and writings.

In so doing, I register the ways Stein's multiple manifestations of masculinity 'resonated' with yet diverged from officially sanctioned early twentieth-century and contemporary genders.[29] In view of Kate Thomas's argument for the importance of attending to 'the resonances that both produce and emanate from queer alliances between cross-temporal texts' despite differences between historical contexts, I aim to differentiate instead of flatten what Elizabeth Freeman calls time's 'wrinkles and folds'.[30] *Gertrude Stein's Transmasculinity* therefore positions Stein's transmasculinity – formed when both homosexuality and cross-gender identification were theorised as 'inversion' – as *akin to* but not *identical to* early twentieth-century, mid-century and contemporary genders. This avoids assuming that masculinity's forms and significance are consistent even as I highlight Stein's trans-generational kinship with past and present transmasculine persons.

As Stryker and Aren Z. Aizura observe, transgender studies not only asks us to avoid 'the presentist fallacy of ontologizing a current framework and imposing it on the strangeness of the past' but also 'compels attention to emergent forms of relationality involving novel types of social actors'.[31] Gayle Salamon further argues through recourse to psychoanalysis and phenomenology that trans- embodiment should not be reduced to the body's material contours but should be understood as a felt sense that emerges as 'a product of relation' to others.[32] This transsubjectivity is relational and depends upon recognition even as it splits the subject. Although the desire to transition or the act of transitioning may be important to some forms of transsubjectivity, Salamon stresses the importance of transpeoples' lived experiences of gender as they play out in various relationships and communities. This capacious account of transsubjectivity is especially useful for theorising the gendered embodiments of those who do (or did) not have access to technologies for sex reassignment or who do (or did) not wish to transition. Although rudimentary techniques for sex reassignment were just becoming available during Stein's lifetime, she expressed no interest in transitioning.[33] Nonetheless, she engaged in multiple 'forms of relationality' that contributed to her shifting transmasculinity in ways that were both internal and external.[34] In focusing on the dual axes of Stein's relationship with Toklas and her masculine homosocial bonds with her colleagues, *Gertrude Stein's Transmasculinity* tracks the ways these ties allowed Stein to fashion an unique and anti-identitarian kind of transmasculinity. Her engagements with others entailed a variety of modes of transmasculine subjectivity she lived out relationally.

The anti-identitarian term 'subjectivity' is important to this approach to Stein's gender. As Freccero explains, this word 'brings together, rather than once again solidifying the divide between, psychoanalysis and other analytics'.[35] Numerous forms of relationality allowed Stein's transmasculine subjectivity to shift in response to the many kinds of queer bonds in which she engaged. Her literary texts and unpublished notebooks suggest that she saw her masculine positionings as bound up with her erotic and masculine homosocial desires. By arguing that her transmasculinity was not an identity but rather a relational mode of shifting subjectivity, *Gertrude Stein's Transmasculinity* registers the interplay between the psychical and the social that took place as she lived out her gender in various contexts. As Roof explains, 'gender is the constant and provisional adjustment an individual makes among objects, desires, and identifications'.[36] Circuits of desire engender forms of gender that cannot be reduced to stable identities but rather split the subject, rendering it internally divided: multiple and conflicted rather than singular and self-identical.

This account of gendered subjectivity informs Salamon's theory of transgender embodiment and entails the same undercuttings of identity as queer theory. As Diana Fuss notes, 'identity is continually compromised, imperiled, one might even say *embarrassed* by identification' because of 'the capacity of identifications continually to evolve and change, to slip and shift under the weight of fantasy and ideology'.[37] Moreover, as Freccero explains, '[s]ubjectivity . . . continues problematically to trouble even queerly deconstructed identitarian and identificatory logics insofar as subjectivity relates only obliquely or metonymically, if at all, to totalizable bodies and agencies' and 'binaristic systems of understanding'.[38] Thus if Fuss is right that identification is 'mobile, elastic and volatile', then 'the meaning of a particular identification critically exceeds the limits of its social, historical, and political determinations'.[39] Even though Stein's masculinity invites comparison to early twentieth-century and contemporary constructs, the transmasculine identifications that subtended her subjectivity make her gender irreducible to any historically specific identity formation.

Instead, Stein's masculinity subsists within what Freeman calls 'structures of belonging and duration that may be invisible to the historicist eye'.[40] Stein's modernism 'trafficked in signs of fractured time. Its signature was interruptive archaisms: flickering signs of other historical moments'.[41] The contrast between her avant-garde posture in *The Autobiography* and her remark in *Paris France* (1939: 1940) about 'how necessary it is to be completely conservative that is particularly traditional in order to be free' suggests that she fashioned her masculinity within 'the double-time of the late nineteenth and early twentieth centuries'.[42] As Stein was well aware, this temporal redoubling 'makes confusion'.[43] In 'How Writing Is Written' (1934–5: 1938), she writes that

> everybody in his generation has his sense of time which belongs to his crowd. But then, you always have the memory of what you were brought up with. In most people that makes a double time . . . When one is beginning to write he is always under the shadow of the thing that is just past. And that is the reason why the creative person always has the appearance of ugliness.[44]

Similar reflections on memory's perils animate Stein's questioning of identity in *Everybody's Autobiography*. Unlike other early twentieth-century queer writers such as Hall, whose *The Well* features a protagonist who uses fine menswear to signify transmasculinity, Stein relied heavily upon context and temporal disjuncture rather than current men's fashions to establish her gender. This bears out Freeman's observation that 'the manipulation of time' can be 'a way to produce both bodies and relationalities'.[45] Before World War I, Stein's masculinity was legible through her avant-garde robes' similarity to her brother Leo Stein's clothing and their contrast to dominant feminine styles.[46] Later, in a move that simultaneously recalled fallen empires and lagged behind dominant early twentieth-century women's hairstyles, she refashioned her persona by using what Wanda Corn and

Tirza True Latimer call her 'Julius Caesar' crop to contrast with Toklas's 'hyperfemininity'.[47] Although figures such as Ernest Hemingway perceived these changes as rendering Stein ugly – in *A Moveable Feast* (1964, 2009) he has Hadley look askance at Stein's 'steerage clothes' and subsequently claims that her short haircut made her look like a 'Roman emperor' – others embraced the redoubled temporality that shifted the ways Stein was seen.[48]

Stein's 1926 crop made her and Toklas look 'decidedly like a traditional male and female couple', as Corn and Latimer note.[49] As Leigh Gilmore argues, Stein and Toklas staged themselves as a butch-femme couple of the sort described by Sue-Ellen Case: their stylised opposition of masculinity and femininity established, made visible, and camped up their gender and sexuality. A limitation of Case's theory, however, is that it makes masculinity and femininity legible only in distinction from one another. The influence of this thinking on Stein scholarship has had the salutary effect of highlighting the importance of her relationship with Toklas to her masculine image. However, this explanation has obscured other ways Stein's masculinity developed. *Gertrude Stein's Transmasculinity* reads Stein's transmasculinity as formed through both her desire for Toklas and her masculine homosocial desires for her colleagues.

By reading Stein's gender as transmasculine, I challenge the assumption that she identified as a woman, which prevails in scholarship approaching her life and work through lesbian studies. Troubling Stein's relationship to categories such as 'female' and 'woman' allows me to decouple her masculinity – and her and Toklas's relationship – from past and present identity categories. I thus distinguish her masculinity not only from early twentieth-century genders but also from more recent identities such as 'butch' and 'lesbian'. Yet given her longstanding relationship with Toklas and public presentation as female, I do not mean to suggest that readings that position her texts as examples of lesbian or 'Sapphic' literature are implausible; her life and writings offer ample support for such arguments. Scholarship that situates Stein as a precursor to mid-century and contemporary butches has also counteracted early studies that stigmatised her masculinity. I nonetheless seek to reframe such work with an eye to the possibility that her subjectivity might have been transmasculine. Halberstam observed in 1998 that what we now call 'butchness' could be understood as either a lesbian or transgender stance, and Roof recently noted that in 'the twenty-first century' the word 'butch' has 'shifted its signification into modes of transgender'.[50] These observations demonstrate the malleability of what Roof calls 'gender regimes', and remind us of the shifting character of Stein's transmasculinity.[51]

By deploying modes of transmasculine subjectivity that 'resonate' with but cannot be reduced to early twentieth-century and contemporary masculinities, Stein created what Freeman describes as a way of 'living aslant to dominant forms of object-choice, coupledom, family, marriage, sociability, and self-presentation' that was happily 'out of synch with state-sponsored narratives of belonging and becoming'.[52] As Stein declares in the opening pages of *The Making of Americans* (1903–11: 1925), '[i]t takes time to make queer people, and to have others who can know it, time and a certainty of place and means'.[53] Abandoning hegemonic genders for a queerer time and place, Stein fashioned masculinity through contingent and often volatile circuits of desire: through her romantic relationship with the feminine Toklas and her homosocial friendships with male and masculine female colleagues. These varied forms of relationality facilitated Stein's gradual 'movement away from' her 'initially assigned gender position' and her eventual embodiment of a shifting and anti-identitarian form of transmasculinity.[54] Underscoring the 'utter contingency and fraught conditions of intelligibility of all embodied subjectivity' and insisting upon its irreducibility to stable identities, *Gertrude Stein's Transmasculinity* examines the ways Stein's deliberate dislocation from her own historical moment mobilised transmasculinity in her life and writings.[55]

Reading Stein slantwise

To do so, *Gertrude Stein's Transmasculinity* reads Stein's writings – and others' literary and visual texts about her – in ways that illuminate the significance of her varied forms of transmasculinity and masculine homosocial bonds with her colleagues. These ties – and therefore Stein's transmasculinity – are persistently inscribed as bound up in desire: most obviously, in her sexual desire for the feminine Toklas; less obviously, but equally importantly, in Stein's homosocial desire for masculine artists and writers. Inscribing her and Toklas's subjectivities as split, Stein's texts consistently reveal and respect their author's masculinity and its embodiment through her desiring relation with her partner, even as her gender shifts in different contexts.[56] Furthermore, her writings register and refract her homosocial desire for male colleagues such as Picasso, Hemingway, Van Vechten and Sherwood Anderson and for masculine women such as Jane Heap (whose dandyism Stein found congenial) and the Duchess of Clermont-Tonnerre (whose short haircut inspired Stein's).

Stein's transmasculinity did not simply imitate maleness, however.[57] Corn and Latimer emphasise that her 1926 makeover refashioned the earlier masculinity she established by disidentifying with femininity. She copied her haircut not from men but from the Duchess of Clermont-Tonnerre, one of Barney's lovers.[58] Stein's crop was crucial because it enabled her to take on a self-authorising form of masculinity. By taking on a short hairstyle, she anticipated Halberstam's 1998 challenge to those that position female and transmasculinities as inferior imitations of maleness.[59] Even Stein's early claim to 'a maleness that belongs to genius' subtly contests such assertions, positing a likeness between herself and the painters without claiming that her 'maleness' mimics theirs.[60] Stein's haircut also undermined her connection of her 'genius' to her identification with others' 'maleness'.[61] Though existing scholarship on Stein tracks the way an increasing interest in feminist and women's concerns accompanied her shift away from her youthful identifications with men, nobody has addressed the implications of her having done so while still inscribing her masculinity.[62] The significance and visibility of Stein's transmasculinity shifted throughout her lifetime, destabilising the early claim to 'maleness' that was only the first of many iterations of her transmasculinity.

In analysing Stein's masculine homosocial bonds, I reinflect Sedgwick's account of 'male homosocial desire' to stress the cultural work done by Stein's masculine gender positionings, which shifted as Stein moved between contexts.[63] This revision of Sedgwick allows me to examine Stein's homosocial desire for a wide range of masculine persons and register her masculine friendships' divergent consequences for desire. As Sedgwick shows, the fuzzy line between between male homo*sociality* and male homo*sexuality* can undercut gender and trouble relationships. Yet Rolf Lundén largely overlooks slippages between homosociality and homosexuality – as well as the volatile forms of relationality they can engender – in his recent analysis of 'Male Friendship' in Stein's portrait 'Men' (1908–12: 1951).[64] As Sedgwick observes, being 'beside' others can provoke 'a wide range of' queer 'relations', such as 'desiring, identifying, representing, repelling, paralleling, differentiating, rivaling, leaning, twisting, mimicking, withdrawing, attracting, aggressing' and 'warping'.[65] This dynamic remains unexplored in studies of Stein's writing even though its destabilising effects are evident in her friendships. Moreover, Sedgwick notes that '[t]he word "queer" itself means *across* – it comes from the Indo-European root *–twerkw*, which also yields the German *quer* (transverse), Latin *torquere* (to twist), English *athwart*'.[66] These crossings are also at play in the word 'trans-', as Jay Prosser's decision to open the first chapter of *Second Skins* with this quotation suggests.[67]

As Joshua J. Weiner and Damon Young argue in reframing Sedgwick, the '"slantwise" orientation of the' queer 'in relation to existing social structures' has meant that 'what we might now call "queerness" . . . has long been invested as at once the site of a symbolic disruption (which is also an antisocial negativity) and a particular relational inventiveness'.[68] E. L. McCallum observes of *The Making of Americans* that Stein's writing 'estranges us from the familiar and reassuring pleasures of ideological forms like family, history' and 'progress' by 'articulating not so much clear opposition to social viability as its pure impossibility'.[69] The social's 'interplay with its own negative' does not tap into 'the death drive' but enables a 'gay play drive' that fuels 'resistances to meaning, the openness to multiple possibilities, a joyful recombination of forms'.[70] This redoubling of antisocial negativity with social generativity ruptured Stein's ties to her family of origin – her bond with Leo never recovered from Toklas's arrival – and animated the vicissitudes of her queer relationality with Toklas, Picasso, Hemingway and Van Vechten. The potentialities and problems of these friendships – bonds 'in which the difficulty of specifying the location of "sexuality" is precisely what is at stake' – fractured and reshaped the trajectories of Stein's masculine homosocial desire in ways that mobilised multiple forms of relationship.[71] Subsisting 'on both the marked and unmarked sides of socially normative systems' in ways that disrupted old and generated new social forms, Stein's homosocial bonds with Picasso, Hemingway and Van Vechten created 'internal rupture[s]' within early twentieth-century discourses of sexuality and gender.[72]

As Roof argues, gender entails 'a complex range of processes, signifiers, and dynamics that do have, albeit distanced and untraceable, some expressive link to subjective drives and desires'.[73] Because 'the modes by which genders are derived, produced, displayed, and altered are many', the vicissitudes of their 'conscious and unconscious' operations are simultaneously 'compelled and voluntary, . . . compliant and perpetually askew'.[74] Due to this complexity, Stein's 'slantwise' relationships with her colleagues led each masculine bond to fracture.[75] Although Stein's connections with Picasso, Hemingway and Van Vechten ranged 'beyond sexual self-recognition' and went beyond 'identitarian positionings' in ways that were 'forever incommensurate' even as they sought to bridge 'differences that' were ultimately 'irreducible', each friendship took a distinct form.[76] Whereas her homosocial desire for Picasso and Hemingway was uneasy and often fraught with negativity, her and Toklas's friendship with Van Vechten was consistently warm, supportive, joyful, and even playful. The varied forms of relationality at work in these queer ties mobilised yet destabilised multiple forms of transmasculinity in Stein's life and writing alike.[77]

These novel masculinities emerged from Stein's '"slantwise" position' with respect to institutionalised forms of homosocial bonding and generated what Michel Foucault calls 'new relational possibilities'.[78] Anderson once wrote that 'Stein is great because she is a releaser of talent. She is a path-finder. She has been a great, a tremendous influence among writers because she has dared, in the face of ridicule and misunderstanding, to try to awaken in all of us who write a new feeling for words.'[79] He points to Stein's capacity to free the word from congealed meanings: to the linguistic openings that have animated decades of scholarship on her pioneering experimental writings. Similarly, her masculine homosocial bonds enabled her to 'reopen affective and relational virtualities' and draw 'diagonal lines . . . in the social fabric' that allowed those 'virtualities to come to light' and create novel forms of relationality.[80] As Foucault observes, queers 'have to invent . . . a relationship that is still formless, which is friendship: that is to say, the sum of everything through which they can give each other pleasure', both physically and socially.[81] By making a life with Toklas and sustaining a variety of artistically driven friendships, Stein dislodged and rearticulated heteronormative familial scripts.

These rearticulations were not consistently progressive, but sometimes 'contradictory and complicit' with rearguard ideological formations, as Halberstam observes.[82] Stein's close ties to gay male Vichy collaborator Bernard Fäy and fractured friendships with sexist modernists Picasso and Hemingway reveal that the innovative forms of transmasculinity she lived out with Toklas and Van Vechten existed alongside investments in more retrograde masculinities.[83] Even though her friendships with men such as Picasso and Hemingway were subject to 'warping' as her anti-sexist transmasculinity conflicted with their attachments to heteronormative social and sexual formations, her 'new feeling for words' and art generated new modes of writing, relationship and gender.[84]

Reading Stein's masculinity

To track the vicissitudes of Stein's desires and transmasculinity, *Gertrude Stein's Transmasculinity* approaches literature and the visual arts as media that have played significant roles in framing twentieth- and early twentieth-century genders. As Pamela Caughie argues, although transgender 'as we study it today emerged out of early twentieth-century scientific discoveries and technologies, such as' the 'synthetic hormones and advances in plastic surgery' so important to transsexual self-realisation, 'it was also engendered by modernist aesthetics, formal innovations responding to and shaping a changing social discourse of sexuality and subjectivity'.[85] This 'makes textual analysis as critical as cultural history to contemporary transgender studies'.[86] Moreover, as Brian Glavey observes, literary form is 'relational' because it solicits but ultimately withholds the reader's '"near-identification"', splitting the subject.[87] Setting this process into motion by inciting her readers' 'interest' and encouraging their 'familiarity', Stein's writing prompts what Sedgwick calls 'the inveterate, gorgeous generativity, the speculative generosity, the daring', and 'the permeability' of 'queer *reading*'.[88] Stimulating readerly creativity, Stein's texts prompt reinventions of literary form and gendered subjectivity alike.

By facilitating relationality, Stein's experimental style provides a means for transmasculine signification and embodiment to emerge. As Joshua Schuster notes of *Tender Buttons* (1912: 1914), 'Stein's preferred keyword to describe her work is "composition"', which suggests 'something material, such as a page of sentences on a given topic or a musical score, but also' an arrangement of 'relationships, positions related to other positions'. Moreover, as Thompson observes, Stein's writing 'stresses the intimacy between text and reader', enabling 'embodiment, fluidity, and immersion in the material world' to be mobilised 'and embodied though reader participation'.[89] This 'democratic relationality' destabilises 'codes of gender that understand genius as masculine' and allows for the categories of 'maleness' and 'genius' to be inhabited in new ways.[90] Thus, for Astrid Lorange, Stein offers 'a performative account of queer embodiment' in poems such as 'Lifting Belly' (1915–17: 1953), which mobilises the 'emergent, contingent, and dynamic' aspects of bodily 'orientations'.[91] Although neither Lorange nor Thompson addresses transmasculine signification, I see it in Stein's radically experimental poetry from the 1910s and 1920s as well as in the texts articulating her sexual desire for Toklas and masculine homosocial desires for her colleagues.

By analysing transmasculine embodiment's significance to Stein's life and writings, *Gertrude Stein's Transmasculinity* engages in what Valerie Rohy calls 'transgender reading'.[92] This approach 'need not name' its subject 'as transgender', but 'must cease to defend' the subject 'against transgender possibilities, recognize that those possibilities may be positive, and engage with current ideas of gender in and around transgender theory'.[93] Although the label 'transgender' was not available in the early twentieth century, many of Stein's writings inscribe her subjectivity in ways that are 'at odds with' the category '"woman"'.[94] I read Stein as 'transmasculine' not to suggest that she identified as transgender in the identitarian sense but to insist that terms such as 'female' and 'woman' are not adequate for understanding her gender. Although I continue to refer to Stein with female pronouns in keeping with her public self-presentation in social and professional contexts, her shifting self-inscriptions as masculine suggest that her subjectivity and gendered embodiment were far more complicated than categories such as 'woman' or 'female' allow us to comprehend.

In reading Stein in this fashion, I challenge those who would rescue her from charges of masculinity. Shari Benstock, for example, attributes accounts of Stein as masculine to the 'many men' who wished to marginalise and discredit her as a 'ridiculous imitation male', and contrasts their depictions with the normatively feminine clothing and hairstyles she wore while at Radcliffe College.[95] Benstock also claims that even with her cropped hair, the skirted Stein 'was never altogether masculine' and 'remained recognizably a woman'.[96] However, Laura Doan has demonstrated that the more famously masculine Hall, too, wore mannishly tailored skirt suits.[97] While it is reasonable to believe that depictions of Stein's masculinity could have been exaggerated by the workings of misogyny and homophobia, other accounts suggest that she left the United States precisely to escape the sartorial norms to which Benstock appeals as evidence of a putatively essential femininity.[98]

Gertrude Stein's Transmasculinity also challenges those who acknowledge Stein's masculinity but judge her negatively for it. Marianne DeKoven, for example, claims in an early study that 'With Alice Toklas as her wife and Pablo Picasso as her peer, Stein was able to live fully the male identification which allowed her to accept herself', claiming '"a maleness that belongs to genius"' only after 'her liaison with Toklas was established'.[99] DeKoven rightfully suggests that Stein's early sense of masculinity may have been formed through simultaneous identification with male colleagues and differentiation from her feminine partner. Despite the insistence of psychoanalysis that identification is multiple and irreducible to identity, DeKoven frames Stein's 'male identification' as a form of 'self-hatred' – a misogynist rejection of her presumably female self.[100] Bettina Knapp even goes so far as to claim that Stein's supposedly 'unbalanced relationship to femininity and to herself as a woman' was caused by the early death of her cold, 'pallid and passive mother': a formulation that unnecessarily pathologises them.[101] These arguments all rest on the essentialist assumption that one's bodily contours should correspond to one's sense of one's gender: on the claim that because Stein's body was female, she must have felt herself to be female and should have identified as a woman.

However, Stein may not have identified as female or a woman. Her insistent yet varied displays of masculinity call that presumption into question, and *Gertrude Stein's Transmasculinity* explores alternative readings of her gender. Yet in directing attention to masculinity's persistence in shifting perceptions of Stein, I also recast earlier work that affirmed rather than derided her masculinity. In the wake of Judith Butler's *Gender Trouble*, scholars have held up Stein as an example of the radical questioning and unfixing of gender.[102] Though Robert Lubar justifiably asks 'how secure' the term 'masculine' is in discussions of Stein, noting shifts in her appearance and perceptions thereof, signifiers of masculinity crop up insistently in depictions of her and reactions to her presence.[103] Moreover, her long-standing relationship with the feminine Toklas and her persistent preference for masculine homosociality reveal her consistent self-inscription as masculine. Stein's example also points, however, to scholars' need to look both at and beyond the visible – at and beyond her mutable outward appearance – to track her transmasculinity. Although Henry Sayre rightfully observes that '[o]ne of the real questions Stein's work raises – and one of the reasons she remains so influential' – concerns the significance of her claim to 'the masculine position', her masculinity was not merely 'a masculine guise' that deployed gender as 'a free-floating signifier' unrelated to her own sense of gendered embodiment.[104] It was instead a mode of transsubjectivity. This is not to say that Stein's identity was fixed, or that her subjectivity was self-identical: her diverse self-positionings suggest elsewise. But it is to say that she consistently inscribed herself as masculine – however overt or covert, however contextually varied and shifting her masculinity's significance was at any given moment.

Stein's relationship to masculinity changed throughout her lifetime, as did the ways she inscribed her gender. Although her desire for bonding with male colleagues and her and Toklas's insider-outsider status within early twentieth-century Parisian Sapphic communities have sometimes been considered evidence of her presumably pernicious 'male identification', I read these trajectories of desire and identification as signs of transmasculinity that undercut stable gender ontologies.[105] As Butler recently observed:

> None of us know precisely who we will 'be' under regimes of ontology that we struggle against or seek to displace. It may be . . . that as we struggle against the categories of gender that secure contemporary ideas of personhood, we no longer know exactly how we are to be named. We might be understood to be in a mode of self-making or self-poesis that involves risking intelligibility, posing a problem of cultural translation and living in a critical relation to the norms of the intelligible.[106]

Stein's writings from the first three decades of the twentieth century employ 'a mode of . . . self-poesis' that works through dominant early twentieth-century masculinities and femininities. By the 1910s and 1920s, her radically experimental poems – along with her and Toklas's love notes – articulate joyful, flexible and feminist transmasculinities in myriad forms. The capacious term 'transmasculine' allows me to register those changes and their implications for Stein's shifting gendered embodiment.

Unlike many modernist texts featuring cross-dressing and other transgender practices, the writings I examine establish Stein's shifting modes of transsubjectivity. As Prosser points out, there are vital distinctions between texts primarily concerned with transsubjectivities (for instance, the *Bildungsroman* narrative of Stephen Gordon's masculinity in *The Well*) and those that deploy figures of gender crossing for other purposes (for example, the appearance of Bella/Bello Cohen as a figure within Leopold Bloom's masochistic fantasy in James Joyce's 1922 *Ulysses*). Yet if Prosser rightfully insists that transsubjectivities are lived and not just metaphorical, we need to remember that representations of them are always already figurative, and that their figurative work matters.

Stryker and Aizura observe that in the present context – in which 'new modes of biopolitical regulation' provide ever narrower definitions of the 'surgical and hormonal bodily transformations' that 'legally define a person's sex or transgender status' – it is vital for '[t]ransgender studies' to 'actively participate in the proliferation and articulation of new modes of embodied subjectivity, new cultural practices, and new ways of understanding the world, rather then becoming an enclosure for their containment'.[107] Transgender studies should create an opening for capacious rather than constrictive accounts of current genders, a project just as urgent for those interested – as I am in this book – in understanding transsubjectivities from the past.

I thus agree with Caughie's assertion that '[r]ather than looking for literal transsexuals in the modernist past, . . . we might look to modernist literature as offering new narratives of embodiment that enable new configurations of gender and sexual identity'.[108] Arguing that such stories constitute a 'transgenre', Caughie reinflects Sandy Stone's 1991 claim that transpeople are 'a *genre* – a set of embodied texts' who disrupt existing forms.[109] Similarly, Prosser – writing of Leslie Feinberg's *Stone Butch Blues* (1993) – defines the 'trans-genre' as 'a text as between genres as its subject is between genders'.[110] Whereas Caughie stresses the varied narrative temporalities through which Virginia Woolf's *Orlando* (1928) offers up its protagonist's fantastic transition as the harbinger of a 'future embodiment' – 'as the deliberate shaping of a narrative of a life that might be lived, and liveable' – Stein uses experimental poetry to inscribe transmasculinity through her varied relations with Toklas and her colleagues.[111] In so doing, Stein's avant-garde writings offer a different kind of 'transgenre' – and a different way 'of understanding the world' – than Woolf's text.[112]

Whereas Caughie argues that *Orlando* 'reconfigures' the genre of 'life writing narratives' to rework dominant 'notions of gender' and 'of time, identity, history, and the very nature of writing and reading', I find in Stein's writings a 'transgenre' that shakes up gendered signification's attachment to narrative forms: temporal, ideological and otherwise.[113] When Stein declares at the opening of 'How Writing Is Written' that 'everybody is contemporary with his period', she asserts that 'the modernist sense of time' is 'synchronous, not linear', as Caughie rightfully notes.[114] This implies that '[h]istoricizing cannot itself be a transhistorical act, flattening out different temporalities in reading across historical time', as scholars who insist upon the irrelevance of contemporary genders to modernist literature claim.[115] Stein's writings about writing show her willingness to experiment with varied temporalities, from the recursively 'prolonged present' of *Three Lives* (1903–6: 1909) to the synchronically 'continuous present' driving her innovative poetry.[116] These textual practices go beyond the complications of diachronic time propelling Woolf's novel.

Stein's formal innovations capture the vicissitudes of 'queer time'.[117] As McCallum argues, Steinian reiteration is not only 'death-driven' but also – and more importantly – 'a projection into a future as an opening within the present that arguably dislodges the very understanding that we have of the present'.[118] This means that the 'continuous present' is not 'a moment in a linear flow of chronology' but 'a propitious opportunity' to generate alternative temporalities.[119] Whereas Woolf's plays with narrative stretch beyond realism's limits to situate Orlando's physical transition in a hypothetical future, Stein's avant-garde poetics inscribe transmasculine embodiment's varied iterations within an endless sequence of 'now[s]'.[120] Like the 'cinema', in which 'no two pictures are exactly alike' but 'each one is just that much different from the one before', the continuous present mobilises successive differences, temporal and otherwise.[121]

Although Stein's explanation of the 'continuous present' in 'Portraits and Repetition' (1934–5: 1935) eschews 'remembering' lest it lock our thinking into static 'repetition' – a mode of reiteration she distinguishes from 'the difference of insistence' that comes from 'varying the emphasizing' – her texts that operate in that mode nonetheless engage the past.[122] Her account of the 'prolonged present' in 'Composition as Explanation' (1926: 1926) is even more explicit about her attention to time's complexities: she writes that 'Melanctha', for instance, entails 'a constant recurring and beginning, . . . a marked direction in the direction of being in the present although naturally I had been accustomed to past present and future'.[123] By complicating linear temporalities, Stein's texts offer what Freeman calls 'a potentially queer vision of how time wrinkles and folds as some minor feature of our sexually impoverished present suddenly meets up with a richer past, or as the materials of a failed and forgotten project of the past find their uses now, in a future unimaginable in their time'.[124] Although Caughie uses Freeman's claim to point to 'a future unimaginable in' Woolf's 'time', which allows her to situate the novelist's preference for the fantastic in *Orlando* as a trans-affirmative feat of imagination, I would like to stress Freeman's recourse to the 'now', whose 'synchronous and recursive' temporality drives Stein's 'continuous present' and probing of time's 'wrinkles and folds'.[125] From what Lisa Siraganian calls the 'internal bell' that tells Toklas that in Stein 'she has recognized a creator of modern time' to Toklas's tendency to recount 'the art world's stunning modernity belatedly' in *The Autobiography*, as if she were 'experiencing literary time from the distant provinces'; from the orgasmic waves of 'As A Wife Has A Cow A Love Story' (1923: 1926) to the irregular rhythms of 'One Carl Van Vechten' (1913: 1922): Stein's varied queer temporalities enable her to mobilise multiple transmasculine positionings.[126]

Experimenting very differently than Woolf's fantastic novel, Stein's poetry registers her erotic desire for Toklas and homosocial desires for her peers, allowing her to live out transmasculine embodiment in her own lifetime, not just as a hypothetical 'future embodiment'.[127] To do so, her writings engage the Lacanian *sinthome*: the unique kind of jouissance experienced by each subject that helps solidify the 'bond between the imaginary, the symbolic, and the real' orders that constitutes subjectivity.[128] Whereas Lacan's *Seminar III* argues that one must accept the 'name of the father' as 'primordial signifier' during subjectification to align the three orders, *Seminar XXIII* identifies 'the father' as only one among a multitude of *sinthomes* that could enable that operation.[129] As Patricia Gherovici argues in her analysis of transsexual memoir, this theory makes it possible to understand transpeoples' writings as 'art that can allow' them 'to love, work, desire'.[130] The *sinthome* allows 'the body' to put 'its anchor in the sea of language' through a 'creative knotting together of the registers of real, symbolic, and imaginary' that enables transgender subjectivity and 'embodiment'.[131] The resultant 'transgenre' makes transpeoples' genders legible to others.[132]

Writing afforded Stein a creative means of inscribing transmasculine embodiment. Her texts exploit reiterations in which each word, like each image in a film, was 'just that much different from the one before'.[133] Using idiosyncratic vocabulary to anticipate contemporary poststructural arguments that reiteration always entails difference, she contends that 'insistence', or 'the inevitable repetition in human expression', involves 'saying the same thing and insisting' while nonetheless 'varying the emphasizing'.[134] '[T]here is no such thing as' exact 'repetition', however, because 'the insistence is different' with each iteration.[135] She claims, moreover, that 'insistence is always alive and if it is alive it is never saying anything in the same way'.[136] If insistence's vitality lies in its ability to generate subtle differences without which 'there is no existing', it also depends upon active engagement with others.[137] Stein observes that when people are 'no longer listening', they are 'beginning repeating, that is . . . ceasing to be insisting'.[138] By pointing to the relational aspect of 'insistence', to the way shifts in signification must be heard to be transformative, this passage also underscores the importance of intersubjectivity to resignification. That listening, like talking, is inevitably imperfect and recognition always undercut by misrecognition only strengthens insistence's generative potential.

As Kathryn Bond Stockton says, '[w]hat we provide between two instances of the same signifier – between the signifiers "queer" and "queer," for instance . . . are bodily experiences, nonce taxonomies (in Sedgwick's sense of one-time namings), and nonce taxonomies *as* bodily experiences'.[139] Stein's avant-garde texts use 'insistence' to bring her transmasculine embodiment into signification, mobilising its implication in her sexual desire for Toklas and masculine homosocial desires for Picasso, Hemingway and Van Vechten. In so doing, Stein creates a poetic 'transgenre' that makes her masculinity's varied modes available for view – not as a hypothetical 'future embodiment' but as a gender that is already 'lived', and continues to be 'liveable', within the 'double time' of her writings' 'continuous present'.[140]

Reading Stein's traces

In Stein's avant-garde texts, open-ended networks of signification mobilise this poetic 'transgenre'. However, one of my assumptions is that my readings will not exhaust the endlessly generative potential of her texts or modernist artworks. As Marjorie Perloff observes, Stein's writings invite a multiplicity of readings; what individual readers find in them 'all depends on our angle of vision'.[141] Viewing Stein's texts from positions conducive to seeing her shifting transmasculinity, I trace its implications for her queer bonds with Toklas and her masculine colleagues. However, Stein's writings may also be seen elsewise; my goal is not to suggest that transmasculinity was her life's singular and determining force or her texts' only mode of signification. This study does not offer a final and totalising pronouncement about Stein's literary 'work' or others' representations of her: an impossible task, given modernist texts' refusals of unambiguous meanings. Rather, I read written and visual artefacts of Stein's life with an eye for her masculinity's textual and cultural significance. In so doing, I do not assume that these texts stand in mimetic relationship to reality, that they are simple reflections of her life. Nor do I assume that Stein's or her colleagues' intentions entirely control those texts' meanings. Instead, I read written and visual texts psychoanalytically: as traces of her life and relationships with her partner and friends.

I do not take these materials as direct expressions of Stein's or her colleagues' psychologies, but as nodal points on various trajectories of intersubjective desire. This method blurs the clear lines that critics of biographical evidence would draw between texts' significations and those who created them. In a polemic against biographical readings, Rosalind Krauss demonstrates through Saussurean linguistics that Picasso's collages found 'the terms of representation on absence' that 'is essential to the operations of the sign'.[142] Representation detaches the artwork from its creator through 'the impersonal workings of pictorial form' and allows collage to interrogate 'the *impersonal* operations of language'.[143] Because language is 'a synchronic repertory of terms into which each individual must assimilate himself', and therefore 'a speaker does not so much speak, as he is spoken by, language', Krauss contends that the artwork's significance unfolds apart from its creator's life.[144] In echoing Roland Barthes's 1968 'The Death of the Author', however, she succumbs to the same fantasies driving high modernists' desire for an impersonal art distinct from its maker and viewer alike.[145]

Assuming that biographical criticism is psychological rather than psychoanalytic, Krauss overlooks the possibilities presented by Lacan's inflection of de Saussure, according to which symbolic and imaginary representations split the subject. This decentred subject's contours may be traced through the representations that constitute it, even though it is irreducible to them and remains haunted by the impossible Real that resists symbolisation. Lacan's description of the subject – in which 'I think where I am not, therefore I am where I do not think'; in which 'I am not wherever I am the plaything of my thought; I think of what I am where I do not think to think' – resembles the line from Arthur Rimbaud – '"Je est un autre." (I is someone [maybe even something] else)' – with which T. J. Clark repudiates biographical readings of Picasso's paintings.[146] It also mirrors the displacements of identity in Stein's reflection in *Everybody's Autobiography* that 'perhaps I am not I even if my little dog knows me'.[147]

Gertrude Stein's Transmasculinity similarly assumes that the subject is split and never fully transparent to itself. Yet unlike Clark and Krauss, I do not assume that decentred subjectivity obviates biographical reading but take Lacan's account of the psyche as a useful caution about the limitations of such evidence. Laurel Recker aptly observes that 'Stein's life and texts dialectically produce one another', even though recent scholarship has tried to disentangle them.[148] I thus take writing and visual artworks not as transparent windows into their makers' consciousnesses but rather as traces of the psyche. What is legible through psychoanalytic reading is not the singular truth of the artwork's meaning or the artist's mind, but residues of the trajectories of desire that make them possible. As Clark says, '[d]esire is a generalizing force', and art 'mimics the process – the geography – of splitting and projection, but only by having those movements of mind and feeling become nothing but moves in an aesthetic game'.[149] Stein's experimental writing operates similarly: it does not express desire so much as transport it onto an aesthetic plane. This does not render Stein's desire irrelevant to her texts, but allows us to situate them in the context of her relationality with others. Psychoanalytic readings are adept at teasing out the textual threads of intersubjectivity, whether between authors or characters, without assuming that language or visual imagery can be reduced to or controlled by authorial psychology. *Gertrude Stein's Transmasculinity* engages in this type of reading by tracking the multiple forms of relationship within which Stein's transmasculinity crystallised.

This methodology pushes back against cultural studies' focus on institutional forces at the expense of other influences on signification. This methodological narrowness risks obscuring equally important considerations, such as intersubjective relations. Refusing any consideration of the author whatsoever also misunderstands key statements by Barthes and Foucault about the author's role in creating and interpreting meaning. Barthes's 'The Death of the Author' and Foucault's 1969 'What Is an Author?' both argue against invoking the author as a limit to interpretation. While Barthes's proclamation of the author's demise might seem to eliminate any consideration of the author whatsoever, he merely challenges claims to authorial originality and sovereignty over meaning. Foucault further argues that the author's name can take on a disciplinary function by constructing an identity that constrains texts' ownership and meaning. He stresses that power relationships establish authorial status and delineate certain writings as authors' 'works' within societies keen to establish individual property rights.[150] Foucault distinguishes the author's existence as a person from the discursively produced 'author-function', a structural position utilised in processes of 'legal codification' to circumscribe texts' significance.[151] Scholars who take Stein's and others' pronouncements about aesthetic objects' autonomy as methodological prescriptions unnecessarily heed the interpretive limits Foucault ascribes to the 'author-function' even as they strive to remove the author from reading.[152]

Foucault's ideas about institutional power have proven valuable for cultural approaches to modernism, but Barthes's emphasis on texts' polyvocality is equally important. Drawing on poststructural linguistics, 'The Death of the Author' insists that 'language' – rather than the author – 'speaks'.[153] This does not render the work autonomous, as Krauss claims, but places its meaning in the reader's rather than the author's hands. Similarly, in his 1971 reply to Foucault in 'From Work to Text', Barthes emphasises the plurality of the 'text' over the filiative nature of the 'Work'.[154] He also clarifies that 'It is not that the Author cannot 'return' in the Text, in his text, but he does so, one might say, as a "guest".'[155] Over and against Foucault's reduction of texts to the power relationships through which they are produced, Barthes enables us to understand the author as one of the 'characters' appearing among many other vectors of signification.[156] Barthes thus claims that the 'Author . . . inscribes himself' in the text as a 'paper author' whose 'life is no longer the origin of his fables, but a fable concurrent with his life'.[157] The author's life does not determine textual meaning but rather is itself 'a text' in the boundless network of signification in which the author's writings participate.

It is in this sense of the author's return to the text as a 'guest' or fictionally produced 'character' that I approach representations of and writings by Stein. In reading her texts for manifestations of transmasculinity and the desires engendering it, I inevitably read queerly: at a slant and in relation to Stein's modernist networks. I take her texts as part of a life project of writing, networking, and self-promotion that extended beyond the boundaries of any single work and engaged the institutions and proponents of modern literature, art and culture among whom Stein positioned herself and her salon. Modernist institutions and networks exerted a significant, though not wholly determining, influence on her emergence, and she used them for her own ends. Her donation of Picasso's 1905–6 *Portrait of Gertrude Stein* (Plate 1) to New York's Metropolitan Museum of Art and her and Toklas's papers to Yale University's Beinecke Library have secured her presence in modernism's archives. These gestures successfully countered gatekeeping institutions such as presses and magazines that did not circulate many of Stein's texts during her lifetime.

The availability of Stein's papers at the Beinecke and the publication of the Yale Edition of the Unpublished Writings of Gertrude Stein, which started in 1951, enabled the scholarship that led to her widespread recognition as a major modernist figure. Moreover, recent work has called attention to Stein's agency in constructing herself as 'a moving picture star in Hollywood' at the historical moment of celebrity culture's emergence.[158] Harcourt's September 1933 publication of *The Autobiography* and the Modern Library's reissue of *Three Lives* provided the occasion for Stein's 1934–5 lecture tour of the United States, which used the rising culture of celebrity to claim her position.[159] Though *The Autobiography* is notoriously inaccurate and cannot be taken as a reflection of reality, it accomplishes something other than mimesis. Using Toklas as narrator to frame Stein and her position within modernism, *The Autobiography* offers a trace of her image as she desires us to see it.

However, as the circulation of Stein's texts and images over the last eighty years in immensely varied contexts has gone on to show, there are many other angles from which to view her. As Roof observes, '[t]he genderscape constantly shifts. Because cultural signifiers, versions of symbolic formations, possible objects of desire, and other modes by which desire is organised culturally constantly change, genderings change as well'.[160] Shifting cultural and institutional factors have affected perceptions of Stein's image, which has vacillated as it has moved across space and time; contemporary institutions and discourses continue to shape the varied ways Stein appears as a queer and modernist icon.

Recent exhibitions brought Stein to the general public's attention in the United States and Europe. In June 2011, two shows on Stein, her family and her professional network were mounted in San Francisco, coincident with the city's LGBT Pride celebration and film festival. *The Steins Collect*, at the San Francisco Museum of Modern Art (SFMOMA), traced the Stein family's impact as early collectors of modern art. Simultaneously, *Seeing Gertrude Stein: Five Stories*, at the San Francisco Contemporary Jewish Museum, drew on visual artworks and Stein's published texts to illustrate the ways she has been perceived by and has exerted influence within familial and professional networks from the early twentieth century to the present. Whereas *Seeing Gertrude Stein* moved on to the National Portrait Gallery in Washington DC, *The Steins Collect* travelled to Paris's Grand Palais and New York's Metropolitan Museum of Art.

As any visitor to gift shops for *The Steins Collect* and *Seeing Gertrude Stein* would have readily noticed, Stein's image is increasingly commodified and circulated in cultural venues both high and low. Postcards, T-shirts, exhibition catalogues and other items featuring Stein's image and quotations are now available. She has also become a cult figure in the queer community. In June 2011, as banners of Stein looked out over neighbourhoods across San Francisco, the Yerba Buena Complex advertised their exhibits with a float for the Pride parade accompanied by actors playing Stein, Toklas and the artists whose work they collected. These proliferations of Stein's image bear comparison to the artefacts Brenda Silver examines in *Virginia Woolf Icon*. Silver observes that diverse contexts and ideologies have produced divergent 'versions' of Woolf's image, which – like Stein's – turns up with stunning frequency in creative and commercial settings.[161] To track different 'versions' of Woolf, Silver draws on Foucault's concept of the 'author-function' and Stuart Hall's theorisation of '"cultural forms and activities as a constantly changing field"'.[162] She uses these concepts from cultural studies while leaving other avenues of interpretation open, such as Richard Dyer's sociological and semiological analysis within which the 'star image' is 'always intertextual and always changing' in ways that are 'contradictory' and multiply 'generative'.[163] Thus 'a work or a star image can be represented as an infinite series of texts, and a specific text can be represented as an infinite series of performances that could, conceivably, produce an infinite series of' images of an author.[164]

My own perspective on Stein is sympathetic to Silver's while leaning more heavily on psychoanalytic and queer approaches to literature and the visual arts. Going beyond the false dichotomy that is all too often drawn between cultural and psychoanalytic readings of literature, I consider writings, visual materials and institutions alike. Departing from Barthes's conclusion that the author should not be taken as a limit for interpretation but may return as a 'guest', I track Stein's emergence as an iconic 'character' in modernist and queer cultures.[165] To do so, I trace out the various forms her masculinity has taken as she has circulated in different textual, visual, cultural and historical contexts. This reveals masculinity's persistence among the signifiers that emerge from Stein's visual and textual lives, even as her gender has shifted in the flux of divergent 'objects, desires, and identifications'.[166]

Gertrude Stein's Transmasculinity

Gertrude Stein's Transmasculinity is comprised of an introduction, seven chapters, and a coda. The introduction and first four chapters focus on moments at which Stein's masculinity surfaces within the visual and the textual: in others' paintings and photographs of her person; in her experimental writings from the first three decades of the twentieth century; and in her self-packaging for mass consumption in *The Autobiography*. Whereas the fourth chapter – on *The Autobiography* – underscores Toklas's support of Stein's masculinity and success as a writer, the final three chapters register the vicissitudes of Stein's masculine homosocial bonds in three friendships with prominent modernists: Picasso, Hemingway and Van Vechten. Stein's connections to Picasso and Hemingway reveal that she was attracted to hegemonic masculinity despite her misgivings about it; their discomfort with this dynamic caused their ties to fray. By contrast, her and Toklas's enduring bond with Van Vechten shows Stein's capacity to find routes for her homosocial desires that embraced alternative masculinities, fostered her feminism, and enabled her to go beyond the oppositions of masculine/feminine and heterosexual/homosexual that underpin reductive understandings of sexuality and gender.

Chapter 1, 'Seeing Stein's Masculinity', considers visual images of and written texts about Stein. Driven by queer reinterpretations of Lacan's theory of the gaze, this chapter reads his work against the grain to analyse representations of Stein by George Platt Lynes, Henri Manuel and Man Ray as well as in their recent reception during *Seeing Gertrude Stein*.[167] Moreover, I use Stein's own comments in *The Autobiography* about being photographed by Man Ray to queer the heteronormative gaze driving James Agee's review of that book in the 11 September 1933 issue of *Time*. Tracking changes between the early twentieth century and the present in attitudes toward Stein's queer sexuality and transmasculinity, this chapter argues that traces of abjection remain in contemporary reactions to her despite greater acceptance of her gender, sexuality and innovative writing.

Chapter 2, 'Reading Stein's Genders: Multiple Identifications in the 1900s', and Chapter 3, 'Reading Stein's Genders: Transmasculine Signification in the 1910s and 1920s', both concern Stein's writings from the first three decades of the twentieth century. Taken together, these chapters demonstrate that her increasingly experimental writings during this period gradually work through dominant early twentieth-century genders, loosening up rigid constructs of masculinity. I first address the implications of Stein's early attraction to Weininger's misogynist *Sex and Character*, and then track how her critical responses to that construct transform from her fictional writings from the 1900s through to her radical experimental texts from the 1910s and 1920s. Chapter 2 focuses on cross-gendered identification in Stein's earliest literary efforts – the prose narratives *Fernhurst* (1904–5: 1971), *Q.E.D.* (1903: 1971), and *Three Lives* (1903–6: 1909). In these works, Stein rejects the category 'woman' while questioning the stability of gender and the limitations of patriarchal ideologies about masculinity and femininity. Chapter 3 argues that her innovative writings from the 1910s and 1920s – such as the long poems 'Lifting Belly' and 'Patriarchal Poetry' (1927: 1953) – use Toklas's feminine positioning to establish Stein's masculinity. Whereas Stein's earlier fiction presented subtler challenges to Weininger, her experimental poems from the 1910s and 1920s explicitly and jubilantly use linguistic innovation to articulate flexible and feminist transmasculinities. In so doing, these texts offer moments of transmasculine jouissance that differ from the 'radical disintegration' and 'humiliation' Leo Bersani attributes to cisgender gay male bottoming.[168] Gleefully affirming the transmasculine subject's ability to shift roles, Stein's innovative writings radically reconfigure gendered embodiment.

Chapter 4, 'Visual Economies of Queer Desire in *The Autobiography of Alice B. Toklas*', uses that text to frame and advance my central argument about the role Stein's transmasculinity played in her homosocial ties with her colleagues. Tracking the dynamics of vision animating *The Autobiography*, I argue that it uses Toklas's loving gaze to establish and recognise Stein's shifting transmasculinity, as well as to highlight her masculine bonds' importance to modernism. *The Autobiography* depicts those ties as very congenial with men such as Sherwood Anderson and masculine women such as Heap, but more fraught – and more likely to induce perspectival vacillation – with Hemingway and Picasso. This multiperspectivalism structures the book and mobilises multiple narratives of modernism's emergence. In so doing, *The Autobiography* reframes Stein's masculinity and relationship with Toklas as part of the appearance of the new that the text initially attributes solely to the formal properties of modern art and writing.

Chapter 5, 'Picasso's Stein / Stein's Picasso: Cubist Perspective / Masculine Homosociality', is the first of three chapters that closely examine Stein's friendships with male modernists. This chapter cross-reads Picasso's paintings that reference Stein – *Portrait of Gertrude Stein*, *Homage a Gertrude* [*sic*] (1909), and *The Architect's Table* (1912) – with her portraits 'Picasso' (1909–10: 1912) and 'If I Told Him A Completed Portrait of Picasso' (1923: 1924) to argue that masculine homosociality was an important force in their dynamic. Tracking the ways their portraits of one another use cubist strategies to register their bond's vicissitudes, I argue that whereas Picasso's portrait of Stein reflects his trepidation about her transmasculinity and their masculine homosociality, her portraits show fondness for him and express concern about his uneven artistic production and imperial masculinity. If Stein's portraits of Picasso ultimately differentiate her queer modes of transmasculinity from his misogynist masculinity, Czech artist Jiří Kolář's reinflections of his portraits further transform the gaze through which her masculinity – and homosocial bond with Picasso – are made available for view.

Chapter 6, '"Torquere": Stein's and Hemingway's Queer Relationality', focuses on Stein's fraught friendship with Hemingway, whose initial supplication to her tutelage transformed into retaliatory aggression in the wake of his observation of Toklas's power over her. Whereas Stein admits in *The Autobiography* to having 'a weakness for Hemingway' despite his faults, Hemingway – who notoriously spoke of wanting to 'lay' her – spitefully attacked her relationship with Toklas in his memoir *A Moveable Feast* in revenge for her calling him 'yellow'.[169] Differences between the public and private Hemingway precipitated crises as he disavowed the possibility that his attraction to the transmasculine Stein may have been driven by a far queerer configuration of gender and desire than the heteronormative logics governing the works he published during his lifetime. Considering *A Moveable Feast* as well as Stein's and Hemingway's shorter poems about one another – Stein's 'Objects Lie on a Table' (1922: 1932), 'He and They, Hemingway' (1923: 1923), 'Evidence' (1929: 1930, 1993), 'Genuine Creative Ability' (1929–30: 1930), and 'Sentences and Paragraphs' (1929–30: 1931); Hemingway's 'The Soul of Spain' (1924) and its sequels – I argue that their dynamic produced troubling vicissitudes that reverberated across their lives and works.[170]

Chapter 7 – 'Stein, Van Vechten and Modernism's Queer Gaze' – offers a counterpoint to Stein's and Hemingway's mutual aggression by focusing on her queerly productive friendship with modernist impresario Van Vechten, which was flirtatious and never soured. Rather than deriding Stein's writing, Van Vechten placed her manuscripts, edited her *Selected Writings*, organised her 1934–5 tour of the United States and took photographs that furthered her celebrity image. To track their bond's vicissitudes, I read Stein's account in *The Autobiography* of her first meeting with Van Vechten; examine her two word-portraits of him, 'One Carl Van Vechten' and 'Van or Twenty Years After' (1923: 1924); and analyse several of his photographs of her and the 'Woojums' family they formed with Toklas. In a circuit of masculine homosocial desire markedly different than those addressed earlier, Stein returned Van Vechten's affection with verbal portraits showing none of the qualms revealed in her writings about Picasso and Hemingway. Instead, Stein's and Van Vechten's portraits of one another affirm their queer bonds, giving them to be seen through a loving gaze. Bearing out Jason Cromwell's observation that 'transsituated' subjectivity undercuts 'the binary of heterosexual and homosexual', generating novel genders and sexualities, friendship with Van Vechten provided vital sustenance for Stein's transmasculinity.[171]

The coda, 'Gertrude Stein Icon', expands on the implications of textual and visual artefacts of Stein's masculine homosocial desires by cross-reading her hesitant reflections on celebrity in *Everybody's Autobiography* with her frequent appearances in the public eye from 2011 to 2012. Although Chapter 1 showed that by the early twenty-first century Stein had emerged as a queer and modernist icon, that high standing is still occasionally challenged. If *Gertrude Stein's Transmasculinity* presents Stein as an important 'character' in the stories of modernism and queer theory – as a 'paper author' whose 'life' does not provide 'the origin of' or the limit to our readings of her texts but is itself 'a fable' – that story will continue as she circulates into new contexts.[172] As more research is done into her masculinity's imbrication with her friendship with Van Vechten and involvement with Fäy, there will likely be further changes to the ways her masculinity is made available for view, with unpredictable consequences for her iconicity. In the meantime, I hope that by calling attention to the varied meanings and 'utter contingency' of Stein's shifting and anti-identitarian transmasculinity, *Gertrude Stein's Transmasculinity* will contribute to this ongoing cultural process.[173]

Notes

1. See Benstock, *Women*, pp. 143–93, for a problematic overview of the different sexual and gender identities present in modernist Paris.
2. See YCAL MSS 76, Box 38, Folder 791 in the Beinecke Rare Book and Manuscript Library, Yale University.
3. That Stein's statement might be a sign of transgender identification has been briefly suggested by Madelyn Detloff, *The Persistence of Modernism*, and Jean E. Mills, 'Gertrude Stein Took The War Like A Man', though much more remains to be said.
4. See Cope, *Passionate Collaborations*; Hovey, *A Thousand Words*; and Thompson, 'Language and Democracy'. See Will, *Gertrude Stein*, for an extended discussion of Stein's engagement with ideas about 'genius'.
5. See the plays with pronouns in Stein's 'As A Wife Has A Cow A Love Story', 'Lifting Belly' and 'Patriarchal Poetry'.
6. See Elfenbein, *Romantic Genius*, pp. 1–16, for a history of genius's late nineteenth- and early twentieth-century association with homosexuality,

and Battersby, *Gender and Genius*, for a feminist critique of historical links between genius and maleness. For analysis of the ways Stein's self-positioning as a 'genius' responds to its conflation with masculinity, see Elliott and Wallace, *Women Artists and Writers*, pp. 90–121.

7. Roof, *What Gender Is*, pp. 28–9. Thanks to Jonathan Eburne for suggesting this book.
8. Halberstam, *Female Masculinity*, xi.
9. Halberstam, ibid., p. 141.
10. Halberstam, ibid., pp. 153–63. Distinguishing between identity categories simultaneously threatens to shore up and destabilise them. Debates over the gender identity of the protagonist of *The Well* ran aground because of the unstable categories scholars invoked: see Doan and Prosser, *Palatable Poison*, in which the irresolvable question of Stephen Gordon's gender cedes to new approaches.
11. Roof, *What Gender Is*, p. 7.
12. Stryker, *Transgender History*, p. 19; Whittle, 'Foreward', p. xi. Stryker offers a carefully nuanced history of transgender; see especially pp. 123–32 for discussion of the 1990s to the present. Debates over transgender are often volatile because of its divergent meanings to self-identified transgender people. As Riggs observes in 'Trans Bodies, Lives and Representations', this 'catch-all term . . . can never adequately refer to a category constituted by people whose standpoints are often incommensurate' (p. 1). Transgender nonetheless remains a useful heuristic for understanding 'variation from gender norms and expectations' (Stryker, ibid., p. 19).
13. Freccero, *Queer / Early / Modern*, p. 3.
14. Freccero, 'Queer Times', p. 20.
15. Hanson, 'Kink in Time'.
16. Derrida, *Archive Fever*, p. 91. Thanks to Melissa Bradshaw for reminding me of this book; I take full responsibility for the conclusions I draw from it.
17. Roof, *What Gender Is*, p. 4, p. 77.
18. Hanson, 'Kink in Time'.
19. Nair, *Secrecy and Sapphic Modernism*, p. 122. Throughout *Gertrude Stein's Transmasculinity*, upon first mention I note in parentheses the composition date of Stein's texts followed by a colon and their first publication date.
20. Stryker and Currah, 'Introduction', p. 8.
21. Foucault, *The History of Sexuality*, p. 43. See Detloff, *The Persistence of Modernism*, pp. 60–2, for a brief analysis of Stein's differences from early twentieth-century and contemporary queer genders. Although Detloff seeks to preserve the 'cultural specificity' and 'particular stylizations of gender performance' of lesbian butch/femme by uncoupling it

from Stein's and Toklas's genderings, I find transhistorical comparisons useful not because they reveal equivalences – they do not – but because they create a context in which the partners' plays on masculinity and femininity can be made legible as manifestations of queer desire.

22. Stein, YCAL MSS 76, Box 38, Folder 791 in the Beinecke Rare Book and Manuscript Library, Yale University.
23. Elliot and Roen, 'Transgenderism and the Question of Embodiment', p. 236.
24. Bernstein, 'Stein's Identity', p. 485.
25. Bernstein, ibid., p. 487, pp. 485–7.
26. Sedgwick, *Tendencies*, p. xii.
27. Stryker et al., 'Introduction', p. 11.
28. Stryker et al., ibid., p. 13; Sedgwick, ibid., p. xii.
29. Thomas, '"What Time We Kiss,"' p. 333.
30. Thomas, ibid., p. 333; Freeman, 'Introduction: Queer Temporalities', p. 163.
31. Stryker and Aizura, 'Introduction', p. 6.
32. Salamon, *Assuming A Body*, p. 59.
33. Prosser, *Second Skins*, p. 141, identifies 1882 as the date of the first 'genital masculinization' but notes that such procedures were not widely available at the time.
34. Stryker and Aizura, 'Introduction', p. 6.
35. Freccero, 'Queer Times', p. 23.
36. Roof, *What Gender Is*, pp. 19–20.
37. Fuss, *Identification Papers*, pp. 9–10.
38. Freccero, 'Queer Times', p. 23.
39. Fuss, ibid., p. 8.
40. Freeman, *Time Binds*, p. xi.
41. Freeman, ibid., p. 7.
42. Stein, *Paris France*, p. 38; Freeman, ibid., p. 7.
43. Stein, 'How Writing Is Written', p. 490.
44. Stein, ibid.
45. Freeman, 'Introduction: Queer Temporalities', p. 159.
46. Corn and Latimer, *Seeing Gertrude Stein*, pp. 31–5.
47. Corn and Latimer, ibid., p. 51.
48. Hemingway, *A Moveable Feast*, The Restored Edition, pp. 24–6. An earlier edition of *A Moveable Feast* was published in 1964; neither is definitive.
49. Corn and Latimer, ibid., p. 51. Earlier Stein scholars assert that in so doing, Stein imitated patriarchy's worst features. Benstock, for example, asserts that Stein's and Toklas's 'model for marriage was a paternal and heterosexual one that duplicated the authority and submission patterns found . . . in the relationship of Stein's own parents . . . or the power

structure of her more recent relationship with Leo', the domineering brother whose 'worst habits' Stein supposedly 'began to imitate' with Alice (*Women*, p. 166). For similar assertions, see DeKoven, *A Different Language*, p. 136; Nair, *Secrecy and Sapphic Modernism*, pp. 119–51; Wagner-Martin, *'Favored Strangers'*; and Will, *Gertrude Stein*.

For approaches in which butch/femme dynamics signify not as copies but repetitions-with-difference of heterosexual gender norms, see Judith Butler, *Bodies That Matter*, *Gender Trouble*, and 'Imitation and Gender Insubordination'; Case, 'Toward a Butch-Femme Aesthetic'; Munt (ed.), *Butch/Femme*; and Nestle (ed.), *The Persistent Desire*. In *Seeing Gertrude Stein*, Corn and Latimer approach Stein through these theories.

50. Halberstam, *Female Masculinity*; Roof, *What Gender Is*, p. 226.
51. Roof, *What Gender Is*, p. 7.
52. Thomas, '"What Time We Kiss"', p. 333; Freeman, *Time Binds*, p. xv.
53. Stein, *The Making of Americans*, p. 21.
54. Stryker, *Transgender History*, p. 19.
55. Stryker and Currah, 'Introduction', p. 8.
56. For work that considers Stein's and Toklas's split subjectivities in light of feminist and queer theory, see Andersen, 'I Am Not Who "I" Pretend to Be'; Blackmer, 'Lesbian Modernism'; Gilmore, 'A Signature of Lesbian Autobiography'; Hovey, *A Thousand Words*; Meese, 'Gertrude Stein and Me'; Smith, *Subjectivity, Identity, and the Body*; and Will, *Gertrude Stein*.
57. Dubious arguments that Stein imitated male masculinity often note her claim to 'maleness' or interest in Weininger; see DeKoven, *A Different Language*, p. 136 and Nair, *Secrecy and Sapphic Modernism*, pp. 119–51, for two examples. Alternatively, Sandra Gilbert and Susan Gubar connect Stein's masculinity to Freud's theory of the 'masculinity complex', according to which a woman's masculinity ostensibly disavows castration. They do not deride Stein for having presumably taken this route; instead, they assert that Freud describes a strategy for circumventing subjugation. See Gilbert and Gubar, *No Man's Land, Vol. 1*, pp. 184–9; and *No Man's Land, Vol. 2*, pp. 238–44.
58. Toklas, *What Is Remembered*, p. 139.
59. Halberstam, *Female Masculinity*.
60. Stein, YCAL MSS 76, Box 38, Folder 791 in the Beinecke Rare Book and Manuscript Library, Yale University.
61. Stein, ibid.
62. See Ruddick, *Reading Gertrude Stein*, p. 53; DeKoven, *A Different Language*, pp. 131–7; Robert Martin, '*The Mother of Us All* and American History'; and Wagner-Martin, *'Favored Strangers'*.
63. Sedgwick, *Between Men*.

64. Although in 'Men in Love?', Lundén is right that 'gay' readings of 'Men' need complication, he is overly defensive in simultaneously acknowledging and denying homosexual desire's effects. See Stein, 'Men'.
65. Sedgwick, *Touching Feeling*, p. 8.
66. Sedgwick, *Tendencies*, p. xii.
67. Prosser, *Second Skins*, p. 21.
68. Weiner and Young, 'Introduction: Queer Bonds', p. 225.
69. McCallum, 'Stein *und Zeit*', p. 239.
70. McCallum, ibid., p. 239.
71. Weiner and Young, 'Introduction: Queer Bonds', p. 226.
72. Weiner and Young, ibid., p. 230, p. 225.
73. Roof, *What Gender Is*, p. 28.
74. Roof, ibid., p. 28.
75. Weiner and Young, 'Introduction: Queer Bonds', p. 225.
76. Weiner and Young, ibid., p. 227.
77. See Lubar for an account of Stein's and Picasso's gender dynamics; see Stein's *The Autobiography of Alice B. Toklas* and Hemingway's retaliatory *A Moveable Feast*, The Restored Edition, for further evidence of her complicated bonds with her male colleagues.
78. Weiner and Young, ibid., p. 225; Foucault, 'The Social Triumph of the Sexual Will', p. 160.
79. Sherwood Anderson, 'Gertrude Stein'.
80. Foucault, 'Friendship as a Way of Life', p. 138. See also Weiner and Young, ibid., for a similar line of argument.
81. Foucault, 'Friendship', p. 136.
82. Halberstam, *Queer Art*, p. 148.
83. The implications of Stein's Vichy complicities are beyond this book's scope. She translated Pétain's speeches and was protected by collaborator Fäy during the war, but her political allegiances remain disputed. Will's *Unlikely Collaboration* is the most comprehensive study of Stein's connections to Pétain and Fäy. Richly contextualised and backed by extensive archival research, *Unlikely Collaboration* nonetheless reduces the political complexities of Stein's wartime texts to the propagandistic purposes motivating her public writing during the Vichy regime. For further debate, see Benstock, 'Paris Lesbianism'; Bernstein (ed.), *Gertrude Stein's war years*; Davis, '"Even Cake Gets to Have Another Meaning"'; Lawrence, 'Who Could Have Read the Signs?'; Lesinska, 'Gertrude Stein's War Autobiographies'; Malcolm, *Two Lives*; Olson, 'Gertrude Stein, William James, and Habit in the Shadow of War'; Souhami, *Gertrude and Alice*, p. 233; Stendahl, 'Why the witch-hunt against Gertrude Stein?'; Catharine Stimpson et al., 'A Play to Be Performed'; Van Dusen, 'Portrait of a National Fetish'; Whittier-Ferguson, 'Stein in Time' and 'The Liberation of Gertrude

Stein'; Will, 'Lost in Translation'; Wineapple, 'The Politics of Politics'; and Zox-Weaver, *Women Modernists and Fascism*.

84. Sedgwick, *Touching Feeling*, p. 8; Anderson, 'Gertrude Stein', p. 3.
85. Caughie, 'The Temporality of Modernist Life Writing', p. 502.
86. Caughie, ibid., p. 502.
87. Glavey, *The Wallflower Avant-Garde*, p. 3.
88. Sedgwick, 'Preface' to *Between Men* (1992), p. x; Glavey, ibid., p. 24.
89. Thompson, 'Language and Democracy', pp. 131–2, stresses William James's and pragmatism's influence on Stein's approach to writing, which is beyond this book's scope, but does not repudiate reading practices not derived from pragmatism.
90. Thompson, ibid., p. 132, p. 149. Stein, YCAL MSS 76, Box 38, Folder 791 in the Beinecke Rare Book and Manuscript Library, Yale University.
91. Lorange, *How Reading Is Written*, pp. 48–51.
92. Rohy, 'Hemingway, Literalism, and Transgender Reading', p. 151.
93. Rohy, ibid., p. 151.
94. Whittle, 'Foreward', p. xi.
95. Benstock, *Women*, p. 171.
96. Benstock, ibid., p. 177.
97. Doan, *Fashioning Sapphism*.
98. See, for example, Daniel, *Gertrude Stein*, p. 50, and Corn and Latimer, *Seeing Gertrude Stein*.
99. DeKoven, *A Different Language*, p. 136. More recently, Nair, in *Secrecy and Sapphic Modernism*, pp. 119–51, argues that Stein identified with a defition of 'genius' grounded in 'maleness' to claim male 'privileges' and underscore her exceptional status in comparison to women writers maligned in her time. For variations on these themes, see Benstock, *Women*, p. 166; Gilbert and Gubar, *No Man's Land*, Vol. 2; Stimpson, 'Gertrice/Altrude', 'Gertrude Stein and the Transposition of Gender' and 'The Mind, the Body, and Gertrude Stein'; Wagner-Martin, *'Favored Strangers'*; and Will, *Gertrude Stein*.
100. DeKoven, *A Different Language*, pp. 135–7. See Fuss, *Identification Papers*, ibid., for extended analysis of uses of psychoanalytic accounts of identification in queer theory.
101. Knapp, *Gertrude Stein*, p. 22.
102. See Gilmore, 'A Signature of Lesbian Autobiography'; Holbrook, 'Lifting Bellies, Filling Petunias, and Making Meanings'; Hovey, *A Thousand Words*; Lubar, 'Unmasking Pablo's Gertrude'; Rehling, 'Taking Patriarchy out of Poetry'; and Smith, *Subjectivity, Identity, and the Body*, for arguments that Stein questions and unfixes gender. See Stimpson, 'Somagrams', and Chessman, *The Public is Invited to Dance*, for pre-Butlerian variants. Some images of Stein suggest that her clothing and self-presentation sent out ambiguous signals

that queered gender. Her many plays with pronouns likewise lend credence to such arguments. As Gilbert and Gubar observe, *Tender Buttons* engages 'the way in which clothing constitutes a sign system that can open or close off meaning', revealing 'the arbitrariness of conventional structures of signification' (*No Man's Land, Vol. 2*, pp. 355–6).

103. Lubar, 'Unmasking Pablo's Gertrude', p. 58.
104. Sayre, 'The Artist's Model', pp. 31–2.
105. DeKoven, *A Different Language*, p. 136.
106. Butler in Butler and Athanasiou, *Dispossession*, p. 67.
107. Stryker and Aizura, 'Introduction', p. 7.
108. Caughie, 'The Temporality of Modernist Life Writing', p. 520.
109. Caughie, ibid., p. 503; Stone, 'The *Empire* Strikes Back', p. 165.
110. Prosser, *Second Skins*, p. 191.
111. Caughie, 'The Temporality of Modernist Life Writing', p. 519.
112. Caughie, ibid., p. 502.
113. Caughie, ibid., p. 502.
114. Stein, 'How Writing Is Written', p. 488; Caughie, 'The Temporality of Modernist Life Writing', p. 505.
115. Caughie, ibid., p. 505.
116. Stein, 'Composition as Explanation', pp. 517–18. For more on temporal variation in Stein's writing, see Folgarait, *Painting 1909*, and Voris, *The Composition of Sense*.
117. Halberstam, *In a Queer Time and Place*, p. 1.
118. McCallum, 'Stein *und Zeit*', p. 240.
119. McCallum, ibid., p. 240.
120. Freeman, 'Introduction: Queer Temporalities', p. 163.
121. Stein, 'Portraits and Repetition', p. 177.
122. Stein, ibid., p. 178, p. 168.
123. Stein, 'Composition as Explanation', p. 517.
124. Freeman, 'Introduction: Queer Temporalities', p. 163.
125. Freeman, ibid., p. 163; Caughie, 'The Temporality of Modernist Life Writing', p. 520; Stein, 'Composition as Explanation', p. 517; Freeman, ibid., p. 163.
126. Siraganian, 'Speculating on an Art Movement', pp. 596–8.
127. Caughie, 'The Temporality of Modernist Life Writing', p. 519.
128. Gherovici, 'The Art of the Symptom', pp. 255–62. Lacan, *The Seminar of Jacques Lacan, Book XXIII*, p. 11. Lacanians have proposed divergent explanations of the *sinthome*'s role in psychical life. Although these debates are beyond this book's scope, my intervention appears as 'Žižek's Antagonism'. Gherovici moves Lacanian thinking away from Millot's transphobic interpretation of the *sinthome* and rehabilitates it for trans-affirmative psychoanalysis.

129. Lacan, *The Seminar of Jacques Lacan, Book III*, p. 96, p. 150; Lacan, *Seminar of Jacques Lacan, Book XXIII*, p. 11. Other *sinthomes* identified in *Seminar XXIII* include 'woman' (p. 84) and 'psychoanalyst' (p. 116).
130. Gherovici, 'The Art of the Symptom', pp. 255–62.
131. Gherovici, 'The Transsexual Body Written', pp. 261–7; Gherovici, 'The Art of the Symptom', pp. 255–62. Although Gherovici's argument concerns transsexual writing, it can be expanded to account for transsubjectivities that do not involve physical or hormonal transition: see Coffman, 'Žižek's Antagonism'.
132. Caughie, 'The Temporality of Modernist Life Writing', p. 503.
133. Stein, 'Portraits and Repetition', p. 177.
134. Stein, ibid., pp. 167–8.
135. Stein, ibid., pp. 166–7. Since 1990, overlaps between Steinian 'insistence' and theories of reiteration in books such as Butler's *Gender Trouble* have fuelled feminist and queer approaches to Stein. Although she uses the term somewhat differently than contemporary theorists, her concept of 'insistence' is philosophically compatible with the post-structural argument (traceable to Jacques Derrida's critique of the idea of the 'origin' in *Dissemination*) that repetition is never perfect and inevitably entails difference.
136. Stein, ibid., p. 171.
137. Stein, ibid., p. 179.
138. Stein, ibid., p. 169, p. 179.
139. Stockton, 'Rhythm', p. 347.
140. Caughie, 'The Temporality of Modernist Life Writing', p. 502, p. 519; Stein, 'How Writing Is Written', p. 490; Stein, 'Composition As Explanation', p. 517.
141. Perloff, 'Poetry as Word-System', p. 76.
142. Krauss, 'In the Name of Picasso', p. 33.
143. Krauss, ibid., p. 39.
144. Krauss, ibid., p. 39.
145. Thanks to Octavio González for suggesting in another context that scholars who repudiate biographical evidence mimic high modernist's theories of aesthetic impersonality. In my view, recent interventions into formalist debates over modernists' approach to the autonomy of the aesthetic object – such as Siraganian's *Modernism's Other Work* – succumb to this fantasy.
146. Jacques Lacan, 'The agency of the letter in the unconscious', p. 166; Clark, *Picasso and Truth*, pp. 9–10.
147. Stein, *Everybody's Autobiography*, 328. Similar language appears in her lecture 'What Are Masterpieces' (1936: 1940) and text called 'Identity A Poem' (1935: 1940).

148. Recker, 'Pitting "Matisse" Against "Picasso"', p. 28.
149. Clark, *Picasso and Truth*, p. 13.
150. Foucault, 'What Is an Author?', pp. 118–25.
151. Foucault, ibid., pp. 124–5.
152. For an example, see Siraganian's analysis of Stein's writings about painting in *Modernism's Other Work*. Arguing that Stein developed her own variant on modernist theories of the autonomous aesthetic object, Siraganian uses them to read Stein's work. See also Voris, *The Composition of Sense*, for similarly constrictive claims.
153. Barthes, 'The Death of the Author', p. 50.
154. Barthes, 'From Work to Text', p. 61.
155. Barthes, ibid., p. 61.
156. Barthes, ibid., p. 61.
157. Barthes, ibid., pp. 61–2.
158. Van Vechten, 'Gertrude Stein', p. 63. For recent work on Stein and celebrity, see Curnutt, 'Inside and Outside'; Glass, *Authors Inc.*; Goldman, *Modernism is the Literature of Celebrity*; Jaillant, '*Shucks, we've got glamour girls too!*'; Leick, *Gertrude Stein and the Making of an American Celebrity*; Siraganian, 'Speculating on an Art Movement'; and Zox-Weaver, *Women Modernists and Fascism*.
159. See Jaillant, ibid., on the importance of the Modern Library's reissue of *Three Lives* to Stein's rise to celebrity in 1933.
160. Roof, *What Gender Is*, p. 34.
161. Silver, *Virginia Woolf Icon*, p. 15.
162. Silver, ibid., p. 15; Stuart Hall, 'Notes on Deconstructing "the Popular"', p. 77.
163. Silver, ibid., pp. 16–17.
164. Silver, ibid., p. 214.
165. Barthes, 'From Work to Text', p. 61.
166. Roof, *What Gender Is*, pp. 19–20.
167. For queer theories of the gaze, see Halberstam, 'The Transgender Look', in *In a Queer Time*, pp. 76–96; Silverman, *Threshold*; and Roof, ibid.
168. Bersani, 'Is the Rectum a Grave?', p. 217.
169. Stein, *The Autobiography*, p. 204, p. 208; Hemingway quoted in Sutherland, 'Alice and Gertrude and Others', p. 297; Stein, *The Autobiography*, p. 204.
170. Portions of Stein's 'Evidence' were first published in 1930; the full text was first printed in *A Stein Reader* in 1993.
171. Cromwell, *Transmen & FTMs*, p. 130.
172. Barthes, 'From Work to Text', pp. 61–2.
173. Stryker and Currah, 'Introduction', p. 8.

Chapter 1

Seeing Stein's Masculinity

> Each generation has something different at which they are all looking . . . The only thing that is different from one time to another is what is seen and what is seen depends upon how everybody is doing everything. This makes the thing we are looking at very different and this makes what those who describe it make of it, it makes a composition, it confuses, it shows, it is, it looks, it likes it as it is, and this makes what is seen as it is seen. Nothing changes from generation to generation except the thing seen and that makes a composition.
>
> Gertrude Stein, 'Composition as Explanation'

Seeing Stein's shifting masculinity requires close attention to the context and varied consequences of the different perspectives from which people see her life. The divergent effects of these factors produce a multiplicity of 'Steins' constituting a variety of responses, from affirmation to derision and everything in between. I inevitably look back at Stein through the lens of the present, in which transgender studies has challenged the assumption that cross-gender identification is a sign of self-hatred. This standpoint allows me to view her masculinity affirmatively to validate a stance she lived out and inscribed in her texts. Yet Stein's transmasculinity has always registered – albeit obliquely, and not always favourably – in others' photographs of and writings about her. Thanks to decades of work by scholars and curators, her masculinity is now more readily available for view than during her lifetime, but this is not to say that evidence of it was not present in the past. It was there: visible to those who knew where to look, yet hidden in plain sight from those who refused to see it.

Lacan's theory of the gaze has been adapted by feminist and queer theorists to elucidate these dynamics.[1] As Roof explains, the 'gaze' – the 'sense of being seen' – 'multiplies the necessary vectors of being looked at to no fewer than three at any given time – looking, being looked at, and what the subject has that is "given to be seen"'.[2] Although '[t]he vector from which this being-seenness emanates is unlocatable', the gaze produces what Roof calls 'vantage'.[3] A 'second-order' formation, 'vantage' provides 'imaginary framing position[s]' that create the 'illusion' of objectivity and naturalise culturally and historically contingent 'gender regimes' that trick us into believing that 'we can see gender for what it is'.[4] Consequently, 'genders are always mis-taken, operating on the objective plane of the fantasies of others'.[5] These 'fantasies' have resulted in varied perspectives on Stein's transmasculinity.

Anamorphic changes have taken place in Stein's dominant image over the years; the meanings attached to her masculinity have shifted through the play of different contexts. Lacan explains anamorphosis through reference to *The Ambassadors*, Hans Holbein's painting in which a foreground element that appears to be a piece of wood when approached frontally transforms into a skull when viewed askance.[6] Whereas Lacan's analysis of *The Ambassadors* posits only two angles of view and two different interpretations of the object at the bottom of the frame, Roof describes this vacillation as an effect of 'vantage', which creates 'an infinite number of' positions for viewing.[7] A queer approach to the visual would thus 'not presume a central or neutral position from which one becomes or moves or deviates', as Lorange argues.[8] Instead, because queer viewing 'always occurs at an oblique angle', Stein's shifting image is best read by attending to the proliferation of perspectives that mobilise a wide variety of 'Steins'.[9]

These varied 'Steins' emerge through shifts in the field of vision. As Roof explains, both the 'look' and the 'gaze' are 'fictive' effects of 'vantage'.[10] What I designate as the Gaze – what Roof calls the general 'sense of being seen' – sets in motion the 'mise en abyme' of the visual, which deploys various gazes and looks to proliferate possibilities for viewing.[11] Silverman's reading of Lacan usefully distinguishes between the latter two concepts. Although both are called *le regard* in French, they describe different aspects of viewing. Whereas 'the gaze' refers to the way the object presents itself to be seen, 'the look' refers to the approach an individual takes toward it.[12] The shifting perceptions and multiple significations inflecting Stein's masculinity at different points in time can all be understood as effects of the play between the Gaze, 'the gaze', and individual 'looks'.

Moreover, as Roof explains, 'Because both the looker and the looked-at are simultaneously subject to and object of the gaze, the look itself circulates among ever-proliferating terms governed by the subject's drives and the cultural modes through which the gazing and gazed constitute privileged sites of desire.'[13] There is thus an intimate connection between sexuality and the vacillation of images. Rose notes that in a reading of a drawing by Leonardo da Vinci, Freud 'relates . . . a failure to depict the sexual act to bisexuality and to a problem of representational space. The uncertain sexual identity muddles the plane of the image so that the spectator does not know where she or he stands in relationship to the picture. A confusion at the level of sexuality brings with it a disturbance of the visual field.'[14] The spectator's sexuality and sexual aspects of the image all play into viewing. These libidinal dynamics inform shifts in the 'gaze' exerted by the image and 'the looks' of spectators viewing it.

However, by conflating maleness with masculinity and femaleness with femininity, Rose assumes that there are only two possible 'sexual identities' – 'male or female' – and uses the unfortunate word 'confusion' to describe the sexual and visual uncertainty resulting from the spectator's inability to fix the image within those terms.[15] Yet importantly, she exposes Lacanian 'sexual difference' as an ideological fantasy that must be 'challenge[d]': she writes that 'our sexual identities as male or female, our confidence in language as true or false, and our security in the image we judge as perfect or flawed, are fantasies' that 'Leonardo's drawing . . . momentarily allow[s] to crumble'.[16] However, her argument does not go beyond this fantasy, instead retaining language about 'sexual difference' consistent with many Lacanians' explanations of sexuation.[17]

Sexuation is said to afford the subject a 'choice of sex as masculine or feminine in assuming an active or passive position vis-à-vis his or her object of desire', as Ellie Ragland puts it.[18] However, in *Seminar XX*, Lacan states that '[m]an and . . . woman . . . are nothing but signifiers'.[19] Because they 'derive their function from . . . saying (*dire*) as a distinct incarnation of sex, . . . [t]he Other . . . can . . . only be the Other sex'.[20] If this 'sex' is 'nothing but signifiers', one need not insist that the only options are '[m]an' and 'woman'.[21] Furthermore, Lacan claims that the 'object *a*' – the object-cause of desire – is '*a*-sexual (*a-sexué*)' and that 'The Other presents itself to the subject only in an *a*-sexual form.'[22] If the 'object *a*' and '[t]he Other' are unsexed and the desiring positions that support them are sustained by 'nothing but signifiers', we can go beyond the language of 'man' and 'woman' Lacan deployed in the 1970s. Rose's insight that 'Leonardo's drawing' collapses the 'fantasies' of 'sexual identities' reveals the fictitious character of the 'masculine' and 'feminine' positions and hints at the possibility that sexuation could work otherwise: a possibility Gherovici explores in her Lacanian account of transgender embodiment.[23] This revision of Lacan suggests an approach to gender, sexuality and vision that does not assume that perspectival vacillation takes place only between the 'masculine' and 'feminine', and remains open to the possibility that it could unfold in many different ways.

The psychical vicissitudes at work in perception vacillate in ways that proliferate different versions of Stein's image. Both individual and collective dynamics inform this process. Silverman's theory of the 'screen' – the image produced by the gaze – accounts for the interplay between normativity and resistance that plays out in perception. She explains that '[t]he full range of representational coordinates which are culturally available at a particular moment in time constitute . . . the "screen"', which includes 'not only . . . normative representations, but also of all kinds of oppositional and subcultural representations'.[24] She points out that only some images constituted by the 'screen' are '"given-to-be-seen"': propped up by hegemony and given the appearance of 'a certain inevitability'.[25] Arguing that the look can be a powerful way of defying hegemonic representation and the gaze that sustains it, Silverman writes that 'the look has all along possessed the capacity to see otherwise from and even in contradiction to the gaze' animating perception of the 'given-to-be-seen'.[26] She emphasises 'the eye's transformative potentiality – its capacity for looking from a position which is not assigned in advance, and for affirming certain ostensibly marginal elements within the screen at the expense of those that are culturally valorized'.[27] Thus, even though it is 'limited by the representational logic and material practices which organize the visual field at any moment in time', and is 'further circumscribed by the imperative placed upon it to apprehend the world via the screen', the look can enact change.[28] Because it is implicated in unpredictable psychical dynamics and 'subject to a complex series of conscious and unconscious "vicissitudes"', it 'can completely transform the value of what is originally seen'.[29] When a look diverges from the angle encouraged by the gaze and works 'in concert with enough other looks' to 'reterritorialize the screen', 'new elements' come 'into cultural prominence' and submerge 'those which . . . constitute normative representation'.[30]

Silverman's theory aptly describes the shifts in the 'screen' and the 'gaze' that have attended Stein's reception as novel possibilities for gaining 'vantage' and seeing her masculinity differently have emerged.[31] Photographs have been important to this process. As Walter Benjamin argues, photography reveals the 'optical unconscious' by capturing elements not immediately visible to the naked eye.[32] Unlike paintings and artworks crafted without the technologies of 'mechanical reproduction', photographs are important sources of historical evidence that instantaneously register materials usually overlooked and unlikely to be emphasised within hegemonic representation.[33] Reading photographs with an eye for these elements is not to engage in retroactive projection but to 'brush history against the grain' and grasp 'an image which flashes up at the instant when it can be recognized' even though the dominant gaze would distract us from it.[34] Many contemporary reactions to photographs of Stein engage this process by emphasising elements of her masculinity that were present but not regularly noticed or affirmed during her lifetime. By encouraging an accumulation of such looks, queer scholars and curators have collectively worked over the last several decades to 'reterritorialize the screen', see signs of Stein's masculinity, and cast it in a positive light. Moreover, the recent rise of transgender studies promises that what Halberstam calls 'the transgender gaze' – which I prefer to call the 'transgender look' – will further this process of reterritorialisation and bring her masculinity into even sharper focus.[35]

As Roof reminds us, 'vantage' creates the false 'illusion' that gender can be viewed objectively.[36] Capitulating to the hegemonic modes of looking fostered by the fantasy of objectivity would assign undue truth-value to others' constructions of the ways 'gender regimes' operated during Stein's historical moment.[37] I would rather acknowledge the personal 'passion' and 'desire' that subtend the study of materials from the past; I would rather keep 'open' than close down the 'interpretive crisis' that Dorothy Stringer, following Benjamin, sees as photography's provocation.[38] Embracing Lacan's insight that fantasy structures rather than diverges from reality, I consciously engage my 'eye's transformative potentiality – its capacity for looking from a position' that is 'not assigned in advance' – to see signs of Stein's transmasculinity in the past and present.[39] Noticing and validating 'ostensibly marginal elements within the screen at the expense of those that are culturally valorized', I employ a transgender look to offer a 'transformative' form of 'vantage' that will shift the gaze through which Stein's masculinity is given to be seen.[40]

In 'Composition as Explanation', Stein herself points to the possibility of profoundly transformative shifts in 'vantage' when she claims that 'Each generation has something different at which they are all looking . . . The only thing that is different from one time to another is what is seen and what is seen depends upon how everybody is doing everything . . . Nothing changes from generation to generation except the thing seen and that makes a composition.'[41] This argument points to the capacity of 'scopic regimes' to reconfigure their terrain by shifting the gaze and changing the 'given-to-be-seen' that forms the image.[42] Suggesting that this process takes place through a generational shift, Stein assumes that the 'given-to-be-seen' is universally experienced by the members of '[e]ach generation'.[43] Though she acknowledges that the gaze can change over time, she does not question its hegemony at any given moment.

However, there are 'oppositional and subcultural representations' within the screen that can elicit individual looks that eventually come together to shift the gaze.[44] Even when originally formed through the hegemonic gaze, images of Stein contain numerous counterhegemonic representations whose significance has transformed over time. Visual artefacts of her life elicit multivalent responses that simultaneously support and contest a homophobic gaze that abjects her masculinity. In the last several decades, images of Stein that were initially deployed with uncertainty or hostility have been taken up as positive signs of queer masculinity, offering a more affirming 'vantage' from which to view her transmasculine subjectivity.[45]

Seeing Stein anamorphically

Divergent perceptions of Stein's gender were thrown into relief in *Seeing Gertrude Stein*, Corn's and Latimer's 2011 exhibition at San Francisco's Contemporary Jewish Museum. The exhibit and catalogue offered richly contextualised archives of representations of Stein and were part of a citywide celebration timed to coincide with San Francisco's June Pride festivities and LGBT film festival. The de Young museum offered a show on Picasso; the San Francisco Museum of Modern Art mounted *The Steins Collect*, on the Stein siblings' activities as art collectors in modernist Paris. Although both versions of *Seeing Gertrude Stein* used images to narrate significant stages of Stein's life and others' reactions to her, subtle differences between them illuminate the anamorphic plays that emerge whenever her image travels into a new context.

The varied ways Stein's image circulated in 2011 San Francisco reveal shifts in the ways she can be seen. That summer, a 1931 photograph of Stein by gay male fashion photographer George Platt Lynes appeared on banners and buses across San Francisco, advertising *Seeing Gertrude Stein* and *The Steins Collect*.[46] As a troupe of performers from the Yerba Buena complex prepared to march in the Pride Parade dressed as Stein, Toklas and cross-dressed iterations of the painters whose work they collected (complete with a drag queen staged as Matisse's *La Femme au chapeau*), Lynes's image of a very butch Gertrude looked out across some 50,000 dykes and transpeople partying in Dolores Park, revving motorcycles, and marching down Valencia Street. By contrast, the original version of Lynes's portrait (Figure 1.1) is in landscape format and shows Stein looking

Figure 1.1 Photograph by George Platt Lynes, *Gertrude Stein in Bilignin* (c. 1931).

out from Bilignin over France's Rhône Valley unfolding to her right. Set in rural France, the image emphasises her head's stern, masculine profile while showing her woman's vest and blouse. The vertical crop used in the banners advertising the 2011 San Francisco exhibits is quite different: it uses a portrait-style format that centres Stein's head and clothing, cutting out the French countryside and redirecting her look toward the cityscape surrounding the image.

By contrast, in the wake of *The Autobiography*'s publication, the 11 September 1933 issue of *Time* featured a vertical crop of Lynes's photograph on its cover. Such a placement was a sign of 'stardom' by the 1930s.[47] Inside, the magazine offered a review of *The Autobiography* by Agee, who glosses Lynes's photo by characterising Stein as 'a sphinx-like, monolithic mass' whose 'close-cropped top' has 'loomed from afar over the hinterland of letters', appearing in the distance '[l]ike a huge squat mountain on a distant border of the literary kingdom'.[48] Emphasising Stein's uncertain image on the literary landscape and replacing the photograph's representation of the French countryside with text figuring shifting perceptions of her work and person, Agee declares that over the last twenty years, 'eyes accustomed to the landscape are beginning to recognize something portentous in her massive outline'.[49] He then figures Stein's physical and linguistic inaccessibility as potential threats to the 'plain reader'.[50]

Agee tells readers that until *The Autobiography*, Stein had only been approached by serious-minded writers such as Hemingway, Anderson, F. Scott Fitzgerald and Van Vechten – 'supposedly sensible' parties whose 'enthusiastic and grateful tales' Agee's wording undermines.[51] He opines that as the text in which 'Mountain Stein' finally deigns to address 'plain readers', *The Autobiography* may help them 'begin to understand why Gertrude Stein's importance as a writer has received so many reiterated testimonials from writers of accredited sanity'.[52] Praising the book's accessibile language, Agee observes that Toklas is no mere literary device but a 'real live companion-secretary . . . who has lived with Gertrude Stein for the last 26 years': after meeting in Paris, 'They set up house together, at No. 27 Rue de Fleurus', and 'have been together ever since'.[53] Breaking paragraph after the phrase 'been together ever since', Agee's wording calls attention to Stein's and Toklas's relationship without naming it. Although his strategy exploits heteronormative readers' denials enabled by 'what Sedgwick describes as the "privilege of unknowing"' in the early 1930s, he also offers Stein's and Toklas's devotion as evidence for positive reports' validity.[54] Moreover, his reference to her fans' 'accredited sanity' also invites readers to re-evaluate dismissals of Stein's writings as products of an infantile or demented mind.[55]

However, Agee's article eventually takes an anamorphic turn. His praise of the couple and *The Autobiography* is followed by a return to Stein's earlier and more experimental work, which he quotes and derides at length at the expense of the book that is his ostensible subject. Even worse, the article is illustrated with an early photograph of Toklas and Stein captioned to appeal to readerly perceptions of her work's absurdity and heighten the suspicions of insanity Agee's backhanded reference to the testimony of her friends of 'accredited sanity' introduces. In this illustration, a seated and gloomy Stein dominates the frame as the couple looks at a group of pigeons, while the caption – a line from *Tender Buttons* that Agee later mocks – reads, 'Toklas & Stein: "Elephant beaten with candy" means something to them.'[56] Insinuating that the couple's connection is as meaningless as a 'pedestrian reader' would find *Tender Buttons*, Agee suggests that Stein's and Toklas's way of making meaning is meaningless, perhaps even crazy.[57] If Benjamin is right that the 'shocks' induced by photographs 'bring the viewer's association mechanism to a standstill' and demand that the photographer supplement the image with a 'caption . . . that implicates photography in the literalization of all the conditions of life and without which all photographic construction is stalled in vagueness', this one furthers rather than contains shock by directing readers to Stein's most opaque statements.[58]

Agee's treatment of this illustration echoes his opening paragraph, which identifies Stein as a writer obscured by her cheerier counterparts and 'by the self-induced fog that hangs around her close-cropped top'.[59] This introduction, which stresses Stein's masculine haircut, foreshadows his closing statement that she has significant 'autobiographical passages which she does not choose to run'.[60] Citing as evidence of Stein's evasiveness the fact that the only confessional moment in *The Autobiography* reveals her to have been 'lonesome' during 'an agony of adolescence', Agee hints at the prospect of depression rather than at Stein's gender presentation or sexual orientation.[61] However, taken in association with the captioned illustration of a gloomy and incomprehensible Stein, the conclusion participates in a common early twentieth-century troping of queers as miserable and insane – even though Agee's testimony to her friends' 'accredited sanity' initially appears to discredit such views.[62] Moreover, the amount of space Stein occupies in the image associates the 'portentous' properties of her 'massive outline' and increasing pull on the literary landscape with her and Toklas's purported penchant for meaninglessness.[63]

Mirroring Stein's account in *The Autobiography* of the shocks to vision supported by her patronage of fauvist and cubist painters earlier in the century, Agee's article subtly figures Stein's size, gender and sexuality as signifiers of disturbing changes in the early twentieth-century landscape.[64] Rather than praise her modernist innovations or offer readers a route into her more difficult writings, he elevates the 'plain reader' as the yardstick by which her work should be judged inadequate.[65] By glossing Lynes's image of Stein's masculine silhouette in this manner and supplementing it with an illustration of her and Toklas captioned to heighten the shock of their difference from *Time*'s middlebrow readership, Agee confirms Stringer's hunch that despite the revolutionary potential Benjamin attributes to photographs' capacity to 'shock' their viewers out of habitual ways of seeing and thinking, the medium can sometimes 'be recuperated to conservative ends'.[66]

However, the 'interpretive crisis' Agee's review strives to contain would remain 'open' as these and other images of Stein travelled into new contexts.[67] His euphemisms for Stein's and Toklas's relationship were common in coverage of their 1934–5 lecture tour of the United States and, as Corn and Latimer observe, could have been understood at the time as designating a queer partnership. They also note that the first edition of *The Autobiography* includes domestic photographs of Stein and Toklas filling in what the written text does not say about their relationship, and features a back cover blurb by Van Vechten whose designation of Toklas as Stein's 'intimate companion' would have increased the likelihood of their being perceived as a couple.[68] Moreover, Corn and Latimer argue that press coverage of the US tour 'treated the two women as a celebrity couple' by depicting their dynamics instead of focusing solely on Stein.[69]

Nonetheless, Corn and Latimer overlook the way the euphemistic character of the term 'companion' also enables *disavowals* of Stein's and Toklas's relationship, as do the journalistic conventions that communicated this information so subtly that it could easily have been overlooked. Although Corn and Latimer convincingly demonstrate that Stein and Toklas were constructed as partners for the gaze and that evidence of their relationship appeared on the 'screen' during the 1934–5 tour, the art historians do not remark upon the way signifiers of the pair's gender and sexuality did not *overtly* challenge the assumptions of heteronormative vision. As Nair observes, *The Autobiography* – the occasion for the lecture tour – turns on heteronormative readers' '"privilege of unknowing"' about queer relationships.[70] Although the text 'insists on the immutability of the relationship between Stein and Toklas', using the latter to view the former and register their 'relationship in writing' through hints allowing savvy queer readers to see them as a couple, the book nonetheless obscures their sexual desire and is only explicit about its heterosexual characters' romantic relationships.[71] Moreover, as Benstock notes, Stein and Toklas guarded their household's privacy: while their relationship was known to friends and colleagues, they phased out the salon and began to control visitors carefully within a few years of Toklas's arrival.[72] Thus, while many subculturally attuned early twentieth-century readers could have readily recognised Stein and Toklas as a couple during their trip to the United States, bearers of heteronormative looks could have easily missed or disavowed their sexuality. Their relationship was visible to those that knew how to look and wished to do so, but remained obscure to those unable or unwilling to see it.

Recent queer scholarship on Stein and Toklas has named their relationship, stabilising the meaning of details that signify it and making disavowal – and the heteronormative gaze that obscures their queerness – impossible to sustain. *Seeing Gertrude Stein* similarly performed the important work of shifting the gaze through which Stein and Toklas are given to be seen. While public awareness of their partnership is much higher now than it was during their lifetimes, the catalogue weaves decades' worth of queer scholarship together with original research to increase general readers' familiarity with their relationship's impact on Stein's *oeuvre*. In so doing, Corn and Latimer offer an affirmative resignification of Stein's masculinity while documenting the effects on representation of hostility to it.

The resignification of Lynes's 1931 photograph of Stein in 2011 San Francisco similarly demonstrates the power of queer-affirmative looks to 'reterritorialize the screen' and shift the way Stein and Toklas are given to be seen.[73] As new material enters the screen through the image's recontextualisation, new 'vantage[s]' emerge to bring Stein's masculinity into the foreground, affirm its value and counter Agee's suggestion of her monstrosity.[74] Unlike his Stein, whose grounding in the Rhône Valley unsettled hegemonic viewers of the literary and artistic terrain with her 'portentous' and 'massive' profile, 2011 San Francisco's Stein attracted few distressed responses.[75] Lynes's image of Stein became an icon of queer masculinity presiding over the city, and she and Toklas were celebrated in the Pride Parade. San Franciscan tropes from the late twentieth century thoroughly overtook the parade's interpretation of Toklas. Despite her embrace of bourgeois dress in early twentieth-century France, her impersonator in 2011 San Francisco wore hippyish clothing and distributed brownies whose reference to her famous Haschish Fudge recipe resonated with the city's countercultural history.[76]

Decades of scholarship had prepared San Francisco's curators, lecturers and performers to accurately communicate the importance of Stein's writing and collecting to art history, literary history and musical history. Hailing both specialist and general-interest audiences, these carefully researched offerings consistently affirmed aspects of Stein's and her work's difference from norms, countering the biases informing earlier portrayals. During *The Steins Collect*, SFMOMA curator Frank Schmigel's public lecture highlighted the impact of her work across the arts. Rejecting early scholarship that maligned Stein for her corpulence, healthy self-esteem, and reiterative writing, Schmigel drew on current scholarship that considers these qualities strengths. Revaluing perceptions of Stein's texts as childish, he traced out the way the general public has gradually caught up with her avant-garde strategies: texts such as 'If I Told Him' were poorly received during Stein's lifetime but have since prompted contemporary experimental poetry and resonances with patterns of reiteration in hip hop.[77] Similarly, in a counterpoint to past attempts to abject Stein for her masculinity, size and intellect, both Schmigel's lecture and *Seeing Gertrude Stein* consistently placed a positive value on these qualities.

Yerba Buena's celebratory approach to Stein was not without its well-placed critics, however. *San Francisco Chronicle* opera critic Joshua Kosman praised Ensemble Parallèle's's 2011 interpretation and performances of her opera *Four Saints in Three Acts* but condescendingly recycled the claims to Stein's purported puerility

Schmigel's lecture refuted.[78] Kosman describes the opera as 'silly', 'naïve', 'cute' and 'chuckle-headed': a 'cloying little theatrical concoction' that 'is the grade-school pageant of the operatic repertoire'.[79] He claims that 'if you're an adult', you must 'pat it on the head, coo indulgently, and wait for it to be over already'.[80] Although Kosman differs from his early twentieth-century counterparts by not explicitly referencing Stein's gender and sexuality, he maligns her writing for its presumed 'immaturity', implicitly criticising her linguistic implication in 'queer time'.[81]

New York Times art critic Holland Cotter also wrote a very uneven review of *The Steins Collect* and *Seeing Gertrude Stein* that maligned Stein's taste in art while championing her innovative writing. He concedes that Stein 'did something right' in her 'early days' by buying Picassos, but does not acknowledge an important point *Seeing Gertrude Stein* makes about her later acquisitions: as Picasso's reputation grew, she was priced out and chose more affordable paintings by the gay male friends he dismisses as 'bush-league surrealists'.[82] Cotter also overlooks the attention *Seeing Gertrude Stein* pays to the cultural impact of Stein's turn to predominantly queer artistic and social networks in the 1920s: a move that also informed her choices as an art collector.

Moreover, Sonia Melnikova-Raich published a review of *Seeing Gertrude Stein* that called attention to the troubling questions Janet Malcolm's *Two Lives* and Will's *Unlikely Collaborations* raise about Stein's complicities with the Vichy Regime during World War II.[83] Once *Seeing Gertrude Stein* reached Washington DC in October 2011, public discourse about Stein's right-wing politics had built to a firestorm. Largely repressed in San Francisco, narratives of Stein's wartime allegiances returned with a vengeance in DC, challenging the positive tone and iconic images that had dominated the exhibit's West Coast iteration. Although scholars had been debating these issues ever since Wanda Van Dusen published Stein's 'Introduction to the Speeches of Maréchal Pétain' in 1996, *Seeing Gertrude Stein* provoked widespread controversy in the popular press.[84] In response, United States President Barack Obama dropped Stein's name from his 2012 Jewish Heritage Month proclamation, excluding her from the body politic.[85]

Halberstam rightfully observes that Stein's wartime activities foreground the uncomfortable question of some queers' complicities with fascism and other noxious ideological formations.[86] Challenging

George Chauncey's '"hidden from history"' model of gay and lesbian studies, Halberstam observes that 'as much as' queer scholars 'have to excavate some histories that have been rendered invisible, we also bury others, and sometimes we do both at the same time. You could say that gay and lesbian scholars also have hidden history, unsavory histories, and have a tendency to select from historical archives only the narratives that please' by offering celebratory accounts of history's queer heroes.[87] Considering 'the history of relations between homosexuality and fascism', Halberstam advocates 'a model of queer history that is less committed to finding heroic models from the past and more resigned to the contradictory and complicit narratives that, in the past as in the present, connect sexuality to politics'.[88] Halberstam rightfully identifies Stein's life story as one such 'narrative'.

Stein's close friendship with a convicted Vichy collaborator – gay male professor and director of the Bibliothèque Nationale, Fäy – reveals that her masculine homosocial desires were not always progressive. Rather, these desires – and Stein's masculinity – were sometimes implicated with reactionary forces. This took place not only through her ties to politically progressive sexists such as Picasso and Hemingway but also through her bonds with right-wing queer men such as Fäy. Viewed from this 'vantage', Lynes's 1931 image of Stein can be seen in a new light.[89] All three iterations of the photograph stress what Corn and Latimer call Stein's masculine, 'imperial' profile, but do so in different contexts.[90] Like the crop Yerba Buena used in its advertising campaign, the 1931 *Time* cover shows Stein in profile, eliminating the landscape within which Lynes originally situated her. However, the original version of the photograph shows her contemplating the rolling hills of the French countryside to which she and Toklas would later retreat during the Occupation, implicitly invoking the rise of fascism by positioning Stein as a general looking out over European terrain. Whereas Agee, writing in modernism's wake, interpreted 'imperial Stein' as a 'sphinx-like, monolithic mass' whose apparent incomprehensibility heralded disturbing changes in the literary landscape, Lynes's photograph of the masculine Stein looking out over the Rhône Valley might seem 'portentous' to contemporary viewers for reasons that have less to to with her writings' experimentation than with the uncomfortable political complicities we now know were to come.[91]

The exhibition's downplaying of Stein's wartime activities *invited* challenges: visitors to museums tend to be well-informed consumers of culture, and questions about Stein's complicities were bound to arise in the wake of Malcolm's and Will's books. However, the catalogue for *Seeing Gertrude Stein* pays scrupulous attention to the questions raised by Stein's activities during World War II and uses a two-page spread of the landscape version of Lynes's 1931 photograph for its title page. The title, authors' names, and publishers are printed on the right side of the image, on top of the Rhône Valley, as if to underscore its importance in Stein's life.

Most importantly, the catalogue and exhibit offer much-needed corrections to the homophobic and transphobic gaze through which Stein's gender, sexuality and writing have been abjected. Attentive to homophobia's effects on the visual archive of her life, both versions of *Seeing Gertrude Stein* offer affirmative glosses of her gender, size and self-esteem. In so doing, *Seeing Gertrude Stein* continues the work of *The Autobiography*, which gives readers a retrospective look at Parisian modernism from the queer perspective of the Stein-Toklas household. Yet at times, Corn and Latimer attend so closely to conventions of fashion, art and photography that they miss the ways Stein's masculinity registers despite the presence of a dominant gaze that would marginalise it. This sometimes leads them to overlook the significance of 'oppositional and subcultural representations' of Stein's masculinity within images staged for the hegemonic gaze.[92]

Seeing Stein's style

Stein's masculinity was articulated differently from that of her early twentieth-century counterparts. While she never wore men's attire or women's clothing modelled on menswear, subtly masculine details – and differentiation from the feminine Toklas – were key to her persona.[93] Stein's appearance also shifted during her time in France. In her 'bohemian' early years in Paris, she chose loose and comfortable clothing that freed her from the constrictive feminine garb of her young adulthood.[94] Her corduroys and sandals 'neutered' her 'femininity' and signified her 'mannishness' by closely resembling Leo's outfits.[95] Their brown corduroy robes exemplified the avant-garde, 'primitivizing' style pioneered by Raymond Duncan; they recalled a broad range of personae such as 'Old Testament prophets, monks and nuns, saints and shepherds, ancient Greeks and Romans'.[96] In 1906, Picasso registered Stein's masculinity in *Portrait of Gertrude Stein* (Plate 1), establishing her as '*une hommesse*' – 'a mannish woman' – by capturing her forward-leaning, space-invading, masculine listening pose.[97] Picasso's masking works in tandem with signifiers of masculinity to strongly distinguish Stein's embodiment from the dominant style of femininity represented in Matisse's *Woman With A Hat*, above which Gertrude and Leo hung the Picasso.[98]

While Corn and Latimer highlight masculine conventions in Stein's clothing and representations of her, they sometimes miss traces of her masculinity in images that attempt to feminise her. After World War I, Stein took up a 'matronly' style of dress that photographers Man Ray and Henri Manuel rendered through feminising imagery.[99] Even in this phase, however, Stein's masculinity was visible but submerged. It remains legible in a 1922 photograph entitled *Gertrude Stein posing for Jo Davidson* (Figure 1.2) that Man Ray took for *Vanity Fair*.[100] In the photograph, Stein's clothing includes details that support Corn's and Latimer's reading of the image as evidence of her 'matronly' phase: she wears a skirt and a ruffled shirt, for instance.[101] However, Corn and Latimer do not remark upon the assertive masculinity of Stein's pose in Man Ray's photograph, nor do they notice the striking similarity between the ruffle she wears in this photograph and the one in Picasso's *Portrait of Gertrude Stein*. The ruffle does not negate the other signifiers of masculinity Corn and Latimer find in Picasso's portrait, nor does it cancel the strongly masculine gestures Stein displays in Man Ray's photograph of her sitting for Davidson. Capturing her spread-open legs, direct look and forward lean, the photograph depicts Stein in a gregarious, masculine posture that defies conventional expectations of femininity and contrasts with the pose 'of a kindly grandmother' into which Davidson sculpts her.[102] In Davidson's sculpture, Stein 'looks down' demurely, 'relaxed and approachable'; she observed that 'Davidson made her "look like the goddess of pregnancy"'.[103] Man Ray's photograph registers the difference between Davidson's gentle matron and his masculine sitter.

Two photographs by celebrity photographer Manuel apply strongly feminine conventions to Stein but fail to suppress her masculinity, which registers in ways Corn and Latimer leave unremarked. They observe that in a 1924 portrait of Stein writing at her desk (Figure 1.3), Manuel stages her as a 'Jan Vermeer letter writer rather than the ambitious woman of letters that she actually was'.[104]

Figure 1.2 Photograph by Man Ray, *Gertrude Stein posing for Jo Davidson* (c. 1922).

Figure 1.3 Photograph by Henri Manuel, *Gertrude Stein* (1924).

Manuel's lighting feminises her features; shallow depth of field blurs the paintings behind her along with her hands and pencil.[105] Though Corn and Latimer are right to describe this photograph as rendering Stein 'as seductive and feminine as any artist ever made her', Manuel's techniques soften but do not negate the serious, direct look that conveys her masculinity.[106]

If the viewer of Manuel's image therefore registers a sense of gender trouble, this effect is even more pronounced in another of his 1924 portraits (Figure 1.4). This photograph shows Stein in an armchair by the fireplace, placed among flowers and other feminine touches that signify 'beauty and domesticity'.[107] The image's framing emphasises these details, leaving Stein's collection of modern art in the periphery. Moreover, her body is curved, draping and feminising her brown robe in a contorted posture that sharply contrasts to most other images' emphasis on her firm stance.[108] Though Corn and Latimer are right that Stein's airbrushed face and vulnerable look reinforce this pose's femininity, they miss the way her hair – uncropped, but photographed to appear short – frames her face as masculine. This unexpected detail likens Stein's face to that of a feminine male. Set upon her body's

Figure 1.4 Photograph by Henri Manuel, *Gertrude Stein* (1924).

curvy pose, her head's discordance with the rest of the scene vertiginously scrambles gender.

Manuel's photographs inadvertently send subtler versions of the gender-bending message Man Ray communicates in the image of Stein he took shortly after her 1926 haircut (Figure 1.5). Man Ray's photograph sets Stein's masculine crop and profile against her feminine make-up and robe, 'dramatiz[ing]' the 'instability' of her gender.[109] *Seeing Gertrude Stein*'s treatment of this photograph's reception offers an excellent example of the look's 'transformative potentiality'.[110] In the exhibition catalogue, Corn and Latimer explain that in 1930, after Stein declined Man Ray's unprecedented request for payment and refused to furnish a copy of her word-portrait of him for a book of his photographs, he ceased photographing her altogether.[111] He then 'took his revenge by using his photograph from 1926 of Stein in heavy makeup to mock her vanity, her sexuality, her body, and her writing' by targeting 'what he took to be her affected masculinity'.[112] By contrast, the curatorial note on that image at the 2011 San Francisco exhibit emphasised the way Man Ray 'played up her gender bending, imagining her as a man in a woman's body – or conversely, a female in male

Figure 1.5 Photograph by Man Ray, *Gertrude Stein* (1927).

drag'.[113] These comments offer an affirmative reading of Stein's queer gender, and do not mention the photographer's vengeful motive. This demonstrates the look's capacity to act 'in concert with enough other looks' to 'reterritorialize the screen, bringing new elements into cultural prominence, and casting into darkness those which . . . constitute normative representation'.[114]

The Autobiography offers another perspective on Man Ray's images of Stein when 'Toklas' recounts an early visit to his hotel room. At that time, he showed them photos of Marcel Duchamp and 'a lot of other people and he asked if he might come and take photographs of the studio and of Gertrude Stein. He did and he also took some of me and we were very pleased with the result. He has at intervals taken pictures of Gertrude Stein and she is always fascinated with his way of using lights. She always comes home very pleased.'[115] This passage presents Man Ray as having initiated a collegial relationship with Stein that 'pleased' her. Much as *The Autobiography* downplays the twists and turns in Stein's friendship with Picasso, the text omits the eventual rupture in her and Man Ray's working relationship.[116] Even when he is 'bother[ed]' by Stein's statement that 'she liked his photographs of her better than any that had ever been taken except one snap shot' by Toklas, *The Autobiography* immediately contains his resistance.[117] Toklas states that on a subsequent shoot, he asked Stein to 'move all you like, your eyes, your head, it is to be a pose but it is to have in it all of the qualities of a snap shot. The poses were very long, she, as he requested, moved, and the result, the last photographs he made of her, are extraordinarily interesting.'[118] Here, Toklas assigns herself and Stein considerable credit for the photographs' aesthetic innovations, much as *The Autobiography* positions her as able to perceive modern art's value before the general public did.[119] In downplaying the tensions between Stein and Man Ray, this passage differs from the text's treatment of other friendships with male modernists that soured: it details her and Matisse's falling-out over her preference for Picasso, and includes an extended attack on Hemingway that he matched with homophobic retaliation in *A Moveable Feast*.[120] Stein's discussion of Man Ray in *The Autobiography* is gentler and leaves no trace of his eventual mockery of her queerness. Instead, her spin on the photographer furthers *The Autobiography*'s goal of advancing her image as a celebrity: she highlights their mutual enthusiasm and encourages readers to align with her 'very pleased' look by viewing his images of her in a positive light.[121] Like the curatorial note at the 2011 *Seeing Gertrude Stein* exhibit valorising his 'gender bending' photograph, *The Autobiography* offers a look at Stein that 'reterritorialize[s] the screen' that would construct her queerness through a hostile gaze, and mobilises a counterhegemonic gaze that affirms Stein's gender and sexuality.[122] Moreover, *The Autobiography* refracts this positive image of Stein through frequent references to differences between its author's perspective and Toklas's focalisations. This multiplies the perspectives through which the book's queer-affirmative gaze gives Stein's image to be seen.

Regardless of how one sees it, Man Ray's image of the short-haired Stein marks her final, 'imperial' stage, during which visual artists reinterpreted her masculinity by relying upon established signifiers for male 'power and authority'.[123] This shift in imagery was prompted by a dramatic change to Stein's appearance in January 1926. Upon the suggestion of the Duchess of Clermont-Tonnerre, Stein cropped her hair into the masculine 'Caesar' cut she kept for the rest of her life.[124] Much like the man-tailored women's couture Hall adopted around the same time, Stein's haircut drew on the current women's fashion of the *coiffure garçonne* to establish her transmasculinity.[125] Her crop was 'reminiscent of the styles worn by monks and ancient rulers', like her corduroy robes.[126] Symbolising a broader shift in women's roles and the 'visual erasure of' gender 'difference', the short haircut offered women a way to claim 'virile power' and consequently elicited widespread disapproval from those eager to preserve gender hierarchy.[127] As Doan and Roberts observe, the *coiffure garçonne* was widely popular in the 1920s and did not always signify 'sapphism', an early twentieth-century precursor to lesbianism.[128] Nonetheless, it is significant that Stein adopted the 'Julius Caesar' haircut in her fifties despite its greater popularity with younger women, and kept it well after it fell out of style.[129] Her decision to retain it suggests her shifting transmasculinity's persistence despite shifts in historical context.

Although Corn and Latimer assert that the 'butch appearance' Stein assumed with the 'Caesar' cut could be read as an instance of the 1920s trend in which 'crossover male-female dress and hairstyle' were used to connote 'homosexuality', she eschewed other common early twentieth-century sartorial signifiers for lesbianism.[130] Even though Corn and Latimer note that Stein 'wore cropped hair, vests, gaiters, and tweeds while other lesbians in the period fashioned themselves in men's ties, longbelted coats, fitted suits, tuxedoes, bowler and fedora hats, and monocles', they do not consider ways those differences might concern gender rather than sexual orientation.[131]

From 1926 onward, the 'Caesar' cut signalled Stein's masculinity across a variety of contexts despite other variations in her appearance. As Corn and Latimer observe, Stein outwardly conformed to conservative gender norms: she continued to wear dresses – rather than masculine-styled women's suits – on formal occasions. In keeping with nineteenth-century etiquette, she wore gowns to deliver evening lectures during her 1926 visit to Oxford and Cambridge and 1934–5 tour of the United States.[132] She similarly appeared in a velvet dress at the 1934 Chicago premiere of *Four Saints in Three Acts*.[133] This attire contrasted with Stein's other clothing: her heavy tweeds struck audiences as outdated yet conveyed a masculinity that remains legible in photographs.[134] Journalists portrayed Stein alternately as masculine or 'grandmotherly': descriptions of her body relied either upon gender-neutral terms referencing her thickness and solidity ('a benevolent Viking'; 'a low, wide tree'; 'a comfortable roly-poly body') or upon echoes of the masculine personae invoked during her early days in Paris.[135] Responses to her soft cap were perplexed but persistently figured it as masculine: as 'a "Baumeister's cap," a "jockey's cap," a "deerstalker's cap,"' 'a '"grouse-hunter's cap,"' or suggestive of 'Robin Hood'.[136] At the same time, her cropped hair – which at one point elicited the remarkable disavowal that 'Her short-cropped hair doesn't look queer' – was also described as 'as right as a cap on a grandmother'.[137] These contradictory representations reveal Stein's masculinity despite others' attempts to feminise her. Shortly after Stein's trip to the United States, her masculinity came into even sharper focus when gay male writer Samuel Steward, reading her palms 'at her insistence', noted that he 'saw what was almost a man's hand, with "physical" fingers'.[138] Steward's insistence on physical signs of Stein's masculinity works in tandem with affirmative observations that her 'Caesar' crop seems 'right as a cap' to counter perceptions that her hair 'doesn't *look* queer'.[139] The play between hegemonic and counterhegemonic responses to Stein's masculinity highlights the anamorphic shifts that have attended perceptions of her gender.

Shifting perceptions of Stein's masculinity continue to animate her contemporary image, even though the current context has transformed the dynamics of her early reception. San Francisco's 2011 cultural offerings made Stein's life and work visible to the general public in ways that substantially altered the early twentieth-century gaze. At the beginning of the twentieth century, Stein's early image was formed in the context of a gaze still dominated by heterosexism and residual nineteenth-century assumptions about art and literature. Stein's challenges to these forces caused widespread uncertainty about her work and transmasculinity, which were often hostilely foregrounded in her image. Now, however, photographic evidence of her masculinity no longer 'shocks' most viewers.[140] Fifty years of scholarship has brought about a significant shift in the hegemonic gaze, which now directs friendlier looks at her transmasculinity and experimental writings alike. The 2011 San Francisco programming reflects those developments.

However, discomfort with Stein's life and work still remains, informing the multiple perspectives at work in her image. While openly homophobic and transphobic depictions are now rare in mainstream cultural institutions, subtler attempts to marginalise her continue. Such responses proceed in the manner of Cotter and Kosman. Avoiding personal attacks on her gender and sexuality, they dismiss her work with dated claims about sophistication and high art, or raise legitimate questions about her Vichy complicities. The latter issues have rightfully retained their shock potential. Stein's image thus remains highly varied and subject to the play between contexts.

The San Francisco context was generally very affirmative of Stein's queerness and experimentalism: *Seeing Gertrude Stein* and other programming reflected up-to-date understandings of her life and work. At the same time, events outside of the cultural institutions' direct control occasionally brought the focus back onto biases that remain visible in Stein's contemporary reception when her dominant image is viewed askance. Explicit homophobia was evident in a subcontracted security guard's foiled attempt to suppress lesbian hand-holding at the *Seeing Gertrude Stein* exhibit, for example. However, the Contemporary Jewish Museum's response – to condemn his actions and host a Hand Holding Day – speaks to the power contemporary cultural institutions continue to exert in shifting the hegemonic gaze through which Stein's masculinity is given to be seen.[141] *Gertrude Stein's Transmasculinity* similarly strives to transform that gaze – and create a new 'vantage' – by bringing internal and external signs of Stein's transmasculinity 'into cultural prominence' and allowing readers to see her gender anew.[142]

Notes

1. See Lacan, *The Four Fundamental Concepts*.
2. Roof, *What Gender Is*, p. 79.
3. Roof, ibid., p. 79.
4. Roof, ibid., pp. 77–8.
5. Roof, ibid., p. 4.
6. Lacan, *The Four Fundamental Concepts*, pp. 79–90.
7. Roof, *What Gender Is*, p. 81, p. 78.
8. Lorange, *How Reading Is Written*, p. 205.
9. Lorange, ibid., p. 205.
10. Roof, *What Gender Is*, p. 79.
11. Roof, ibid., p. 79, p. 81.
12. As a way around this conceptual confusion, I use the phrase 'the look' to designate the visual objectification feminist film theorists such as Mulvey attribute to 'the gaze'.
13. Roof, *What Gender Is*, p. 79.
14. Rose, *Sexuality in the Field of Vision*, p. 226.

15. Rose, ibid., pp. 226–7.
16. Rose, ibid., pp. 226–7.
17. Lacan argues that the goal of psychoanalysis is for the analysand to go beyond the fundamental fantasy that structures subjectivity. See Lacan, *Four Fundamental Concepts*; and Lacan, *The Seminar of Jacques Lacan, Book XXIII*. For explication, see Ruti. For an argument that psychoanalytic queer and trans- theories need to go beyond the fantasy of 'sexual difference', see Coffman, 'The Unpredictable Future' and 'Žižek's Antagonism'; the latter discusses the implications for transgender psychoanalysis of Lacan's *Seminar XX* and *Seminar XXIII*.
18. Ragland, *The Logic of Sexuation*, p. 65. This book offers a detailed discussion of Lacanian 'sexuation' and 'sexual difference' as they overlap with and diverge from sociological understandings of 'gender'.
19. Lacan, *The Seminar of Jacques Lacan. Book XX*, p. 39.
20. Lacan, ibid., p. 39.
21. Lacan, ibid., p. 39.
22. Lacan, ibid., p. 127.
23. Rose, *Sexuality in the Field of Vision*, p. 226; Gherovici, 'The Art of the Symptom' and 'The Transsexual Body Written'. See also Coffman, 'Žižek's Antagonism', for an extended argument that Lacanian psychoanalysis needs to theorise the possibility that signifiers other than 'man' and 'woman' might be at play in sexuation.
24. Silverman, *Threshold*, p. 221, p. 179.
25. Silverman, ibid., p. 221.
26. Silverman, ibid., p. 156, p. 221.
27. Silverman, ibid., p. 182.
28. Silverman, ibid., p. 222.
29. Silverman, ibid., p. 223.
30. Silverman, ibid., p. 223.
31. Roof, *What Gender Is*, p. 79.
32. Benjamin, 'Small History', p. 68. See also Benjamin, 'The Work of Art', pp. 235–7.
33. Benjamin, 'Small History', p. 68; Benjamin, 'The Work of Art', p. 217.
34. Benjamin, 'Theses', pp. 255–7.
35. Halberstam, *In a Queer Time*, pp. 76–96.
36. Roof, *What Gender Is*, p. 77.
37. Roof, ibid., p. 78.
38. Derrida, *Archive Fever*, p. 91; Stringer, *Not Even Past*, p. 110.
39. Silverman, *Threshold*, p. 182. Slavoj Žižek's many books offer wide-ranging examples of the implications of Lacan's argument that fantasy structures reality. For queer and trans- readings of his work, see Coffman, 'Queering Žižek' and 'Žižek's Antagonism'.
40. Silverman, *Threshold*, p. 182; Roof, *What Gender Is*, p. 77.

41. Stein, 'Composition as Explanation', p. 513.
42. Roof, *What Gender Is*, p. 34; Silverman, *Threshold*, p. 221.
43. Silverman, ibid., p. 221; Stein, 'Composition as Explanation', p. 513.
44. Silverman, *Threshold*, p. 179.
45. Roof, *What Gender Is*, p. 79.
46. For more on Lynes's queer photographic aesthetic, see Brown, 'Queering Glamour in Interwar Fashion Photography'.
47. Silver, *Virginia Woolf Icon*, p. 79.
48. Agee, 'Stein's Way', p. 57.
49. Agee, ibid., p. 57.
50. Agee, ibid., p. 57.
51. Agee, ibid., p. 57.
52. Agee, ibid., p. 57.
53. Agee, ibid., p. 57.
54. Nair, *Secrecy and Sapphic Modernism*, p. 120.
55. Agee, 'Stein's Way', p. 57. For a notorious account of Stein's writings as animated by a disturbed and infantile mind, see Skinner, 'Has Gertrude Stein a Secret?'
56. Agee, 'Stein's Way', p. 57.
57. Agee, ibid., p. 58.
58. Benjamin, 'Small History', p. 93.
59. Agee, 'Stein's Way', p. 57.
60. Agee, ibid., p. 60.
61. Agee, ibid., p. 60.
62. Agee, ibid., p. 57. See Coffman, *Insane Passions*, for an analysis of the early twentieth-century stereotype of the 'crazy lesbian'.
63. Agee, 'Stein's Way', p. 57.
64. Stein, *The Autobiography*, pp. 31–3.
65. Agee, 'Stein's Way', p. 57.
66. Benjamin, 'Small History', p. 93; Benjamin, 'Theses', pp. 262–3; Stringer, *Not Even Past*, p. 111. The prospect of 'conservative' uses of shock is implicit in Benjamin's depiction of Eugène Atget's photographs of early twentieth-century Paris: observing that they appear to reveal 'a crime scene', Benjamin suggests that 'every photographer' should 'expose guilt on his pictures and identify the guilty' (Stringer, ibid., p. 111; Benjamin, 'Small History', p. 93). This emphasis on policing differs markedly from his radical argument in 'Theses' that shock may be harnessed for historical materialist thinking that challenges official histories.
67. Stringer, *Not Even Past*, p. 110.
68. Stein quoted in Corn and Latimer, *Seeing Gertrude Stein*, pp. 212–15; pp. 236–7. The contempory edition of *The Autobiography* published

by Vintage does not include photographs of Stein and Toklas; see Corn and Latimer, ibid., pp. 212–13.

69. Corn and Latimer, *Seeing Gertrude Stein*, p. 237.
70. Nair, *Secrecy and Sapphic Modernism*, p. 120.
71. Nair, ibid., p. 121.
72. Benstock, *Women*, p. 168.
73. Silverman, *Threshold*, p. 223.
74. Roof, *What Gender Is*, p. 79.
75. Agee, 'Stein's Way', p. 57.
76. Toklas, *The Alice B. Toklas Cookbook*, p. 259.
77. As an example of transfers between Steinian insistence and hip hop, Schmigel cited a performance by children from Oakland Elementary of Stein's 'Every Afternoon', available at http://mediamogul.seas.upenn.edu/pennsound/authors/Softpalate/Softpalate-Stein_02_Every-Afternoon.mp3 (last accessed 19 September 2017).
78. Kosman, '"Four Saints in Three Acts" review'. Thanks to Lee Callahan for this item.
79. Kosman, ibid.
80. Kosman, ibid.
81. Halberstam, *Queer Art*, p. 73. See also Halberstam, *In a Queer Time*, pp. 1–21.
82. Cotter, 'Modern Is Modern Is . . .'. Thanks to Melissa Bradshaw for this item and to her and Deborah Cohler for fruitful discussion of it. See Corn and Latimer, *Seeing Gertrude Stein*, p. 170, for an explanation of Stein's neoromantic acquisitions.
83. Melnikova-Raich, 'Exhibit leaves out how Gertrude Stein survived Holocaust'; Malcolm, *Two Lives*; Will, *Unlikely Collaborations*.
84. Van Dusen, 'Portrait of a National Fetish'.
85. Mozgovaya, 'Obama corrects controversial Jewish Heritage Month proclamation'.
86. Halberstam, *Queer Art*, pp. 159–60.
87. Halberstam, ibid., p. 148.
88. Halberstam, ibid., p. 148.
89. Roof, *What Gender Is*, p. 79.
90. Corn and Latimer, *Seeing Gertrude Stein*, pp. 51–5.
91. Corn and Latimer, ibid., pp. 51–5; Agee, 'Stein's Way', p. 57.
92. Silverman, *Threshold*, p. 179.
93. Corn and Latimer, *Seeing Gertrude Stein*, p. 51.
94. Corn and Latimer, ibid., pp. 31–5.
95. Corn and Latimer, ibid., p. 35.
96. Corn and Latimer, ibid., pp. 31–5.
97. Corn and Latimer, ibid., pp. 28–36.

98. For further analysis of signifiers of masculinity in Picasso's *Portrait of Gertrude Stein*, see Corn and Latimer, *Seeing Gertrude Stein*, p. 36; Giroud, *Picasso and Gertrude Stein*, pp. 17–34; Lubar, 'Unmasking Pablo's Gertrude', pp. 70–1 n. 89; and Richardson, *A Life of Picasso. Vol. I*, p. 403.
99. Corn and Latimer, *Seeing Gertrude Stein*, p. 41.
100. Corn and Latimer, ibid., p. 46.
101. Corn and Latimer, ibid., p. 41.
102. Corn and Latimer, ibid., p. 44.
103. Corn and Latimer, ibid., p. 44.
104. Corn and Latimer, ibid., p. 47.
105. Corn and Latimer, ibid., p. 47.
106. Corn and Latimer, ibid., p. 49.
107. Corn and Latimer, ibid., p. 49.
108. Corn and Latimer, ibid., p. 49.
109. Corn and Latimer, ibid., pp. 51–4.
110. Silverman, *Threshold*, p. 182.
111. Corn and Latimer, *Seeing Gertrude Stein*, pp. 56–7.
112. Corn and Latimer, ibid., p. 57.
113. This note is reproduced along with Man Ray's image at http://www.npg.si.edu/exhibit/stein/pop-ups/01-06.html (last accessed 19 September 2017).
114. Silverman, *Threshold*, p. 223.
115. Stein, *The Autobiography*, p. 186.
116. See Stein, ibid., pp. 182–3 and pp. 199–200.
117. Stein, ibid., p. 186.
118. Stein, ibid., p. 186.
119. See Stein, ibid., pp. 31–3.
120. Stein, ibid., p. 14, pp. 60–3, pp. 203–8; Hemingway, *A Moveable Feast*, The Restored Edition, pp. 117–19.
121. Stein, *The Autobiography*, p. 186. See Curnutt, 'Inside and Outside'; Goldman, *Modernism is the Literature of Celebrity*; Leick, *Gertrude Stein and the Making of an American Celebrity*; and Zox-Weaver, *Women Modernists and Fascism*, on Stein's construction of her celebrity image.
122. Silverman, *Threshold*, p. 223.
123. Corn and Latimer, *Seeing Gertrude Stein*, pp. 51–5.
124. Toklas, *What Is Remembered*, p. 139; Corn and Latimer, ibid., p. 51.
125. See Doan, *Fashioning Sapphism*. I read Doan's analysis of Hall – and Corn's and Latimer's analysis of Stein's sartorial choices (ibid.) – not as decisively negating the possibility that either of them might have had identities that anticipate contemporary formations of transgender, but as demonstrating the range of styles that were available in the early

twentieth century to construct masculinities. I follow Halberstam's *Female Masculinity* in not conceiving of female and transmasculinities as mutually exclusive.

126. Corn and Latimer, *Seeing Gertrude Stein*, p. 51.
127. Roberts, 'Samson and Delilah Revisited', p. 74, p. 69.
128. Doan, *Fashioning Sapphism*; Roberts, ibid.
129. Corn and Latimer, *Seeing Gertrude Stein*, p. 51.
130. Corn and Latimer, ibid., p. 51.
131. Corn and Latimer, ibid., p. 51.
132. Corn and Latimer, ibid., pp. 88–9.
133. Corn and Latimer, ibid., pp. 226–7.
134. Corn and Latimer, ibid., pp. 230–1.
135. Quoted in Corn and Latimer, ibid., pp. 230–1.
136. Quoted in Corn and Latimer, ibid., pp. 230.
137. Quoted in Corn and Latimer, ibid., p. 231.
138. Steward, 'The Memoir', p. 63.
139. Quoted in Corn and Latimer, *Seeing Gertrude Stein*, p. 231.
140. Benjamin, 'Small History', p. 93.
141. The guard's actions drew vocal protests from witnesses and were not endorsed by the Contemporary Jewish Museum, which immediately dismissed him and issued a public apology. See Nevius, 'Guard cracks down on hand-holding at Stein exhibit'. Thanks to Deborah Cohler for keeping me apprised of these developments.
142. Roof, *What Gender Is*, p. 79.

Chapter 2

Reading Stein's Genders: Multiple Identifications in the 1900s

> None of us know precisely who we will 'be' under regimes of ontology that we struggle against or seek to displace. It may be . . . that as we struggle against the categories of gender that secure contemporary ideas of personhood, we no longer know exactly how we are to be named. We might be understood to be in a mode of self-making or self-poesis that involves risking intelligibility, posing a problem of cultural translation and living in a critical relation to the norms of the intelligible.
>
> Judith Butler, *Dispossession: The Performative in the Political*

From 1900 to 1920, as Stein was beginning to experiment with different modes of masculinity, she gradually worked through the ideologies she encountered as a reader of Weininger's *Sex and Character*, a dubious contribution to sexology that valorises masculinity and denigrates femininity.[1] Because Weininger's misogyny was a reaction against late nineteenth- and early twentieth-century feminisms, it is unsurprising that early feminist work on Stein assumes on the basis of her interest in *Sex and Character* that she suffered from a self-hating form of 'male identification' – and a consequent repudiation of 'female identity' – that moderated with age.[2] These studies ground such assertions in the young Stein's claim to 'a maleness that belongs to genius', positioning her lifelong relationship with the feminine Toklas as mimicry of patriarchal gender roles.[3] However, critics approaching Stein's work through lesbian studies – which documents significant differences between lesbian butch-femme relationships and heteronormative gender binaries – have shown that Stein's masculinity was not a tool for dominating Toklas. Instead, her gender was negotiated in the context of what Gilmore calls the 'coupled' subject: a split form of subjectivity in which the masculine Stein and the feminine Toklas were mutually dependent.[4]

Even those scholars whose work presents Stein's masculinity as a positive aspect of a 'lesbian' relationship frame her and her writings as concerned with 'women's' or 'female' bodies, however. While my argument shares with lesbian scholarship a strong critique of the claim that Stein's and Toklas's embodiment of gender difference mimicked patriarchy, I also question the assumption – implicit in the term 'lesbian' – that Stein identified unproblematically as a 'woman' or 'female'. Her texts trouble these presumptions as early as *Q.E.D.* (1903: 1971) and *Three Lives* (1903–6: 1909). Thus, rather than take Stein's early claim to 'maleness' as evidence of a woman's self-hatred, I read it as an incipient form of transmasculine subjectivity.[5]

Stein's assertion of maleness does not capitulate to Weiningerian misogyny. Although she took an early interest in *Sex and Character*, much scholarship exaggerates Weininger's regard for masculine females and her investment in his ideas. While he rates female masculinity higher than femininity, he also argues on the basis of anecdotal evidence that '*there are women with some of the characteristics of genius, but there is no female genius, there never has been one* (even among the masculine women named in history and discussed in the first part) *and there never can be one*'.[6] Thus, as Lorange observes, 'the crucial point of his system is that *no* woman, no matter how "manly," ever comes close to the most feminine man'.[7] Even though Stein's assertion of 'a maleness that belongs to genius' problematically reflects Weininger's view that genius is exclusively masculine, her statement defies his system by claiming that status for herself. This does not suggest that she identifies as the type of masculine woman Weininger describes but rather that she rejects and transcends his gender system.

Stein further distinguished herself from Weininger by expressing feminist views. She was always a vocal supporter of university education for women, but her self-confidence was shattered upon her move from the supportive context of Harvard and Radcliffe to the openly misogynist environment of the Johns Hopkins medical school.[8] Stein's troubling statements about this period of her life do not necessarily reflect anti-feminist ideology. Although *The Autobiography* notes that Stein ignored those who begged her to stay in medical school to advance 'the cause of women', Cynthia Secor argues that this should be viewed not as a refusal of feminism but as a sign of her newfound commitment to writing.[9] Stein did not 'mind' such 'causes'; she simply decided to become a writer rather than a doctor or an activist.[10] As a writer, she was vocal about misogyny motivating hostile responses to her work.[11] Her willingness to challenge sexism shows her considerable differences from Weininger, even as her assertion of her own 'maleness' differentiates her from woman-identified feminists.[12]

Stein's reactions to *Sex and Character* and the misogyny of Johns Hopkins were early points in the trajectory of her work, which later troubled Weiningerian ideologies. As Maria Damon observes, Weininger 'understood psycho-linguistic flux, polyvocality, multiple identity, and diffuse proliferation' – traits he attributed to femininity and non-Aryan peoples – 'as atavistic and profoundly detrimental to the progress of a rational humanity'.[13] By contrast, starting with *Three Lives*, Stein's writing featured innovative 'verbal styles – repetition, circularity, "imprecision," unconventional syntactic and semantic constructions – that were despised as primitive and that were literally thought to mark the speaker or writer as less than fully human'.[14] As Damon points out, these decentring strategies revalue qualities Weininger denigrated. Using 'insistence' to split the subject, Stein's texts employ discourses of race and gender to displace forms of masculinity and femininity that were hegemonic in white American culture in the first three decades of the twentieth century.[15]

Stein's writings from the 1900s place characters who favour 'verbal styles' such as 'repetition, circularity, and "imprecision"' in dialogue with Stein figures who subscribe to a gender system equating masculinity with reason and the lack of visible emotion.[16] This form of relationality critically reworks Weininger's gender ideologies as her fiction gradually begins to associate its Stein figures with a broader range of gender constructs than a strictly Weiningerian framework would allow. *Fernhurst* (1904–5: 1971) displays her initial attraction to Weininger's ideas as well as her first challenges to them. Whereas *Q.E.D.* – a thinly veiled fictionalisation of Stein's involvement in a love triangle – locates her masculinity and attraction to women in the hyperrational and emotionally blocked Adele, *Three Lives* fractures these qualities across several characters. As Lisa Ruddick argues, Melanctha and her lover, Jeff Campbell, are 'the products of Stein's imaginative self-splitting'.[17] Her masculinity and middle-class values appear in Jeff, who disapproves of Melanctha's sexual 'wanderings' and repeatedly insists that she and other blacks abandon such patterns.[18] But Stein's queerness manifests in Melanctha's bisexuality and the text's reiterative language.[19] Though they do so only partially, *Fernhurst*, *Q.E.D.* and *Three Lives* all begin to undermine Weininger's ideology, allowing Stein to reject the rigid construction of masculinity as a consistent identity free of subjective division. The very traits he dehumanised gradually became Stein's sources of innovation, enabling her to reject the concept of stable identity and embrace 'verbal styles' whose insistence splits the subject. Through this movement, Stein's texts enact shifts in gender and genre that inform the radically anti-identitarian transmasculinities in her experimental writings from the 1910s and 1920s.

To read signs of incipient transsubjectivity in Stein's life and writings, we must understand the process through which this transformation takes place. As Prosser forcefully argues, transpeople exert agency as 'constructing subjects' who relationally write 'their own plots in dialogue with medical discourse' rather than in submission to it.[20] Although he is principally concerned to distinguish transsexuals' self-understandings from the frameworks of the clinicians upon whom they depend for sex reassignment, his argument is also relevant to other forms of transgender. These, too, often exist in dialogue with medical constructs without being reducible to them.

However, Stein's writings engage medical discourse in a different manner than the texts informing Prosser's work. This leads to significant divergences between the transsubjectivities articulated in her texts and those featured in *Second Skins*. Hall's *The Well*, a key early twentieth-century text for Prosser, opens with a forward by sexologist Havelock Ellis and develops its protagonist's masculinity through explicit references to his and Richard von Krafft-Ebing's studies of congenital inversion. Unlike *The Well*, Stein's writings do not dialogue with sexological discourse, nor do they feature inverts who use men's fashions to make their masculinity visible. That Stein ultimately neither embraced those ideas nor Weininger's suggests that her transsubjectivity did not rely upon the visible embodiment of cross-gendered identification but was formed through the relationality of her identifications with her characters and her playful self-inscription as Toklas's husband.

The playfulness and multiplicity of Stein's style – which begins with her subtle mockery of Jeff in *Three Lives* and becomes more pronounced in the 1910s and 1920s – also distinguishes her inscriptions of transsubjectivity from those in other transgender texts. As Salamon argues in response to Prosser, transmasculine embodiment need not be governed by a desire for congruity but can be relationally shifting, anti-identitarian, and characterised by subjective division.[21] Prosser emphasises texts that use narrative to bring coherence and resolution to an initial gap between the body's exterior surface and a transperson's internal sense of gender identity. By contrast, Stein's writings from *Three Lives* onward refuse to reduce gendered subjectivity to a singular identity that remains stable over time.[22] Instead, her avant-garde textual practices inscribe the vicissitudes of relationship and defy the rules of genre to shake up early twentieth-century 'regimes of' sexual and gender 'ontology' that she found unworkable in young adulthood.[23] These texts' varied forms of relationality allow her to mobilise a wide variety of masculinities.

The pliability of genders in Stein's texts is crucial to her displacement of masculinity's misogynist forms. As Michael Moon suggests, when Stein asks 'what is the use of being a boy if you are going to grow up to be a man' in her lecture 'What Are Masterpieces and Why Are There So Few of Them' (1936: 1940), she gives a 'belated kiss-off to' Weininger's misogynist version of adult masculinity.[24] This rejection of Weininger happened much earlier than 1936, however, and early scholarship on Stein presents it as evidence that she gradually came to understand herself as a woman. Ruddick asserts that this change took place shortly after Stein finished *Three Lives*, whereas DeKoven claims that Stein did not make such as shift until 1927.[25]

Although I agree that Stein's relationship to gender shifted significantly in the first three decades of the twentieth century, I contest earlier scholarship's timelines and assumption that Stein's subjectivity was that of a 'woman'. As Biddy Martin observes, one's relationship to one's gender can change, even as key components of it may remain constant. Over time, a person's or character's 'identifications' with hegemonic masculinity and its 'supporting disidentifications' with femininity can come to 'shatter', breaking down 'defense[s]' against femininity and leading to significant 'affective and behavioral' changes without fundamentally altering 'the configuration of sexual differences consolidated over time'.[26] In Stein's case, this transformation engendered an anti-identitarian feminist mode of transmasculine subjectivity rather than 'female identity'.[27]

Stein's writings from the first three decades of the twentieth century gradually move through this process, which is recursive rather than linear and plays out differently in each text. In the 1910s and 1920s, Stein's radically experimental poems mobilised supple and explicitly anti-patriarchal transmasculinities in a variety of relational contexts, fashioning a poetic 'transgenre'.[28] To reach the point at which she could write in ways that rendered this flexible form of transsubjectivity 'liveable', however, Stein's fiction from the 1900s first destabilised and worked through the rigid gender ideologies that initially attracted her.[29]

Driven by conflicted relationships, *Fernhurst*, *Q.E.D.* and *Three Lives* register the fraught forms of relationality that emerged as early twentieth-century genders changed. These works of prose fiction gradually yet unevenly work through dominant ideologies about feminine inferiority and masculine superiority as well as the forms of desire and relationship they entail. Because they are three of Stein's earliest texts, they are often read together in scholarship that traces her process of coming to terms with lesbianism.[30] While I, too, take these texts as concerned in displaced form with the nature of Stein's desire, I am also interested in reconsidering its relationship to her gendered embodiment. Prior work that takes a negative view of Stein's cross-identification during this period draws heavily on her personal notebooks and fiction, but the latter reveal a more complex relationship to embodiment than earlier research describes. Whereas *Fernhurst* upholds the rigidly misogynist masculinity promoted by Weininger, *Q.E.D.* reproduces some of its elements while challenging others. *Three Lives*, by contrast, systematically undermines attempts to stabilise masculine identity, insisting that it is a form of split subjectivity.

Gender and identification in *Fernhurst* and *Q.E.D.*

As DeKoven observes, *Fernhurst* is focalised through a narrator who shares Weininger's biases and contradictions: she valorises dominant masculine values and is sceptical of women's ability to attain them. This narrator praises Fernhurst College's 'ostensible ideals' as 'Honorable and manly' but – in a claim verging on paranoia – charges its powerful female Dean, Helen Thornton, with manipulatively undermining 'the male ideal' of student-driven governance to which her institution aspires.[31] Faulting Thornton for promoting 'the doctrine of the superiority of women' and thereby misleading her charges, the narrator asserts that:

> Had I been bred in the last generation full of hope and unattainable desires I too would have declared that men and women are born equal but being of this generation with the college and professions open to me and able to learn that *the other man* is really stronger I say I will have none of it.[32]

Fernhurst tracks the distortions produced by the narrator's pervasive sense of exhaustion by the effort to achieve masculinist ideals.[33] Persistently associating Thornton with decadence and institutional clout, the novel registers both the Dean's power and the narrator's disavowal of it.

However, it is important to note – which DeKoven does not – that despite the narrator's attitude, the Dean and her college emerge victorious. By the novel's end, Philip Redfern – Thornton's rival for Janet Bruce's love – has been forced out of Fernhurst and left in uncertain professional circumstances while the women remain 'in their very same place' at the college.[34] The novel's maintenance of the lesbian couple's power on the Fernhurst campus differs sharply from the real-life events that inspired Stein's novel: the love triangle at Bryn Mawr that led English professor Mary Gwinn to leave future college President Helen Carey Thomas to elope with Philosophy professor Alfred Hodder.[35] By rewriting its source materials, *Fernhurst* overcomes its narrator's internalisation of the ideology of feminine weakness and confirms the possibility that women can succeed in positions of power. The novel remains Weiningerian, though, in noting that after Redfern's departure, Thornton eventually 'regained all property rights' in Bruce.[36] This statement reflects the patriarchal assumption that women are objects of exchange and attributes a misogynist form of female masculinity to Thornton. While *Fernhurst* elevates her and dethrones Redfern, the novel's depiction of Thornton's masculinity does not move beyond Weininger's ideologies.

Like *Fernhurst*, *Q.E.D.* offers a trace of Stein's early masculine identifications. It is often read as a lesbian love triangle in which Mabel and Adele vie for Helen's affections. As John Carlos Rowe observes, 'all three female characters in *Q.E.D.* display characteristics of Stein's actual and ideal self-conception around 1903', even though Adele is the dominant Stein-figure.[37] After Mabel and Helen challenge Adele's middle-class values, the latter explicitly disidentifies with the category 'woman'. Proclaiming that '"I always did thank God I wasn't born a woman"', Adele rejects the cultural construct 'woman' as descriptive of herself.[38] Ruddick reads this statement as evidence that Adele has 'disowned' her 'gender', an interpretation that conflates sex with gender and erroneously assumes that repudiating an ill-suited gender construct amounts to self-alienation.[39] This is the first step in Stein's disidentification with 'woman' and embrace of masculinity that culminates in her cross-writing of herself as Jeff in *Three Lives*. Although DeKoven glosses Adele's statement as evidence of 'lesbian gender indeterminacy', I read her as asserting transsubjectivity.[40]

Adele's transmasculinity remains within dominant early twentieth-century gender constructs, however. Her self-definition upholds the binary opposition between disembodied masculine reason and embodied feminine passion that Stein's later writings break down.[41] Yet by presenting desire's embodied expression as a problem for the masculine Adele, *Q.E.D.* reveals the blockages produced by the gendered mind/body split. Though this highly discursive text frequently discusses passion, it is rarely displayed. Adele advocates a 'middle-class ideal' in which 'respectable' people 'avoid excitements and cultivate serenity', rejecting 'passions' taken up 'simply for the sake of an experience'.[42] She repudiates all 'passions' from her 'scheme of things' except the 'moral' ones, which 'are distinctly of it'.[43] She also vocalises an 'almost puritanic horror' of 'physical passion', and experiences her beloved Helen's kisses as coming from radically outside of herself.[44] When Helen finally kisses Adele, the latter '[s]uddenly . . . felt herself intensely kissed on the eyes and on the lips', but 'felt vaguely that she was apathetically unresponsive'.[45] After Adele explains that she had been caught up in thinking, the latter asks with exasperation, '"Haven't you ever stopped thinking long enough to feel?"'[46] Explaining that '"[t]hinking is a pretty continuous process"' for her, Adele sits up and Helen bends down to kiss her 'warmly' before leaving.[47]

Despite this moment and Adele's growing awareness of her attraction to women, she continues to experience embodied desire as coming from outside of herself. On a subsequent occasion, she again finds 'herself at the end of a passionate embrace' by Helen.[48] This formulation speaks to Adele's continued repression by staging her as the passive object of Helen's passion. It also suggests that the split between thinking and feeling is a continuing issue for Adele. At one point, she observes that 'I want things . . . only in order to understand them', and that '[a]ll I want to do is to meditate endlessly and think and talk'.[49] She then says to Helen that 'you believe it necessary to feel something to think about and you contend that I don't give myself time to find it. I recognize the justice of that criticism and I am doing my best these days to let it come'.[50] She does not succeed, however. After describing Helen's personality as divided by contradictions, Adele realises that her scientific tone has hurt her lover's feelings. Apologising profusely, Adele tells Helen that she never 'realized that you were in pain', and explains her behaviour as a manifestation of 'my cursed habit of being concerned only with my own thoughts'.[51]

Later, Adele is better able to identify her own 'anger' and Helen's 'pain'.[52] Nonetheless, Adele continues to fear the emotions her affair with Helen has roused. Returning to New York after a long absence, Adele realises that she had stayed away because she 'rather dreaded losing herself ' with Helen.[53] This time, however, the 'feeling' of distance 'between them gradually disappeared', and Adele 'yielded herself to the complete joy of simply being together'.[54] Although they 'lost themselves in happiness', it proves short-lived.[55] As 'intimacy' increases and Adele's sexuality becomes more active, her relationship with Helen moves from attraction to repulsion and she experiences 'revulsion'.[56] A 'kiss that seemed to scale the very walls of chastity' causes her to fling herself 'away on the instant filled with battle and revulsion', and she loses 'herself in the full tide of her fierce disgust' – a condition from which she never fully recovers.[57]

The 'puritan instincts' behind Adele's reaction remain a problem for her and Helen.[58] Even though Adele realises that 'the Calvinistic influence that dominates American training . . . has interfered with my natural temperament', she cannot get past the resulting blockage.[59] Though her 'completeness of revulsion never occurred again', it still divides them:[60]

> Adele realized that Helen demanded of her a response and always before that response was ready. Their pulses were differently timed. She could not go so fast and Helen's exhausted nerves could no longer wait. Adele found herself constantly forced on by Helen's pain. She went farther than she could in honesty because she was unable to refuse anything to one who had given all.[61]

Although Adele admits that her sexuality is mediated by North American Calvinism, she nonetheless uses the biological metaphor of 'pulse' to invoke the mismatch between her and Helen's patterns of desire, and blames Helen's 'exhausted nerves' for physical and emotional 'pain'.[62] Adele's and Helen's incompatibility heightens the problems created by their triangulation with Mabel Weeks, eventually leading to the relational 'dead-lock' that ends the narrative.[63]

Despite this ending, *Q.E.D.* subtly challenges hegemonic ideas about gender and sexuality. This novel is the first of Stein's texts to include implicit references to the denaturalisations of gender that become more explicit in her later work. *Q.E.D.* begins with an epigraph from Shakespeare's *As You Like It* that references female-to-male cross-dressing. This citation denaturalises gender, undercutting the narrator's biological metaphors and exposing Adele's rigid form of transmasculinity as a construct. Moreover, the text's mobilisation of both Adele's and Helen's perspectives calls dominant constructs of rational masculinity into serious question. Unlike *Fernhurst*, which features a female narrator who upholds Weininger's ideology of male superiority by using it to judge the characters, *Q.E.D.* avoids such commentary.

Moreover, as Hovey argues, *Q.E.D.* gradually 'frees' Adele from American Puritanism and places her in a European setting conducive to 'sensual' expression, albeit after her split from Helen.[64] To accomplish this change, Stein draws on troublingly 'racist colonizing tropes' to enable her protagonist to go '"primitive"': to embrace an identificatory mode that allows her to become 'earthier, aboriginal and more native', '"large, abundant, full-busted and joyous"'.[65] Hovey argues that these tropes mobilise 'multiple and simultaneous positions' that gradually expand Adele's ability to live out lesbianism.[66] I agree that her sexuality and gender are less rigidly defended at the end of the novel than at the beginning. However, I view Adele not as achieving a supple relation to lesbian sexuality by the narrative's conclusion but as coming to inhabit a form of transmasculine subjectivity that accommodates her desire for women.

Gender and multiple identification in *Three Lives*

Stein underwent a parallel transformation after completing *Q.E.D.*, wandering through Paris in androgynous robes that drew on similarly 'primitivizing' tropes.[67] This change in attire, like *Q.E.D.*'s primitivism, provided an outward sign of her move into a flexible form of transmasculinity. Shortly thereafter, the troubling racial discourses animating Adele's transformation in *Q.E.D.* reappear in the centrepiece novella of *Three Lives*, 'Melanctha'. They do so in different guises, however, as Stein disperses her identification into a staid African American doctor, Jeff, and his 'wandering' lover, Melanctha.[68]

If in *Q.E.D.*, Adele's declaration that '"I always did thank God I wasn't born a woman"' repudiates white American middle-class womanhood, *Three Lives* furthers this rejection by cross-writing Stein as Jeff and Melanctha.[69] Through this process, Stein displaces her own concerns about sexuality and gender into debates about how black Americans should live. All three narratives in *Three Lives* concern their characters' entrapment by middle-class sexual repression. The protagonist of 'The Good Anna', the opening story, is a white German immigrant who scolds her dog for mounting her neighbours' pets; the lead character in 'The Gentle Lena', which closes the collection, is another white German immigrant who dies in childbirth after being pushed by her family into a loveless marriage. The centrepiece, 'Melanctha', features a black man determined to counter whites' stereotypes of African Americans by insisting upon his sexual propriety.

As Hovey notes, many of Adele's puritanical qualities resurface in Jeff.[70] Both display a strong preference for thinking over feeling that reveals their investment in what Rowe calls 'Euroamerican traditions of knowledge' and reason.[71] Exemplifying the philosophical approach to identity against which Stein later positioned herself, they assume that linguistic meaning is stable and that the thinking subject is consistently self-identical. While both *Q.E.D.* and *Three Lives* concern conflicts created by Adele's and Jeff's hyperrationality and prudishness, Stein's attribution of masculine qualities to them also works through her own transmasculinity and its connections to her desires for women. Stein's simultaneous identification with these two characters' sexual conservatism and Melanctha's sexual 'wanderings' loosened up the rigid masculinity with which she initially identified, paving the way for the flexible and feminist transmasculinity that emerged in her later texts.

As Nathaniel Mackey observes, 'Melanctha' does Stein's identifications in 'blackface'.[72] Through what Hovey describes as 'racial drag', the text uses 'dissident sexuality . . . to buttress racial stereotypes rather than contest them' while unsettling dominant early twentieth-century genders.[73] The narrator subtly mocks Jeff's internalisation of hegemonic white constructs of feminine propriety and masculine stability even as Stein continues to identify with him, troubling the white masculinity with which she identified in Adele. Moreover, *Three Lives* makes not only the orthodox Jeff but also the sexually open Melanctha available for Stein's identification. These multiple identifications pave the way for the flexible and feminist transmasculinities that emerge in her radically experimental writings from the 1910s and 1920s.

Three Lives experiments with the form of prose narrative to a far greater extent than *Fernhurt* and *Q.E.D.*, introducing the first of many variants on the reiterative style for which Stein is now famous. As Stein explains in 'Composition As Explanation', 'Melanctha' employs the 'prolonged present', a temporal mode that paved the way for her later writings' use of the 'continuous present': 'there was a constant recurring and beginning there was a marked direction in the direction of being in the present although naturally I had been accustomed to past present and future, and why, because the composition forming around me was a prolonged present'.[74] As Freeman demonstrates, however, Stein's distinction between these two temporalities is 'contradictory' and does not fully account for the temporal variability of 'Melanctha'.[75] For Freeman, Melanctha occupies an 'atelic' way of being in time that is 'shapeless' and allows her to live 'aslant from . . . social' norms.[76] By inhabiting Steinian 'insistence', Melanctha experiences modes of 'vitality' and 'animacy' that enact '*chronocatachresis*' by violating the 'dominant regimes of time' that characterise 'chrononormativity'.[77]

Although Stein's 'prolonged present' and Freeman's 'chronocatachresis' depart from linear time in ways that provide alternatives to the 'ideological forms' constraining the texts' characters and Stein alike, these novel temporalities do not free them completely.[78] While Stein was breaking away from the idea that time moves from 'past' to 'present' and 'future' and instead capturing the sense of 'being in the present', the text's recursive movements of 'recurring and beginning' reveal vestiges of linear time that keep her narratives and characters stuck in temporal and ideological formations that eventually undo them.[79] While Stein's writings do not successfully rearticulate hegemonic genders and sexualities until the 1910s and 1920s, *Three Lives* questions their most pernicious aspects and undoes her identification with the damaging version of masculinity that initially attracted her.

Stein's double identification with Jeff and Melanctha allowed her to explore possibilities for a masculinity that neither takes the form of the self-identical subject nor is driven by the 'regular' temporality of middle-class norms.[80] Carla Peterson argues that while Stein primarily identifies with Jeff, she also shares Melanctha's temperament. First introduced as a character who 'wondered, often, how she could go on living when she was so blue', Melanctha frequently displays moodiness that recalls Stein's depression while in medical school and confirms Freeman's argument that 'Melanctha' concerns 'chronic' illness.[81] Melanctha is established as a 'blues woman' through rhythms drawn from African American musical forms.[82]

As Stringer explains, 'women blues artists were . . . spurs to thinking new forms of relationality' because their performances connected their own situations to others'.[83] In writing about Melanctha's attempt to form a new type of relationship with the conservative Jeff, Stein opened up sites for her own identification by introducing irregular rhythmic patterns to narrative. Bruce Barnhart notes that at the level of 'sentences and paragraphs', blues patterns and ragtime 'syncopation' animate the novella's linguistic experimentation.[84] As Peterson observes, this displacement of 'traditional Western notions of prose regularity' innovates within genre.[85] Although this does not create a 'transgenre', the experimentation of *Three Lives* loosens up Stein's masculinity and sets the stage for her radical experimentation in the 1910s and 1920s.[86]

The rhythms Peterson and Barnhart describe are evident throughout the text, especially when it addresses the violence Melanctha experiences from men. At one point, the narrator says that when Melanctha's 'father began fiercely to assail her, she did not really know what it was that he was so furious to force from her. In every way that he could think of in his anger, he tried to make her say a thing she did not really know.'[87] As DeKoven observes, this passage 'rushes forward freely and then halts at each '-er' rhyme' such that 'the rhythm enhances the overall incantatory, hypnotic effect of the repetition'.[88] Peterson notes that this effect is primarily associated with Melanctha, whose speech parallels the narrator's 'stylistic . . . tendency toward a form of mind-wandering marked by repetition, offbeat stresses, and lack of subordination'.[89] However, syncopated rhythms also insinuate themselves into Jeff's language when he is most under her influence. When he explains that '"you see, Melanctha, really, it's just like this way always with me. You see, Melanctha, its like this way now all the time with me"', his reiterations illustrate his claim that 'You see Melanctha, it's like this way with me. I got a new feeling now, you been teaching to me, just like I told you once, just like a new religion to me.'[90] Jeff's verbal patterns mimic Melanctha's as he begins to question normative masculinity's split between thinking and feeling. Jeff's 'new religion' bears out M. Lynn Weiss's observation that '[r]epetition in blues does not simply destabilize meaning, but through the use of musical and verbal irony, it provides an atmosphere in which analysis can take place and another meaning can be provided'.[91] In 'Melanctha', bluesy reiteration challenges and reworks hegemonic masculinity, dispersing Stein's identification between Melanctha and Jeff while undercutting the latter's ideologies. This double movement suggests that Stein was as drawn to Melanctha's sexual freedom as to Jeff's conservatism and was using racialised aesthetic displacements to work through conflicting attitudes about gender and sexuality while writing *Three Lives*.

There are limits to the text's challenges to hegemonic forms of gender, sexuality and racialisation, however. Despite the passages whose surface-level displacements of regularity interest DeKoven and Peterson, Barnhart notes that the novella's use of a third-person narrator – rather than the first-person persona of blues lyrics – suppresses the genre's 'commitment to the participatory values of imbrication and entanglement' as well as the 'vertiginously affective response the blues pulls from its listeners'.[92] Moreover, he points out that Melanctha's eventual fate reveals that Stein only superficially assimilated the blues' formal innovations. Unlike Melanctha, '[t]he protagonist of a blues performance never ends up dead because blues narration occurs in the first person' and mobilises the listener's identification with – rather self-distancing from – the narrative.[93] As a result, '[t]he detachment that characterizes the relationship between Melanctha and the narrator' enables the reader's condescension toward '"Poor Melanctha"' because '"surely her love had made her mad and foolish"'.[94]

These distancing tactics distinguish Stein's 1900s fiction from her 1910s and 1920s poems, which encourage more direct modes of relationality than those through which *Three Lives* solicits her identifications. However, in identifying the ways in which 'Melanctha' retreats to the safety of the third person, Barnhart fails to see that Stein's innovative use of 'insistence' displaces and renews rather than reifies meaning. He claims, for example, that 'Melanctha' largely relies upon the kind of 'exact repetition that dominates the American imagination' and that, like its 'clearest expression' in accounting, remains within a temporality 'indebted to the ideals of possessive individualism' challenged by the more irregular patterns of blues, jazz, and ragtime.[95] However, in 'Portraits and Repetition', Stein rejects the dominant concept of perfect 'repetition' in favour of 'insistence', asserting that 'I am inclined to believe that there is no such thing as repetition . . . That is what makes life that the insistence is different, no matter how often you tell the same story if there is anything alive in the telling the emphasis is different.'[96]

In *Three Lives*, insistence allows Stein to identify with her characters even if she sets herself apart from them in some ways. By using a third-person narrator, she takes distance from Melanctha and appears to side with Jeff's preference for regularity. However, Stein also collapses this distance by identifying with Melanctha's moodiness and employing her bluesy rhythms to displace dominant ideologies. The rhythmic 'insistence' of Stein's prose ultimately destabilises Jeff's and the third-person narrator's attempts to distance themselves from the protagonist. This movement does not radically revise the gendered and raced subject positions upon which Stein relies in *Three Lives*, nor does it rescue the rebellious Melanctha from an early death.

In the 1910s and 1920s, Stein's experimental poems mobilised transmasculinities that mix Jeff's masculinity with Melanctha's sexual openness and unpredictability, departing from his belief in a masculinity grounded in self-identical subjecthood and enabling new forms of relationship. Before Stein could reach this point, however, 'Melanctha' employed aesthetic techniques drawn from black cultures to re-invent literature and question dominant early twentieth-century gender ideologies.

Stein's growing interest in the visual arts both aided in and thwarted this process.[97] As Corinne Blackmer and Michael North show, in 'Melanctha' Stein develops an innovative form of linguistic masking that works like Picasso's Iberian and African masks. Blackmer notes that as the story progresses, 'slight discrepancies begin to appear' in the characters' 'various attributes', much like the shifting planes on Picasso's masks.[98] Rose Johnson, for example, is initially depicted through classically racist tropes as 'a real black, tall, well built, sullen, stupid, childlike, good looking negress', but one page later is described as 'coarse, decent, sullen, ordinary, black' and 'childish'.[99] The contradictions that emerge through these reiterations' differences exemplify Stein's method in 'Melanctha'. The text 'defamiliarizes and denaturalizes mimetic modes of narrative representation and therefore radically alters conventional assumptions regarding the interrelationships among stereotype, character, voice, and discourse'.[100] As Adrian Piper observes, this strategy encourages 'a self-consciously critical rather than unselfconsciously participatory or involved evaluational perspective toward' Stein's characters and enables her to appropriate African art to serve her own aesthetic goals.[101] Presenting her characters through techniques borrowed from Paul Cézanne, Stein shows them as 'great complexes of continuously shifting verbal planes' whose 'warping' challenges realism's linear conception of space and time.[102] As a result, her characters are not 'static configurations' but relationally 'kinetic forms, mobile tones', and 'fragmented bits and pieces'.[103] This foreshadows the split subjectivity that undercuts the stability of identity even more overtly in Stein's later writings.

As Rowe argues, Stein's strategy in 'Melanctha' emphasises 'the artifice of skin color', allowing it 'and the related conventions of race, gender, sexuality, and other forms of identity' to become '"visible" only through their deformation or "estrangement" by unconventional, literary language'.[104] Anne Cheng identifies both the 'flat, clean, denuded, endlessly appealing glossy surface' of Stein's writing and 'Cézanne's planar surfaces' as examples of a modernist 'preoccupation with surface' prompted by the 'invention of plastic, that most twentieth century of materials'.[105] Cheng stresses that a plasticky malleability also characterised Josephine Baker's controversial performances, which deployed her dark skin along with primitivising casings (such as her infamous banana skirt) to entertain popular audiences. Widespread fascination with these 'surfaces' is evidence of modernism's 'dream of a second skin – of remaking one's self in the skin of the other'.[106]

Like Cheng, I do not deny that there are problematically racist and primitivist elements at work in Baker's dance. In soliciting spectators' stereotypes of black people, Baker's performances play to the same fantasies as 'blackface' – another practice exemplifying modernism's 'preoccupation with surface'.[107] Mackey argues that Steinian 'repetition advances a critique of language that is not unrelated to the one we see in the minstrel show', which mocks 'language's . . .

insecure hold on the world'.[108] Pointing to meaning's tenuousness and pliability, Stein's linguistic and visual manipulations of skin colour and masking are problematic forms of 'atavism' that participate in modernism's 'dream of a second skin'.[109]

Cheng describes Baker as engaged in 'impersonation': she 'is expertly skilled at *making models of herself*, which both shield and reveal her' by using 'her nudity – and her images – like second skins'.[110] Using language much like Cheng's, Hovey describes Stein's *Autobiography* as treating her and Toklas's genders as 'impersonations' by playing on concepts such as 'wives' and 'geniuses'.[111] 'Melanctha', too, mimics early twentieth-century constructs by using masking and skin colour to resignify gendered embodiment while undercutting the concept of the self-identical subject. Yet unlike Baker's performances, Stein's text mobilises the modernist fantasy of a 'second skin' to work through issues that entail both skin colour *and* gendered embodiment.[112] Crossing racial, gendered and sexual formations alike, 'Melanctha' displaces *Q.E.D.*'s concerns with gender and sexuality onto Jeff's and Melanctha's skin colour.

Like Cheng's analysis of race, Prosser's account of transsexuality in *Second Skins* draws on Didier Anzieu's concept of the 'skin ego'. Whereas Cheng's book stresses the 'architectural/spatial elements' at work in Freud's description of the ego as '"itself the projection of a surface"' and Anzieu's explanation of it as '"the projection on the psyche of the surface of the body"', Prosser uses these claims to insist upon the psyche's 'corporeal dependence'.[113] Although Prosser's critique of Butler's theory that the body is an 'illusory psychic projection' productively insists upon the importance of the somatic, Salamon draws on Paul Schilder's notion of the 'body schema' to emphasise that the body and its parts are 'only given, only accessible, through a mediating psychic structure'.[114] Thus 'the body is not an envelope for psyche, and the skin is not an envelope for the body': because the subject is split rather than self-identical, 'both body and psyche are characterized by their lability rather than their ability to contain'.[115] I consider Salamon's insistence on the body schema's porousness and flexibility applicable to racialised and gendered embodiments alike.[116]

Inspired by but going beyond 'Cézanne's planar surfaces', Stein's *Three Lives* uses language rather than paint as the source of the 'conventions' through which she reworks racialised, gendered and sexualised embodiment.[117] Both Rowe's attention to the interplay between skin colour and other 'conventions' in *Three Lives* and

Cheng's concept of modernism's 'dream of a second skin' help us understand the role of Stein's early fiction in working through her transmasculinity.[118] '[E]strangement' provides Stein with a metaphorical means of re-imagining the body, as Jeff's and Melanctha's blackness signifies multiple bodily differences between Stein and her previous incarnation in *Q.E.D.*[119]

Most scholarship has focused on the racial aspects of Stein's internal self-displacement into black characters in 'Melanctha'. Yet the text's attention to the body's exterior surface and its interplay with the psyche's internal rhythms also suggest a desire for a 'second skin' in both Cheng's and Prosser's senses. Revising Prosser, Salamon observes that '[t]he body image is multiple (any person always has more than one), it is flexible (its configuration changes over time), it arises from our relations with other people, and its contours are only rarely identical to the contours of the body as it is perceived from the outside'.[120] Similarly, Cheng reads Adolf Loos's plan for a house for Baker as suggesting 'the pliability of bodily boundaries. Loosian cladding, as an extension of skin, opens and extends the body's boundary into the exterior world, rendering that body at once imperial and porous.'[121] Porousness and multiplicity are at work in *Three Lives* and Stein's later articulations of embodiment.

As Stein cross-writes herself into Jeff and Melanctha, their skin colour stands in for other bodily transformations that *Three Lives* does not – or will not – articulate. These possibilities are ultimately less about race than about gendered embodiment. Yet if for Cheng, modernists' 'dream of a second skin' worked both ways – as 'a *mutual* fantasy, one shared by both Modernists seeking to be outside of their own skins and by racialized subjects looking to escape the burdens of epidermal inscription' – for Stein it was a one-way street.[122] Whereas Baker's performances tried to 'suture' the 'ruptures' effected by racist treatment of the black female body, Stein's racialised cross-writing enacts something quite different.[123] Rather than undercutting atavistic 'notions of racialized embodiment', 'Melanctha' plays into them.[124] Yet for all its preoccupations with the racialised body, the text is less interested in undoing racial prejudice than in using blackness to work toward a more flexible form of masculinity than Jeff's. The desire for transformation signalled in 'Melanctha' – and, more broadly, in Stein's early writings – is not simply that of becoming black, or becoming a man. Instead, that desire is for an embodied masculine sexuality that is more flexible than Jeff's hegemonic masculinity.

'Melanctha' routes this desire for a new masculinity through Stein's dual identification with Jeff and Melanctha, attempting to work through their conflicts but ultimately leaving them stuck in the patterns they brought to their relationship. Drawing on techniques from the visual and performing arts, Stein uses estrangement to induce formal 'warping'.[125] The resulting distortions critique Jeff's discourse of 'racial uplift', mock his internalisation of dominant white gender ideology, and reroute Stein's early identification with his rigid masculinity through Melanctha's sexual openness.[126]

Jeff shares Adele's puritanical worldview and middle-class emphasis on regular, hard work. However, *Three Lives* transports these discourses from the white, bourgeois context of *Q.E.D.* into the poor, black neighbourhood Jeff serves as a doctor.[127] In his view, blacks should avoid the 'excitements' to which they all too often succumb.[128] He declares that:

> 'No I ain't got any use for all the time being in excitements and wanting to have all kinds of experience all the time . . . I don't believe much in this running around business and I don't want to see the colored people do it. I am a colored man and I ain't sorry, and I want to see the colored people like what is good and what I want them to have, and that's to live regular and work hard and understand things, and that's enough to keep any decent man excited.'[129]

Indulging in the stereotype of the hypersexualised black woman, Stein displaces onto Melanctha the open expression of desire that takes place in a more stilted fashion between white women in *Q.E.D.*[130] Unlike Jeff, Melanctha prefers to learn through 'real experience', and 'wandered very widely' in both sexual and nonsexual realms to develop 'wisdom'.[131] 'Melanctha' does two things as it works through Stein's simultaneous identification with these characters. First, the narrator subtly mocks Jeff's prudish form of masculinity and Stein's own identification with it. Second, the text offers Melanctha's 'wandering' search for 'wisdom' as a challenge to Jeff's linear worldview and an example of a way sexuality can afford people opportunities to connect with and learn from others.[132] In so doing, 'Melanctha' enables Stein to radicalise her approach to her masculinity and desires for women.

As Michael Trask argues, Stein rehearses 'the dominant concerns of the psychology of persons' at the turn of the century by using the conflict between Jeff and Melanctha to explore 'the antithesis between desire and habit, between wandering and regularity, between disobedience and obedience'.[133] Although structurally, *Three Lives* juxtaposes these characters in an apparent opposition between masculine thinking and feminine feeling, the text breaks down that binary very quickly. From the first moment Melanctha challenges Jeff's belief in 'living regular and quiet' while avoiding 'excitements', she taps her experiences for thinking even though her embodied cognitive style differs from Jeff's cerebral approach.[134] Melanctha calls attention to Jeff's 'contradictory and unintelligible logic', creating 'a chasm between his abstract values and concrete experience'.[135] Noting that Jeff's work as a physician puts him in contact with the types of people his ideology condemns, Melanctha points out that he is consistently non-judgemental: 'You are just as free and easy as any man can be Dr. Campbell, and you always like to be with Jane Harden, and she is a pretty bad one and you don't look down on her and you never tell her she is a bad one.'[136] Based on this observation, Melanctha argues that 'It don't seem to me Dr. Campbell, that what you say and what you do seem to have much to do with each other.'[137] He replies by reiterating the dominant ideology of living 'regular': 'you shouldn't try to know everybody just to run around and get excited'.[138] In this exchange, Melanctha's observations about Jeff seem far more reasonable than his irrational repudiation of feeling and reiteration of the imperative to live 'regular'.[139] As the story progresses, Jeff vacillates between suppressing feeling and losing 'all himself in a strong feeling' for Melanctha.[140] In the latter moments, which come when 'wandering' with her, he will 'find himself' and 'not know how or what it was he had been thinking'.[141] *Three Lives* thereby breaks down the opposition between masculine thinking and feminine feeling that drives *Q.E.D.*

Three Lives also undermines what at first appears to be a clear distinction between Jeff and Melanctha. Perloff argues that the book's mimicry of Cézanne complicates readings that present these characters as polar opposites; instead, the text's linguistic fragmentation scrambles time in ways that render them 'unknowable and indefinable'.[142] This indeterminacy shows in the inconsistency Melanctha observes between Jeff's behaviour and belief system. Her willingness to call him out on this discrepancy turns on the assumption that the subject should be self-identical, and supports Perloff's claim that the seemingly different Jeff and Melanctha 'often seem to coalesce'.[143] At this moment, she is acting much like him by expecting consistency. Nonetheless, Melanctha's questioning challenges the assumption that a person must have a stable identity: an attitude informing Jeff's frustration with and misunderstandings of Melanctha. These characters' contradictions complicate gender, calling Jeff's rigid form of masculinity into question.

Stein aestheticises Jeff's and Melanctha's conflict in ways that loosen up gender constructs and sexual identifications. Despite Melanctha's well-reasoned arguments, Jeff continues to reiterate his expectation that people exhibit stability and consistency. This moves from the characterological to the aesthetic realm when he complains about his shifting perceptions of Melanctha:

> Sometimes you seem like one kind of a girl to me, and sometimes you are like a girl that is all different to me, and the two kinds of girls is certainly very different to each other, and I can't see any way they seem to have much to do, to be together in you. They certainly don't seem to be made much like as if they could have anything really to do with each other.[144]

In this scene, Jeff echoes Adele's criticism of Helen in *Q.E.D.*: he is disturbed to see multiple Melancthas in the same woman. His distress at this perception mirrors the reaction an aficionado of nineteenth-century realism would likely have had when first confronted with a Cézanne or Picasso. Without the stable viewpoint provided by traditional perspective, the spectator perceives vacillations in objects' appearance, so the picture is not as expected.

Three Lives anticipates Stein's early portraits of modern painters when Jeff credits Melanctha with the capacity to manifest 'what is certainly a thing, like a real beauty'.[145] Despite his desire for 'certainty', his language points to the opacity and variability of this beautiful 'thing'.[146] This resonates with Stein's 1912 portrait of Picasso, which reiterates phrases such as 'Something had been coming out of him, certainly it had been coming out of him' to mobilise multiple perspectives.[147] The turns taken by the word 'thing' – which is variably 'solid', 'charming', 'lovely', 'perplexing', 'disconcerting', 'simple', 'clear', 'complicated', 'interesting', 'disturbing', 'repellent' and 'pretty' to its implied viewers – are similar to Jeff's vacillating perceptions of Melanctha.[148] He, too, sees his object as both a 'real beauty' and 'very ugly'.[149]

These similarities between 'Melanctha' and 'Picasso' suggest that the varied forms of 'attracting', 'aggressing', 'repelling' and 'warping' that characterise the relationality of the Sedgwickian 'beside' are at play in Jeff and Melanctha's relationship and the spatiotemporal manipulations of modernist art.[150] Stein claims that Picasso held that 'he who created a thing is forced to make it ugly' to estrange its viewers, and her early portrait of him illustrates the resulting vacillation between attraction to and repudiation of new and unfamiliar canvasses that are alternatively 'charming' and 'repellent'.[151] This dynamic resonates with her statement in 'How Writing Is Written' that 'the creative person always has the appearance of ugliness'.[152] Melanctha provokes in Jeff the sense of 'double time' that 'makes confusion' and 'ugliness' for those trapped between the 'sense of time which belongs to his crowd' and the 'persistent drag of the habits that belong to you'.[153] In Jeff's case, this 'double time' is ideologically charged as he is caught between Melanctha's sexual openness and his disapproval of those who seek 'excitements'.

As Laura Doyle observes, 'Melanctha' uses reiterations in which 'the stability of words like really and certainly certainly dissolves' to undermine Jeff's desire to 'live regular'.[154] Unlike the speaker in 'Picasso', who merely registers the vicissitudes of spectatorial attraction and repulsion induced by his painting, Jeff attempts to suppress the effects of Melanctha's undecidability by denying the reality of actions that perturb him. Eschewing the claims to ontological certainty he initially makes for the 'thing' that 'certainly . . . comes out' of Melanctha, he attempts not to believe that she 'mean[s]' anything by behaviours that defy his belief in 'living regular': he denigrates them as 'ways so bad, I can't believe you mean them hardly'.[155] This strategy is ineffective, though. Even when he is 'rich with' the feelings inspired by the 'real beauty' he can sometimes see in Melanctha, 'that other girl' returns, makes their relationship seem 'ugly', and undermines his trust.[156] Melanctha's deviations from Jeff's assumptions operate like a modernist painting's rejection of traditional rules of composition: divergence from expectations elicits incredulity and leads to repulsion. By reiterating scenes in which these characters' conflicts lead Jeff to such shifts, *Three Lives* employs the 'prolonged present' to mobilise perspective in ways similar to modern art.[157] By shocking perspective, the book dramatises the transition from nineteenth- to early twentieth-century aesthetics and sexual attitudes alike.

Jeff's dogged belief in linguistic meaning's stability and identity's consistency underpins his attraction to and repulsion from Melanctha. At one point, he responds to her criticism of his own inconsistencies with the assertion that 'I don't mean this except only just the way I say it. I ain't got any other meaning Miss Melanctha.'[158] He cannot grasp that meaning's indeterminacy has contributed to their misunderstandings, so his perceptions of Melanctha oscillate throughout the novella.[159] At one point, he declares that 'I certainly don't know anything at all about you' and that 'I certainly never do feel I could be very trusting with you.'[160] Here, Jeff stumbles upon a paradox: the only thing about which he can be certain is his uncertainty about Melanctha. This undecidability is unsettling: it upends his perceptions of Melanctha, confidence in linguistic meaning's clarity, and belief in the concept of the self-identical subject. The clash between these ideas and Jeff's beliefs exacerbates the unsettling sense of 'double time' – and accompanying vacillation between 'beauty' and 'ugliness' – he experiences with Melanctha.

Stein claims to have reacted quite differently when faced with a similar problem of perception. In *The Autobiography*, she positions herself as an avant-garde spectator who can understand artistic innovations others find distressing. She claims that upon first seeing *La Femme au chapeau* at the 1905 Salon d'Automne, she thought the painting was 'perfectly natural' even though it uses colour and space in ways that violate nineteenth-century realist conventions.[161] There may be an element of *Nachträglichkeit* in this statement: whereas in the first decade of the twentieth century Stein was beginning to assimilate modern art's innovations by working them into compositions such as *Three Lives*, in *The Autobiography* she retroactively claims to have perceived them as nothing new. This move allows Stein to subtly put down Matisse and promote herself as avant-garde by claiming to be ahead of the general public, who saw what she considered to be an ordinary painting as 'not attractive' and reacted with fury.[162] However, her writings from the first decade of the twentieth century reveal a more nuanced process of adapting modern painting's innovations for literature.

The 'warping' of perspective that emerged from Cézanne's and Picasso's experiments went on to create similar reverberations in *Three Lives*.[163] Although it shares more stylistic similarities with Cézanne's and Picasso's paintings from the 1900s than with *La Femme au chapeau*, Stein composed *Three Lives* in the wake of her visit to the 1905 Salon. By mocking Jeff's prudish reaction to Melanctha, Stein shows her difference from him: he resists being unsettled by the revolutionary aspects of modernity, and instead deems the new 'ugly'.[164] *Three Lives* aestheticises this conflict to work through Stein's early identification with Jeff's rigid masculinity.

To do so, Stein does not imitate Matisse's 'perfectly natural' *La Femme au chapeau* but instead mimics the 'warping' style of an even more radical portrait by Cézanne.[165] The latter painting 'had not seemed natural' at first, but she and Leo purchased it nonetheless.[166] It took 'her some time to feel that it was natural' even as her writing came to be influenced by it.[167] Stein's reaction to the Cézanne suggests the same kind of disturbance by the 'lovely' but 'disconcerting' innovations in painting that her 1912 portrait of Picasso tracks in initial reactions to cubism.[168] Her vacillating perception of the Cézanne as 'natural' and 'not . . . natural' animates the 'stylistic strangeness' of her literary deployment of his style.[169] These innovations animate the movement in *Three Lives* that ultimately allows Stein to succeed where Jeff does not in radicalising her response to dominant early twentieth-century genders and sexualities.

As Rowe observes, in 'The Gentle Lena' Stein mimics Cézanne in another way by treating 'Lena Mainz's skin color as if it were paint on canvas', thereby 'calling attention to the "compositional quality of racial designations"'.[170] Similarly, in 'Melanctha' Stein highlights the 'racial hybridity' signaled by her protagonist's 'pale yellow' skin, revealing that race is a 'social fiction'.[171] Stein's self-dispersal into the 'pale yellow' Melanctha and the 'light brown, grey haired' Jeff uses the 'artifice of skin color' to denaturalise gender constructs.[172] However, I read the gender Stein achieves through racialised cross-writing as a different kind of fiction than the 'social fiction' of 'race' that Rowe describes.[173] Although the text's mimicry of Cézanne destabilises both, revealing them to be 'conventions', its treatment of gender does not parallel the 'neoprimitivism' Rowe rightfully finds so problematic in Stein's racist tropes.[174] Will argues that Stein was undergoing a 'category crisis' while composing 'Melanctha' and grasped out at 'clichés' about blacks as a way of accepting her own 'Jewish difference'.[175] In my view, this 'category crisis' also concerned gender.[176]

All three stories in *Three Lives* feature protagonists who are undone by oppressive early twentieth-century gender ideologies.

Because of this, the book might seem to treat gender as conservatively as race. However, 'Melanctha' registers Stein's crises while also destabilising gender ontology, furthering the movement toward transmasculine embodiment heralded in *Q.E.D.* with Adele's declaration that she wasn't 'born a woman'.[177] *Three Lives* goes further than *Q.E.D.*, though, by routing Stein's identifications through both Jeff and Melanctha. Repudiating Jeff's rigid insistence upon the self-identical subject, *Three Lives* makes possible the anti-identitarian and feminist transmasculinities in Stein's poetry from the 1910s and 1920s.

Unlike Stein, whose experimental poems and love notes to Toklas in the 1910s and 1920s eventually loosen up bourgeois ideas about gender and sexuality, Jeff is increasingly bothered by Melanctha's sexual openness, which reflects early twentieth-century challenges to dominant notions of feminine propriety. *Three Lives* uses aesthetic distortions to present her 'wandering' as part of the modernist appearance of the new.[178] Much as art aficionados used to traditional perspective were upset by Cézanne's and Picasso's warpings, so is Jeff distressed because Melanctha's assertive sensuality defies his expectations for women and black people alike. He does not adjust easily to these changes.

Jeff's repudiation of Melanctha is in its early stages when he sees 'two kinds of girl' in her; his revulsion intensifies as the text fractures perspective to register her continued 'wanderings'.[179] However, unlike *Q.E.D.*, which emphasises its female characters' repression of 'physical passion', *Three Lives* makes Melanctha's erotic openness – rather than her and Jeff's sexual relationship – the source of his distress.[180] Though he struggles with her differences from hegemonic femininity throughout their relationship, his pain becomes particularly intense when he learns from Jane that Melanctha's sex life has included 'many things' she 'had not yet taught him' – things that made him 'sick'.[181] As Jeff begins to 'see much clearer' into her past, he begins to experience disgust – 'to feel very sick inside him' – and 'to know what it was to have deep feeling'.[182] Blocked by rigid ideas about proper masculinity and femininity, he is unable to face Melanctha.

Melanctha eventually writes to Jeff to call him out on his withdrawal and silence, a refusal of relationality she characterises as 'one of the queer kind of ways you have' of 'repenting of yourself all of a sudden'.[183] Declining to respond directly to Melanctha's suggestion that he is more sexually open than he claims, he asserts that he finds her past distressing because he believes in stability and consistency. He complains that Melanctha lacks 'understanding' for 'all I have to suffer to keep straight on to really always to believe in you and trust you': that is, for the difficulties he encounters as 'a man, who thinks like I was always thinking, not to think you do things very bad very often'.[184] Here Jeff points not only to his philosophical and sexual normativity but also to his efforts to bend his beliefs: he refers to his 'thinking' in the past tense, as if he had changed his mind.[185] Instead of calling his belief in the self-identical subject's unity 'straight', he foregrounds his difficulty in keeping 'straight on' in trusting Melanctha despite her defiance of his values.[186] This reveals Jeff's continued willingness to diverge from his ideology of living 'regular' and abstaining from 'excitements'.[187]

Jeff's difficulties with Melanctha's challenges to hegemonic masculinity and femininity nonetheless continue to produce revulsion. *Three Lives* aestheticises these emotions. Like a modern painting whose 'warping' challenges conventional perspective and standards of aesthetic beauty, Melanctha's past challenges Jeff's attitudes about race, gender and sexuality, making their relationship seem 'ugly'.[188] Once he finally brings himself to see Melanctha again, he tells her that:

> I knew you had been free in your ways, Melanctha, I knew you liked to get excitement the way I always hate to see colored people take it. I didn't know, till I heard Jane Harden say it, you had done things so bad, Melanctha. When Jane Harden told me, I got very sick, Melanctha. I couldn't bear hardly, to think, perhaps I was just another like them to you, Melanctha. I was wrong not to trust you perhaps, Melanctha, but it did make things very ugly to me.[189]

Jeff locates the problem in Melanctha's 'bad' behaviour, although he acknowledges that his values inform his judgement.[190] Although he concedes that he should not have allowed their differences to have undermined his trust, he still experiences disgust and continues to see their situation as 'very ugly'.[191] The word 'ugly' aestheticises the fractures that appear in Jeff and Melanctha's relationship because of their different temperaments and clashing values. It suggests that something is distorted, not right, in their interactions – that they are not beautiful in ways that meet his standards.

While Jeff vacillates between love and disgust, his physical distress returns unexpectedly once they have recovered from his discoveries about Melanctha's past.[192] Resting after sex during a period otherwise characterised by 'much joy' as they lose 'themselves in warm wandering', Jeff begins to wonder:

> What was it that Melanctha did, that made everything get all ugly for them? What was it that Melanctha felt then, that made Jeff remember all the feeling he had had in him when Jane Harden told him how Melanctha had learned to be so very understanding? Jeff did not know how it was that it had happened to him. It was all green, and warm, and very lovely to him, and now Melanctha somehow had made it all so ugly for him. What was it Melanctha was now doing with him?[193]

Although it initially affords him 'freedom' and 'joy', Jeff's loss of control eventually produces revulsion.[194] He externalises the situation, perceiving it as 'ugly' and positing Melanctha as the calculating agent of his undoing. Yet sexuality – a key difficulty for Adele – does not cause Jeff's pain. Stein has resolved Adele's problems with 'desiring' by cross-writing herself as a heterosexual man capable of 'much joy' in his lover's body.[195] At stake is the system of bourgeois heterosexual monogamy Jeff defends and Melanctha defies – a system dependent on a rigid understanding of masculinity and feminine purity. Melanctha's challenge to this worldview thrusts Jeff into a disorienting experience of 'double time' that 'makes confusion' and 'ugliness'.[196] This causes him to attempt to regain stability by reiterating his linear doctrine of 'living regular'.[197]

From the beginning of Jeff and Melanctha's relationship, however, Steinian reiteration has undermined this ideology. Echoing Jeff's earlier bout of feeling 'sick' about Melanctha's past, his sense of ugliness gradually turns to a 'strong disgust inside him' and he reiterates his view that 'colored people' should focus on 'living regular' and not want 'to be always having new things, just to keep on, always being in excitements'.[198] He states that his disgust is

> [n]ot for Melanctha herself, to him, not for himself really, in him, not for what it was that everybody wanted, in them; he only had disgust because he could never know really in him, what it was he wanted, to be really right in understanding, for him, he had only disgust because

> he never could know really what it was really right to him to be always doing, in the things he had before believed in, the things he before had believed in for himself and for all the colored people, the living regular, and the never wanting to be always having new things, just to keep on, always being in excitements. All the only thinking now came up very strong inside him. He sort of turned away then, and threw Melanctha from him.[199]

The clash between Jeff's life with Melanctha and his conservative system of values once again turns sexual bliss into revulsion. At stake at this moment, however, is Jeff's fear of losing the stable standards dominant masculinity provides for feminine beauty and goodness. He stops defending his beliefs, admitting that 'he never could know really what it was really right to him to be always doing'.[200] He repeats the word 'really' as a ballast against the sense of 'double time' induced through his loss of belief in identity's stability and consistency.[201] However, the force of the resultant psychical and linguistic undecidability causes him to repudiate Melanctha.

Whereas in *Q.E.D.*, an 'almost puritanic horror' of 'physical passion' eventually breeds a 'fierce disgust' that precipitates the demise of Adele's relationship with Helen, in *Three Lives* Jeff's disgusted rejection of Melanctha does not resolve as quickly because its causes are more complex.[202] Like Adele and Helen, Melanctha and Jeff experience difficulties with pacing. The latter two characters temporarily resume their relationship shortly after Jeff 'threw Melanctha from him', and continue until he begins to perceive that 'he had to go so fast' to keep up with her.[203] Yet *Three Lives* eschews the earlier book's characterisation of these differences as a matter of biological 'pulses', instead emphasising the characters' relational dynamics.[204] Jeff believes that 'Melanctha somehow never seemed to hear him' as 'they were getting strong to get excited', and perceives that she is 'making him feel, always, how good she was and how very much she suffered in him'.[205] This endows her with a combination of masculine sexual assertiveness and feminine manipulativeness.

Much as he thinks that Melanctha is not 'strong enough inside her to stand any more of his slow way of doing', he fears that he is not 'very strong inside him' because he capitulates under pressure.[206] He attributes his and Melanctha's relational difficulties not to biology but to his ostensibly flawed character: he cannot be 'straight out, and real honest' about his needs, so he 'had to go fast', against his temperament, to please her.[207] This means that his actions are 'far ahead of his own feeling' and contribute to misperceptions because 'he always had to show more to Melanctha than he was ever feeling'.[208] This leads him not to 'like it very well these days, in his true feeling', because he cannot make his actions 'right, inside him'.[209] This dynamic makes Jeff 'uneasy', which becomes a 'weight' and a 'real torment' as he and Melanctha no longer feel 'inside all right, as they once did, to be together'.[210]

Their relationship unravels once Jeff realises that 'Melanctha was too many for him' – an objection to her subjective splitting that echoes and complicates Adele's declaration that Helen is 'one too many for me'.[211] After Jeff learns that Melanctha has begun to 'wander' with 'others' again, he realises he does 'not want her' any more.[212] Embittered at having harboured the 'illusion' that Melanctha loved him, Jeff terminates their relationship and resumes his 'quiet' life of 'working'.[213] Despite the unsettling oscillations mobilised during his time with Melanctha, Jeff concludes that he 'had behaved right and he had learned to have a real love in him'.[214] Although Jeff's hegemonic masculinity has been unsettled by his relationship with Melanctha, offering Stein a wider range of options for identification, he reaffirms it at the end of his part of the narrative.

Unlike *Q.E.D.*, however, 'Melanctha' does not end in narrative 'dead-lock'.[215] Jeff disappears, but Melanctha's story continues. She enters into what eventually becomes a failed engagement with Jem Richards, a gambler whose personality and lifestyle suit her penchant for excitement.[216] Jem's freewheeling masculinity offers a counterpoint to Jeff's rigidity. Although Jem's and Melanctha's temperaments make them a good match, their high tolerance for unpredictability eventually leads to their relationship's demise. A turn of terrible luck in gambling causes Jem to experience a financial crisis that leads him to distance himself from Melanctha and leave town in search of work. Although Melanctha and Jem stand as examples of new forms of femininity and masculinity that were beginning to emerge in the early twentieth century, Jeff's conservative approach to gender informs the ending of 'Melanctha' despite his disappearance from its narration.

Despite Jem's presence until the end of the story, Melanctha's greatest love, Rose, emerges in the final pages to reinforce hegemonic gender ideology. Rose's and Melanctha's different approaches to gender ultimately cause their friendship to end. They had been very close – perhaps even lovers – before Melanctha met Jem, but Rose had stopped sleeping in Melanctha's home after she married Sam Johnson, a 'workman' whose 'stable', 'serious' and 'kindly' behaviour makes him a more 'simple' version of Jeff.[217] Sam, too, only 'wanted . . . to have a little house and to live regular and to work hard'.[218] Blackmer points out that unlike Jeff, Rose has contradictory attributes and seems to perform respectability as a masquerade to 'acquire power within her community and secure her material and social position'.[219] This suggests that like Jeff's, Sam's style of masculinity might be a public performance designed to enhance his and Rose's social standing.

Nonetheless, Rose's insistence on the importance of playing to normative standards of femininity and masculinity eventually informs her repudiation of Melanctha, who refuses to play Rose's game. Like Jeff, Rose lays down a standard of conduct and turns Melanctha's sexual choices into an issue of trust. After hearing rumours about the 'awful kind of things' Melanctha has been doing with men, Rose attempts to advise her about how to 'act real right'.[220] Rose claims that her friend responds to her advice affirmatively, saying 'yes all right Rose, I do the way you say it', but then 'don't never noways do it'.[221] Melanctha mimics Rose's speech but not her actions, leading Rose to conclude that 'Melanctha no way is really honest'.[222] Judgement rather than compassion also informs Rose's reaction to the depressive Melanctha's suicide threats: Rose describes her friend's behaviour – and the life patterns that inform it – as 'no kind of way any decent girl ever had ought to do'.[223] As rumours about Melanctha's supposed indecencies grow, Rose drops her for declining to follow oft-repeated injunctions about the 'way to act right'.[224] Rose's actions parallel Jeff's: both characterise Melanctha as untrustworthy and reject her for her variation from their rules of feminine decency. Rose is the greatest of Melanctha's losses, as she had 'wanted Rose more than she had ever wanted all the others'.[225] After Rose's rejection, Melanctha 'never had any strength alone ever to feel safe inside her'.[226] Jem breaks up with Melanctha shortly thereafter, and she eventually dies of consumption in a facility for the poor.

Even though Jeff, Sam and Rose survive Melanctha, the text systematically questions and rejects their ideology of living 'regular'.[227] Rose performatively denaturalises feminine decency even as she vocalises it. Moreover, as Jayne Walker observes, the story's treatment of language as a problem of representation gradually breaks down the rigid binaries between 'good' and 'bad' informing these characters' moral framework.[228] Reiteration undercuts those words' force. Even though Jeff remains alive at the story's end, his ideals have been undermined and he lacks an object of desire. The story's conclusion thus calls his middle-class masculinity into serious question.

As Stein was writing *Fernhurst*, *Q.E.D.* and *Three Lives*, she was working through her youthful investment in gender and sexual norms; 'Melanctha' undoes hegemonic masculinity in ways Stein continued to pursue throughout her lifetime. In her own life, Stein eventually came to inhabit a masculinity that was open to the idea that women may exercise sexual agency. Her disidentification with Jeff's constrictive assumptions about feminine decency and the stability of the self-identical masculine subject was the first step in her gradual process of shedding her attraction to misogynist masculinity and its dependence on denigrations of femininity.

Three Lives' literary inflection of techniques from modern art and music innovates in prose narrative and forges a path for her sexually open and flexible transmasculinities in the 1910s and 1920s. In so doing, 'Melanctha' resists generic expectations by embracing what Freeman calls the 'intensity' of Melanctha's 'chronic' condition without the 'futural directionality' implied by narratives of 'recovery'.[229] Unlike Melanctha, Stein did 'intensity' differently in the decades following *Three Lives*. Spending the rest of her life working as an avant-garde writer, resignifying heteronormative genders and marriage constructs, she found a rhythm that left her neither stuck in nor undone by the rigid gender formations the recursive iterations of her early book's 'prolonged present' displace.[230] Unlike Melanctha, whose 'chronocatachresis' allows her to live and die from the 'intensity' of the 'insistence' of 'excitements' that diverge from bourgeois temporal norms, Stein established life rhythms that were at odds with dominant temporalities yet enabled her survival.[231] And unlike Jeff, who is left loveless at the end of 'Melanctha', Stein maintained a lifelong relationship with Toklas, embracing rather than rejecting her sexual strength.

If narrative ultimately did not afford Stein the opportunity it did Woolf to create a 'transgenre', radically experimental poetry in the 1910s and 1920s did.[232] By placing Stein in a 'critical relation to the norms of the intelligible', these texts engage in 'a mode of self-making', of 'self-poesis', that flexibly and non-hierarchically articulates her transmasculinity.[233] This allows feminist transmasculinities to appear in her writings, refashioning gender and genre into a 'transgenre' through which Stein's shifting and anti-identitarian transmasculine subjectivity was both 'lived, and liveable' in relation to Toklas's femininity.[234]

Notes

1. Weininger, *Sex and Character*. See Sengoopta, *Otto Weininger*, for an argument that *Sex and Character* is an extreme manifestation of widespread preoccupations of *fin-de-siècle* Viennese discourse on gender and sexuality.
2. DeKoven, *A Different Language*, p. 136, p. 36. See Sengoopta, ibid., pp. 31–6 for discussion of Weininger's place in *fin-de-siècle* feminist and anti-feminist discourse. For work offering critiques of Stein's masculine identification similar to DeKoven's, see Benstock, *Women*; Bridgman, *Gertrude Stein in Pieces*; Doane, *Silence and Narrative*; Elliott and Wallace, *Women Artists and Writers*, p. 96; Gilbert and Gubar, *No Man's Land*, Vol. 1 and Vol. 2; Knapp, *Gertrude Stein*; Rule, *Lesbian Images*; Smith, *Subjectivity, Identity, and the Body*; Stimpson ('Gertrice/Altrude'; 'Gertrude Stein and the Transposition of Gender'; and 'The Mind, the Body, and Gertrude Stein'); and Wagner-Martin, *'Favored Strangers'*. The questionable assumption that Stein and Toklas's relationship uncritically mimics patriarchal genders underpins these arguments.
3. Stein, YCAL MSS 76, Box 38, Folder 791 in Yale University's Beinecke Library.
4. Gilmore, 'A Signature of Lesbian Autobiography', p. 222. As Biddy Martin shows in *Femininity Played Straight*, p. 3, the interpretation of female masculinity as 'male identification' rests on the questionable assumption that 'virtually any expression of gendered style, whether femme or butch', is a function of patriarchy – a premise Judith Butler trenchantly challenges in *Gender Trouble*. Butler also destabilises the distinction between 'sex' and 'gender' on which Stein's initial feminist reception depended.

   For examples of criticism that uses these developments to read Stein through lesbian culture and theory, see Blackmer, 'Lesbian Modernism'; Gilmore, 'A Signature of Lesbian Autobiography'; Hovey, *A Thousand Words* and 'Sapphic Primitivism'; Johnston, 'Narratologies of Pleasure'; McCabe, '"A Queer Lot"'; Meese, 'Gertrude Stein and Me'; and Merrill, 'Gertrude Stein and Autobiography'. Stimpson was among the first to view Stein's sexuality favourably, but her early work – for example, 'Gertrice/Altrude', pp. 122–39 – questionably casts aspersions on Stein's masculinity and treatment of Toklas. This moderates in 'The Somagrams of Gertrude Stein', which reads Stein's and Toklas's dynamic more generously.

5. See YCAL MSS 76, Box 38, Folder 791 in the Beinecke Rare Book and Manuscript Library, Yale University.
6. Weininger, *Sex and Character*, p. 163. See Sengoopta, *Otto Weininger*, pp. 46–58, for analysis of these ideologies. Also see Sengoopta, ibid., pp. 29–31, for a history that traces Weininger's misogyny – especially the widespread early twentieth-century belief that women lack reason – to nineteenth-century philosophers such as Immanuel Kant, Friedrich Nietzsche and Arthur Schopenhauer.
7. Lorange, *How Reading Is Written*, p. 214.
8. Linda Wagner-Martin, *'Favored Strangers'*, pp. 46–7. See Brenda Wineapple, 'Gertrude Stein and the Lost Ark', for an archivally based argument that at Johns Hopkins and in the years that immediately followed, Stein espoused the view of the futility of the 'New Woman's' efforts that she ascribes to Adele in *Fernhurst* and even composed an unpublished essay decrying 'Degeneration in American Women'.
9. Stein, *The Autobiography*, pp. 77–8; Secor, 'Gertrude Stein: The Complex Force of her Femininity', pp. 29–30. See Nair, *Secrecy and Sapphic Modernism*, pp. 138–41, for an argument that this passage shows Stein's refusal to embrace 'causes that would obscure her inimitability'.
10. Stein, *The Autobiography*, p. 78.
11. Wagner-Martin, *'Favored Strangers'*.
12. Stein, YCAL MSS 76, Box 38, Folder 791 in the Beinecke Rare Book and Manuscript Library, Yale University.
13. Damon, 'Gertrude Stein's Jewishness', pp. 499–500.
14. Damon, ibid., pp. 499–500.
15. Stein, 'Portraits and Repetition', p. 166. 'Race' is not a biological fact but a cultural construct: see Gates, Jr, 'Writing, "Race," and the Difference It Makes', pp. 1893–4; and Peterson, 'The Remaking of Americans', pp. 143–4.
16. Damon, 'Gertrude Stein's Jewishness', pp. 499–500.
17. Ruddick, *Reading Gertrude Stein*, p. 13.
18. Stein, *Three Lives*, p. 117.
19. Much scholarship on *Three Lives* focuses on Stein's cross-writing as Jeff and on his and Adele's similarities; see Bridgman, *Gertrude Stein in Pieces*; DeKoven, *A Different Language* and *Rich and Strange*; Leon Katz, 'Introduction'; Rule, *Lesbian Images*; and Walker, *The Making*

of a Modernist. However, Ruddick, *Reading Gertrude Stein*, pp. 52–3, notes that 'Melanctha absorbed features of her author's history', and Hovey (in 'Sapphic Primitivism') reveals that Melanctha's lesbian relationships critique of the turn-of-the-century homophobic hypocrisies also challenged in *Q.E.D.* In *'Favored Strangers'*, Wagner-Martin, too, sees traces of Stein in both Jeff and Melanctha.

20. Prosser, *Second Skins*, pp. 8–9.
21. Salamon, *Assuming a Body*, p. 41.
22. For additional accounts of Stein's troubling of identity, see Ashton, 'Our Bodies, Our Poems'; Bernstein, 'Stein's Identity'; and Lorange, *How Reading Is Written*.
23. Butler in Butler and Athanasiou, *Dispossession*, p. 67.
24. Stein, 'What Are Masterpieces', p. 499; Moon, 'Do You Smoke?', p. 64. Similar language appears in Stein's 'Identity A Poem' and *Everybody's Autobiography*.
25. Ruddick, *Reading Gertrude Stein*, p. 53; DeKoven, *A Different Language*, pp. 131–7. See also Robert K. Martin, '*The Mother of Us All* and American History'; and Wagner-Martin, *'Favored Strangers'*.
26. In *Femininity Played Straight*, Biddy Martin develops this argument by reading Aimée Duc's *Are They Women?* (1901), which features a character whose early adoption of early twentieth-century misogynist masculinity is eventually supplanted by a suppler masculinity that does not require repudiating femininity (p. 67).
27. DeKoven, *A Different Language*, p. 36.
28. Caughie, 'The Temporality of Modernist Life Writing', p. 503.
29. Caughie, ibid., p. 519.
30. See Knapp, *Gertrude Stein*; Wagner-Martin, *'Favored Strangers'*; and Stimpson, 'The Mind, the Body', for different accounts of this time in Stein's life. As Knapp observes, *Q.E.D.* reveals Stein's 'distress' at realising that her desires were unacceptable to dominant North American culture (p. 75). However, Knapp's claim that Stein was neither attracted to men nor attractive to them has been complicated in subsequent scholarship (p. 76).
31. Stein, *Fernhurst*, pp. 5–7.
32. Stein, ibid., pp. 6–8, emphasis added.
33. See Blankley, 'Beyond the "Talent of Knowing"', for an argument that *Fernhurst* repudiates the 'New Woman'.
34. Stein, *Fernhurst*, p. 49.
35. Wagner-Martin, *'Favored Strangers'*, pp. 76–7.
36. Stein, *Fernhurst*, p. 49.
37. Rowe, 'Naming What Is Inside', p. 230.
38. Stein, *Q.E.D.*, p. 58.
39. Ruddick, *Reading Gertrude Stein*, p. 53.

40. DeKoven in Stein, '*Three Lives*' *and* '*Q.E.D.*', p. 181 n. 2.
41. DeKoven, *A Different Language*, pp. 133–4. See this book and Stimpson, 'The Mind, the Body', for early scholarship on Stein's treatment of the mind/body split.
42. Stein, *Q.E.D.*, p. 59. See Hovey, 'Sapphic Primitivism', pp. 560–1, for a discussion of this ideology's 'bourgeois' and 'masculine-identified' features in the context of *fin-de-siècle* fears about 'decadence'.
43. Stein, *Q.E.D.*, p. 59.
44. Stein, ibid., p. 59.
45. Stein, ibid., p. 66.
46. Stein, ibid., p. 66.
47. Stein, ibid., p. 66.
48. Stein, ibid., p. 78.
49. Stein, ibid., p. 80.
50. Stein, ibid., pp. 80–1.
51. Stein, ibid., p. 82.
52. Stein, ibid., p. 88.
53. Stein, ibid., p. 102.
54. Stein, ibid., p. 102.
55. Stein, ibid., p. 102.
56. Stein, ibid., p. 102.
57. Stein, ibid., p. 102.
58. Stein, ibid., p. 103.
59. Stein, ibid., p. 103.
60. Stein, ibid., p. 104.
61. Stein, ibid., p. 104.
62. Stein, ibid., p. 104. See Blackmer, 'African Masks', pp. 238–40, for further analysis of biological language in this passage.
63. Stein, *Q.E.D.*, p. 102, p. 133.
64. Hovey, 'Sapphic Primitivism', p. 564.
65. Hovey, ibid., pp. 563–4; Stein, *Q.E.D.*, p. 118.
66. Hovey, 'Sapphic Primitivism', p. 564.
67. Corn and Latimer, *Seeing Gertrude Stein*, pp. 31–5.
68. Stein, *Three Lives*, p. 117.
69. Stein, *Q.E.D.*, p. 58.
70. Hovey, 'Sapphic Primitivism', pp. 560–1.
71. Rowe, 'Naming What Is Inside', p. 231.
72. Mackey, 'Other: From Noun to Verb', p. 528.
73. Hovey, 'Sapphic Primitivism', pp. 548–64.
74. Stein, 'Composition as Explanation', pp. 517–18. See Voris, *The Composition of Sense*, pp. 4–5 for discussion of the ways Stein and others ultimately exceed these categories. For more on temporal variation in 'Melanctha', see Folgarait, *Painting 1909*.

75. Freeman, 'Hopeless Cases'. See also Voris, *The Composition of Sense*, pp. 4–5.
76. Freeman, 'Hopeless Cases', pp. 335–8.
77. Freeman, ibid., pp. 340–6.
78. Stein, 'Composition as Explanation', p. 517; Freeman, 'Hopeless Cases', p. 346; McCallum, 'Stein *und Zeit*', p. 239.
79. Stein, 'Composition as Explanation', pp. 517–18.
80. Stein, *Three Lives*, p. 117.
81. Stein, ibid., p. 87; Freeman, 'Hopeless Cases', pp. 335–9.
82. Peterson, 'The Remaking of Americans', p. 152. For a similar approach to 'Melanctha', see Weiss, '"Among Negroes"'. See Barnhart, *Jazz in the Time of the Novel*, for analysis of transfers between the formal properties of blues, jazz, and ragtime and modernist novelistic form.
83. Stringer, *Not Even Past*, p. 135.
84. Barnhart, *Jazz in the Time of the Novel*, p. 173.
85. Peterson, 'The Remaking of Americans', p. 149.
86. Caughie, 'The Temporality of Modernist Life Writing', p. 503.
87. Stein, *Three Lives*, p. 95.
88. DeKoven, *A Different Language*, p. 43.
89. Peterson, 'The Remaking of Americans', p. 149.
90. Stein, *Three Lives*, p. 158.
91. Weiss, '"Among Negroes"', p. 118.
92. Barnhart, *Jazz in the Time of the Novel*, p. 178.
93. Barnhart, ibid., p. 178.
94. Barnhart, ibid., p. 178.
95. Barnhart, ibid., p. 175.
96. Stein, 'Portraits and Repetition', pp. 166–7.
97. The links between Stein's and the modernist painters' innovations have long been a subject of scholarship, with Cézanne and Picasso the most frequent comparisons. See Benstock, *Women*; Blackmer, 'African Masks'; Brinnin, *The Third Rose*; Brogan, 'The "Founding Mother"'; DeKoven, 'Gertrude Stein and Modern Painting'; Dubnick, *The Structure of Obscurity* and 'Two Types of Obscurity'; Grahn, *Really Reading Gertrude Stein*; Heldrich, 'Connecting Surfaces'; Katz, 'Introduction'; Madeline, 'Preface'; North, 'Modernism's African Mask'; Perloff, '"A Fine New Kind of Realism"' and 'Poetry as Word-System'; Peterson, 'The Remaking of Americans'; Rowe, 'Naming What Is Inside'; Ruddick, *Reading Gertrude Stein*; Scobie, *Earthquakes and Explorations*; Siraganian, 'Out of Air'; Steiner, *Exact Resemblance to Exact Resemblance*; Sutherland, *Gertrude Stein*; Voris, *The Composition of Sense* and 'Interpreting Cézanne;' and Walker, *The Making of a Modernist*.
98. Blackmer, 'African Masks', p. 244.
99. Stein, *Three Lives*, pp. 85–6.

100. Blackmer, 'African Masks', p. 242.
101. Piper, 'The Logic of Modernism', p. 576.
102. Knapp, *Gertrude Stein*, p. 88; Sedgwick, *Touching Feeling*, p. 8.
103. Knapp, *Gertrude Stein*, pp. 88.
104. Rowe, 'Naming What Is Inside', p. 223, p. 226. Stein discusses connections between her writings and Cézanne's painting in 'A Transatlantic Interview', pp. 502–4. For more on transfers between Cézanne's painting and Stein's *Three Lives*, see Dubnick, *The Structure of Obscurity* and 'Two Types of Obscurity'; Knapp, *Gertrude Stein*, p. 88; Mitrano, *Gertrude Stein*; Perloff, 'Poetry as Word-System', p. 92; Ruddick, *Reading Gertrude Stein*; Walker, *The Making of a Modernist*; Voris, *The Composition of Sense* and 'Interpreting Cézanne'; and Will, *Gertrude Stein*, pp. 116–21.
105. Cheng, *Second Skin*, p. 114, p. 10, p. 114. This is Stein's only mention in *Second Skin*.
106. Cheng, ibid., p. 13.
107. Mackey, 'Other: From Noun to Verb', p. 528; Cheng, *Second Skin*, p. 13.
108. Mackey, 'Other: From Noun to Verb', pp. 526–7.
109. Cheng, *Second Skin*, p. 4, p. 13.
110. Cheng, ibid., p. 66.
111. Hovey, *A Thousand Words*, p. 101.
112. Cheng, *Second Skin*, p. 13.
113. Freud and Anzieu quoted in Cheng, ibid., p. 30; Prosser, *Second Skins*, p. 42.
114. Prosser, ibid., p. 42; Salamon, *Assuming a Body*, p. 28, p. 35.
115. Salamon, ibid., p. 28.
116. Salamon, ibid., pp. 25–8.
117. Cheng, *Second Skin*, p. 10; Rowe, 'Naming What Is Inside', p. 226.
118. Rowe, ibid., p. 226; Cheng, ibid., p. 13.
119. Rowe, 'Naming What Is Inside', p. 226.
120. Salamon, *Assuming a Body*, p. 29.
121. Cheng, *Second Skin*, p. 56.
122. Cheng, ibid., p. 13.
123. Cheng, ibid., p. 120.
124. Cheng, ibid., p. 152.
125. Sedgwick, *Touching Feeling*, p. 8.
126. Blackmer, 'African Masks', p. 248.
127. See Rowe, 'Naming What Is Inside', pp. 227–9, for detailed analysis of Jeff's 'endorsement of the dominant culture's scientific epistemology' and the implications of Melanctha's resistance to it.
128. Stein, *Three Lives*, p. 117.
129. Stein, ibid., p. 117.

130. In ‘Sapphic Primitivism’, Hovey traces this trope from Stein’s student themes at Radcliffe College through *Q.E.D.* and *Three Lives*.
131. Stein, *Three Lives*, p. 116, p. 108.
132. Stein, ibid., p. 117, p. 108.
133. Trask, *Cruising Modernism*, p. 104.
134. Stein, *Three Lives*, p. 117.
135. Blackmer, ‘African Masks’, p. 248.
136. Stein, *Three Lives*, p. 120.
137. Stein, ibid., p. 117.
138. Stein, ibid., p. 117, p. 120.
139. Stein, ibid., p. 117.
140. Stein, ibid., p. 154.
141. Stein, ibid., p. 154.
142. Perloff, ‘Poetry as Word-System’, p. 92.
143. Perloff, ibid., p. 92.
144. Stein, *Three Lives*, p. 138.
145. Stein, ibid., p. 138.
146. Stein, ibid., p. 138.
147. Stein, ibid., p. 138; Stein, ‘Picasso’, p. 142.
148. Stein, ‘Picasso’, p. 143.
149. Stein, *Three Lives*, p. 138, p. 151.
150. Sedgwick, *Touching Feeling*, p. 8.
151. Picasso paraphrased in Stein, *Picasso* (1938: 1938), p. 14; Stein, ‘Picasso’, p. 143.
152. Stein, ‘How Writing Is Written’, p. 490.
153. Stein, ibid., p. 490.
154. Doyle, ‘The Flat, the Round, and Gertrude Stein’, p. 268; Stein, *Three Lives*, p. 117 [*sic*].
155. Stein, ibid., p. 138, p. 117, p. 138.
156. Stein, ibid., p. 138, p. 151.
157. Stein, ‘Composition as Explanation’, pp. 517–18.
158. Stein, ibid., pp. 121–2.
159. Stein, ibid., p. 138.
160. Stein, ibid., p. 87.
161. Stein, *The Autobiography*, p. 32.
162. Stein, ibid., p. 32. See Siraganian, ‘Speculating on an Art Movement’, for analysis of Stein’s slights to Matisse.
163. Sedgwick, *Touching Feeling*, p. 8.
164. Stein, *Three Lives*, p. 151.
165. Stein, *The Autobiography*, pp. 31–2; Sedgwick, *Touching Feeling*, p. 8.
166. Stein, ibid., p. 32.
167. Stein, ibid., p. 32.
168. Stein, ‘Picasso’, p. 143.

169. Stein, *The Autobiography*, p. 32; Will, *Gertrude Stein*, p. 38.
170. Rowe, 'Naming What Is Inside', p. 224.
171. Rowe, ibid., p. 222; Stein, *Three Lives*, p. 86; Rowe, ibid., p. 222.
172. Stein, ibid., p. 86, p. 11; Rowe, 'Naming What Is Inside', p. 223.
173. Rowe, ibid., p. 222.
174. Rowe, ibid., p. 226, p. 234.
175. Will, *Gertrude Stein*, pp. 38–9.
176. Will, ibid., p. 39.
177. Stein, *Q.E.D.*, p. 58.
178. Stein, *Three Lives*, p. 117.
179. Stein, ibid., p. 138.
180. Stein, *Q.E.D.*, p. 59.
181. Stein, *Three Lives*, p. 144.
182. Stein, ibid., p. 144.
183. Stein, ibid., p. 145.
184. Stein, ibid., p. 146.
185. Stein, ibid., p. 146.
186. Stein, ibid., p. 146.
187. Stein, ibid., p. 117.
188. Sedgwick, *Touching Feeling*, p. 8; Stein, *Three Lives*, p. 155.
189. Stein, ibid., p. 151.
190. Stein, ibid., p. 151.
191. Stein, ibid., p. 151.
192. Stein, ibid., p. 155.
193. Stein, ibid., p. 155.
194. Stein, ibid., pp. 144–5.
195. Sedgwick, *Touching Feeling*, p. 8; Stein, *Three Lives*, p. 155.
196. Stein, 'How Writing Is Written', p. 490.
197. Stein, *Three Lives*, pp. 155–6.
198. Stein, ibid., pp. 155–6.
199. Stein, ibid., pp. 155–6.
200. Stein, ibid., p. 156.
201. Stein, ibid., p. 156; Stein, 'How Writing Is Written', p. 490.
202. Stein, *Q.E.D.*, p. 59, p. 102.
203. Stein, *Three Lives*, p. 156, p. 163.
204. Stein, *Q.E.D.*, p. 104.
205. Stein, *Three Lives*, p. 163.
206. Stein, ibid., p. 163.
207. Stein, ibid., p. 163.
208. Stein, ibid., p. 163.
209. Stein, ibid., p. 163.
210. Stein, ibid., p. 163, p. 171, p. 173.
211. Stein, ibid., p. 175; Stein, *Q.E.D.*, p. 81.

212. Stein, *Three Lives*, p. 184, p. 190.
213. Stein, ibid., p. 193.
214. Stein, ibid., p. 206.
215. Stein, *Q.E.D.*, p. 133.
216. See Peterson, 'The Remaking of Americans', for a discussion of Jem's roots in stereotypes from 'Coon Songs' and an argument that *Three Lives* follows African American performers in challenging those images (pp. 146–9).
217. Stein, *Three Lives*, p. 211.
218. Stein, ibid., p. 229.
219. Blackmer, 'African Masks', p. 244.
220. Stein, ibid., p. 228.
221. Stein, ibid., pp. 228–9.
222. Stein, ibid., p. 229.
223. Stein, ibid., p. 229.
224. Stein, ibid., p. 232.
225. Stein, ibid., p. 233.
226. Stein, ibid., p. 233.
227. Stein, ibid., p. 117.
228. Walker, *The Making of a Modernist*, pp. 32–6.
229. Freeman, 'Hopeless Cases', p. 346, p. 335.
230. Stein, 'Composition as Explanation', pp. 517–18.
231. Freeman, 'Hopeless Cases', p. 346, p. 338; Stein, *Three Lives*, p. 117.
232. Caughie, 'The Temporality of Modernist Life Writing', p. 503.
233. Butler in Butler and Athanasiou, *Dispossession*, p. 67.
234. Caughie, 'The Temporality of Modernist Life Writing', p. 503, p. 519.

Chapter 3

Reading Stein's Genders: Transmasculine Signification in the 1910s and 1920s

Stein's radically experimental texts from the 1910s and 1920s go well beyond the destabilisation of masculinity offered in *Three Lives*. Her early novels subtly displace misogynist masculinity without offering 'a narrative of a life that might be lived, and liveable' in defiance of dominant expectations without significant penalty.[1] By contrast, Stein's avant-garde poems from the 1910s and 1920s explicitly rework gender and power. Engaging in 'a mode of . . . self-poesis that involves risking intelligibility', Stein's writings from this period denaturalise and rearticulate her early claim to 'a maleness that belongs to genius', using her relationality with Toklas to mobilise pliable, feminist, anti-identitarian transmasculinities.[2] In so doing, Stein successfully utilises a 'transgenre' to write '"a set of embodied texts"' that undo and refashion existing genders.[3] In the 1910s and 1920s, Stein achieved in poetry what she was unable to accomplish in narrative in the 1900s: articulations of transgender embodiment that pushed generic limits and enabled her and Toklas to live out varied genderings in their relationship.

In this experimental poetry – written in what Joan Retallack calls the 'present sensual' tense rather than the distanced third person of 'Melanctha' – the eroticised play between Toklas's femininity and Stein's masculinity is overt and embodied.[4] Breaking with normative generic and linguistic structures; toying with gendered pronouns: these writings explicitly and jubilantly use linguistic experimentalism to articulate flexible and feminist transmasculinities. Whereas much early feminist scholarship frames Stein's avant-garde writings as concerning her relationship to female or women's embodiment, enacted through a lesbian relationship with Toklas, I contend that Stein's self-inscriptions in her poems from the 1910s and 1920s cannot be contained by the categories 'woman' or 'lesbian'. Instead, these anti-identitarian texts eschew stable ontologies and 'struggle against categories of gender'.[5] By mobilising a variety of anti-patriarchal transmasculinities, her avant-garde poetics reiteratively asserts, destabilises, and renegotiates a variety of masculine and feminine embodiments.

This view of Stein's masculine self-inscriptions in the 1910s and 1920s differs markedly from early Stein scholarship. DeKoven asserts that Stein 'essentially thought of herself as a man' during 'her radically experimental period', when she supposedly transferred self-hatred into linguistic rebellion.[6] DeKoven argues that this 'male identification did not shift until the late twenties, when there is evidence that Stein began to feel better about her female identity'.[7] Rejecting the assumption that Stein identified as a 'woman' and that her masculine gender positioning was self-hating allows for a more nuanced reading of her innovative texts' genderings. Her experimental writings from the 1910s and 1920s mobilise masculinities that depend neither on Weininger's repudiation of femininity nor on the bourgeois notions of feminine propriety wielded against Melanctha. Instead, they fold feminine erotic stances into an anti-patriarchal, feminist transmasculinity that breaks through normative constructs of patriarchal masculinity well before her mid-1930s rejection of dominant understandings of being 'a man'.[8]

The avant-garde poetic techniques Stein introduced in the 1910s and 1920s also distinguish her inscriptions of transgender from the narrative forms of transmasculine writing discussed by Prosser.[9] Whereas for Prosser, narrative affords transsexuals a way to 'create a coherent subject' that resolves a 'split' between past and present, Salamon's approach to embodiment refuses this search for bodily 'plenitude and fullness'.[10] Salamon's Lacanian approach undercuts the assumption that transsubjectivity must be self-identical and coherent rather than divided.[11] Similarly, Stein's love notes and experimental texts persistently inscribe transmasculine embodiment across a variety of contexts, producing a plurality of meanings and modes of subjectivity.

Thus far, feminist scholarship has focused on experimental writing's challenges to patriarchy while only partially exploring its reworking of gender constructs. Though Elisabeth Frost rightfully notes that the term 'experimental writing' remains 'vague', a discrete set of concerns animates scholarship on twentieth-century feminist experimentalism.[12] Ellen G. Friedman and Miriam Fuchs argue that experimentation breaks 'patriarchal fictional forms' and replaces them with 'radical forms' driven by 'nonlinear, nonhierarchical, and decentering' strategies.[13] Barbara Page further observes that these displacements 'write against norms of "realist" narrative'.[14] In Page's sense, Stein's work could be described as 'experimental' as early as *Three Lives*, whose linguistic indeterminacy sets the stage for Stein's more radical attacks on language, regulatory behaviour, and dominant genders in the 1910s and 1920s. Stein's texts from the first decade of the twentieth century also begin to destabilise Weininger's misogynist masculinity, as Damon has shown.[15] However, Stein mounts even more thoroughgoing challenges to hegemonic masculinities in her experimental poems. Obliterating boundaries between genre and gender, these writings resist misogyny and inscribe shifting modes of transmasculine embodiment.[16]

Deploying 'the art of punning . . . to mix genders with impunity', these texts position Stein as masculine while destabilising masculinity and denaturalising its relationship to patriarchy.[17] Merrill Cole rightfully argues that texts such as 'Patriarchal Poetry' (1927: 1953) turn 'on shaking up patriarchy's confidence in identification' through ever-shifting significations.[18] An implication of this argument Cole does not develop is that these shifts open up new possibilities for gender. As Jennifer Ashton observes, much thinking about feminist experimental poetry assumes that 'women's formal experiments partake of the distinctiveness of women's bodies'.[19] This work was influenced by Hélène Cixous's and Luce Irigaray's essentialist theories of *écriture féminine* and feminine jouissance, respectively; it holds that Stein writes the female body through linguistic play suppressed by patriarchy.[20] However, these theories founder on the limitations of the reverse discourse at work in their insistence on the subversive potential of the embodied femininity repressed by patriarchal language. This framework leaves femininity trapped within the very paradigm it strives to shatter and fails to theorise transmasculinities at all.

Challenging such accounts, Harriet Scott Chessman argues that Stein's language is neither 'phallogocentric' nor 'wholly or essentially "female"'.[21] Rather, her poetics leaves gender 'identification . . . open to question', inscribing gender and embodiment through a non-hierarchical and 'dialogic form' that uses relationality with Toklas to rework dominant genders.[22] Though Chessman does not explore this possibility, her approach hints that transmasculinities are at play in Stein's work. Taking seriously the possibility that Stein may not have identified as either 'female' or a 'woman', and that her texts' proliferation of genders need not be grounded in either of those identities, enables more nuanced accounts of her shifting masculinity – and its relationship to misogyny and patriarchy – than earlier scholarship considered. Stein's textualisations of transmasculine subjectivity are productively unstable, both in the forms they take across time and their relationship to social and linguistic structures that privilege masculinity and denigrate femininity.

Salamon's capacious account of transgender embodiment offers an especially useful framework for reading Stein's transmasculinity. Distinguishing 'between the body as it is seen, as object, and the body as it is felt and phenomenologically experienced', Salamon situates embodiment as 'a product of relation' rather than objectively verifiable matter.[23] Toklas performed the vital function of validating, indeed loving, Stein's lived gender. As Ulla Dydo and others document, Stein often moved between writing love notes to Toklas and composing literature, often using the former to stimulate the latter.[24] While the resulting texts can be read in a variety of ways that need not be limited to the autobiographical, it is clear that they formed an important part of Stein's and Toklas's everyday life and were influenced by it. As Dydo observes, some of Stein's texts – such as *A Book Concluding With As A Wife Has A Cow A Love Story* (1923: 1926) – draw explicitly on her and Toklas's sexual vocabulary, which also appears elsewhere in Stein's notebooks and published writings.[25] Earlier scholars have situated these erotic exchanges as evidence of lesbianism. However, given Stein's consistently masculine self-inscriptions, I read them through Salamon as evidence of Toklas's importance in forming and articulating Stein's transsubjectivity. Seen through this lens, what Gilmore describes in reference to *The Autobiography* as the 'coupled' subject of Stein/Toklas can be read as something other than lesbian.[26] Through their exchanges of love notes and erotic poetry, Toklas's and Stein's relationship elicited their gendered embodiments and provided vital sustenance for Stein's shifting and anti-identitarian transmasculinity.

Reading Stein's transmasculine significations through Salamon's account of embodiment allows me to reframe earlier scholarship that offers a respectful account of Stein's and Toklas's relationship while privileging lesbian desire. Penelope Engelbrecht asserts that 'For Stein, to speak *is* to act; she conflates text and reality, makes the flesh word/makes the word active flesh.'[27] While I concur with Engelbrecht's argument that Stein's experimental writing enacts an embodied poetics, I disagree with her suggestion that Stein's playfulness with pronouns is a mere 'disguise' for lesbian desire.[28] This assumes that Stein's embodiment was unproblematically 'female' and that she identified as a 'woman'. Yet as Susan Holbrook argues, texts such as 'Lifting Belly' (1915–17: 1953) produce 'meanings' that are always 'variable, multiple, and provisional'.[29] They undercut 'moments of clear referentiality' to enact a 'radical questioning', 'disruption' and denaturalisation of 'normative gender figurations' and the heteronormative sexualities they support.[30] Yet Stein takes this troubling of gender even further than Holbrook theorises. The experimental poems from the 1910s and 1920s introduce innovative genres and genders that go beyond – rather than merely contest – the binaries of man/woman, heterosexual/homosexual. What Holbrook aptly calls the 'trans- poetic' of Stein's textual 'polyvalence' mobilises not only queer language and desire but also transgenderings.[31] I label these desires both 'queer' and 'trans-' because – as Cromwell observes – people with 'transsituated identities and bodies' desire in ways that undermine 'the binary of heterosexual and homosexual', proliferating new ways of experiencing gender and sexuality.[32] Much like Cromwell's and Salamon's subjects, Stein's innovative writings from the 1910s and 1920s go well beyond 'questioning' heteronormative genders and desires to mobilise constantly shifting transgenderings that radically rework gendered embodiment.

However, unlike Kay Turner suggests, Stein's writings do not engage in radically anarchistic freeplay with gender; her masculinity persisted in varied forms throughout her lifetime.[33] Moreover, Stein's experimental works from the 1910s and 1920s play with authoritarian and anti-authoritarian masculinities, showing both an attraction to hegemonic masculinities and an inclination to question them. In so doing, her texts challenge dominant masculinities in ways that differ from other feminist experimental writings: they inscribe masculinity without being masculinist and offer important alternatives to misogynist masculinities.

Radical genders, radical sexualities: 'babies', 'cows' and 'Caesars'

The plays with gendered pronouns in 'As A Wife Has A Cow' are often read as examples of a well-established pattern in which 'Stein, the husband . . . makes love to Toklas, the wife.'[34] Dydo has established that despite Stein's experimentalism, 'husband' and 'wife' – and their associated gendered pronouns – are quite stable in the notebooks at the Beinecke Library. Whereas Toklas usually – though not always – is the figure who has the 'cows' to which 'As A Wife Has A Cow' and the love notes refer, the former produces manuscripts they call 'babies'.[35] However, these 'cows' and 'babies' are always 'joint creations' rather than the product of a metaphorical 'mother' or 'father'.[36] Observing that Stein's invocations of her 'babies' and Toklas's 'cows' depend on the language of 'patriarchal gender', Dydo underestimates the implications of their queer resignification of marriage terminology.[37] Although Kathryn Kent reads Stein's and Toklas's inscriptions of gender as 'analogous to what Judith Butler describes as "gender parody"', I see their writings as playfully but seriously reworking dominant ideas about what it means to be a wife or a husband, feminine or masculine.[38]

Neil Schmitz notes that 'Lifting Belly' emphasises 'the belly as its choicest figure, not the phallus', and Catharine Stimpson contends that '[t]he phrase "lifting belly" becomes both a repetitive synecdoche for a repeated, repeatable sexual act and a generalized metonymy for Stein's life'.[39] As Lorange argues, the 'queer bodies' in Stein's poems 'present a challenge to the dominant semiotics . . . predicated on the repression of the body and the assumptions of heteronormativity'.[40] Rather than reading 'Lifting Belly' as 'lesbian erotica', Lorange contends that it is 'a performative account of queer embodiment'.[41] The insistently reiterated 'phrase "lifting belly" . . . indexes bodily modality' in ways that cannot be reduced to stable meanings but instead should be taken as signs of 'the capacity for bodily life'.[42] Viewed through this lens, 'Lifting Belly' and Stein's other writings inscribe the body's 'orientations' as 'emergent, contingent, and dynamic' in ways that are 'potentially radicalizing' because they defy stable notions of identity.[43] With this anti-identitarian understanding of Stein's texts in mind, I am interested in tracking the ways the varied genders at play in her writings resonate with transgender sexualities.

Transgender sexual practices often turn on renaming genitalia and expanding sexual vocabularies – acts that sidestep normative understandings of bodies to register the partners' felt senses of gender and embodiment.[44] Although lesbian-feminist scholarship on Stein's erotic writings often attributes 'cows' to Toklas, reading this word as signifying both orgasms and faeces, at various points the masculine figure also has 'cows'.[45] 'Caesars' also often connotes orgasm in Stein's texts. Less frequently discussed, it is associated with Stein's and others' masculinity. Early scholarship on Stein asserts that she encodes lesbian desire by eroticising this language. Although Lorange suggests that such work prudishly presents us with 'a queerness abstracted from Stein and made legible as textuality', she, too, overlooks Stein's overt sexual inscriptions.[46] I view Stein's references to 'cows' and 'Caesars' as enacting a radical and openly erotic uncoupling of sexuality from binary sex. The significance of 'cow' and 'Caesar' shifts as these words traverse new sexual and bodily contexts, registering transmasculine sexuality.

Though consistently masculinised, the relationship of 'Caesars' to the act of penetration varies. Stein's textual practice addresses the way that, as Ann Cvetkovich puts it, 'Different kinds of penetration' – and different kinds of sex – '*mean* different kinds of things, a complexity sometimes effaced in a phallocentric culture'.[47] In 'A Sonatina Followed By Another' (1921: 1953), 'Caesars' are associated with female ejaculation and the kind of orgasm that comes from penetration and stimulation of the Gräfenberg Spot (G-spot).[48] The 'tenderness' prompted by a 'pump' that 'can pump other things than water' is a sensation that 'grows and it grows' to 'fill a cow full of filling' with a substance that 'comes out of the way of the Caesars'.[49] Stein's puns on 'Caesars' are polyvalent, suggesting but not unambiguously denoting penetration. In 'Lifting Belly', her use of 'Caesars' proliferates rather than restricts pleasures and diminishes rather than aggrandises the phallus. After producing 'Big Caesars. / Two Caesars. / Little seize her.', a speaker asks, 'Did I do my duty. / Did I wet my knife.'[50] Exploiting a pun on 'wet' and 'whet', this question playfully asks whether penetration took place with a 'knife' – a violent phallic symbol – yet leaves the matter unsettled. 'Caesars' diminish into 'little seize her[s]' as the phallus is put under erasure and supplanted with a masculinity oriented not toward self-satisfaction but the pleasure of the other.

'Caesars' are explicitly non-penetrative at another point in 'A Sonatina'. Stein writes that 'Caesars stay they do not stray . . . they permit indeed they insist indeed they cause indeed they aid they do not pause they cause and we register with a smile and a nod that *there is no need of a prod* indeed we register that satisfaction has been obtained.'[51] Rather than emphasising the action of a partner prompting a lover's 'Caesars', Stein underscores the orgasmic body's productive capacities. The 'Caesars' 'stay' and 'insist'; they 'permit' and 'aid' their own pleasures; they are their own 'cause'.[52] 'Lifting Belly' includes similar formulations, such as reiterations of 'Lifting belly is so strong'.[53] This phrase – along with lines such as 'Lifting belly is so able. / Lifting belly is so able to be praised' – presents the body as its own source of erotic strength, and the lovers register fulfilment only in the passive voice.[54] In the poem's larger context – which inscribes Stein and Toklas as a 'couple[d]' subject – the body is not a passive object incited by an active, masculine partner but is mutually animated by the partners' interaction.[55] In 'A Sonatina', the 'couple[d]' subject appears only at the end of the aforementioned passage as the 'we' that 'register[s] that satisfaction has been obtained'.[56] Nobody exerts physical or linguistic control; the lovers simply signal 'with a smile and a nod' their approval that 'there is no need of a prod' to incite the body's self-generating 'Caesars'.[57]

In 'Lifting Belly', Stein also writes that 'Caesars' stand '*in relation to* a cow'.[58] As Rebecca Mark observes, 'Caesar' – as well as related 'patriarchal symbols of man' such as 'sun', 'general', 'king', 'Ford' and 'monument' – 'lose their power to dominate' and become 'relational' in the text.[59] Mark's reading recalls Sedgwick's Deleuzian argument for thinking the 'beside', which offers a valuable alternative to 'dualistic thinking' pitting one party against another in a struggle for dominance.[60] By drawing attention to 'planar relations', the term 'beside' allows us to think about the ways 'a number of elements may lie alongside one another' in peace or hostility.[61] Similarly, the significance of words such as 'cows', 'Caesars' and 'lifting belly' unfolds both vertically and horizontally in Stein's experimental texts. Midway through 'Lifting Belly', a speaker asks 'Why can lifting belly please me', and the amused response – 'because it is an occupation I enjoy' – is followed by a well-known Steinian eroticisation of laterally shifting signifiers: 'Rose is a rose is a rose is a rose.'[62] This phrase mobilises a variety of sounds, including 'eros'. References to wind and water appear throughout the poem, signifying sexual energy, bodily fluids and lateral movements of nature mobilising the body's ups and downs. 'Lifting belly high' happens after the 'wind' blows and the speakers reference 'water' coming from 'Not exactly an ocean' but 'a sea'.[63] Shortly thereafter, a speaker observes that 'Lifting belly is such a windmill', implying that sexuality works rhythmically to harness nature's energies.[64] Above all, 'Lifting belly is so kind' – the text's most frequently reiterated phrase – highlights the gentleness with which the partners physically and psychologically touch one another.[65] A sole instance of 'Mixing belly is so kind' breaks down the partners' mental and physical boundaries in a temporary moment of erotic fusion, of the 'beside'.[66] Multiple iterations build to the declaration that 'Lifting belly connects. / Lifting belly naturally celebrates. / We naturally celebrate. / Connect me in places. / Lifting belly. / No no don't say that. / Lifting belly oh yes.'[67] This phrasing does not emphasise hierarchy but affirms connection.

Mark thus argues that 'Lifting Belly' undercuts the binary opposition between 'private' and 'public' by mobilising 'lesbian sex in the world, participating, relating and transforming everything it encounters'.[68] Although it is reasonable for Mark to take Stein's and Toklas's gender play as an expression of lesbianism, it can also be read otherwise: as evidence of their eroticisation of Stein's transmasculinity. Unlike hierarchical male masculinities, Stein's transmasculinity is lateral: her 'Caesars' take place 'in relation to a cow'.[69] 'Lifting Belly' reworks dominant forms of masculinity by situating it in non-hierarchical 'relation' to femininity.

The poem also rearticulates hegemonic masculinity by toying with dominance and submission in the context of more persistent iterations of lateral, connective and 'kind' erotic scenarios.[70] At one point, roughness turns to pleasure in a formulation that parodies and undermines imperialist masculinity. Chessman argues that puns on '"Caesar"' / "sees her" / "seize her"' lead 'not to rape or occupation, but to "cows" (an image of both the pastoral and female orgasm) and kisses'.[71] Stein's statement that '"Caesar . . . is plural"' 'suggests a dialogue between different "Caesars"' rather than a violent colonisation of the feminine.[72] At another point, the phrase 'Lifting belly captures' is followed by 'Lifting belly excuses'; these words are interspersed between iterations of 'oh yes' and references to 'swimming', shortly thereafter described as 'Bathing bathing in bliss'.[73] Suggesting oceans, this passage resituates sexual satisfaction on a horizontal plane. The speaker goes on to express 'kindness to my wife' and present their activity as 'Lifting belly to a throne'.[74] This elevates Toklas to the status of a queen – a word that also appears in the notebooks and 'If I Told Him'.[75] This language positions sexuality as the source of royal power and the feminine Toklas – rather than the masculine Stein – as its figurehead.

'Lifting Belly' offers numerous erotic scenarios that suggest that gender is continually in process. Much scholarship stresses the scenes in which a 'husband' gives 'cows' to his 'wife', picking up echoes of the wavelike cadences of 'In came in there, came in there come out of there . . . Feeling or for it, as feeling or for it' that build to the wife's orgasmic release in 'As A Wife Has A Cow'.[76] That poem emphasises the movement of the wife's 'cows' rather than their active incitement by her partner. Whereas 'As A Wife Has A Cow' suggests a masculine partner eliciting the feminine jouissance whose wavelike rhythms dominate the poem, 'Lifting Belly' also mobilises forms of eroticism in which both partners are submissive. Both enjoy their 'new game' called 'filling petunia': an image for vaginal penetration implying that it is 'not the same' activity as 'lifting belly' (which connotes the position taken by a woman receiving oral sex) but is indeed 'the same' in that both produce 'cows'.[77] 'Filling petunia' is like 'lifting belly' in that it entails similarity to but distinctness from heterosexuality. This play between sameness and difference is a recurrent topic of philosophical reflection in Stein's texts. She writes that 'Lifting belly is so kind. / Darling wifie is so good. / Little husband would. / Be as good. / If he could. / This was said. / Now we know how to differ. / From that. / Certainly. / Now we say. / Little hubbie is good. / Every Day.'[78] With 'From that', this passage pivots from a discussion of Stein's and Toklas's power dynamic to an assertion of their difference '[f]rom that': the heteronormative constructs of masculinity and femininity from which they have 'Certainly' learned 'how to differ'.[79] While this passage emphasises the gender difference through which Toklas is positioned as feminine and Stein as masculine, the latter is described in diminutive terms – 'Little husband' and 'Little hubbie' – that reconfigure masculinity's meaning and subvert hierarchical oppositions between masculinity and femininity.

This diminution of masculinity turns to self-shattering jouissance in a particularly proliferative passage in one of Stein's notebooks from 1923. She writes, 'She is constantly the darling . . . going to have her cow now. Masterpieces of yes; Oh yes masterpieces oh yes, master in pieces, oh yes.'[80] This passage's shattering of masculine mastery is part of a larger critique of gendered power relations running throughout several of her experimental texts, including those concerning her larger social and aesthetic context, in the early 1920s: well before her mid-1930s interrogation in 'What Are Masterpieces' of the value of being 'a boy if you are going to grow up to be a man'.[81] The 1923 note in which the 'master' falls to 'pieces' appears in a notebook that also includes early materials for 'If I Told Him'.[82] Like Stein's celebration of the 'master' in 'pieces', 'If I Told Him' undercuts patriarchal mastery by mocking its subject's – and Stein's own – Napoleonic aspirations. 'Lifting Belly' and 'Patriarchal Poetry' take up the same topic. Though written ten years apart, these two texts can be fruitfully read together as critically playing with patriarchal gender. 'Lifting Belly' often references 'Caesars' in passages that concern 'throne[s]', 'seat[s]' and 'title[s]'.[83] Moreover, at one point, the text's discourse mirrors the linguistic usages 'Patriarchal Poetry' mocks: the speaker 'explain[s]' and clarifies what he 'meant' to an interlocutor who has 'addressed me as Caesar' and whom he admonishes to 'do your duty and do not forget that I establish myself'.[84] This sudden turn into authoritarian discourse is jarring, calling attention to the fact that the speaker's power is not natural but constructed through verbal exchange. Shortly thereafter, a woman leaves to have a child with another woman, and another speaker answers the command to 'Call me semblances' with the response that 'I call you a cab sir.'[85] This dismissal of mimesis prompts a thoroughgoing questioning of gender ontology: 'What is a man. / What is a woman. / What is a bird.'[86] Eventually, the speakers interpellate one another as gendered beings: a request to 'Please be the man' is met with the affirmation that 'I am the man.'[87] This exchange is dialogic rather than hierarchical. Stein's masculine stance is desirously invited by Toklas; it emerges in response to a call. Appearing dialogically within a text that presents sexuality as relational, connective and 'kind', Toklas's invitation playfully questions and draws out – rather than imposes – Stein's masculinity.[88] 'Lifting Belly' stages the provisional assignment of gender as a process continually subject to negotiation and consent.

Stein on Stein's genders: 'masterpieces of yes'

The phrase 'oh yes' – signal of consent par excellence – also appears in 'Lifting Belly', which offers it as an invitation for the 'cow' to 'come out'.[89] Like the language in Stein's 1923 notebook, this passage invokes jouissance, which I describe elsewhere as 'the experience of ecstasy that exceeds symbolic inscriptions . . . by tapping into the drive in the' Lacanian 'Real'.[90] However, the forms of jouissance in Stein's writing differ from what most psychoanalysts and queer theorists have analysed thus far. In *Seminar XX*, for example, Lacan distinguishes between 'feminine jouissance' and 'phallic jouissance', neither of which results from anatomical difference: as he clarifies in *Seminar XXIII*, 'phallic jouissance is certainly not penile jouissance'.[91] Nor does 'feminine jouissance' follow naturally from female embodiment, as Cixous and Irigaray assume in their important critiques of early psychoanalysis's inadequate understanding of the pleasures afforded the female body.[92] Instead, Lacan's two modes of jouissance correlate to the feminine and masculine positions presumably available during sexuation. The subject is free to adopt either of these stances irrespective of 'anatomy or gender'.[93] Once this choice has been made, '[e]ach structure of desire establishes a pattern connecting it to jouissance depending on the way lack . . . is filled in reference to the' master signifier 'and the object (*a*) that marks the primordial subject as real'.[94] As Shanna Carlson argues, the resulting masculine and feminine positions are distinct from gender and 'signal two different logics, two different modes of ex-sistence in the symbolic, two different approaches to the Other, two different stances with respect to desire, and (at least) two different types of jouissance'.[95] Whereas Carlson is interested in the possibility that some transgender subjects may occupy the feminine position within this logic of sexuation, I see in Stein's erotic writings an opportunity to interrogate the mode of jouissance associated with both positions and, in turn, to question the ways Lacanians have interpreted sexuation.

As Carlson suggests, there may be more than two modes of jouissance. Yet based on the assumption that only the masculine and the feminine stances are available to subjects and that jouissance devolves from those positions, Lacan states that whereas 'phallic *jouissance*' stands in non-relationship to 'feminine *jouissance*', the latter is 'beyond the phallus' and woman 'knows nothing if not that she experiences it'.[96] However, it is possible to introduce novel master signifiers to articulate other modes of sexuation than the masculine and feminine positions.[97] This expands our understanding of jouissance.

Lacan's concept of the *sinthome* affords each subject the opportunity to achieve an idiosyncratic iteration of jouissance connecting the imaginary, symbolic and Real orders. Because any signifier can be the *sinthome*, jouissance is not limited to the varieties outlined in

Seminar XX. As Gherovici argues, Lacan's theory of the *sinthome* allows for theorisations of trans- embodiment, providing 'a novel way to think about sexual difference' that does not hinge on the subject's acceptance of 'the phallus or the Name-of-the-Father' as master signifiers.[98] Instead, through 'writing', transpeople can touch the 'unsymbolizable' Real and achieve 'a different form of embodiment in which the body finds its anchor in a sea of language'.[99]

As the 'creative *sinthome*' allowing Stein to achieve transmasculine embodiment through her relationship with Toklas, Stein's erotic writings offer innovative alternatives to Lacan's distinction between 'feminine *jouissance*' and 'phallic *jouissance*'.[100] These texts negotiate sexual agency in flexible ways that complicate the opposition between masculine activity and feminine passivity underlying the assumption that sexuation requires a person to choose an 'active or passive position' with respect to their partner.[101] Stein's texts also displace Lacan's presumption that 'phallic *jouissance*' entails no relation 'to the Other as such'.[102] By utilising the contiguities offered by the 'planar relations' of Sedgwick's 'beside', stressing the wife's 'cows' and rendering sexuality lateral, Stein's texts inscribe flexible masculinities and femininities that go beyond Lacan's antagonistic division between activity and passivity.[103] By suggesting that there are more than two modes of jouissance, Stein's writings articulate transgender embodiment and challenge Lacan's assumption that there are only two ways – masculine and feminine – of undergoing sexuation and becoming a subject.

In the 1923 love note reiterated in 'Lifting Belly', Toklas's feminine jouissance causes Stein's masculinity to fragment; their different forms of subjective dissolution prompt the cry 'oh yes'. As the 1923 note's jubilant acceptance of jouissance that leaves the 'master in pieces' suggests, Stein's experimental writings mobilise flexible and feminist transmasculinities that move laterally between active, submissive and collaborative forms of relationship. These transmasculinities undercut rather than uphold traditional associations between masculinity and artistic 'genius'. In the 1923 notebook, Stein's iterations of 'masterpieces of yes' turn the 'master' to 'pieces', invoking and fragmenting the notion of authorial mastery on which the patriarchal concept of 'masterpieces' depends. Turner and others have documented that Stein's and Toklas's eroticisation of the writing process queerly resignified the heteronormative metaphor according to which desire produces textual 'babies'.[104] Will further observes that the phrase 'masterpieces of yes' performs 'a critique of the fiction of the author as transcendental (phallic) signifier' by subjecting the concept of '"genius"' to a 'dialogic' process that 'level[s] textual hierarchies'.[105] Although Will does not make this connection, Stein's 'Patriarchal Poetry' also enacts this movement by using reiteration to inscribe its subject as a genre that produces 'master piece[s]' that her mocking iterations leave 'in pieces'.[106] Similarly, at one point in 'Lifting Belly', the speaker references 'Big Caesars. / Two Caesars. / Little seize her', and at another, both 'Caesars and cow come out.'.[107] The passage thereby inscribes both feminine and transmasculine jouissance.

Lorange rightfully observes that 'Stein writes something like the bliss text' as described by Barthes: going well beyond pleasure, textual 'bliss' precipitates a '"crisis"' in 'language' and subjectivity.[108] Stein's texts eroticise that experience in ways whose implications for her sense of gendered embodiment are worth exploring. Especially remarkable is the queering of gender and embodiment that emerges in the 1923 note's play on Stein's and Toklas's roles in the making of 'cows' and 'babies' through jouissance. Written in the wake of *Ulysses*, Stein's 1923 note can be read as an exuberant reworking of Molly Bloom's polylogue, which is often read as *écriture féminine.*[109] Stein's note inscribes not only the jouissance of Toklas's 'cow' but also the erotic shattering of Stein's transmasculine subjectivity. Unlike Molly's orgasms, Toklas's take place in Stein's arms, not those of Blazes Boylan – and the differences between these masculine figures matter. Stein's masculinity and transmasculine jouissance differ significantly from Lacan's 'phallic *jouissance*', which involves individual bliss but refuses a relation 'to the Other as such'.[110] By contrast, the Stein-figures in her texts from 1915 through the 1920s attend carefully to Toklas's bliss. The passage praising 'masterpieces of yes' mixes orgasm with literature, writing with the body, as Stein's transmasculinity prompts Toklas's jouissance. In so doing, the significance of the phrase 'oh yes' well exceeds the jouissance associated with *écriture féminine* and mobilises anti-patriarchal transmasculinities.

Moreover, the 1923 love note invites multiple readings that question the ownership of the 'masterpieces' Stein's and Toklas's eroticism produces. Although Stein is the masculine 'master' who falls to 'pieces', Toklas – who has 'cows' and occasionally wields the phallic 'pen' – also occupies that role.[111] That Toklas and figures for her wield considerable power in Stein's texts and life is clear in their love notes, which show the former refusing and reworking patriarchal models of wifely obedience to gain the upper hand.[112] 'Lifting Belly' similarly interrogates and inverts conventional structures of masculine authority. While at one moment that text reiterates the phrase 'Oh yes the Caesar' shortly after the line 'Yes sir' – thereby suggesting a conventional arrangement of masculine dominance and feminine submission – 'Lifting Belly' later offers the command 'Husband obey your wife'.[113] That his obedience leads to 'Caesars' that are not the same as 'a cow' repositions Stein as the 'master' who is 'in pieces', her subjectivity shattered in writerly and erotic jouissance.[114]

At one point, 'Lifting Belly' also states that '[h]e has' had 'a cow', produced from the 'filling' of his 'petunia'.[115] This moment in 'Lifting Belly' suggests that Stein's masculinity is not grounded in impenetrability. This passage also recalls Cromwell's observation that transgender sexuality involves resignifying the body. Here, Stein retains masculinity as a renamed orifice – the 'petunia' – is penetrated. The 'cow' that comes from the 'filling' of Stein's 'petunia' recalls Gayle Rubin's observation that '[g]ay men . . . have role models for men who are passive or subordinate in sexual encounters but retain their masculinity'.[116] Though Rubin makes this point to make butch-butch sexuality visible, her insight also applies to scenarios involving femme dominance and transmasculine submission.[117] These acts of masculine sexual receptivity call into question Halberstam's distinction between the lesbian butch and the untouchable, 'stone', 'transgender' butch.[118] Stein retains masculinity during erotic submission, even though her sense of mastery falls to 'pieces'.

By rearticulating our language for embodiment, the poem goes beyond the understanding of sexuation and 'sexual difference' grounding Lacan's account of 'feminine' and 'phallic' jouissance.[119] Stein's transmasculine jouissance shatters patriarchal constructs of language, gender and sexuality. Unlike the symbolic order of *Seminar XX*, whose structures of desire and jouissance are anchored by the phallic signifier, 'Lifting Belly' allows jouissance to unfold in the context of dialogic reiterations whose shifting significations undercut stable gender ontologies and linguistic meanings. In so doing, Stein's writing exceeds *écriture féminine*'s subversions, which depend on an embrace of the femininity repressed by patriarchal language. Moreover, because Stein's transmasculinity is disentangled from patriarchal gender, the poem is able to mobilise both a transmasculine jouissance that differs from Lacanian 'phallic *jouissance*' and a novel form of feminine jouissance distinct from that of *écriture féminine*.

Stein's transmasculine jouissance is also different from the masculine self-shattering Leo Bersani attributes to male homoerotic sexual receptivity. Bersani makes the case for the 'strong appeal of powerlessness, of the loss of control' in sexual submission, which takes the form of a 'radical disintegration and humiliation of the self' that transgresses the ego's limits.[120] Cvetkovich observes that his emphasis on 'humiliation of the self . . . emerges in the context of how a specifically *masculine* self is humiliated, and hence threatened with disintegration, by anal penetration'.[121] To put it more precisely, Bersani addresses *cisgender* male masculinity's shattering through sexual submission. The crucial difference between the cisgender gay male submission at stake in Bersani's work and the kind of transmasculine jouissance emerging through the 'filling' of Stein's 'petunia' in her experimental writing is that the former uses subjective destitution to enact the trauma of powerlessness whereas the latter uses it to produce the joy of sexual affirmation.

All forms of jouissance use sexuality to push the subject to the point of temporary dissolution. Bersani and Cvetkovich emphasise different ways this experience can be traumatic, whether by inducing self-shattering or engaging past traumas. Of Stein's writings from the 1910s and 1920s, *Tender Buttons* contrasts with texts such as 'Lifting Belly' by offering the most sustained exploration of the traumatic aspects of jouissance, 'a violent kind of delightfulness'.[122] As DeKoven observes, *Tender Buttons* eroticises what Stein describes in 'Poetry and Grammar' (1934–5: 1935) as a broader programme in which 'Poetry is concerned with using with abusing, with losing with wanting, with denying with avoiding with adoring with replacing the noun.'[123] Through this assault on the noun, *Tender Buttons* inscribes traumatic jouissance in a wide variety of gendered scenarios.[124] Notably, the end of the book's 'Objects' section figures both phallic transmasculine jouissance and feminine jouissance as traumatic. Inscribing a form of transmasculine sexuality that approximates Lacan's definition of phallic jouissance, the 'BOOK' section 'Suppose[s] a man a realistic expression of resolute reliability suggests pleasing itself white all white and no head.'[125] Focusing exclusively on the masculine subject's satisfaction and rejecting the Sedgwickian 'beside', the text states that he has 'little chance to beside beside rest'.[126] The next section – suggestively headed 'PEELED

PENCIL, CHOKE' – sets out to 'Rub her coke'.[127] As Ruddick suggests, this phrase proliferates gender by suggesting both 'rubbing "her" out' and rubbing 'her cock'.[128] The final entry – 'THIS IS THE DRESS, AIDER' – concludes with the line 'A jack in kill her, a jack in, makes a meadowed king, makes a to let.'[129] Suggesting violence to the phallus and the penetrated partner alike, these passages inscribe both masculine and feminine jouissance as traumatic.[130] At the same time, *Tender Buttons*' larger context suggests that these experiences are also 'tender' forms of 'delightfulness'.[131]

By contrast, 'Lifting Belly' and other of Stein's experimental writings from the 1910s and 1920s inscribe largely non-traumatic forms of sexuality that rearticulate hegemonic masculinity and femininity. Though the phrase 'Lifting belly is anxious' appears early on, it is one of very few hints at this mood in the entire poem.[132] Power exchanges appear in playful contexts; their aggression quickly dissipates. One passage opens with 'Shall I chat' and goes on to inscribe an exchange in which the speaker's clarification that 'I mean pugilists' is met with 'Oh yes trainer. / Oh yes yes.', followed by a request to 'Say it again to study'.[133] In this dialogue, trauma is toyed with rather than violently imposed. The text speedily folds this speculative moment back into the lovers' 'sweet' and affirmative murmurs about 'Lifting belly' being 'very well' after having 'been perfectly fed'.[134] Shortly thereafter, one speaker declares that 'Baby is so good to baby'.[135] Even when the text toys with aggression, it places an overwhelming emphasis on the joys of sexual pleasure and the kind of subjective dissolution that accompanies jouissance without staging it as traumatic.[136]

Stein's masculinised 'Caesars' are similarly playful rather than traumatising, as the lines 'Big Caesars. / Two Caesars. / Little seize her' suggest.[137] In this passage, the locus of masculine power multiplies and diffuses – yet the effect is to make '[l]ittle' the 'seiz[ure]' of the feminine party. Moreover, the 1923 love note in which the 'master' falls to 'pieces' associates self-shattering with pleasure's proliferation rather than the strategies for working through past experiences of sexual violation Cvetkovich finds in 1950s and contemporary butch/femme sexualities.[138] Whereas Bersani claims that the 'radical disintegration . . . of the self' makes sexuality an 'anticommunal, antiegalitarian, antinurturing', and 'antiloving' force, many of Stein's experimental writings and her and Toklas's love notes tap the jouissance of submission and subjective dissolution for their loving and communal potential, reworking genders in the process.[139]

A 1925 entry in one of Stein's notebooks shows the culmination of that process. She writes, 'it is husband who is trying he is trying and he is succeeding, he is succeeding he is trying and he is succeeding and what is he trying he is trying his wife's cow and it is a good cow and she and he are satisfied, We call it three and free.'[140] Here, Stein presents herself as a 'husband' embracing the submission of 'trying his wife's cow' – as happily flipped and reveling in transmasculine jouissance, far from the 'abstracted' and 'desexualized' Stein to whom Lorange refers.[141] Moreover, the passage's reference to 'three and free' suggests that the 'cow' has produced a third element. Turner reads Stein's 'cows' as faeces; given her eroticisation of writing, they could also be manuscripts.[142] Similar invocations of faeces occur in 'Lifting Belly' when Stein writes that 'Lifting belly is to jelly. / Holy most is in the sky. / We see it in three. / Yes we see it every night near the hills. This is so natural. Birds do it.'[143] Here, the poem insinuates that the element Stein and Toklas 'see' in 'three' is faecal matter, which 'birds' as well as lovers produce. It is also associated with the 'jelly' – vaginal fluid – produced through 'lifting belly'. Whether faeces, fluid or a piece of writing, these references to a product – made by but 'free' from the two lovers – points to the way their desire is subtended by split subjectivity, producing this third element as what Lacan calls the *object a*. Tim Dean argues that 'the turd' is the 'prototype for object *a*': that phantasmatic object, produced by the symbolic yet partaking of the Real, around which desire circles.[144] Noting that 'whether or not we're all . . . missing the phallus, certainly we've all lost objects from the anus', Dean contends that the phallus – which orthodox Lacanians often position as the master signifier – is 'incidental' rather than essential to 'Lacan's account of fantasy, sexuality, and desire'.[145] Stein's and Toklas's notes are persistently scatological, freeing them from phallogocentric structures of desire. Occupying the role of the transmasculine subject trying 'his wife's cow', Stein experiences a freeing rather than traumatising jouissance. The husband's sense of mastery is left 'in pieces', but he and his wife are both 'satisfied' by the third term that allows them to break 'free' of rigid gender constructs and loosen up their desires' trajectories. Stein's erotic poetry and love notes to Toklas demonstrate that they privately rejected and resignified hegemonic masculinity well before Stein publicly questioned it in the mid-1930s.[146]

All of these passages exceed the parameters of Lacanian jouissance by inscribing and interrogating their author's transmasculine subjectivity. Only six years after Stein distinguished her sense of superior 'maleness' from what she then believed was her inferior feminine other, she came to use her experimental writing to engage in an anti-identitarian 'mode of . . . self-poesis' that deployed her masculinity for feminist purposes.[147] Eschewing stable gender ontologies, Stein's writings playfully toy with gendered power relationships, mocking masculine self-aggrandisement and supporting feminine strength. Undermining masculinity's hierarchical expressions and developing its lateral possibilities, her texts rework it by exploring its gentle and submissive potential. Produced in desiring relation with Toklas – in loving rather than antagonistic relation to the feminine – Stein's gendered inscriptions point to masculinity's instability and capacity to challenge patriarchy. Rendering Stein's and Toklas's sexualities and genders queer, these '"embodied texts"' offer examples of a 'transgenre' that uses poetic innovation to make Stein's transmasculinity 'liveable' through her relationship with Toklas.[148] Stein's experimental writings from the 1910s and 1920s thereby mobilise a shifting transmasculine embodiment, offering an important alternative to misogynist masculinities.

Notes

1. Caughie, 'The Temporality of Modernist Life Writing', p. 519.
2. Butler in Butler and Athanasiou, *Dispossession*, p. 67.
3. Caughie, 'The Temporality of Modernist Life Writing', p. 503.
4. Retallack, 'High Adventures in Indeterminacy', p. 251.
5. Butler in Butler and Athanasiou, *Dispossession*, p. 67.
6. DeKoven, *A Different Language*, p. 36.
7. DeKoven, ibid., p. 36.
8. Stein, 'What Are Masterpieces', p. 499; see also Moon, 'Do You Smoke?'
9. In *The Formation of 20th-Century Queer Autobiography*, Johnston similarly argues that Stein creates alternatives to inaccurate medical and psychoanalytic approaches to lesbianism.
10. Prosser, *Second Skins*, p. 102; Salamon, *Assuming a Body*, p. 41.
11. Salamon, ibid.
12. Frost, *The Feminist Avant-Garde in American Poetry*, p. xxv. See Christine Brooke-Rose, 'Illiterations' and Stephens, 'What Do We Mean by "Literary Experimentalism"', for two genealogies of the term 'experimental writing', and Mix, *A Vocabulary of Thinking*, for a study of its feminist inflections.

13. Friedman and Fuchs, 'Contexts and Continuities', p. 3.
14. Page, 'Women Writers and the Restive Text'.
15. Damon, 'Gertrude Stein's Jewishness'.
16. See Johnston, *The Formation of 20th-Century Queer Autobiography*, and Thompson, 'Language and Democracy', for analysis of feminist experimentation in Stein's poetry. Though problematic for its treatment of Stein's masculine identifications, Wagner-Martin's *'Favored Strangers'* offers ample evidence of feminist stances she took as an adult.
17. Ruddick, *Reading Gertrude Stein*, p. 213. Ruddick's early study both depends upon the conceptual framework of *écriture féminine* and goes beyond it by acknowledging gender's plurality in Stein's work.
18. Cole, 'Remaking Sense', p. 85.
19. Ashton, 'Our Bodies, Our Poems', p. 170.
20. Cixous, 'The Laugh of the Medusa'; and Irigaray, *This Sex Which Is Not One* and *Speculum of the Other Woman*. See Salamon, *Assuming a Body*, pp. 131–44 for a revision of Irigaray that better registers transsubjectivities' complexities.

    For scholarship that reads Stein's writing as *écriture féminine*, see Benstock, *Women*; DeKoven, *A Different Language*; and Ruddick, *Reading Gertrude Stein*. For the theoretical underpinnings of the argument that patriarchal language suppresses linguistic playfulness, see Cixous, 'The Laugh of the Medusa'; and Kristeva, *Desire in Language* and *Revolution in Poetic Language*. For a critique of the elision of masculinity in scholarship that reads Stein's writing as *écriture féminine*, see Chessman, *The Public is Invited to Dance*. See Engelbrecht, '"Lifting Belly Is a Language"'; and Johnston, *The Formation of 20th-Century Queer Autobiography*, for postmodern lesbian challenges to readings of Stein's writing as *écriture féminine*; see Holbrook, 'Lifting Bellies, Filling Petunias', for an argument that such interpretations misread Kristeva's work; and see Stimpson, 'Somagrams', for an argument that Stein is 'a visionary of the "post-post-Oedipal"' (p. 651).
21. Chessman, *The Public is Invited to Dance*, pp. 5–6.
22. Chessman, ibid., p. 3.
23. Salamon, *Assuming a Body*, p. 63, p. 59.
24. Dydo, *Gertrude Stein*, pp. 27–30. See also Meese, 'Gertrude Stein and Me', and Turner, 'This "Very Beautiful Form of Literature"'.
25. Dydo, *Gertrude Stein*, pp. 28–9.
26. Gilmore, 'A Signature of Lesbian Autobiography', p. 222.
27. Engelbrecht, '"Lifting Belly Is a Language"', p. 99.
28. Engelbrecht, ibid., p. 98, p. 101. Engelbrecht continues a long tradition of reading Stein's writing as encoding lesbianism: see Benstock, *Women*; Bridgman, *Gertrude Stein in Pieces*; DeKoven, *A Different Language*; Dickie, 'Recovering the Repression in Stein's Erotic Poetry'; Rule, *Lesbian Images*; and Stimpson, 'The Mind, the Body, and Gertrude

Stein' and 'Gertrude Stein and the Lesbian Lie'. See Stimpson's 'Somagrams' for an argument that Stein's work offers not an 'evasion' of lesbianism but rather a lesbian 'anti-language' (p. 648); see Gilmore, 'A Signature of Lesbian Autobiography' and Susan McCabe, '"A Queer Lot" and the Lesbians of 1914', for reversals of the thesis of lesbian encoding; see Glavey, *The Wallflower Avant-Garde*, and Nair, *Secrecy and Sapphic Modernism*, for compromise positions; and see Blackmer, 'Lesbian Modernism', and Meese, 'Gertrude Stein and Me', for arguments that Stein's inscriptions of lesbianism are open, not covert.

29. Holbrook, 'Lifting Bellies, Filling Petunias', p. 759.
30. Holbrook, ibid., p. 759, pp. 764–5.
31. Holbrook, ibid., pp. 751–2.
32. Cromwell, *Transmen & FTMs*, p. 130.
33. Turner, 'This "Very Beautiful Form of Literature"', p. 18.
34. Dydo, *Gertrude Stein*, p. 28.
35. Dydo, ibid., p. 28.
36. Dydo, ibid., p. 28.
37. Dydo, ibid., p. 28. In *Rescued Readings*, Elizabeth Fifer similarly presumes that Stein's use of heterosexual marriage vocabulary capitulates to hierarchical gender roles.
38. Kent, *Making Girls into Women*, p. 157.
39. Schmitz, *Of Huck and Alice*, p. 202; Stimpson, 'Somagrams', p. 647.
40. Lorange, *How Reading Is Written*, p. 51.
41. Lorange, ibid., p. 48.
42. Lorange, ibid., p. 49.
43. Lorange, ibid., p. 51.
44. Cromwell, *Transmen & FTMs*, pp. 130–4.
45. See Meese, 'Gertrude Stein and Me: A Revolution in the Letter', and Turner, 'This "Very Beautiful Form of Literature"', for two lesbian readings of Steinian 'cows'. For examples of Stein's scatological references, see 'Lifting Belly', which contains commands to 'Come out cow . . . Yes oh yes cow come out', followed by references to an 'odor' that 'I smell sweetly' (pp. 30–1). See Turner, 'This "Very Beautiful Form of Literature"', for a lesbian-feminist reading of references to faeces in Stein's and Toklas's love notes. See Ruddick, *Reading Gertrude Stein*, for an early argument that this indicates a pre-Oedipal fixation, and Lorange, *How Reading Is Written*, for a recent critique of those claims. Thanks to Stephanie Hsu and William Spurlin for encouraging me to think about the scatological significance of Stein's 'cows'.
46. Lorange, *How Reading Is Written*, p. 198.
47. Cvetkovich, *An Archive of Feelings*, p. 60.
48. Stein, 'A Sonatina', pp. 287–315.

49. Stein, ibid., p. 309.
50. Stein, 'Lifting Belly', p. 22.
51. Stein, 'A Sonatina', p. 312, emphasis added.
52. Stein, ibid., p. 312.
53. Stein, 'Lifting Belly', pp. 6–8, pp. 11–17.
54. Stein, ibid., p. 12.
55. Gilmore, 'A Signature of Lesbian Autobiography', p. 222.
56. Gilmore, ibid., p. 222; Stein, 'A Sonatina', p. 312.
57. Stein, ibid., p. 312.
58. Stein, 'Lifting Belly', pp. 46–7, emphasis added.
59. Mark, 'Introduction', p. xx.
60. Sedgwick, *Touching Feeling*, p. 8.
61. Sedgwick, ibid., p. 8.
62. Stein, 'Lifting Belly', p. 35.
63. Stein, ibid., pp. 8–9.
64. Stein, ibid., p. 12.
65. Stein, ibid., pp. 10–11, pp. 20–3, pp. 28–9.
66. Stein, ibid., p. 12.
67. Stein, ibid., p. 23.
68. Mark, 'Introduction', p. xix.
69. Stein, 'Lifting Belly', pp. 46–7.
70. Stein, ibid., p. 10.
71. Chessman, *The Public is Invited to Dance*, pp. 106–7.
72. Chessman, ibid., p. 107.
73. Stein, 'Lifting Belly', pp. 24–5.
74. Stein, ibid., p. 25.
75. Stein, 'If I Told Him', p. 464.
76. Stein, 'As A Wife Has A Cow', p. 461.
77. Stein, 'Lifting Belly', p. 53.
78. Stein, ibid., p. 49.
79. Stein, ibid., p. 49.
80. Stein, YCAL MSS 76, Box 92, Folder 1710 in the Beinecke Rare Book and Manuscript Library, Yale University.
81. Stein, 'What Are Masterpieces', p. 499; see also Moon, 'Do You Smoke?'
82. Stein, YCAL MSS 76, Box 92, Folder 1710 in the Beinecke Rare Book and Manuscript Library, Yale University.
83. Stein, 'Lifting Belly', pp. 25–6.
84. Stein, ibid., pp. 25–8.
85. Stein, ibid., p. 29.
86. Stein, ibid., p. 32.
87. Stein, ibid., p. 51.
88. Stein, ibid., p. 10, p. 51.

89. Stein, ibid., p. 30. Whereas I propose a queer revision of Lacanian 'jouissance', Lorange reads Stein through Deleuze's theory of 'jouissance' in which pleasure is productive (pp. 201–2).
90. Coffman, 'Unpredictable Future', p. 44.
91. Lacan, *The Seminar of Jacques Lacan, Book XXIII*, p. 43.
92. See Cixous, 'Laugh of the Medusa'; Irigaray, *This Sex Which Is Not One* and *Speculum.*
93. Ragland, *The Logic of Sexuation*, p. 65.
94. Ragland, ibid., p. 98.
95. Carlson, 'Transgender Subjectivity', p. 64.
96. Lacan, *The Seminar of Jacques Lacan. Book XX*, p. 74.
97. For further explanation, see also Coffman, 'The Unpredictable Future' and 'Žižek's Antagonism'.
98. Gherovici, 'The Transsexual Body Written', pp. 261–7.
99. Gherovici, 'The Art of the Symptom', pp. 255–62.
100. Gherovici, ibid., p. 262.
101. Ragland, *The Logic of Sexuation*, p. 65.
102. Lacan, *The Seminar of Jacques Lacan. Book XX*, p. 9. In 'The Laugh of the Medusa', Cixous challenges the phallogocentric premises on which this idea depends and proposes a theory of writing the body that shatters the Lacanian symbolic.
103. Sedgwick, *Touching Feeling*, p. 8.
104. Turner, 'This "Very Beautiful Form of Literature"', p. 17.
105. Will, *Gertrude Stein*, p. 87.
106. Stein, 'Patriarchal Poetry', p. 133.
107. Stein, 'Lifting Belly', p. 30, p. 22.
108. Lorange, *How Reading Is Written*, p. 201.
109. See Cixous, *The Exile of James Joyce*, for one example.
110. Lacan, *The Seminar of Jacques Lacan. Book XX*, p. 9.
111. Turner, 'This "Very Beautiful Form of Literature"', pp. 16–17.
112. Stein, *Baby Precious*, pp. 158–60.
113. Stein, 'Lifting Belly', p. 27, p. 47.
114. Stein, ibid., pp. 46–7.
115. Stein, ibid., p. 53.
116. Rubin, 'Of Catamites and Kings', p. 473.
117. Rubin, ibid., p. 471.
118. Halberstam, *Female Masculinity*, p. 148.
119. For readings of Lacan founded on strict readings of 'sexuation' and 'sexual difference', see Dean, *Beyond Sexuality*; Ragland, *The Logic of Sexuation*; and Shepherdson, 'The *Role* of Gender and the *Imperative* of Sex'.
120. Bersani, 'Is the Rectum a Grave?', p. 217.
121. Cvetkovich, *An Archive of Feelings*, p. 62.

122. Stein, *Tender Buttons*, p. 462.
123. DeKoven, *Rich and Strange*, p. 198; Stein, 'Poetry and Grammar', p. 231.
124. See Kent, *Making Girls into Women*, for discussion of *Tender Buttons*' queerly gendered erotics.
125. Stein, *Tender Buttons*, p. 476.
126. Stein, ibid., p. 476.
127. Stein, ibid., p. 476.
128. Ruddick, *Reading Gertrude Stein*, pp. 211–13.
129. Stein, ibid., p. 476.
130. Stein, ibid., p. 462.
131. Stein, ibid., p. 462.
132. Stein, 'Lifting Belly', p. 10.
133. Stein, ibid., p. 24.
134. Stein, ibid., p. 24.
135. Stein, ibid., p. 24.
136. Stein, ibid., p. 24.
137. Stein, ibid., p. 22.
138. Contemporary and 1950s North American butch/femme cultures comprise the bulk of Cvetkovich's archive; Detloff, *The Persistence of Modernism*, notes significant differences between these couples' and Stein's and Toklas's genders (pp. 60–2).
139. Bersani, 'Is the Rectum a Grave?', p. 217, p. 215.
140. Stein, YCAL MSS 76, Box 92, folder 1720 in the Beinecke Rare Book and Manuscript Library, Yale University.
141. Lorange, *How Reading Is Written*, p. 198.
142. Turner, 'This "Very Beautiful Form of Literature"', pp. 25–33.
143. Stein, 'Lifting Belly', p. 19.
144. Dean, *Beyond Sexuality*, p. 264.
145. Dean, ibid., p. 264. Chapter 2 of *Beyond Sexuality* unfortunately capitulates to Millot's pathologisation of transsexuality in *Horsexe*.
146. Stein, 'What Are Masterpieces'.
147. Butler in Butler and Athanasiou, *Dispossession*, p. 67.
148. Caughie, 'The Temporality of Modernist Life Writing', p. 503, p. 519.

Chapter 4

Visual Economies of Queer Desire in *The Autobiography of Alice B. Toklas*

Whereas Stein's avant-garde poetry from the 1910s and 1920s utilises 'self-poesis' to articulate a variety of feminist transmasculinities, *The Autobiography* (1932: 1933) – mass-marketed experimental non-fiction – plays with perspective to hide her masculinity in plain sight and position it as the source of modernist innovation.[1] Stein's masculinity signifies multiply within *The Autobiography*, yet discerning its significance demands that one look askance – from a novel 'vantage' – at the 'given-to-be-seen'.[2] Though Stein played with signifiers of gender throughout adulthood with varied results, *The Autobiography* stresses that it was not until 1926 that she took up the iconic 'Julius Caesar' haircut through which her gender is often retrospectively read.[3] The text emphasises that Stein decided on her 1926 crop after seeing it on the Duchess of Clermont-Tonnerre; it only subsequently elicited comparisons to men.[4] Sidestepping rather than engaging in the logic of male imitation with which Stein is often charged, *The Autobiography* highlights the way she achieved her masculinity through a complex process of signification and attribution. The text thereby demonstrates that Stein's transmasculinity does not function mimetically but shifts in different settings.

The Autobiography stresses, however, that Stein's masculinity is not a 'free-floating signifier' with which she toys on a whim, but a shifting mode of embodied transsubjectivity lived out daily in relation to Toklas and her male colleagues.[5] On the one hand, a logic of opposition distinguishes Stein from the feminine Toklas; on the other hand, non-mimetic association establishes Stein's masculinity through contiguity with male artists and writers. As Siraganian observes, *The Autobiography* is driven by 'the sociality of the art world and its celebrity culture', offering 'the reader the life story of that "social-artistic-intellectual organism" from both a personal viewpoint and from a community-directed' standpoint.[6] Yet as Nair notes, *The Autobiography* focuses on Stein's and Toklas's friendships with heterosexual colleagues such as Matisse, Picasso, Anderson and Hemingway – all of whom arrive at 27, rue de Fleurus with 'wives' – while downplaying sexual relationships between the queer characters in the background.[7] Catering to heterosexist readers' enjoyment of 'the "privilege of unknowing"', *The Autobiography* relies upon intertextual references and queer readers' in-group knowledge to make characters' same-sex relationships legible.[8] In so doing, the book deploys perspective transformatively: Stein's use of Toklas as narrator reorients the gaze through which Stein's masculinity – and the masculinist scene of Parisian modernism – is given to be seen.

Driven by what Gilmore describes as the mutually constitutive split between Toklas's femininity and Stein's masculinity, *The Autobiography* deploys Toklas's look – and those of the text's readers – to align with the queer couple's '"slantwise" orientation . . . to existing social structures'.[9] This invites us to see Stein's masculinity and her pivotal role in early twentieth-century Paris's male-dominated avant-gardes through Toklas's loving eyes: from a perspective ordinarily sidelined in patriarchal and heterosexist accounts of modernism. By using Toklas to direct attention to Stein's masculinity and express amusement about her friendships with male modernists, *The Autobiography* reveals the fractures engendered by her masculine homosocial bonds. Those ties produced varied forms of queer relationality – such as 'desiring, identifying, representing, repelling, paralleling, differentiating, rivaling, leaning, twisting, mimicking, withdrawing, attracting, aggressing' and 'warping' – that animate the manipulations of perspective through which *The Autobiography* gives Stein's masculinity – and the scene of Parisian modernism – to readers to be seen.[10]

Stein's Caesar

The Autobiography offers two different perspectives on the 1926 cropping of Stein's hair into the masculine 'Caesar' cut.[11] The first, appearing early on, states that:

> Only a few years ago when Gertrude Stein had had her hair cut short, she had always up to that time worn it as a crown on top of her head as Picasso had painted it, when she had had her hair cut, a day or so later she happened to come into a room and Picasso was several

> rooms away. She had a hat on but he caught sight of her through two doorways and approaching her quickly called out, Gertrude, what is it, what is it. What is what, Pablo, she said. Let me see, he said. She let him see. And my portrait, said he sternly. Then his face softening he added, mais, quand même tout y est, all the same it is there.[12]

This account of Picasso's response to Stein's haircut emphasises that his initial hostility emerged in reaction to a forced reorientation of vision. Highlighting the distance between them and the framing provided by 'two doorways' at this moment of visual startlement, this passage figures the multiple perspectives characterising Picasso's and Stein's cubist practice.[13] We see Picasso initially apprehending Stein from 'several rooms away', shuttling 'through two doorways' with his view of her hair obstructed by her hat.[14] These shifts in Picasso's perception of Stein suggest parallax – 'how the same phenomena looks different from a different angle or perspective or by extension how human events look different to a different perceiver' – which, as Daniel Schwartz suggests, has 'a kinship with cubism'.[15] Nair observes that even though the analogy between Stein's writing and cubist painting is imperfect, she 'shared with her Cubist counterparts an interest in destabilizing assumptions surrounding perception and perspective'.[16] *The Autobiography* thus shows that Picasso's and Stein's art and writing demand changes to previous ways of looking and reading – shifts *The Autobiography* presents as central to modernism's force.

This passage appears in a section of *The Autobiography* detailing the public's initial enragement by modern art's challenge to nineteenth-century ways of seeing and positioning Stein as before her time as one of modernism's first champions. Whereas *The Autobiography* presents modern art as meeting with decades of hostility before acceptance, the book's account of Picasso's reaction to Stein's haircut tracks a far more rapid process of adjustment. This painter – famous for his work's reorientation of vision – is startled by her masculine crop, but quickly adjusts to its demand for a new way of seeing and reorients his stance.

By highlighting Picasso's concerns about the crop's implications for his portrait of Stein, *The Autobiography* calls attention to her power to transform modernism's legacy. The masculine haircut shifts the gaze mobilised by his painting, challenging the narrative of modernism centred on Picasso's work. His quick adjustment to this new angle of vision accepts the cut's challenge to its predecessor's aesthetics and the changed narrative it implies for his work's and modernism's legacy. His realisation that 'all the same it [his portrait] is there' points to his – and Stein's – capacity to mobilise multiple viewpoints on and narratives about modernism's origins.[17]

The text's emphasis on Picasso's ability to move between different 'vantage[s]' to see his early portrait of Stein in her 1926 haircut also recalls the struggle he experienced while painting her.[18] As Lubar argues, a 'complex process of psychic transference' caused Picasso to stall while finishing *Portrait of Gertrude Stein* (Plate 1); he ultimately painted Stein's face using perspectival distortions that marked his first step into analytic cubism.[19] In *The Autobiography*, when Picasso recognises that even with the new hairstyle, 'all the same it [his portrait] is there', his statement reveals his continuous perception of Stein's masculinity – which persists despite the visual field's shifting coordinates – and betrays the disorientation he experienced as he came to grips with her gender.[20]

At first mention, however, *The Autobiography* neither explicitly addresses the 'Caesar' cut's masculine connotations nor the subtle masculinity Stein's persona conveyed before it. By the time readers are prompted to re-envision Stein's short hairstyle at the end of *The Autobiography*, though, we have been eased into the queerer version of modernism the 'Caesar' cut implies. The second account of the haircut highlights the Duchess of Clermont-Tonnerre's role in prompting the change. In the later passage, the new style provokes immediate approval rather than shock:

> Madame de Clermont-Tonnerre came in very late to one of the parties, almost every one had gone, and her hair was cut. Do you like it, said Madame de Clermont-Tonnerre. I do, said Gertrude Stein. Well, said Madame de Clermont-Tonnerre, if you like it and my daughter likes it and she does like it I am satisfied. That night Gertrude Stein said to me, I guess I will have to too. Cut it off she said and I did.
>
> I was still cutting the next evening, I had been cutting a little more all day and by this time it was only a cap of hair when Sherwood Anderson came in. Well, how do you like it, said I rather fearfully. I like it, he said, it makes her look like a monk.
>
> As I have said, Picasso seeing it, was for a moment angry and said, and my portrait, but very soon added, after all it is all there.[21]

Unlike Picasso, Stein immediately approves of the Duchess's changed appearance and asks Toklas to give her the same cut. This response – driven by identification and supported through affirming looks – reflects the way Stein and the Duchess always 'delighted in each other's understanding'.[22] Anderson – a consistent ally of Stein's throughout *The Autobiography* – offers his approval with a simile highlighting the cut's masculinity: 'it makes her look like a monk'.[23] Neither shock nor vacillating vision informs these responses. However, the text also uses reiteration to call the reader back to the earlier account in which Picasso follows his displeased reaction with a quick adjustment. This reiteration underscores the difference between these two perspectives on the cut.

By using reiteration to reveal divergent responses to Stein's new image, *The Autobiography* employs temporal 'wrinkles and folds' to reframe her transmasculinity as part of the appearance of the new that the earlier segment of the book attributes to the formal properties of modern painters' art and her writing.[24] Looking back from 1934, *The Autobiography* refuses to offer a singular narrative of modernism's emergence and instead deploys multiple perspectives on its origins and innovations. In the two passages approaching Stein's short crop from different angles, the text's play with surfaces underscores Picasso's and her different visions of modernism. Yet the book's tracking of different reactions to her haircut also emphasises that it is not shocking from all standpoints – and that these differences in reaction matter.

The economies of vision at work in these two scenes illuminate some significant features of *The Autobiography*. First, even though it is more accessible to its mass-market readership than Stein's more avant-garde writings, *The Autobiography* still disorients traditional ways of looking in ways similar to the modern paintings whose influence the book's first sections highlight. Toklas – the text's narrator – self-consciously references this phenomenon: she remarks that upon first visiting the Stein atelier, she thought that 'The pictures were so strange that one quite instinctively looked at anything rather than at them just at first.'[25] She also states that 'the beginning of my life in Paris . . . was based upon the rue de Fleurus and the Saturday evenings and it was like a kaleidoscope slowly turning'.[26] This formulation uses the kaleidoscope as a metaphor for the disorientation of perspective her encounter with modernism engendered, highlighting the numerous plays with surfaces and shifting perspectives mobilised through Toklas's narration.

Margot Norris observes that *The Autobiography* employs both the 'postimpressionistic principle of the homogenized composition' – that is, 'the idea of each part of a composition being as important as a whole . . . one human being is as important as another human being . . . a blade of grass has the same value as a tree', as Stein puts it in 'A Transatlantic Interview' (1946: 1962–4) – and 'the homogenized perspective of cubism, in which every perspective is as operationally important as every other'.[27] The narrator asks readers to view Stein's new hairstyle from several standpoints by offering divergent accounts of its reception. This approach approximates cubism and allows one to read *The Autobiography*'s figurations of gender and desire as inscribed through – rather than hidden by – its language, which mobilises multiple significations and shifting viewpoints. This strategy is apparent throughout the text.

The book's visual vacillations are conveyed through the ruse animating its narrative strategy. Entitled *The Autobiography of Alice B. Toklas*, the narrative is ostensibly told from Toklas's perspective but was actually written by Stein, as the ending reveals. Gilmore observes that this ploy mimics a trick of representation used in the visual arts: 'an autobiography, like a photograph, simulates the action of the eye in a way that obscures how the apparatus of representation works on and within the scene it depicts'.[28] Working 'on and within the scene' of 27, rue de Fleurus, *The Autobiography* achieves a *trompe l'œil* effect through a *mise-en-abîme* of 'posing': 'Alice poses for Stein's portrait of her, and Stein poses Alice and depicts herself.'[29] The text thus employs 'the coupled subject' of Stein/Toklas as 'a space from which to write' and 'also a space' from which to manipulate 'perspective, a defining aspect of photography and portraiture'.[30] Although I see *The Autobiography* as operating more like a cubist painting than the cinematic 'space-off' Gilmore offers as an analogy, I concur with her suggestion that the book manipulates perspective to trick the reader into a new way of seeing.[31] The text's queering of vision brings both Stein's and Toklas's erotic partnership and the former's transmasculine positioning into view by subtly warping the visual field.

Gilmore shows that far from being an objectionable appropriation of Toklas's voice – as some early critics charged – Stein's choice of narrator mutually implicates their subjectivities, destabilising rather than reaffirming hegemonic genders.[32] Georgia Johnston further illuminates the narratological innovations *The Autobiography* employs to show Stein's and Toklas's lives 'through multiple perspectivism, collectivity, and fragmentation'.[33] However, scholars have paid little attention to the way the text's displacements register in divergent visual economies. Vacillating perspectives on the couple's and modernism's reception are particularly apparent in the book's staging of Picasso's, Stein's and Anderson's different perceptions of the 'Caesar' crop. Stein's inclusion of hair-cropping scenes strongly suggests that her masculinity registers in the book's fragmentation, mobilising its visual economies.

Stein's queer modernism

The text's treatment of Stein's masculinity obliquely inflects its account of her early years in Paris, although her gender's relevance is not immediately apparent. *The Autobiography* foregrounds modernism and the art world's rising stars, recounting Stein's career as a writer and art collector before telling about her childhood. Toklas emphasises that Stein's capacity for perception is superior to others' in that she recognised modernist painting's innovations well before the general public did. Toklas claims that upon first viewing *La Femme au chapeau* at the 1905 Salon d'Automne, most 'people were roaring with laughter at the picture and scratching at it. Gertrude Stein did not understand why, the picture seemed to her perfectly natural . . . This picture by Matisse seemed perfectly natural and she could not understand why it infuriated everybody.'[34] This passage substantiates Stein's assertion in 'How Writing Is Written' that 'if there are any of you who are going to express yourselves contemporarily, you will do something which most people won't want to look at'.[35]

Although this gesture informs the way Stein situates herself in *The Autobiography*, this passage's implications go beyond the idea that Matisse and Stein were ahead of their time. As she notes in 'Composition As Explanation', 'No one is ahead of his time, it is only that the particular variety of creating his time is the one that his contemporaries who also are creating their own time refuse to accept.'[36] This implies that temporal warpings animate *The Autobiography*'s narrative structure. As with her haircut's reception, her account of seeing *La Femme au chapeau* at the Salon d'Automne is narrated retrospectively, twenty years after the exhibit – once Matisse's work ceased to shock the general public. Toklas positions Stein as ahead of her time and possessed of an unusual capacity to see from a perspective other than that of the hegemonic gaze elicited by earlier styles of painting. Her *vision* is advanced, and her look at Matisse's painting is different from those around her. Moreover, Toklas's statement that Stein found *La Femme au chapeau* 'perfectly natural' subtly suggests that the painting was ordinary, even a throwback. As Siraganian observes, *The Autobiography* positions Stein as 'a creator of modern time' and Toklas as 'a shrewd market watcher' whose calculations do not favour Matisse.[37] Whereas the Yale key for 27, rue de Fleurus exemplifies the couple's status as early adopters of the 'brand everyone would eventually acquire', their decision to have their cook 'fry eggs for Matisse instead of making him an omelette' communicates that '[t]he public has priced him at fried eggs' and that Toklas's 'bell' would never 'ring' to rate his genius as equivalent to Stein's.[38]

Much as the text's juxtaposition of Picasso's, Stein's and Anderson's divergent ways of looking at the 'Caesar' cut mobilises the fracturing of perception accompanying challenges to the dominant gaze, the passage on *La Femme au chapeau* foregrounds the multiplicity of perspectives initially at play in its reception. Though Toklas asserts that 'the picture seemed . . . perfectly natural' to Stein, this apparently essentialist phrase's larger context destabilises the assumption that there is a normative way for a painting to elicit the gaze or for a viewer to look at it.[39] Later, far more viewers agreed with Stein's assessment and their looks, acting 'in concert with enough other looks', shifted the hegemonic gaze.[40] This changed the 'given-to-be-seen': dominant images that appear to enjoy 'a certain inevitability' but that can be 'reterritorialize[d]' when many viewers approach them differently.[41] In the case of *La Femme au chapeau*, a painting the text claims initially to have been considered unviewable within the hegemonic gaze was eventually revalued as a masterpiece by the general public.[42] As Siraganian suggests, however, *The Autobiography* also invites us to question this newly dominant perception – to be sceptical of the way 'the market' now 'easily and instantaneouly appraises' Matisse 'highly' – and to align our looks with Toklas to view Stein, but not him, as an avant-garde genius.[43]

Stein's reference to *La Femme au chapeau* as 'perfectly natural' also shows none of the struggle evident in Picasso's portrait of her and recalled in *The Autobiography* by his initial reaction to her 1926 haircut. The text thereby suggests that whereas Picasso's painting of Stein challenges dominant modes of perception by registering his disorientation by her gender and unsettling his works' viewers in turn, Stein's challenge to the hegemonic gaze works differently. The split between Toklas's femininity and Stein's masculinity conditions the text's fractured visual economy. As Will contends, 'The instability of Alice's position within the text, and the way in which this position unsettles conventional modalities of seeing and knowing, correlates with Jacques Lacan's notion of *le regard* (the gaze) . . . In foregrounding the gaze as well as what eludes the gaze, *The Autobiography* appropriates its genre's claims to authority, mastery, and by extension, "genius," and emphasizes their fictitiousness.'[44] This move destabilises perspective in ways that direct readers into following Stein's and Toklas's looks rather than looking upon them in shock. The text uses this playful twist on autobiography to counter the effects of initial misogynist and homophobic devaluings of Stein's writing and queer changes to the dominant mode of perception the book positions as modern art's consequences.

The Autobiography thus implies that initial responses to Stein's writing were linguistic and aesthetic manifestations of the same shocks that prompted the formal innovations of Picasso's *Portrait of Gertrude Stein* and attended modern painting's early reception. To reorient perceptions of Stein's place in the avant-garde, the text connects initial responses to her writing to what she characterises as the dominant reaction to *La Femme au chapeau*. The crowd's reaction to Matisse's painting 'bothered [Stein] and angered her because she did not understand why because to her it was so alright, just as later she did not understand why since the writing was all so clear and natural they mocked at and were enraged by her work'.[45] This establishes the radical aesthetics and value of Stein's work by comparing its ability to disturb to that of Matisse's painting. But there is more to this passage than the writer's self-promotion. Toklas emphasises Stein's anger at the picture's reception – her vexation by the crowd's furious response and similar reactions to her own writing. By depicting this cycle, *The Autobiography* offers a figure for the disorienting of vision prompted by Stein's writing and transmasculinity. However, the book's narrative strategy works to counter the hegemonic gaze assumed by such responses by allowing Toklas – and her steadfast support of Stein's genius – to shape what is given to readers to be read and seen.

Thus, though both of these passages are overtly concerned with establishing Stein as a major figure of the Euro-American avant-garde, the queerness animating *The Autobiography*'s reiterative narrative strategy offers readers multiple opportunities to recontextualise the book's opening portrayal of modernism and the significance of Stein's masculinity within it. These shifting gazes and looks continue to inflect *The Autobiography*'s inscription of Stein's relationship with Toklas and masculine homosocial bonds with colleagues. This visual economy illuminates trajectories of queer desire that have been obscured in disputes over the book's treatment of Stein's and Toklas's marriage. These debates ask whether the text masks Stein's and Toklas's relationship by encoding what an early article by Catharine Stimpson calls 'the lesbian lie' or whether it hides its protagonists' sexuality in plain sight by making it visible to those that know how to look.[46] The book's economy of vision strongly suggests the latter.

Moreover, when viewed from an alternative angle, *The Autobiography* reveals trajectories of masculine homosocial desire by using Toklas to position Stein as a masculine genius among her peers. This strategy establishes her masculinity as an effect of her texts' playful renditions of desire. Yet by placing Toklas in the pivotal role of narrator rather than that of a woman exchanged 'between men', *The Autobiography* departs from the pattern of male homosocial desire Sedgwick tracks in eighteenth- and nineteenth-century English literature.[47] Employing Toklas to reveal their own '"slantwise" . . . relation to existing social structures' and the vicissitudes of her masculine homosocial bonds with a variety of modernist figures, Stein's book demonstrates the queerly 'relational inventiveness' animating her experience of modernist Paris.[48] In so doing, *The Autobiography* strategically positions Stein as one of its masculine geniuses while destabilising the very concept of 'genius'.

Heterogendered Stein

The Autobiography highlights Stein's masculinity by deploying a heterogendered form of social organisation in which the implicitly masculinised Stein sits with the 'geniuses' and Toklas with their 'wives'.[49] Stein's use of Toklas as narrator cleverly deploys through narrative focalisation what Halberstam describes as a 'transgender gaze': one that recognises the subject's gender as they wish it to be seen.[50] This 'transgender look', as I prefer to call it, is grounded in imaginary reflections that are ultimately *mis*recognitions.[51] Yet Salamon demonstrates the intersubjective look's vital role in constituting transsubjectivity, however much its apparent 'identity is always already marked by nonidentity or difference'.[52] In *The Autobiography*, Toklas's self-positioning among the 'wives of geniuses' identifies Stein with the 'geniuses', designating her as a 'husband' within the salon's heterogendered frame and constructing Stein as a masculine 'genius' within Toklas's affirmative gaze. Though Stimpson claims in an early article that *The Autobiography*'s denouement, which reveals Stein's authorship of Toklas's story, 'erases Alice as the gaze, the eye, that fixes Stein's identity', this reading misses that Alice's look – like all looks – entails an illusory yet enabling *méconnaissance*.[53] The text's eventual revelation that these looks are ruses does not cancel the significations they enabled. The text turns on its conclusion's inability to erase the inscriptions of gender its earlier linguistic and visual plays mobilised. Toklas's desiring look recognises and validates Stein's masculine gender even as the text's narrative strategy complicates imaginary fantasies of perfect recognition and subjective plenitude.

This economy of vision works in conjunction with the book's well-known destabilisation of Stein's and Toklas's genders to allow Stein to take up 'a masculine stance' as she 'chats companionably with Carl Van Vechten and Sherwood Anderson'.[54] Yet far from setting Stein up against her male colleagues' putatively more 'real' masculinity, the 'Toklas' narrator inserts them into a context in which the identities of 'wives' and 'geniuses' all figure as 'impersonations'.[55] As Hovey observes, Toklas describes herself as having '"sat with wives who were not wives, of geniuses who were not real geniuses"', with wives '"of geniuses, of near geniuses, of would be geniuses"', and so destabilises those identities.[56] Moreover, as Stimpson writes of 'As A Wife Has A Cow', 'the knowledge . . . that both "husband" and "wife" might be women severs a sense of the necessity of the putative connections between femaleness and femininity, maleness and masculinity'.[57] This highlights *The Autobiography*'s staging of gender as relational rather than essential. The text persistently places Stein in the category of masculine 'genius' and Toklas in the role of feminine 'wife' – however constructed and actively taken on those genders may be.

However, Gilmore convincingly argues that writing Gertrude's story in Alice's voice does not appropriate the latter's identity, as is frequently charged. Rather, *The Autobiography* depends upon the 'coupled', or 'doubled' nature of its subject: on the way its inscriptions of 'Stein' and 'Toklas' blur the boundary between self and other, making them mutually dependent at the very scene of representation.[58] As Corinne Andersen observes, this strategy 'allow[s] Stein to view her own subjectivity from the vantage point of the Other', undercutting 'the illusion of the ego's stability' premising criticism of Stein's purported egotism.[59] Even though 'Toklas' is Stein's narrative device, this feminine figure powerfully shapes the story – and the characters' and readers' looks.

Moreover, Norris observes that the book's title – unlike others Stein considered – 'situates the "wife" as a subject' narrating the story from her own perspective.[60] This role enables 'readers to assume the sight and interest of Alice's implied reader of *The Autobiography*: that of a wife'.[61] Johnston similarly notes that while Stein 'retains control' of the story voiced through Toklas, *The Autobiography* 'displaces' their subject positions, creating an 'alternative reading practice' that plays upon their different perspectives.[62] Schmitz argues that this technique creates at least three different portraits of Stein through an 'act of transgression' that allows her to refuse 'her proper place in Cubism' and 'declare her own artistry', contesting Picasso's *Portrait of Gertrude Stein* and challenging the 'prejudicial exclusion' of her 'genius from the Pantheon of Modern Art'.[63] Norris observes that the book's cubism also calls attention to Toklas's subjectivity, differentiating *The Autobiography* from conventional forms of portraiture that deploy a painter's wife as a '"face"' that '"becomes immortalized" as a muse and survives as a residue of inspiration, with all of her labor – domestic, economic, and artistic – effaced in the art'.[64] *The Autobiography* instead makes visible Stein's position within networks of modernist 'geniuses' and the way these artists' and writers' work was integrated with Toklas's practice of domestic arts.[65] The book's 'cubist gesture of multiperspectivism' thus animates its transfeminism.[66]

Stein uses her early portrait 'Ada' (1910: 1922) to inscribe Toklas in *The Autobiography*. As Johnston notes, this move encourages intertextual reading by refusing 'textual closure and' producing 'a new reading position' that proliferates perspective.[67] By rendering 'vantage' multiple and mobile, this intertextuality counteracts *The Autobiography*'s surface-level heterosexism and enables queer ways of looking.[68] References to this portrait also exemplify the text's interimplication of Toklas's and Stein's subjectivities and strengthen the latter's self-inscription as a masculine genius. Stein's use of Toklas as narrator and privileging of 'Ada' differentiate the partners, highlighting the importance of their heterogendered form of homosexuality to the former's subjectivity and artistic trajectory. Moreover, as Margaret Dickie observes, *The Autobiography* privileges 'Ada' – rather than the better-known portraits of Cézanne,

Matisse and Picasso – as the first of Stein's portraits, and thereby positions Toklas, rather than the painters, 'as the person who launched [Stein] into portraits'.[69] This textual strategy situates Toklas 'both as a source and as a subject' for Stein's writing and reinforces the latter's placement among geniuses.[70]

Furthermore, as Gilbert and Gubar observe, 'Ada' figures Toklas's and Stein's mutual talking and listening as a process of doubling identified with the latter's 'genius'.[71] They note that in 'Portraits and Repetition', Stein declares that 'being a genius, I am most entirely and completely listening and talking, the two in one and the one in two'.[72] In *The Autobiography*, this doubling undercuts stable identities. Will contends that the resultant 'queering of narrative agency . . . extracts "genius" from the domain of the autonomous artist and relocates it in the shifting and polymorphous terrain of same-sex desire, explicitly making sexuality part of the equation of "talking and listening"'.[73] This 'positions Toklas as possessing a "genius" that is developed or awakened by engagement with Stein's own'.[74] Moreover, as Chessman argues, Stein's dialogic textuality makes '[b]iology . . . comically elusive' and renders gender 'open to question', making 'it possible to imagine male or female speakers within either masculine or feminine modes of language'.[75] Chessman's approach enables radical destabilisations in which language – rather than bodily materiality – figures gendered embodiment. Viewed from this perspective, intertextual connections between *The Autobiography*, 'Ada' and 'Portraits and Repetition' extend and complicate Stein's construction of herself as a masculine 'genius' by claiming the brilliant discursive practices through which her 'listening and talking' are redoubled in and reflected by Toklas's genius.[76]

By assigning 'Ada' priority in its narrative of Stein's literary portraiture, *The Autobiography* also constructs Toklas as her sitter, much as Picasso's women lovers were his sitters. Norris argues that like Matisse's and Picasso's portraits of their wives and lovers, 'Ada' effaces Toklas into a '"face"' that 'subsume[s]' her 'into the aesthetic signature of the genius's style', transforming her into 'a mirror of the artist'.[77] However, her reading overlooks dialogue's importance in 'Ada'. Chessman persuasively argues that 'Ada' and other pieces blend Stein's and Toklas's voices instead of silencing the latter.[78] This distinguishes Stein's portrait of Toklas from the painters' portraits of their wives by rendering her more than a static 'face'.[79] *The Autobiography* figures this dialogism by presenting Stein and Toklas as recognising one another perfectly through the look: the latter declares that she is 'very often able to read' Stein's 'illegible' handwriting when its author cannot.[80] This underscores Stein's opacity to herself and thus the text's splitting of her and Toklas's subjectivities. It toys with Stein's role as the text's author and points to the possibility that Toklas's subjectivity and voice register in both pieces – not just *The Autobiography*, as Norris claims.[81]

Stein's use of Alice as a sitter for 'Ada' is also significant. Emphasising both the painter's and the sitter's agency, Lubar argues that portraiture involves 'a highly complex economy of psychic and social exchanges between the painter and the sitter'.[82] Both the act of painting and the portrait are 'located within a symbolic economy that is mediated by the gaze', and, I would add, the Gaze.[83] The critic can trace these intersubjective dynamics by reading the portrait as 'a trap for . . . the gaze'.[84] Lubar's insistence upon the sitter's agency is a helpful response to the false charge that Stein appropriated and exploited Toklas in *The Autobiography* and life. Yet whereas the act of sitting generally involves incommensurability between the artist's fantasies and those of the portrait's subject, Stein's placement of 'Ada' within *The Autobiography* presents a special case because Stein both refers to her portrait of her partner and scripts Toklas's reactions to it. *The Autobiography* thereby self-consciously figures an exchange that is only implicit in other forms of portraiture.

The Autobiography offers two very different scenes of 'Ada's' reception and multiple ways of looking at its portrayal of Toklas. Stein first has Toklas incorporate 'Ada' into her narration and vouch for its accuracy. The latter states that in 'Ada', Stein 'has given a very good description of me as I was at that time' – Toklas's childhood, depicted in *The Autobiography*'s first chapter.[85] Turning on *Nachträglichkeit* (deferred action), Toklas's gesture invests her and Stein's pasts with the significance of their eventual relationship and aligns their views of 'Ada'.[86] This is a different manifestation of the identification to which *The Autobiography* attributes Stein's decision to get the 'Caesar' haircut. Stein and Toklas seem to share 'the look' in *The Autobiography* and thus what appears to be the same subject position. However, this apparent alignment is split through the former's deployment of the latter's viewpoint to construct the gaze through which their household is given to be seen. This narrative ruse destabilises perspective and reveals that identification – and, in turn, imitation – also multiplies differences, which register in the text's interimplication of Stein's and Toklas's subjectivities.[87] This mobilises a cubist proliferation of perspectives.

Multiperspectivalism also informs the book's inscription of Toklas's reaction to Stein's representation of her in 'Ada'. As Norris observes, in a second and later reference to 'Ada' in *The Autobiography*, Toklas 'allegorizes the politics of the genius and the wife as a competition between fine art and domestic art staged as a marital quarrel'.[88] This playfully highlights Toklas's resistance to her portrayal in 'Ada' and *The Autobiography* and 'dramatizes' her 'resistance to having her own domestic art, the hot meal, categorically displaced by Stein's invention of a new genre of portraiture'.[89] When Stein prevails by stopping Toklas's meal to share 'Ada', her

> victory is provisional at best, for the marital conflict, and Alice's inability to 'see' herself in the signature portrait by Gertrude, obliges her to invent a new genre of portraiture all over again: one that will restore Alice's domestic art to Stein's fine art, and one that will allow Alice to 'see' herself as *she* sees herself, rather than as Stein sees her.[90]

For Norris, this scene implies that 'Stein's signature portrait of Alice as "Ada" is such a narcissistic "face" that it must be redrawn in *The Autobiography* in order to erase Stein's signature style and let Alice's Alice, the wife's portrait by the wife, achieve a fictional self-representation' more convincing than the early portrait.[91]

However, Norris misses the portrait's dialogic inscription of Toklas's voice and the way *The Autobiography* offers two different perspectives on Toklas's reaction to 'Ada'. As Norris observes, the second version underscores Toklas's resistance to the effacement of her culinary art, but the first version emphasises the portrait's representational accuracy: Toklas calls it a 'very good description' of her early years.[92] It is thus not that 'Ada' misrepresents Toklas but that it does not fully register the significance of her marriage to Stein. Nor does Toklas's first remark about 'Ada' merely call attention to the difference between its style and the ruse of representation animating *The Autobiography*. Her qualification that the portrait registers her subjectivity 'at that time' highlights the temporal gaps accompanying *The Autobiography*'s mobilisation of shifting perspectives.[93] This defiance of linear temporality works alongside the text's narrative strategy to decentre its subjects and refract perspective.

Stein uses this narrative apparatus to inscribe herself and her partner within a heterogendered social order in which Toklas's positioning with the 'wives' conditions Stein's placement with the 'geniuses' – however playful, denaturalised and resituated within a domestic reworking of modernist aesthetics those positionings may be. This highlights the difference between Stein's feminist masculinity and that of Hemingway, Matisse and Picasso. As Norris shows, unlike these men – who exploited their wives' labour at home and in the studio only to discard and marginalise them once they no longer proved useful – Stein stayed with Toklas for the rest of her life, making her voice and domestic artistry central to modernism in *The Autobiography*.[94]

By making Stein's relationship with Toklas the lynchpin of its narrative strategy, *The Autobiography* also minimises her brother Leo's role in establishing the salon. However, what the text includes about Leo – with whom Gertrude first came to Paris and hosted the salon – provides hints about early iterations of her masculinity. The portion of *The Autobiography* that features him focuses on the siblings' activities as modern art collectors and salon hosts, presenting them as equals in dealing with visiting 'geniuses'. This parallelism subtly establishes the masculinity Gertrude reinforces by figuring Toklas as her 'wife', and sets the stage for the exclusive claim to the role of family 'genius' Gertrude makes upon Leo's departure. The fracturing of his and Gertrude's bond anticipates the difficulties that eventually emerged in her fraught homosocial bonds with heterosexual male colleagues such as Matisse, Picasso and Hemingway.

Homosocial Stein

Though biographers have established that Stein befriended and networked with both men and women, *The Autobiography* highlights the play between her heterogendered desire for Toklas and homosocial desire for her male colleagues.[95] Using the contrast between these forms of queer relationality to establish Stein's masculinity, the text's reiterations underscore her longing for homosocial bonds while highlighting their potential to fracture. As Charles Caramello argues, in *The Autobiography* 'Stein wants Toklas to concoct a family romance that represents Stein as competing with male siblings and as succeeding fathers; she allows Toklas, in effect, to show Stein as preoccupied with rivals, as competitive toward Picasso as an artist, and as resentful toward Picasso and Hemingway as men who had attained, by 1932, the wealth and celebrity that Stein lacked.'[96] Toklas directs readers' attention to moments at which Stein's and her friends' looks either align (in Anderson's case) or cross (in Hemingway's, Matisse's and Picasso's cases), and also offers her own perspective on their interactions. By using this strategy, Stein mimics the perspectival multiplicity of cubist painting, mobilising multifarious views of her tricky homosocial alliances. *The Autobiography* displays her strong attraction to and identification with colleagues such as Anderson; at the same time, it registers the forms of 'differentiating, rivaling, leaning, twisting, . . . withdrawing, . . . aggressing' and 'warping' that emerge as her friendships with Hemingway and Picasso unravel.[97]

The Autobiography strategically highlights Stein's affiliation with famous male writers and artists to bolster her reputation, using associative contiguity with masculine modernist luminaries to foreground her celebrity and masculinity. Emphasising *The Autobiography* and other texts that concern her relationships with fellow modernists, Goldman analyses the way Stein established her celebrity through affiliation with other stars.[98] He argues that, like Stein's experimental writing, this logic of association parallels de Saussure's theory of the sign: value is established through elements' differential positioning within a signifying system, rather than grounded in a claim to inherent worth.[99] 'Stein' takes on value within this star system through contiguous positioning among 'Matisse', 'Picasso' and others.

Though Goldman's theory aptly accounts for Stein's self-positioning in *The Autobiography*, his assertion that the roles of Gertrude as 'husband' and Alice as 'wife' are 'divorced from the body and attached to the idea of celebrity' needs to be complicated.[100] He claims that 'Stein categorizes husbands and wives as entities divided into public and private rather than male and female.'[101] However, this formulation overlooks several decades of scholarship documenting Stein's persistently masculine identifications, plays with pronouns, and cross-writing. These masculine self-inscriptions in Stein's life and writing suggest that in *The Autobiography*, too, 'husband' continues to be gendered (though not sexed) as masculine even as it designates stardom. If in *The Autobiography*, 'husbands are celebrities . . . whose names refer beyond the text to their position in the differential system of the public sphere', the position of 'husband' can be 'divorced' from the male body but not from masculinity.[102]

Stein's transmasculinity registers in *The Autobiography* through her positioning as Toklas's 'husband' and affiliation with other 'geniuses' in a circuit of masculine homosocial desire. However, Stein's transmasculinity is distinct from her colleagues' cisgender male masculinities, so the homosocial desires animating their friendships often fracture. Stein's strategy of writing back against those who courted her patronage and mentoring in their twenties but later devalued her represents a challenge to the institutional forces that influenced their asymmetrical career trajectories – forces that played out over time and whose complexities cannot be captured by a purely synchronic approach to *The Autobiography*'s logic of celebrity.

By striking back against their misogynist characterisations of her person and work, *The Autobiography* analyses the dynamics through which 'desiring', 'attracting' and 'identifying' transform into 'rivaling', 'twisting', 'warping' and 'repelling'.[103] The text emphasises Stein's role at the early stages of Picasso's and Hemingway's careers while also challenging their retroactive efforts to minimise her assistance. As a struggling young artist in Montmartre, Picasso courted Stein's patronage – her financial capital. But once he was established and she tried to leverage his cultural capital to enhance her own reputation, their friendship soured. Similarly, Hemingway initially sought out her and Anderson's mentoring only to turn on them once he had become a successful writer. *The Autobiography* highlights Stein's impact on these men and critiques their poor treatment of her, suggesting that it was only after they became famous and Stein attempted to benefit from their reputations that their friendships soured. *The Autobiography* also recruits Anderson as a sympathetic peer whose actions parallel Stein's to counter their mutual targeting by the ungrateful Hemingway's wrath. Thus, while countering hostile portrayals, *The Autobiography* also points to Stein's potential to have viable friendships with men.

Moreover, *The Autobiography* suggests that Stein's masculine homosocial attractions were not limited to males but extended to masculine women such as the dandy Jane Heap.[104] This vector of homosocial desire denaturalises the putatively essential connection between masculinity and maleness. Halberstam's *Female Masculinity* makes a compelling case for this conceptual move's feminist potential but does not explore the forms of bonding that could be its consequence. By contrast, *The Autobiography*'s dual attention to Stein's heterogendered romantic relationship and the vicissitudes of her masculine homosocial desires for men and masculine women establishes her transmasculinity and deploys it for feminist purposes. Both varieties of masculine homosocial desire contribute to the book's cubism, multiplying masculinities while denaturalising their relationship to maleness.

This dynamic shows in *The Autobiography* when Toklas recounts a luncheon hosted by Stein and attended by both Matisse and Picasso. The meal takes place when a crisis of triangulated desire emerges through jealousy expressed as aesthetic differences. Matisse displaces his irritation at Stein's growing intimacy with Picasso onto the claim that her preference for 'local color and theatrical values' should make a 'serious friendship' with him impossible.[105] Stein bridges this gap temporarily by manipulating the look and the gaze as conduits of desire. At the luncheon, she places each artist in front of his own work, directing their looks differently. This stratagem maintains harmony until Matisse steps out of position and looks at the room from another spot. His wider angle reveals Stein's tactics and leads him to believe that she 'had lost interest in his work'.[106] Like the text's treatment of Stein's short haircut, this scene turns on shifting the look. All is harmonious until Matisse takes an angle of approach Stein did not prescribe for him, causing him to see that his work is not her sole object of desire. His revaluation of the luncheon contributes to their friendship's breakdown over her interest in Picasso.

Paralleling the text's two showings of Stein's 'Caesar' crop and the 'Ada' portrait, *The Autobiography* precedes the above story with an earlier version. The first account makes no mention of Matisse's and Picasso's rivalry, emphasising that the artists were very 'happy' with the luncheon.[107] Matisse alone notices Stein's ruse – retroactively, not 'until just as he left' – and considers it evidence that she is 'very wicked'.[108] Underscoring the *méconnaissance* in Stein's arrangement of the painters' looks and her conversations with them, Matisse observes that 'the world is a theatre for you, but there are theatres and theatres, and when you listen so carefully to me and so attentively and do not hear a word I say then I do say that you are very wicked'.[109] This highlights the role of visual and verbal differences in Stein's and Matisse's difficulty. The reiteration of this scene reveals differences that heighten the 'warping' *The Autobiography* employs to register their friendship's termination.[110]

The later account of the luncheon heightens this distortion by using the visual to short-circuit Stein's and the painters' homosocial desires. By offering this view of the luncheon well after an account focused exclusively on its celebration of modernist painters' aesthetic innovations, *The Autobiography* mobilises multiple perspectives on its role in modernism's development – some playing up the painters' aesthetic differences, others highlighting Stein's transmasculinity and role within a fractured circuit of triangulated desire. These multiple perspectives show that *The Autobiography*'s simultaneous articulation of questions of aesthetics and desire is crucial to understanding Stein's queer relationality with her colleagues. In the second version of the lunch, the men look at paintings affirming their value as artists and thereby sustain a circuit of desire in which Stein plays only a supporting role. Stein, by contrast, seeks to elicit a gaze affirming all of their importance. In so doing, she occupies both the masculine role of the 'genius' and the feminised position of the object of jealousy that emerges between men. This differentiates her transmasculinity from Matisse's and Picasso's male masculinities. However, *The Autobiography* also emphasises Stein's agency in redirecting the looks through which triangulated desire circulates. The text's narrative strategy furthers her attempt to step out of the role of object by foregrounding both her affiliation with men and her differentiation from the feminine Toklas. The latter is presented as controlling the narration, and thus as refusing the role of object exchanged between men. Because Stein and Toklas are positioned '"slantwise" . . . in relation to existing social structures' such as the male-driven art world, this mode of storytelling has a 'warping' effect on the scene of modernism that is heightened by the text's temporal 'wrinkles and folds'.[111]

The Autobiography takes a more understated approach to the eventual ruptures in Stein's and Picasso's friendship, subtly deploying the look and the gaze to track shifts in Stein's and the painter's desires. Between the two world wars – when Stein and Picasso 'always talked with the tenderest friendship about each other to any one who had known them both but . . . did not see each other' – Stein speaks fondly to Picasso's mother of how he was 'remarkably beautiful' during their friendship's early years.[112] When Stein portrays Picasso as 'illuminated as if he wore a halo', his mother responds that

> if you thought him beautiful then I assure you it was nothing compared to his looks when he was a boy. He was an angel and a devil in beauty, no one could cease looking at him. And now, said Picasso a little resentfully. Ah now, said they together, ah now there is no such beauty left.[113]

Particularly noteworthy is the physical attraction to Picasso this passage attributes to Stein. By pointing to Picasso's youthful illumination, Stein stages his appearance as eliciting a gaze in which he appears beautiful and suggests that her masculine homosocial desire sometimes could be homoerotic. His mother, in turn, suggests that the gaze he staged as a child was even more compelling because he appeared simultaneously as 'an angel and a devil'.[114] Stein and his mother both agree, however, that after the war 'there is no such beauty left' – that the gaze has shifted so they look at him differently than before.[115] By showing Picasso's capacity for initially 'attracting' but eventually 'repelling' Stein, this passage's shifting perspectives reveal the short-circuiting of the desire that initially animated his and Stein's personal and professional attraction to one another – an attraction whose complexity also registers in his portrait of her and reaction to her 1926 haircut.[116]

At other times, a complicated vacillation between sympathetic homosocial association and hostile aggression registers in *The Autobiography*, with Anderson consistently appearing in the former guise and Hemingway in the latter. Much as the text compares the effect of Stein's writings to that of modern painting, *The Autobiography* uses masculine affiliation to align her view of Hemingway with Anderson's and position her as a modernist innovator. Anderson first appears in *The Autobiography* as a celebrated writer who 'moved and pleased' Stein by affirming her work's importance to his own; therefore 'Gertrude Stein and Sherwood Anderson have always been the best of friends.'[117] He later resurfaces as a colleague who shares her view of Hemingway as a 'pupil' who left them 'both a little proud and a little ashamed of the work of their minds'.[118] *The Autobiography* consistently aligns Stein's look with Anderson's in this regard.

In contrast to Anderson, whom Toklas consistently presents as 'attracting' Stein and 'paralleling' her look, *The Autobiography* emphasises Hemingway's inconsistency: his volatile movements between 'desiring, identifying' with, 'mimicking', 'rivaling' and 'aggressing' against his mentors.[119] In a pivotal move, Toklas reveals Stein's and Anderson's shared 'weakness for Hemingway:

> They both agreed that they have a weakness for Hemingway because he is such a good pupil. He is a rotten pupil, I protested. You don't understand, they both said, it is so flattering to have a pupil who

> does it without understanding it, in other words he takes training and anybody who takes training is a favorite pupil. They both admit it to be a weakness.[120]

The Autobiography portrays Stein and Anderson as flattered by Hemingway's obedience – even though they label it 'yellow' – but also uses Toklas to unmask and label as 'rotten' the aggression leading him to retaliate.[121] The text characterises Hemingway as a man who submits to mentoring, repays his supporters with attacks, and fears the consequences. Toklas tells us that

> Hemingway had at one moment, when he had repudiated Sherwood Anderson and all his works, written him a letter in the name of american [*sic*] literature which he, Hemingway, in company with his contemporaries was about to save, telling Sherwood just what he, Hemingway thought about Sherwood's work, and, that thinking, was in no sense complimentary. When Sherwood came to Paris Hemingway naturally was afraid. Sherwood as naturally was not.[122]

This passage stages Hemingway as a cliché driven by the 'anxiety of influence', and Anderson – and by extension, Stein – as a writer so confident as to have no need of the Oedipal model of masculinity or fear of its rebellious sons.[123] This is why Hemingway 'looks like a modern' but 'smells of the museums': in attempting to 'save' American literature from its forebears, he ironically displays his enslavement to tradition and submission to the very masters he resents.[124] This act of 'warping' is the 'real story of Hemingway' Stein and Anderson lament that he will never tell, but that Toklas exposes to the readers of *The Autobiography* nonetheless.[125] This passage also hints at the weakness hidden behind Hemingway's famed bravado and – in stating that he 'smells of the museums' – presents his masculinity as amusingly anachronistic in comparison to Stein's.

Although Toklas critiques Hemingway's pattern of behaviour, which differs markedly from Anderson's, her narration also foregrounds his and Stein's enabling of the younger writer. In teasing Stein and Anderson for their 'weakness for Hemingway', Toklas shows far more fondness for her partner's and friend's vulnerability to sycophants than for Hemingway's duplicity. But Toklas also hints that the former are attached to the same power dynamic driving the latter's supplication, even though Stein shows far more susceptibility to flattery than interest in submission in *The Autobiography*. This gesture suggests that a subtle form of 'parallelling' is at work in Stein's, Anderson's and Hemingway's queer relationality despite the older writers' attempt at 'differentiating' themselves from their 'pupil'.[126] This is why Stein and Anderson admit to being 'a little proud and a little ashamed of the work of their minds'.[127] *The Autobiography* betrays Stein's own submissive tendencies – and her own masculinity's fragility – even though she shows it in the most flattering of available lights by deploying a gaze constituted through Toklas's loving look at her genius.

Stein's use of Toklas to critique her male colleagues' cowardly gender politics becomes even more apparent in the text's depiction of Picasso's homophobic treatment of Jean Cocteau. Although Caramello rightfully observes that *The Autobiography* 'has Toklas . . . overtly attack Hemingway' but only 'covertly critique Picasso' – a dynamic I see in the contrast between the book's open mockery of the former's servility and its far subtler reference to the disappearance the latter's 'halo' – the section on Cocteau more pointedly criticises the painter.[128] Toklas begins by attributing a remark to Picasso that characterises Cocteau as obsessed with his youthful image: 'It was at this time that Jean Cocteau who prides himself on being eternally thirty was writing a little biography of Picasso, and he sent him a telegram asking him to tell him the date of his birth. And yours, telegraphed Picasso.'[129] This characterisation of Cocteau continues when the text recounts an interview Picasso gave to a Catalan newspaper assuming it would not be translated into French. He spoke more freely than usual, and 'said that Jean Cocteau was getting to be very popular in Paris, so popular that you could find his poems on the table of any smart coiffeur'.[130] This portrays Cocteau as a vain middlebrow who catered to a popular gay audience rather than elite aficionados of high art. *The Autobiography* tells readers that once the interview was translated, Cocteau sought out Picasso, who hid and attempted to attribute it to Francis Picabia, who denied it. Picasso's wife then lied to Cocteau's mother, leading her to believe her husband was innocent.[131] Whereas Hemingway betrays his weakness by submitting to his mentors and turning on them with aggression, Picasso reveals his own cowardice through his refusal to own his remarks about Cocteau.[132] Toklas, by contrast, reveals Picasso's homophobic statements and his attempts to deny them.

Stein's covert aggression about these events is noteworthy: she does not openly challenge Picasso's attack on Cocteau but deploys Toklas to reveal and critique the painter's conduct. Though Picasso's disparaging of femininity is part of the dominant construct of masculine homosociality in which Stein participates by engaging him and Hemingway, *The Autobiography* also shows her difference from it by using Toklas to critique its homophobia and regain the upper hand. If Anderson directly displays self-confidence despite Hemingway's vitriol, Stein routes her response through Toklas. Through this act of ventriloquy, the text's cubist warpings give a variety of masculinities to be seen.

Thus, even though Toklas relates that it was during the summer of Picasso's attack on Cocteau 'that Gertrude Stein, delighting in the movement of the tiny waves on the Antibes shore, wrote the Completed Portrait of Picasso, the Second Portrait of Carl Van Vechten, and The Book of Concluding With As A Wife Has A Cow A Love Story this afterwards beautifully illustrated by Juan Gris', *The Autobiography* stresses the fractures in the circuit of desire animating these texts.[133] Whereas 'As A Wife Has A Cow' enacts Stein's and Toklas's sexual bliss, their jouissance contrasts to Stein's gentle mockery of Picasso's Napoleonic self-centredness in 'If I Told Him'. The latter text's subtle critique of hegemonic male masculinity reverberates within portrayals of Stein's counterhegemonic trans-masculinity, as her other texts' playful references to their author as 'Caesar' suggest.

The Autobiography's explicitness about Hemingway's attacks and its subtler allusion to the time between the two world wars during which Stein and Picasso 'were not seeing each other' both suggest that her homosocial desire for these men – and for association with their dominant masculinities – is fractured and warped by difference.[134] Toklas's choice of vision as a metaphor for Stein's and Picasso's mutual withdrawal between the wars foregrounds their divergent perspectives and echoes the latter's earlier explanation for his delayed completion of Stein's portrait. *The Autobiography* tracks the visual reverberations of his reaction to Stein by refracting it through her, his and Toklas's looks. Toklas relates that 'all of a sudden one day Picasso painted out the whole head. I can't see you any longer when I look, he said irritably. And so the picture was left like that' to be finished later.[135] She also notes that Picasso finally finished the head 'without having seen Gertrude Stein again'.[136] Both of these passages underscore the portrait's fragmenting of vision. However, Toklas also states that upon seeing the finished picture – and Stein's masked face – both 'he and she were content' with its appearance.[137] In this instance, their looks are parallel.

This alignment of looks differs markedly from the reaction Lubar finds in Picasso's portrait. He argues that in the finished picture, Stein's hollowed eyes result from the painter's disturbance by and 'refusal to see' her gender.[138] Anticipating analytic cubism, the painting warps perspective and reanimates Picasso's reaction for viewers. The portrait's mobilisation of the gaze is thus quite different than the resolution of conflict *The Autobiography* suggests when it recounts the two parties' pleasure in the portrait and tracks Picasso's prompt shift in reaction to Stein's 1926 haircut. Though this early passage claims a parallel between Stein's and Picasso's looks at the completed portrait, *The Autobiography* goes on to use Toklas's look (itself orchestrated by Stein) to shift the gaze and prompt the reader to look at the portrait – and Stein's and Picasso's divergent masculinities – from another 'vantage'.[139] This alternative perspective induces perspectival warping, revealing the gender trouble underpinning their friendship.

The Autobiography also inscribes Stein's gender by registering her interest in other queer modernists – even though their sexualities are not remarked upon. The explicitly queer routing of Stein's homosocial desires would intensify in the 1920s; the final chapters note her connections to the lesser-known gay male artists, composers and writers that formed her inner circle as her friendships with Picasso and Hemingway frayed.[140] Stein's ties with queer men in the 1920s underscore her persistent interest in homosocial bonding. As Stimpson and Nair observe, however, *The Autobiography* does not remark upon the same-sex relationships that flourished between pairs of men and women in Stein's and Toklas's network.[141] These occlusions contrast to the attention early chapters pay to the female partners of Stein's male colleagues. This dynamic suggests that *The Autobiography* is less interested in tracing out the forms of relationality queers in Stein's networks enjoyed with one another than in leveraging her and Toklas's '"slantwise" orientation' toward her heterosexual male colleagues' behavioural patterns to place 27, rue de Fleurus – and Stein's transmasculine genius – at the centre of Parisian modernism. The book's eventual move toward alliances with queer people does suggest, though, a shift away from the fraught bonds with heterosexual men she cultivated earlier in her career. This move promises another perspective on Stein's transmasculinity, albeit one whose queerness would not be brought into the foreground of dominant representation until *Seeing Gertrude Stein* in 2011.

The Autobiography does, however, occasionally figure Stein's masculinity in relation to other queers by calling attention to her interest in masculine women. That not all of Stein's homosocial desires are for males indicates the anti-essentialist character of her masculinity. Unlike her responses to men, both imitation and affiliation are at work in the book's portrayal of her connections to these women. Whereas the former motivated the 'Caesar' crop Stein copied from the Duchess of Clermont-Tonnerre, the latter characterises the book's treatment of Stein's friendship with Jane Heap, the female dandy who arranged for the publication of two of her texts – 'the Birthplace of Bonnes and The Valentine to Sherwood Anderson' – in *The Little Review*.[142] In a statement paralleling passages showing Stein's gratitude toward men such as Anderson, Hemingway and Ford Madox Ford (all of whom facilitated the publication of her work), Toklas tells readers that her partner 'had always liked Jane Heap immensely, Margaret Anderson interested her much less'.[143] Here, Toklas both signals Stein's preference for Heap, the more masculine member of the couple who ran *The Little Review*, and references the 'valentine' that simultaneously thanks Sherwood Anderson for his introduction to *Geography and Plays* and offers 'a love poem to Toklas'.[144] The reference to a popular genre for romantic love in Stein's tribute to Anderson suggests that it sustains multiple trajectories of desire. Though Dydo is right that 'A Valentine' – like many of Stein's writings – expresses her love for Toklas, this circuit of desire also implicates the man named in the title. When 'A Valentine' appears in the context of *The Autobiography*, Stein's desires are both heterogendered (for Toklas) and homosocial (for Heap and Sherwood Anderson), with the latter trajectory running through male-bodied and female-bodied masculine persons alike.

Whereas *The Autobiography* emphasises Stein's affiliation with the dandy Heap, positioning them both as fellow masculine modernists, it uses affiliation and identification to track the effects of the 'Caesar' haircut that became a powerful feature of Stein's image. In showing the crop, the text mobilises multiple angles of vision: Stein's identificatory look at the Duchess, Anderson's approving look at Stein, and Picasso's uneasy looks at her. These occur in the context of yet more looks – Stein's look at *La Femme au chapeau*, Picasso's and Matisse's crossed looks at their own paintings, and Stein's and Anderson's parallel looks at Hemingway – all of which are orchestrated by Toklas's bemused yet loving look upon Stein and their milieu. Given to be seen through Toklas's gaze – and the cubist fracturings the book's plays between varied looks and gazes engender – Stein's transmasculinity appears kaleidoscopically, in '"slantwise"' relationship to male masculinities, in the 'wrinkles and folds' of cubism's queer temporality.[145] *The Autobiography* thereby denaturalises and resignifies masculinity, allowing the reader to imagine both Stein's gender and the scene of modernism anew.

Notes

1. Butler in Butler and Athanasiou, *Dispossession*, p. 67.
2. Roof, *What Gender Is*, p. 79; Silverman, *Threshold*, p. 227.
3. Corn and Latimer, *Seeing Gertrude Stein*, p. 51.
4. See Halberstam's *Female Masculinity* for a powerful account of the originary capacity of female and transmasculinities.
5. Sayre, 'The Artist's Model', p. 32. See Nair, *Secrecy and Sapphic Modernism*, p. 123 for further analysis of the relationality of the text's narrative mode.
6. Siraganian, 'Speculating on an Art Movement', pp. 593–4.
7. Nair, *Secrecy and Sapphic Modernism*, pp. 119–51.
8. Nair, ibid., p. 120.
9. Gilmore, 'A Signature of Lesbian Autobiography'; Weiner and Young, 'Introduction: Queer Bonds', p. 225.
10. Sedgwick, *Touching Feeling*, p. 8.
11. Corn and Latimer, *Seeing Gertrude Stein*, p. 51.
12. Stein, *The Autobiography*, p. 53.
13. See Caramello, *Henry James, Gertrude Stein*, p. 167, for analysis of the ways *The Autobiography* reproduces Henry James's framing of 'Isabel Archer in doorways' in *Portrait of a Lady*.
14. Stein, *The Autobiography*, p. 53.
15. Schwartz, *Reconfiguring Modernism*, p. 142. As Schwartz's reference to 'kinship' suggests, Stein's writing does not perfectly mimic cubist painting. There has been substantial debate about the extent of the parallels between painterly and literary cubism. See Walker, *The Making of a Modernist*, pp. 127–49, for a detailed discussion of cubist strategies in *Tender Buttons*. She and Dubnick (*The Structure of Obscurity*, pp. 28–44, and 'Two Types of Obscurity') see *Tender*

Buttons as imitating synthetic cubism, whereas Scobie ('The Allure of Multiplicity', pp. 103–7; *Earthquakes and Explorations*, pp. 110–14) critiques Dubnick for drawing too 'neat' a 'dichotomy' between the analytic cubism of *The Making of Americans* and the synthetic cubism of *Tender Buttons*. While he praises Walker for being more nuanced than Dubnick, he ultimately rejects Walker, too, stressing metonymy's importance in cubist painting. DeKoven also underscores the limits of the analogy between cubist literature and painting in an essay sensitive to Stein's feminist differences from Picasso; see 'Gertrude Stein and Modern Painting'. Perloff finds similarities between *Tender Buttons* and the '*reduction*' in Marcel Duchamp's 'early Dada paintings of 1912–1913' – a style, termed 'Orphic Cubism' by Guillaume Apollinaire, in which 'the relation between signifier and signified becomes even more tenuous' than in analytic cubism ('Poetry as Word-System', pp. 99–100). Hilder's 'After all one must know more than one sees' examines Stein's cubism on her own terms rather than those of cubist painting. See also Brinnin, *The Third Rose*; Brogan, 'The "Founding Mother"'; Steiner, *Exact Resemblance*; Voris, *The Composition of Sense* and 'Interpreting Cézanne'.

Departing from readings of Stein as a cubist, Siraganian ('Out of Air', p. 659) argues that Stein's approach to the visual arts situates 'the work of art in relation . . . to the beholder' rather than 'its referent', as linguistically oriented formalist and poststructuralist critics assume. See also Siraganian, *Modernism's Other Work*.

16. Nair, *Secrecy and Sapphic Modernism*, p. 127.
17. Stein, *The Autobiography*, p. 53.
18. Roof, *What Gender Is*, p. 79.
19. Lubar, 'Unmasking Pablo's Gertrude', p. 59.
20. Stein, *The Autobiography*, p. 53.
21. Stein, ibid., p. 233.
22. Stein, ibid., p. 233.
23. Stein, ibid., p. 233. In 'Anglophones in Paris', Abravanel observes that Anderson's preface to Stein's *Geography and Plays* 'rewrites Stein's sexuality as a study in American masculinity'. Refuting the image of Stein as a 'languid' sipper of 'absinthes' and insisting upon her 'striking vigor' and 'powerful mind', Anderson presents her as 'nearly a stereotype of American masculinity' (Sherwood Anderson, 'Preface', p. 6; Abravanel, 'Anglophones in Paris', p. 94).
24. Freeman, 'Introduction: Queer Temporalities', p. 163.
25. Stein, *The Autobiography*, p. 9.
26. Stein, ibid., p. 84.
27. Norris, 'The "Wife" and the "Genius"', p. 85; Stein, 'A Transatlantic Interview', p. 502; Norris, ibid., p. 85.

28. Gilmore, 'A Signature of Lesbian Autobiography', p. 200.
29. Gilmore, ibid., p. 218.
30. Gilmore, ibid., p. 222.
31. Gilmore, ibid., p. 222.
32. Gilmore, ibid. See also Andersen, 'I Am Not Who "I" Pretend to Be"'; Blackmer, 'Lesbian Modernism'; Corn and Latimer, *Seeing Gertrude Stein*; Johnston, *The Formation of 20th-Century Queer Autobiography* and 'Narratologies of Pleasure'; Meese, 'Gertrude Stein and Me'; and Merrill, 'Gertrude Stein and Autobiography', for sympathetic characterisations of Stein's placement of Toklas as narrator. These writers respond to earlier work that positions Stein as a female patriarch who exploited Toklas. For examples, see Benstock, *Women*; Gilbert and Gubar, *No Man's Land*, *Vol. 1* and *Vol. 2*; and Stimpson ('Gertrice/Altrude' and 'Gertrude Stein and the Transposition of Gender'). The latter of Stimpson's essays moves from the argument that Stein mimed patriarchal gender and appropriated Toklas's voice to the more nuanced claim that some of her texts challenge this model. See Friedman, 'Women's Autobiographical Selves', for an ambivalent account of *The Autobiography*'s gender politics; see Norris, 'The "Wife" and the "Genius"', for an argument that assumes that Stein and Toklas mimed heterosexual gender differences but that also offers a sympathetic account of the latter's role as narrator of *The Autobiography*.
33. Johnston, 'Narratologies of Pleasure', p. 594. Phoebe Stein Davis similarly underscores the book's tendency to repeat the 'same stories' from different standpoints to expose 'the constructed nature of memory in autobiography' and the 'importance of allowing for the validity of different perspectives': see 'Subjectivity and the Aesthetics of National Identity', p. 23.
34. Stein, *The Autobiography*, p. 32.
35. Stein, 'How Writing Is Written', p. 488.
36. Stein, 'Composition as Explanation', p. 514.
37. Siraganian, 'Speculating', p. 596.
38. Siraganian, ibid., p. 596.
39. Stein, *The Autobiography*, p. 32.
40. Silverman, *Threshold*, p. 223.
41. Silverman, ibid., p. 156, p. 221, p. 223.
42. This account of the Fauvists' initial reception is a myth: see Harrison et al., *Primitivism, Cubism, Abstraction*, p. 46.
43. Siraganian, 'Speculating', p. 600.
44. Will, *Gertrude Stein*, p. 142.
45. Stein, *The Autobiography*, pp. 32–3.
46. Stimpson, 'Gertrude Stein and the Lesbian Lie'.

47. Sedgwick, *Between Men*.
48. Weiner and Young, 'Introduction: Queer Bonds', p. 225.
49. Stein, *The Autobiography*, p. 81.
50. Halberstam, *Queer Time*, pp. 76–96.
51. See Lacan, 'The mirror stage'; see Merrill, 'Gertrude Stein and Autobiography', for a reading of *The Autobiography* through Lacan's theory of imaginary *méconnaissance*. While valuable, Halberstam's account of 'the transgender gaze' in *In a Queer Time* conflates it with the 'look'. I thus distinguish between these two facets of vision.
52. Salamon, *Assuming a Body*, p. 23.
53. Stimpson, 'Gertrude Stein and the Lesbian Lie', p. 318.
54. Schmitz, *Of Huck and Alice*, p. 216.
55. Hovey, *A Thousand Words*, p. 101.
56. Hovey, ibid., p. 101. See Gilmore, 'A Signature of Lesbian Autobiography', for a related analysis, and Nair, *Secrecy and Sapphic Modernism*, pp. 132–3, for an argument that Stein adhered to masculinist conceptions of 'genius' while destabilising the category of 'wife'. See Elliott and Wallace, *Women Artists and Writers*, p. 99, and Nair, ibid., for arguments that Stein positioned 'herself in ways that corresponded to prevailing myths of masculine genius' to which Hovey, *A Thousand Words*, and Will, *Gertrude Stein*, respond.
57. Stimpson, 'Gertrude Stein and the Transposition of Gender', p. 12; Stein, 'As A Wife Has A Cow A Love Story'.
58. Gilmore, 'A Signature of Lesbian Autobiography', p. 60, p. 68. See also Andersen, 'I Am Not Who "I" Pretend to Be'; Blackmer, 'Lesbian Modernism'; Meese, 'Gertrude Stein and Me'; Merrill 'Gertrude Stein and Autobiography'; Smith, *Subjectivity, Identity, and the Body*; and Will, *Gertrude Stein*, for different inflections of the argument that *The Autobiography* enacts the partners' split subjectivities. See Friedman, 'Women's Autobiographical Selves', for a discussion of the book as 'a lesbian rejection of the self as an isolate being' and as figuring Stein's and Toklas's 'fluid identity' (pp. 54–5).
59. Andersen, 'I Am Not Who "I" Pretend to Be', p. 30.
60. Norris, 'The "Wife" and the "Genius"', p. 86. Similarly stressing that the text positions Toklas not as a figure of 'martyrdom' but rather as a woman who found 'freedom' and feminist agency in her partnership with Stein, Caramello, *Henry James, Gertrude Stein*, p. 167, nonetheless presumes that the latter identified as an 'expatriate female genius' even as he refuses to devalue her writing or stigmatise her masculinity.
61. Norris, 'The "Wife" and the "Genius"', p. 86. Norris oddly insists that the book's '"separate but equal" representational politics' fails because contemporary readers are presumably uncomfortable 'positioning themselves as wives'; her suggestion that the book's gender politics remain

'valid only for the world of her text' ignores the contemporary resurgence of butch/femme lesbianism and the possibility that some heterosexual wives might identify with Toklas's marriage to Stein (p. 96).

62. Johnston, 'Narratologies of Pleasure', p. 596.
63. Schmitz, 'Portrait, Patriarchy, Mythos', p. 69; Schmitz, *Of Huck and Alice*, p. 204. In the former, Schmitz argues that the 'three portraits' of Stein in *The Autobiography* are the Gertrude of Picasso's portrait; the 'Gertrude's Alice's Gertrude' constructed by 'Toklas' as narrator; and Gertrude Stein as 'the I' who finally reveals her presence and 'seizes Alice's discourse' in the conclusion.
64. Norris, 'The "Wife" and the "Genius"', p. 88.
65. Stein, *The Autobiography*, p. 85.
66. Norris, 'The "Wife" and the "Genius"', p. 89.
67. Johnston, 'Narratologies of Pleasure', p. 597.
68. Roof, *What Gender Is*, p. 79.
69. Dickie, 'Recovering the Repression in Stein's Erotic Poetry', p. 6.
70. Dickie, ibid., p. 6. While Stein is 'open' about the importance of 'Ada' to her development, its queerness may not have been obvious to *The Autobiography*'s early readers.
71. Gilbert and Gubar, *No Man's Land, Vol. 2*, p. 241. Unfortunately, Gilbert and Gubar contradict their affirmative reading of Stein's genius by denouncing her treatment of Toklas; ibid., pp. 250–7. Though they acknowledge that Toklas 'used the role of subordinate to sustain her own power and serve her own ends', they do not sufficiently reflect on its implications for her and Stein's relationship (ibid., p. 253).
72. Stein, 'Portraits and Repetition', p. 180.
73. Will, *Gertrude Stein*, p. 137.
74. Will, ibid., p. 140.
75. Chessman, *The Public is Invited to Dance*, p. 6.
76. Stein, 'Portraits and Repetition', p. 180.
77. Norris, 'The "Wife" and the "Genius"', p. 88.
78. Chessman, *The Public is Invited to Dance*, pp. 63–7.
79. Norris, 'The "Wife" and the "Genius"', p. 88.
80. Stein, *The Autobiography*, p. 71. See Gilmore, 'A Signature of Lesbian Autobiography', for analysis of this aspect of Stein's writing.
81. See Smith, *Subjectivity, Identity, and the Body*, for a similar argument about *The Autobiography*.
82. Lubar, 'Unmasking Pablo's Gertrude', p. 57.
83. Lubar, ibid., p. 63.
84. Lubar, ibid., p. 57.
85. Stein, *The Autobiography*, p. 4.
86. In *The Language of Psycho-Analysis*, LaPlanche and Pontalis define Freudian *Nachträglichkeit* as the revision of 'past events at a later date'

that invests them with 'significance or even with efficacity or pathogenic force' (p. 112).

87. Chessman, *The Public is Invited to Dance*, p. 65.
88. Norris, 'The "Wife" and the "Genius"', p. 91.
89. Norris, ibid., p. 91.
90. Norris, ibid., p. 91.
91. Norris, ibid., pp. 88–9.
92. Stein, *The Autobiography*, p. 4.
93. Stein, ibid., p. 4.
94. Norris, 'The "Wife" and the "Genius"', pp. 96–7. See Caramello, *Henry James, Gertrude Stein*, pp. 119–68, for a similar discussion.
95. See especially Wagner-Martin, '*Favored Strangers*', for a correction to claims that Stein slighted women.
96. Caramello, *Henry James, Gertrude Stein*, pp. 161–2.
97. Sedgwick, *Touching Feeling*, p. 8.
98. See Curnutt, 'Inside and Outside'; Glass, *Authors Inc.*; Goldman, *Modernism is the Literature of Celebrity*; Jaillant, '*Shucks, we've got glamour girls too!*'; Leick, *Gertrude Stein and the Making of an American Celebrity*; Siraganian, 'Speculating on an Art Movement'; and Zox-Weaver, *Women Modernists and Fascism*, for further analysis of the strategies through which Stein promoted her celebrity.
99. Goldman, *Modernism is the Literature of Celebrity*, pp. 81–110.
100. Goldman, ibid., p. 94.
101. Goldman, ibid., p. 94.
102. Goldman, ibid., p. 94.
103. Sedgwick, *Touching Feeling*, p. 8.
104. See Corn and Latimer, *Seeing Gertrude Stein*, for a discussion of Heap's 'dandified masculine demeanor' (p. 184).
105. Stein, *The Autobiography*, p. 61.
106. Stein, ibid., p. 61.
107. Stein, ibid., p. 14. For discussion of Stein's early portraits of Stein and Matisse in light of their rivalry, see Recker, 'Pitting "Matisse" Against "Picasso"'.
108. Stein, *The Autobiography*, p. 14.
109. Stein, ibid., p. 14.
110. Sedgwick, *Touching Feeling*, p. 8.
111. Weiner and Young, 'Introduction: Queer Bonds', p. 225; Sedgwick, ibid., p. 8; Freeman, 'Introduction: Queer Temporalities', p. 163.
112. Stein, *The Autobiography*, p. 182.
113. Stein, ibid., p. 208.
114. Stein, ibid., p. 208.
115. Stein, ibid., p. 208.
116. Sedgwick, *Touching Feeling*, p. 8.

117. Stein, *The Autobiography*, p. 185.
118. Stein, ibid., pp. 203–4.
119. Sedgwick, *Touching Feeling*, p. 8.
120. Stein, *The Autobiography*, p. 204.
121. Stein, ibid., p. 204.
122. Stein, ibid., p. 203.
123. Bloom, *The Anxiety of Influence*. See Abranavel, 'Anglophones in Paris', p. 99, on how Hemingway retrospectively described his 'feud with Stein' in 'Oedipal' terms.
124. Stein, *The Autobiography*, p. 204.
125. Sedgwick, *Touching Feeling*, p. 8; Stein, ibid., p. 204.
126. Sedgwick, ibid., p. 8; Stein, *The Autobiography*, p. 204.
127. Stein, ibid., pp. 203–4.
128. Caramello, *Henry James, Gertrude Stein*, p. 161; Stein, *The Autobiography*, p. 208.
129. Stein, ibid., pp. 208–9.
130. Stein, ibid., p. 209.
131. Stein, ibid., p. 210.
132. See Richardson, *A Life of Picasso. Vol. III*, pp. 413–14, for an argument that Picasso's treatment of Cocteau was both 'loyal' and 'sadistic'.
133. Stein, *The Autobiography*, p. 210.
134. Stein, ibid., p. 182.
135. Stein, ibid., p. 44.
136. Stein, ibid., p. 53.
137. Stein, ibid., p. 53.
138. Lubar, 'Unmasking Pablo's Gertrude', p. 62.
139. Roof, *What Gender Is*, p. 79.
140. See especially Corn and Latimer, *Seeing Gertrude Stein*, pp. 139–52, for analysis of these networks. As Garrity and Latimer observe in 'Queer Cross-gender Collaboration', these friendships have rarely been studied and deserve further investigation.
141. Stimpson, 'Gertrude Stein and the Lesbian Lie', p. 317; Nair, *Secrecy and Sapphic Modernism*, pp. 145–51.
142. Stein, *The Autobiography*, p. 208.
143. Stein, ibid., p. 208. See Nair, *Secrecy and Sapphic Modernism*, pp. 144–7, for an argument that Stein praises Heap because she and Margaret Anderson helped facilitate the publication of Stein's work.
144. Dydo, *A Stein Reader*, p. 376. See also Corn and Latimer, *Seeing Gertrude Stein*.
145. Weiner and Young, 'Introduction: Queer Bonds', p. 225; Freeman, 'Introduction: Queer Temporalities', p. 163.

Chapter 5

Picasso's Stein/Stein's Picasso: Cubist Perspective/Masculine Homosociality

Stein's transmasculinity was refracted through her homosocial bonds with male colleagues – a process particularly visible in the visual and linguistic traces of her friendship with Picasso. Take, for instance, the jacket of Wendy Steiner's 1978 *Exact Resemblance to Exact Resemblance*, which features two images by Czech artist Jiří Kolář. The front displays a collage placing the head from Picasso's 1907 *Self-Portrait* over that of his 1905–6 *Portrait of Gertrude Stein* (Plate 1); the back offers a crumplage of the latter 'whose witty distortions', says Steiner, 'show Stein as Picasso might have painted her . . . when he was much deeper into the exploration of Cubist space and when Stein was composing her first verbal portrait of him'.[1] Steiner contends that Kolář's images 'celebrate the birth of modernist portraiture through a set of postmodernist devices: the mutual interplay of sitter and painter, the founding of image upon image upon image, the game of copying to achieve originality and uniqueness'.[2] However, Steiner's reading overlooks the way Kolář's images – and the works upon which they are founded – undercut notions of artistic 'originality', autonomy, genius and the stable genders on which those concepts depend.[3]

The substitution of Picasso's head for Stein's in the first of Kolář's images raises several questions about the dynamics of portraiture. We know that Picasso took brush to canvas and painted *Portrait of Gertrude Stein*; we also know that Stein took pen to paper and composed two portraits, 'Picasso' (1909–10: 1912) and 'If I Told Him' (1923: 1924). Yet these facts of composition belie the complexity of

Stein's and Picasso's exchanges. As Kolář suggests through collage, Picasso may have also been engaged in self-portraiture while painting Stein. And as Ulla Haselstein points out, Stein's verbal portraits were developed through a relational process of '"talking and listening"' that implicates them in the transference and renders her poems 'self portraits as well'.[4] Cope emphasises that this makes Stein and Picasso collaborators, complicating the claims to artistic autonomy, agency and originality on which conventional accounts of masculine genius are founded.[5]

As Johanna Drucker argues, Picasso 'embodied, for modernism, the very essence of artist/genius – he was a childhood prodigy, a foreign outsider, a male whose virility was flaunted in his biography and in his work (process and themes), whose inventiveness and originality were the trademarks of his productivity'.[6] He offered a modernist reshaping of the 'image of the artist with self-production as the central dynamic – disruptive, decentralizing, and resisting unity' – while simultaneously asserting 'his potency through the structuring activity of the visual space'.[7] Drucker asserts that '[m]uch of his output can be read in terms of a compensation for male performance anxiety', beginning with 'the original trauma represented by' the *Demoiselles d'Avignon* (1907, Plate 2) and continuing until his death.[8] Cope and Lubar similarly find gender anxiety in Picasso's reaction to Stein. Lubar offers a psychoanalytic mapping of the 'complex process of psychic transference' in Stein's and Picasso's exchange, reading her masked face in *Portrait of Gertrude Stein* as the trace of fears prompted by her strong presence.[9] Cope further argues that Stein's and Picasso's friendship entailed '*mésalliances* of gender' that are 'marked in and through' their 'works of art' and reveal ambivalence about their positions within modernist networks.[10] While Cope and Lubar rightly point to Stein's and Picasso's gender trouble, they rely on vague concepts such as anxiety and ambivalence that insufficiently illuminate the complications that arose during the writer's and painter's friendship.

Sedgwick argues that gender anxiety can emerge through the slippage between male homo*sociality* and male homo*sexuality*.[11] Weiner and Young further observe that in bonds 'in which the difficulty of specifying the location of "sexuality" is precisely what is at stake', the effort to go 'beyond sexual self-recognition' and 'identitarian positionings' results in an 'incommensurate' tie between those with 'irreducible' differences.[12] This formulation points to the possibility that the erotic undercurrents that subtended friendships such as Stein's and Picasso's produced a difficulty that went well beyond that of gender anxiety and exceeded available categories for identity. The 'slantwise' desires that emerged through their *méconnaissances* and '*mésalliances*' – as well as the differences between Picasso's hegemonic male masculinity and Stein's counterhegemonic transmasculinity – rendered their friendship volatile and contributed to their bonds' frays in ways taken up in the portraits.[13]

Ultimately, Stein's and Picasso's masculine homosocial desire was fraught in ways that produced the disorientations their portraiture exploits. It has long been established that Stein's use of perspective was influenced by the kinds of modernism practised by others in her network, especially Cézanne, Picasso and Georges Braque – all famous subjects of her poems. Like them, Stein uses form to invite multiple perspectives and reshape the reader's perception of objects. For Lubar, the act of portraiture involves a psychical exchange whose product serves as 'a trap for . . . the gaze'.[14] Because the gaze is subtended by fantasy, the scene of portraiture implicates visual and fantasmatic exchanges between sitter and painter.[15] In the gaze of the Other, the subject's confrontation with the other's look results in a 'disorganization of perception' that fragments representation and proliferates possibilities for looking.[16] Stein's *The Autobiography*, her portraits of her colleagues, and their portraits of her track this play between the 'look' and the 'gaze', self-consciously exploiting its perspectival multiplicity.

In cubist painting, 'meaning is relational, not intrinsic'; the vicissitudes of Stein's and her colleagues' homosocial bonds further their works' plays with the look and the gaze.[17] Their portraits of one another reveal the traces of their homosocial desire *and* the forms of *méconnaissance* that sometimes led their ties to fray. Alternately 'desiring, identifying, representing, repelling, paralleling, differentiating, rivaling, leaning, twisting, mimicking, withdrawing, attracting, aggressing' and 'warping', the psychical and formal effects of Stein's and Picasso's queer relationality were crucial to modernism's reorientations of language and vision.[18] Their bond's effects fragment perception in cubist painting and literature alike.[19] Much as *The Autobiography* destabilises the notion that its subjects are 'geniuses', so do Stein's and Picasso's portraits of one another undercut the concept of 'genius' by multiplying perspectives and shifting the gaze.[20]

As Silverman argues, 'the eye's transformative potentiality' enables the look to 'completely transform the value of what is originally seen' by highlighting 'oppositional and subcultural representations' and downplaying 'normative representations'.[21] Stein's and Picasso's portraits of one another deploy both 'normative' and 'oppositional' representations.[22] Picasso's masking of Stein's face reveals his fascination with and disturbance by her gendered and erotic differences from him – effects produced through and fractured by their homosocial bond.[23] Mobilising a hegemonic gaze, the portrait draws on techniques of masking from Iberian sculpture to construct her transmasculinity as primitive.[24] By contrast, Stein's portraits of Picasso perform a more complex work on masculinity, showing her affection and misgivings. Whereas 'Picasso' uses reiteration to inscribe her desire for the 'charming' painter and offer an implicit critique of primitivist representations in their earlier work, 'If I Told Him' inflects their homosociality by critiquing their masculinities.[25] Lovingly mocking both of their Napoleonic aspirations to genius, the latter portrait shifts the dominant gaze and proliferates counterhegemonic looks. The gender trouble instigated by their masculine homosocial bond ultimately produces a modernist multiperspectivalism that reveals gender and sexuality to be tenuous and shifting, subject to the vicissitudes of viewer and viewed alike.

Stein's and Picasso's masculine homosocial bond has long been visible, even though its relationship to their portraits' reorientations of perspective has been underappreciated. Accounts of their early friendship emphasise the strength of their initial attraction. Picasso's biographer John Richardson uses language that implicitly calls attention to their homosocial desire by slipping between the homosocial and the homosexual. He writes that upon Picasso's and Stein's first meeting, she 'was immediately attracted to this "good-looking bootblack", as he was to this extraordinarily intense and warm yet granite-like young woman with her striking unfeminine head and "deep temperamental life quality"'.[26] Richardson also notes Stein's masculinity, stating that she 'thought and acted like a modern-minded man – self-assured, forthright, disarmingly jovial'.[27] This highlights Stein's attraction to Picasso's youthful masculinity and his fascination by her gender. Fernande Olivier, Picasso's partner at the beginning of his and Stein's friendship, is even more explicit in stating that he was drawn to her 'physical personality': her intellect was 'lucid and organized, and her voice and her appearance were masculine'.[28] Art dealer Daniel-Henry

Kahnweiler suggests that these traits contributed to Stein's standing within her family and avant-garde networks: he asserts that of the Steins, Gertrude was 'the "great man" of the family'.[29] His language positions Stein as Picasso's equal within a construct of masculine 'genius' that her writings complicate.

Biographies of Picasso consistently depict a man whose collegial relationships were almost exclusively with men; his early letters to Stein use affectionate, masculinising language to describe her as well. On 31 March 1911, he addresses a postcard to 'Mademoiselle Gertrude Stein, man of letters', and on 8 January 1918 includes her with Guillaume Apollinaire and Braque as an 'old pal and pard'.[30] The latter gesture interpellates Stein into an avant-garde male 'cameraderie'.[31] Picasso's affinity for Stein led him to establish an 'elective brotherhood' and 'fraternity' with her but exclude Leo Stein.[32] Richardson compares the painter's interest in Gertrude to Hemingway's statement that '"Gertrude Stein and me are just like brothers"', and states that 'Picasso's feelings for Gertrude could also be described as fraternal.'[33] Picasso's folding of Stein into his avant-garde fraternity points to the masculine homosocial nature of their ties.

Theirs was a complicated homosociality, though, because Stein's transmasculinity simultaneously supported and troubled the homosocial order that would define her as an object of exchange between men. Her strategy for pursuing her literary aspirations set her apart from most women modernists drawn to early twentieth-century Paris: she maintained friendships with them while joining a male-driven avant-garde.[34] Corn and Latimer thus interpret Picasso's 1909 *Homage a Gertrude* (Plate 3) – a painting of several women designed for Stein's and Toklas's bedroom ceiling – as staging their shared alliance with masculine modernism.[35] *The Autobiography* also highlights Stein's active participation in her network's circuits of masculine homosocial desire. However, as Caramello argues, the text simultaneously pushes back against the tendency of Matisse's and Picasso's 'patriarchal painting' toward 'abstracting women' and the female body.[36] Stein's involvement in a predominantly male avant-garde incorporated her attraction to women and refused the desire to be a male artist's object or drop out from the circle of exchange entirely. Tamar Garb therefore argues that *Homage a Gertrude* points to her and Picasso's common love for women, yet as Pierre Daix emphasises, he shared not only homosocial bonds but also space and female lovers with his male colleagues.[37] Stein was no object of exchange, nor did she position Toklas as the object of masculine homosocial rivalry. Stein's transmasculinity distinguishes her and Picasso's masculine homosocial bond from the ties 'between men' that are Sedgwick's subject.[38]

This 'internal rupture within' modernism's economy of gender and sexuality animated the vicissitudes of Stein's and Picasso's friendship.[39] His reactions to her show a move from 'desiring' to 'differentiating' and 'withdrawing' – a shift from respecting her writing to devaluing it for artistic and personal reasons.[40] His initial response to her work was effusive albeit narcissistic: upon the publication of her first portrait of him in 1912, he wrote that 'you will be the glory of America'.[41] However, his enthusiasm for her writing waxed and waned. Kahnweiler takes Picasso's failure to complete his promised illustrations for Stein's *Birthday Book* between 1924 and 1929 as a form of 'passive resistance' driven by his sense of artistic individuality and hesitance to collaborate, even on a volume dedicated to his son Paulo.[42] Others claim the painter looked down on Stein because he harboured reservations about her claim to practise literary cubism. For example, Richardson quotes one of Picasso's sceptical statements about her – that '"With lines and colors one can make patterns, but if one doesn't use words according to their meaning, they aren't words at all"' – as evidence that he viewed her as inferior.[43] Richardson also questionably cites Stein's tentative assertion that '"Pablo and Matisse have a maleness that belongs to genius . . . *Moi aussi* perhaps"' as evidence that her claim to genius was quite thin.[44] These readings highlight the difference between Stein's identificatory 'parallelling' and 'mimicking' of Picasso and his 'differentiating' and 'withdrawing' from her.[45]

These reactions to Stein's persona overlook the ways the art world and publishing industry systematically advantaged Picasso and disadvantaged her: a dynamic she subtly critiques in *The Autobiography*, as Caramello observes.[46] The possibility that she could have been a legitimate rival against whom the painter struggled does not register in these responses. Nor do they consider that the role of this 'not-quite-woman' as one of Picasso's first buyers and champions might have made him uncomfortable because it undermined claims to his artistic autonomy.[47] Nor does Lubar, who calls attention to Picasso's struggle with Stein's power, fully illuminate the way her aspiration to masculine genius – and thus to a status that rivalled the painter's – was likely also at stake in their exchange.[48] As Cope argues, Stein's and Picasso's efforts to claim the role of self-sustaining genius animate the gender trouble at work in their masculine homosociality.[49] As their reservations about their ties grew, their portraits of one another mixed 'desiring' and 'paralleling' with 'withdrawing' and 'differentiating'.[50] The resulting 'warping[s]' reveal traces of their affectionate but unsteady friendship.[51]

Picasso's Stein

These forces inform Picasso's *Portrait of Gertrude Stein*, which assaults hegemonic perspective while sustaining a dominant gaze that invites viewers to fear Stein's masculinity. Although Picasso was drawn to Stein, her masculine persona stymied the assumptions about gender underpinning his approach to portraiture. As Sayre observes, Picasso often engages the erotic dimensions of the 'ambiguous relation between the artist and his model': a 'deeply problematized terrain, in which questions of representation were fully and openly implicated in questions of sexual politics, questions of power and control, mastery and desire'.[52] Stein removed herself from the position of feminised 'object' and took up 'the masculine position' even as she 'submitted herself' to Picasso's painterly look.[53] Thus, despite their initial attraction, *Portrait of Gertrude Stein* registers his misgivings about her gender.

Portrait of Gertrude Stein therefore 'represents a moment when the rupture of conventional pictorial and sexual codes intersects and destabilizes systems of representation and notions of identity', as Garb observes.[54] This leads to several conflicting consequences for the look and the gaze. Downplaying her women's fashions – her ruffled blouse and bun, for example – Picasso draws on well-established conventions to depict her posture as masculine. His portrayal of her robe was likely modelled on Auguste Rodin's 1898 *Monument to Balzac*, which shows its subject in similar garb.[55] The monk's robe appears frequently in sculptures of nineteenth-century male artists and gives 'its wearer a monumental physical presence' not associated with women of the time.[56] Picasso thus suggests that Stein uses the robe to signify masculinity. His painting also poses her solid frame in the 'reverse' position of the 'authoritative' stance taken by Louis-François Bertin in Jean Auguste Dominique Ingres's 1832 portrait.[57] The 'corpulence' and 'dominance of pictorial space' shown in Ingres's picture of Bertin are nineteenth-century signifiers of men's success.[58] Moreover, Picasso places Stein's hands on her knees in a masculine fashion.[59] The only overtly feminine signifiers in the painting are her brooch and ruffled shirt. The latter was typically feminine clothing at the time, but also resembles the white shirt and collar Bertin wears in Ingres's painting. Beyond these details, there are no feminine trappings in Picasso's portrait, which plays up Stein's masculine stance.

Foregrounding this masculinity, Lubar presents Picasso's Stein as even more imposing than Ingres's Bertin: her 'pose is more dynamic' than his, and she 'appears to exceed the spatial boundaries of the picture' whereas he does not.[60] Stein's hand also contrasts to Bertin's: a 'prosthetic phallus', the former's 'limp' appearance signifies and neutralises Picasso's fears of her masculinity.[61] Lubar thus argues that Stein's 'adoption of masculine norms' provoked a sense of 'symbolic castration' that called Picasso's gender identity into question and stalled his completion of the head on her portrait.[62] In a delayed reaction, he finished the picture several months later, pushing past his blockage by painting Stein's head as a mask. The mask 'marks Pablo's recognition of Gertrude's power, but also his refusal to see', for its 'dark, cavernous openings for eyes' avoid meeting her look.[63] The mask's formal fracturings challenge dominant ways of using perspective to mobilise the gaze and serve as 'trace[s]' of Picasso's trepidation over Stein's challenge to gender norms.[64] These effects go well beyond anxiety, however, by psychically and formally enacting the 'twisting' and 'warping' Sedgwick finds in queer relationality.[65]

These queer effects are also engendered by the primitivist formal borrowings that have made *Portrait of Gertrude Stein* and the paintings that came in its wake so troubling. As Susanna Pavloska and Walker have shown, Picasso's use of Iberian sculptures as models for Stein's masked face initiates the painting's rupture from the conventions of realism and modernism's break from nineteenth-century forms.[66] Reading Picasso's 1947 reflection on an early visit to the Musée d'Ethnographie du Trocadéro, Cheng argues – without denying primitivism's 'invidious appropriation' – that his 'act of painting "seizes power" *not* by dispelling threats but by "giving form" to terror and desire'.[67] Painting does not defend the boundaries of the subject against external menaces but instead 'congeals . . . the memory of violence' by transforming the artwork into an 'artifact' of 'desire and its trauma'.[68]

Yet if in the Trocadéro, Picasso's traumatic encounter with modernism's 'imperial origins' cracked open 'sites of contamination that point to other kinds of relationality' that cannot 'be easily categorized', and thereby created an opening for modern art's formal innovations, his encounter with Stein – while inflected through Iberian sculpture – also entailed other forms of shock.[69] As the circuits of his homosocial desire were jolted by Stein's similarities to and differences from male masculinity, Picasso called upon his memory of being 'sickened' by 'the residue of imperial violence' at the Trocadéro to give form to both traumas and register his disturbance by the masculinity that initially attracted him.[70] By treating Stein's masculinity as traumatic primitivism, Picasso reveals a significant difference from her. Unlike Stein, he does not embrace self-shattering jouissance, thrilled that 'the master' has fallen to 'pieces'.[71] Rather than exclaiming 'oh yes' to that possibility and revelling in powerlessness, Picasso defends against the challenge to his gender system implied by his attraction to her masculinity, transforming his shock into cubism's aesthetic innovations.[72]

The distortions of traditional perspective that resulted from this act have divergent effects. By using masking to contend with Stein's masculinity, Picasso's *Portrait of Gertrude Stein* draws upon primitivist style to innovate in aesthetic form and challenge hegemonic ways of looking. As Sayre argues, Picasso thereby suggests that Stein assumes 'the masculine position' as 'a kind of mask, a free-floating signifier laid upon something entirely other'.[73] Yet the '"transvestite" look' that results 'does not so much transform the feminine position as it does submit the masculine position . . . to the level of discourse'.[74] As a result, *Portrait of Gertrude Stein* inspired the literary inflection of masking at work in *Three Lives* and Stein's 'assumption of the identity of Alice B. Toklas' in *The Autobiography*, a text whose gendered masks figure and affirm Stein's and Toklas's lived genders.[75] Moreover, *Portrait of Gertrude Stein* initiated the technique of masking that pushed Picasso toward analytic cubism, and – much later – toward synthetic cubism's strategies of collage. On a formal level, these innovations challenge hegemonic ways of looking.

On the level of content, however, Picasso's *Portrait of Gertrude Stein* supports rather than contests the way gender and sexuality are constructed by the dominant gaze. Picasso's primitivist masking of Stein's face heightens the portrait's inflection of the fears incited by her masculinity. Cope suggests that whether consciously or unconsciously, Picasso was 'seduced' by Stein's 'presence' and in crisis over his own gender while 'painting and repainting' her face.[76] When '*Faced with Stein, he felt compelled to return to some "primitive" or primal experiences, open himself up to something quite unsettling, forceful, delirious, strange*' – and produced the first of his cubist distortions by masking her face.[77] This mask's primitivism metonymically invokes Stein's heavy robe. A 'sartorial form of primitivizing', this garment was a sign of Stein's masculinity and part of a 'bohemian style of dress' she and other avant-garde figures adopted as everyday attire in the first decade of the twentieth century.[78] Even as it challenges dominant visual aesthetics, *Portrait of Gertrude Stein* mobilises and heightens the effects of a hegemonic gaze that associates her masculinity with primitivism.

However, it is not enough to note – as does Lubar – that Picasso's nervousness about Stein's gender made *Portrait of Gertrude Stein* a pivotal work in the history of modern art; that the portrait marks Picasso's first foray into analytic cubism; and that the picture initiates an aesthetic shift that culminated in *Les Demoiselles*, whose primitivism has prompted even more controversy than *Portrait of Gertrude Stein*.[79] Nor is it enough to point out, as does Cope, that 'painting the portrait of Stein allowed Picasso access to a different bodily form': '[l]iteral, massive, not-quite-right, not-quite-or-more-than-a-woman, Stein spoke a language and gestured toward the expression of a gender unknown to Picasso until he met her'.[80] None of these claims address the vicissitudes of masculine homosocial desire that contributed to Picasso's simultaneous attraction to and inability to grapple with Stein's gender. Alternately 'desiring', 'repelling', 'differentiating', 'twisting', 'withdrawing', 'attracting', 'aggressing' and 'warping', Picasso's queer 'relations' with Stein drew upon negativity to mixed effect.[81] Her '"slantwise"' relation to gender norms led to 'irreducible' differences between her and Picasso, ultimately making their queer relationality 'incommensurate'.[82] These relational difficulties were productive in some ways: their 'twisting' and 'warping' prompted modern art's aesthetic innovations.[83] Yet in other ways, these problems were counterproductive, contributing to the portrait's failure fully to shift the gaze through which Stein's masculinity is presented for view.

Despite the role of his misgivings about Stein's masculinity in fraying their homosocial desire, Picasso's portrait was a key moment in the development of her masculine image. Corn and Latimer note that 'at some point between her college days and her portrait by Picasso, Stein became *Gertrude Stein*': 'a singular figure, an intense intellectual, a talkative and fearless émigrée, an original dresser, a Jew, an American, an *hommesse*'.[84] One of the earliest images that recognises and registers Stein's transmasculinity, Picasso's *Portrait of Gertrude*

Stein traces within the visible an identification that was, at the time of her sitting, cloaked in her androgynous robe's subtle masculinity. Stein recognised herself in the gaze constituted by the painting, approving of it in 1906.

In 1938, Stein reaffirmed that she was 'satisfied' with Picasso's portrait, declaring that 'for me, it is I, and it is the only reproduction of me which is always I, for me'.[85] She compared the experience of looking at Picasso's style to the way the 'child sees the face of its mother': 'the child sees it from very near, it is a large face for the eyes of a small one, it is certain the child for a little while only sees a part of the face of its mother, it knows one feature and not another, one side and not the other', much like the viewer of a cubist painting.[86] As Garb observes, this describes a relational experience in which the viewer's sensory encounter with 'charged fragments' is more important than understanding the whole.[87] It also shows Stein's 'acknowledgement' of the portrait's exposure 'of the fissure between image and referent, organ and sense', that revealed her 'complex splitting of subjectivity' and anticipated her own writings.[88] In the kaleidoscopic vision mobilised by *The Autobiography*'s split narration, the potentially 'oppressive meaning' of Picasso's 'capture' of Stein's image is 'displaced' and thereby freed from 'Picasso's frame of reference'.[89] As we are reminded as we step through the doorways reframing Stein's image – and Picasso's vision – in *The Autobiography*'s second chapter, in 1926 she took on her iconic 'Caesar' haircut.[90] In so doing, Stein made visible and explicit the masculinity Picasso's portrait only intimated. This change in look shifted the gaze through which her gender was presented for view.

Stein's Picasso

Stein suggests in *The Autobiography* that her cropped hairstyle forced Picasso to look at her anew and recognise that despite her new image, 'all the same it [his portrait] is there'.[91] Her new haircut caused him to assume 'the transvestite look' and reorient the gaze through which he saw Stein and her role in modernism.[92] Yet even before her crop and *The Autobiography*, her portraits of fellow modernists shifted the gaze through which they – and she – were given to be seen. If Picasso's portrait of Stein introduced cubism to the world by attempting to thwart her masculine look, her textual responses offer traces of her look in its imbrication with his. As Glavey notes, Stein's portraiture is relational, encouraging 'us to relate to it the way we might relate to an autonomous individual as opposed to an autonomous artifact'.[93] At the same time, Stein's portraits split the subject. Asking their readers to swap 'an eye for an I' and shift between different sensory modes, these texts refuse 'closure' and 'the illusion of coherence', paralleling Lacan's work.[94] The masculine homosocial desires animating Stein's counterhegemonic look at Picasso are thus put into play yet fragmented within her portraits of him. These poems make Picasso available for view from multiple angles and challenge the hegemonic gaze that abjects Stein's masculinity.

Just as Picasso's portrait of Stein is influenced by his desire for her, Stein's portraiture is inflected by her psychical investments in her subjects; it traces out her desire for and identification with powerful figures of the male avant-garde. As Haselstein observes, Stein's writing has a different 'aesthetic objective' than that of the cubist painters in that she 'upheld the notion of the portrait as a psychological analysis of the individual, whereas the cubists . . . restricted themselves to the visual representation of the face and body'.[95] While Lubar rightfully demonstrates that Picasso's portrait of Stein registered the effects of the transference that emerged during her sittings, this was an inadvertent consequence of the painter's work rather than its aim.[96] Stein, by contrast, describes composition as driven by a relational interplay of '"talking and listening"'.[97] Because Stein's writing process is explicitly relational and implicates the transference, Haselstein views her portraiture as a medium for the 'circulation of social power and the narcissistic erotics of self-presentation'.[98] Stein's poems about her colleagues register 'intersubjective perception and recognition', revealing the 'emotional and artistic nexus of friendship and enmity, patronage, competition, and solidarity that had developed' between her and the painters.[99] Stein's and her colleagues' masculine homosocial bonds are among the social factors implicated in these intersubjective exchanges. Her and Picasso's portraits of one another may thus be read as artefacts of the transference at work in their masculine homosociality.

Although Stein's work involves a literary 'mimicking' of cubist painting, differences between language and paint produce divergent effects.[100] Stein's portraiture uses language to reshape the gaze through which her and her colleagues' masculinities are made available for view. This linguistic emphasis distinguishes her work from that of her colleagues in the visual arts and allows her to inscribe their masculine homosocial bonds in her own way. As Perloff notes,

Stein takes 'words out of their usual contexts and create[s] new relationships among them', suspending grammatical conventions and prompting readers to decontextualise and recontextualise individual words.[101] She takes from Cézanne the notion that 'in composition one thing was as important as another thing' and from cubism the idea that 'every perspective is as operationally important as every other'.[102] This strategy enables Stein to prompt readers to see her subjects anew – though she does so through different means and to different ends than modern paintings. The resulting incommensurability subtended Stein's and Picasso's aesthetic differences and distinct 'positions' with regard to gender and sexuality.[103] Eager to differentiate himself from the masculine Stein and reduce any appearance of genuine rivalry, Picasso distanced himself from her literary cubism and discredited her project rather than looking for signs of its novelty – for the ways it may have reiterated his own aesthetic strategies with a transformative difference.[104]

However, there are limits to the innovations Stein achieves by drawing on Cézanne to shift the gaze through which her masculine homosocial bonds can be seen. Walker observes that Stein's literary imitation of Cézanne uses primitivism to break away from dominant nineteenth-century literary realism.[105] Much as Picasso's portrait of Stein uses primitive style to register his troubled reaction to her transmasculinity, her portraits use a similar – though not identical – strategy to offer a trace of her initial response to him. However, like Picasso's primitivism – which contributes to his paintings' formal innovations while leaving dominant racial and gender biases unchallenged – Stein's stylistic primitivism does not always reshape dominant ways of seeing. While scholarly opinion is divided about whether her use of 'verbal styles . . . that were despised as primitive' challenges or exacerbates stereotypes of race and gender, the text in which those constructs are most explicit – 'Melanctha' – mobilises a discourse on gender and race that does not contest dubious claims about black women's purported hypersexuality.[106] Stein's work thus does not thwart all culturally overdetermined 'ways of seeing' any more than Picasso's *Demoiselles*; instead, 'Melanctha' sustains the primitivist gaze and aligns with Picasso's hegemonically masculine angle of view.[107] Stein's portraits of Picasso, by contrast, deploy primitivist styles stripped of *Three Lives*' racialising elements, deriving their form from the aesthetic challenges Stein and others faced in apprehending Picasso's paintings. Less rocked by 'trauma' than

Picasso's *Portrait of Gertrude Stein* was by her, Stein's portraits of him draw on primitive stylistics to stress the 'identifying', 'paralleling' and 'mimicking' characterising her desire for him while only subtly registering her misgivings.[108]

Stein's portraits of Picasso nonetheless shift the gaze through which their homosocial bond and divergent masculinities are made visible. In so doing, her texts offer a different angle from which to look at their friendship and exceed the painter's challenge to dominant systems of representation. Her poems' insistence on each word's equal value mobilises a gaze ungoverned by hegemonic genders and desires. Stein's portraits thereby make possible a variety of looks and actively support counterhegemonic ways of seeing that contest the dominant gaze.[109] This process allows Steinian portraiture to challenge not only the prevailing aesthetic tenets of realism but also the ideologies of gender and sexuality at work in dominant modes of vision. In so doing, Stein's portraits of Picasso offer a different way of looking at their fractured homosocial alliance than does his portrait of her. However, her two poems about him handle desire and masculinity quite differently.

Stein's 'Picasso' (1909–10: 1912)

Stein's masculine homosocial desire subtends 'Picasso', which concerns responses to the painter and his work. Stein began composing 'Picasso' while sitting for *Portrait of Gertrude Stein*; their open-ended dialogue informs her text's approach to its subject.[110] Her homosocial desire for Picasso is implicated in the process of perception that registers in the portrait, revealing her '"slantwise" orientation' with respect to 'existing social structures'.[111] Although the poem goes beyond Stein's perspective to track the painter's reception in modernist Paris, her masculine homosocial desire for him functions as 'the site of a symbolic disruption . . . and a particular relational inventiveness' inflecting the formal features through which the text offers multiple ways of looking.[112] The shifting relationality fostered by Paris's modernist networks is evident not only in the portrait's thematic content – which emphasises from the outset that 'some were certainly following . . . one who was completely charming' – but also in the text's mobilisation of perspective.[113] Refusing to describe Picasso as an object, Stein's portrait treats 'meaning' as 'relational' and uses reiteration to highlight the divergent ways he is viewed.[114]

Garb argues that Picasso's *The Architect's Table* (1912, Plate 4) is similarly relational, incorporating a 'reworking, in stippled paint, of Gertrude Stein's calling card' to 'flatter her' and encourage her continued patronage.[115] Moreover, Garb suggests that this painting mimics the style of Stein's 'Picasso'. With 'the straight lines and right angles of the set square . . . dispersed across the picture so that its character as an object is mimicked in the reiteration of its rectilinear shape throughout the oval canvas', *The Architect's Table* deploys '[a] straight thing, a square thing, a scattered thing' to demonstrate that 'the character of the tool is undermined even as its indispensability is demonstrated'.[116] So too, is meaning's stability undercut by the picture's reorientation of perspective. Because Stein's name is 'painted at an angle', *The Architect's Table* suggests that '[t]hings cannot easily be named and names do not easily adhere to things, least of all when identities and sexualities are at stake'.[117]

Picasso's and Stein's 'slantwise' homosocial desire for one another thus carries back and forth between his paintings and her writings from this period in a *mise-en-abîme* of imitation.[118] As Walker argues, Stein's texts from this time use a 'limited' vocabulary to create 'a heightened surface texture that both asserts its own poetic qualities and creates a network of semantic associations, independent of syntax'.[119] Some of these writings were composed during Picasso's '"grey period," the years between 1910 and 1912 when he was producing his most austere cubist canvases' by limiting 'his palette to shades of gray and ocher', but others – such as 'Picasso' – were written earlier and may have influenced his tonal restrictions.[120] Stein's textual practices and Picasso's visual techniques force readers out of their ordinary patterns of reading and looking, producing multiple perspectives and 'sensory transposition[s]' that trace the play between the look and the gaze.[121] Stein thereby uses musical elements to register 'the "rhythm" of Picasso's "personality"', presenting his creative process 'as an insistent series of near-repetitions'.[122] The portrait thus raises 'the question of the rhythm or production of' Picasso's 'appearance', drawing on senses that animate his creativity to mobilise the shifts in perception attending his work's reception.[123]

These divergent ways of looking are animated by Stein's masculine homosocial desire. She was 'charming and flirtatious', solicitous of 'male attention' despite her attraction to women.[124] Though she does not inscribe herself as 'I' within her first portrait of Picasso, as the third-person narrator she implicitly stages herself as somebody 'following' the 'charming' painter.[125] Mirroring her own charm with that of her subject, she inscribes her desire for him in the text. The piece begins with an incantation identifying Picasso as a 'completely charming' individual that 'some were certainly following'.[126] Reiterating several permutations of 'charming', 'certainly' and 'following' in the opening paragraph, Stein portrays Picasso as drawing many followers.[127] As Haselstein suggests, Stein's stance toward her subject is one of 'absorbed . . . adoration' – at least in the opening passages.[128] By engaging the process of perception and therefore the transference, she combines 'the subject and the object of portraiture'.[129] Stein's absorption contrasts with the 'warping' in Picasso's *Portrait of Gertrude Stein*.[130] Animating desires for Picasso that include but exceed the homosocial and homosexual, the portrait's opening positions her in an affectionate rather than a conflicted relationship to him.

However, the portrait cannot be reduced to Stein's own viewpoint or desire for the painter. Instead, the piece mixes her look with the dominant gaze to track Picasso's shifting reception, tracing out the dynamics of the desires that circle around him while refusing to indicate their nature or the genders of those experiencing them.[131] Are these desires aesthetic, professional, sexual, or some combination thereof? Leaving the gender of Picasso's admirers and the nature of what is 'coming out of him' unspecified, the portrait encourages a plurality of readings and views of the painter.[132] Facilitating both hegemonic and counterhegemonic looks, the poem mobilises multiple perspectives and trajectories of desire.

As the portrait progresses and angles for looking proliferate, reiteration linguistically enacts cubist shifts of perspective. Yet reading involves a different experience of time than viewing cubist painting, which does not steer the reader through time. Stein's portrait of Picasso guides the reader through an opening invocation of the painter 'charming' his 'following' and then through a dynamic depiction of him 'working' on 'something', the meaning of which is never as 'clear' nor as 'solid' as she teases us into believing because that 'meaning' shifts depending on the verbal context of the 'thing'.[133] As Garb observes, 'the object of creation' in this portrait 'cannot be named' because, '[l]ike a fragment in a Cubist painting, its meaning is relational, not intrinsic'.[134] The object of Stein's aesthetic and homosocial desires – and of other followers' varied desires – thus proves elusive.

Illustrating Picasso's view that 'he who created a thing is forced to make it ugly', the resulting image shades into the abject halfway through the portrait: the 'solid', 'charming' and 'lovely' thing 'coming out of' Picasso becomes simultaneously 'lovely', 'perplexing' and 'disconcerting'; 'simple', 'clear' and 'complicated'; 'interesting', 'disturbing', 'repellent' and 'pretty'.[135] These cadences also animate Stein's 1938 account of Picasso's deliberate production of the 'ugly' and its ability to shift the gaze through which art is given to be seen. She writes that 'In the effort to create the intensity and the struggle to create this intensity, the result always produces a certain ugliness, those who follow can make of this thing a beautiful thing because they know what they are doing, the thing having already been invented.'[136] With the benefit of hindsight, Stein suggests that initial disapproval of Picasso's work eventually shifted to approval – and to the emergence of cubism as a major artistic movement – because followers remained open to this new way of seeing even as they were discomfited by it. As she notes, 'a picture may seem extraordinarily strange to you and after some time not only it does not seem strange but it is impossible to find what there was in it that was strange'.[137]

Stein's 'Picasso' portrait registers the dynamics attending the first stage of this process of reception. Tracking the modes of Stein's and Picasso's queer 'relations' – and generalising them to all of the latter's 'following' – the poem first stresses 'desiring' and 'attracting' then highlights 'warping' and 'repelling'.[138] The temporality of Stein's sentences emphasises these paradoxical incursions of the abject, pointing to Picasso's challenges to hegemonic ideas about aesthetic beauty and social acceptability. This produces shocks within the flows of aesthetic, social and sexual desire that cause the piece's shifts in perspective to enact a different – and more indeterminate – form of 'warping' than the gender trouble in Picasso's portrait of Stein.[139] Unlike Picasso's painting, which presents Stein as masculine yet masks his fears about her strength, her portrait of him suggests a different trajectory of desire and gives readers few hints about the reasons for her misgivings.

Written in the wake of Picasso's *Portrait of Gertrude Stein* and *Demoiselles* as well as her own 'Melanctha', Stein's 'Picasso' tracks the way she and her contemporaries were both attracted to and disturbed by these troublingly primitivist representations. Although 'Picasso' uses primitivist style to trace these reactions, it does not reproduce the racial stereotypes driving 'Melanctha', whose 'wandering' protagonist enjoys more sexual agency than the prostitutes confined by the male gaze of Picasso's *Demoiselles.*[140] Shifting the site of shock and 'trauma' into the aesthetic realm, 'Picasso' implicitly critiques early racist routings of Stein's and Picasso's masculine homosocial desire.[141] Although it does not explicitly refuse readers' sexist, homophobic or racist approaches, 'Picasso' shifts the gaze in a way *Portrait of Gertrude Stein*, *Les Demoiselles* and 'Melanctha' do not. Eschewing problematic racial representations, 'Picasso' emphasises the troubled reactions of the followers whose desire Picasso initially attracted. In so doing, the text's paradoxical language speaks to cubism's fracturing of perspective and shattering of aesthetic conventions. These twists are enabled by the language through which the portrait opens the viewing process to multiple vectors of desire and by its sudden turn from positive to equivocal affect.

From this point forward, the portrait's language becomes less positive than at the beginning, and everybody becomes less active: though 'some' people are 'still following' Picasso, he is not consistently 'working' even though the 'things' he produces still have 'meaning'.[142] By the end, Picasso is 'almost always working', 'not ever completely working', and 'not one working to have anything coming out of him'.[143] Even though '[h]e always did have something come out of him', it does have 'meaning', and '[s]ome were certainly following him', the portrait ends with the statement that '[h]e was not ever completely working'.[144] This emphasis on Picasso's lags in 'working' and diminishing 'following' focuses attention on his artistic output and shifting status as the object of others' desires.

Stein's 'Picasso', then, tracks her initial attraction to but eventual disappointment in the 'one who was completely charming', showing her mixed feelings about the person by whom she was initially 'charm[ed]'.[145] Although it is animated by Stein's masculine homosocial desire, this text is not overtly about Picasso's gender. Instead, Stein points to Picasso's capacity to 'disturb' his followers and suggests that a representational impasse causes his and their flagging energy.[146] This crisis is aesthetic, calling dominant notions of beauty into question, but is also gendered and sexual. By using the shifting vicissitudes of Stein's desire for the painter to track his 'charming' of his followers, 'Picasso' interrogates the libidinal implications of modernism's shocks to representation.[147]

To do so, 'Picasso' stages its subject as a significant individual being followed, positioning him as an autonomous genius. However, the portrait's gradual turn from 'desiring' to 'warping' and 'repelling' subtly challenges his role as the Great Man who led a network of struggling artists at the beginning of the century and later came to dominate the modernist art world.[148] In this poem, Picasso's diminution relates to the uneven patterns of production that reduce his 'following' and fray circuits of desire, including Stein's.[149] This 'symbolic disruption', both sexual and aesthetic, enables Picasso's and the text's 'inventiveness', shifting affect and perspective by fracturing his and Stein's masculine homosocial bond.[150]

Stein's 'If I Told Him: A Completed Portrait of Picasso' (1923: 1924)

Stein's 'Picasso' reveals frays in their masculine homosocial bond that foreshadow their friendship's twists and turns. It hit a rough patch after World War I, but recovered by early 1923, when Stein and Toklas visited Picasso in Antibes.[151] While there, Stein and Picasso so effectively 'stimulated' each other's creativity 'that everyone felt recharged'.[152] This relational energy animates Stein's work from that year, from 'As A Wife Has A Cow' to 'If I Told Him'. Linda Voris rightfully observes that the latter poem's 'method' depends upon 'myriad transitive relations'.[153] Although she sees this relationality as purely formal, I consider it to be inextricable from, yet not entirely defined by, the interpersonal relations that prompted it. As Haselstein explains, because Stein's texts from this period are mutually implicated, 'If I Told Him' can be read as 'an interior monologue by Stein on her relationship with Picasso'.[154] The poem's tone is affectionate yet its content is playfully equivocal: more openly so than the earlier portrait, written before Picasso's career was well established. Consequently, Stein's later portrait is more explicit than its predecessor in working through the varied implications of their masculine homosocial bond. In so doing, the text shifts the gaze through which Stein's and Picasso's masculinities are presented for view.

Opening with a question reiterated through chiasmus and punctuated with full stops rather than question marks – 'If I told him would he like it. Would he like it if I told him.' – the second portrait immediately interpellates both Stein and Picasso, interrogating and destabilising their masculine homosocial bond.[155] The text incorporates multiple substitutions of 'Napoleon' for 'he' within reiterations of the opening question. As Thompson notes, 'the close proximity of the two names' – 'Picasso' and 'Napoleon' – hints at 'associations between the two men' that the reader must actively interpret.[156] The portrait's opening affectionately mocks and questions Picasso's masculinity by comparing him to 'Napoleon', an icon of overweening masculinity and a significant model for nineteenth-century writers' understandings of 'genius'.[157] Moreover, as Amy Blau observes, Stein compares herself to 'Napoleon' because she and Picasso were both '"kings" of their respective movements in art'.[158] 'If I Told Him' therefore both inscribes and examines her masculinity in relation to Picasso's.

Because the poem teases Picasso about his Napoleonic qualities, Will describes 'If I Told Him' as an 'assault on male "genius"'.[159] However, I hear both negatives and positives in the portrait, which establishes Stein's and Picasso's masculine homosocial alliance while playfully referencing their heterogendered sexual orientations. Appearing within the relational movements of texts 'in which the difficulty of specifying the location of "sexuality" is precisely what is at stake', the portrait's rhythms echo the orgasmic waves of 'As A Wife Has A Cow' even as they figure what Dydo calls 'Picasso's creative energy', 'conquering armies', fragile 'power, . . . fickle sexuality, misogyny, and flattery'.[160] Yet Dydo misses Stein's implication in questioning these qualities. She, too, possessed an immense 'creative energy', charm and imperial masculinity even though she lacked Picasso's 'armies' of institutional support.[161] By the middle of the 1920s, she sported what critics frequently describe as her 'Caesar' haircut – a name that, like 'Napoleon', connotes military masculinity and appears along with 'cow' as a signifier for queer eroticism in her writings.[162]

However, transmasculinities and cisgender male masculinities often differ; tonal dissonance within 'If I Told Him' interrogates not only Picasso's posture as a 'male genius' but also its similarities to and divergences from Stein's transmasculinity.[163] Her masculinity signifies differently than his because it is situated '"slantwise" . . . in relation to existing social structures'.[164] Published in tandem with 'If I Told Him', 'As A Wife Has A Cow' reverses the dynamic of *The Autobiography*, which uses Toklas's look to focus on Stein, and is driven by a speaker who backgrounds her own subjectivity to stress the 'cows' enjoyed by her 'wife'.[165] By attending to her partner's pleasure, the imperial Stein differs significantly from Picasso, whose misogyny even sympathetic biographers consider to have undermined 'most of his relationships with women'.[166] Stein's and Picasso's differences inflect their masculine homosocial bond, producing multiple perspectives.

'If I Told Him' works through affinities and divergences between Stein's and Picasso's masculinities, intensifying the first portrait's pared-down style, heightening attention to sound, and foregrounding 'the arrangement of words in compositional space'.[167] Voris thus argues that 'If I Told Him' provides 'a model for looking that was not looking for resemblance or verisimilitude but looking for the composition of relations and therefore a spatial homology for composition'.[168] She notes that like cubist painting, Stein's portraits exploit 'referential details' semiotically for non-referential purposes through 'intratextual elaboration'.[169] However, Voris goes too far when she insists that the poem's reiterations of 'Napoleon' are purely non-referential and that biographical interpretations focusing on Picasso are impertinent. 'If I Told Him' does exceed the notion that a portrait should 'be a likeness of its subject'; however, it does so not by rendering Picasso irrelevant but by mixing its analysis of him with reflections on Stein's similarities to and differences from his Napoleonic qualities.[170] If – as Voris acknowledges – the portrait's reiterative language does not abandon referentiality altogether but destabilises the portrait's referents in a way that utilises their non-referential possibilities, then it does not stand to reason that biographical detail is irrelevant to interpretation. It only means that the portrait's significations go well beyond its author's and subject's lives. This proliferation multiplies perspectives from which Stein's and Picasso's masculine homosociality may be seen.

The resulting 'twistings and warpings' in perspective are enabled by Stein's transmasculinity.[171] The shared rhythms of 'As A Wife Has A Cow' and 'If I Told Him' animate the latter poem's interrogation of the similarities and differences between Stein's and Picasso's genders – and thus of their masculine homosocial bonds. Going beyond the first portrait's implicit homosociality, Stein presents herself as parallel to Picasso by stating that 'I judge judge. / As a resemblance to him.'[172] This play with patriarchal poetry undercuts rather than sustains its modalities by introducing and undermining the referential notion that the writer might be 'a resemblance to' the painter.[173] Invoking Picasso and his many lovers, Stein writes that 'kings' are feeling 'full for it': much like 'Shutters shut and open', 'so do queens'.[174] Though Voris argues that this 'passage does not concern denotation (whether the shutters shut), but instead creates a pronounced rhythm that abstracts the expression "to shut"', in my view Stein's reiterations of 'Shutters shut' mix 'denotation' with semiotic proliferation.[175] Both 'negativity' and 'inventiveness' characterise the portrait's treatment of representation and relationality.[176] As DeKoven observes, in 'If I Told Him' 'obliteration or intensification of meaning alternately emerges, becomes "visible," as the other disappears'.[177] Although Thompson reads this passage's references to camera shutters as feminising 'the inferior act of repetition without a difference', which Stein repudiates for its association with mimetic representation, it is important to consider them in light of the poem's own reiterations.[178] The cadences reverberating throughout 'If I Told Him' inform – and are informed by – the rhythmic movements of the texts Stein wrote in 1923. Recalling window and camera shutters, the passage uses images from the visual arts to multiply perspectives and mobilise many other significations, including those concerning similarities and differences between Stein's and Picasso's masculinities.

Implicating multiple forms of relationality, 'If I Told Him' echoes the resignifications of gendered jouissance at play in 'As A Wife Has A Cow'. If Thompson is right that the former makes it possible for Stein to identify herself with 'kings' whose linguistic experimentation is anti-mimetic, undermining 'expected codes of language' and 'gender' in a 'linguistic drag act', we need not understand the resultant opening in 'gendered space' as enabling anti-feminist transmasculine identification with kings over and against 'queens'.[179] Read through the gender politics of Stein's experimental poems from the 1910s and 1920s, the portrait's image of opening and shutting shutters invokes feminine sexuality as a visual vacillation contrasting with the kings' excessive fullness – a sense of plenitude and wholeness Stein undercuts by referencing 'Napoleon' and his notorious overcompensation. Stein's toyings with her 'resemblance' to the painter place herself as another of the 'kings' and Toklas as one of the 'queens'. However, the poem thereby reproduces and recontextualises the orgasmic waves of 'As a Wife has a Cow', which evokes Stein's and Toklas's sexual relationship through reiterative language that builds gradually to orgasm. The rhythm of 'As A Wife Has A Cow' is smooth, even though it is not driven by a linear build-up to a singular climax. And notably, the piece focuses on the pleasure of the 'wife' having the 'cow' – not on her partner. This reverses the phallogocentrism often at work in hegemonic male masculinities and re-orients the masculine partner toward feminine jouissance.[180] Yet the orgasmic waves of 'As A Wife Has A Cow' transform into the more hesitant stutterings of the non-'Completed' portrait of Picasso as masculine mastery's fragility – rather than queer feminine jouissance's ecstasy – claims centre stage. In 'If I Told Him', 'Shutters' may 'shut and open' and 'so do queens', but the emphasis is less on female orgasm than on the playfulness with patriarchal poetry Stein uses to critique Picasso's egocentrism and mobilise an alternative transmasculinity. In so doing, the poem's 'twisting' and 'warping' of the cadences of 'As A Wife Has A Cow' mobilises multiple perspectives on gender, highlighting convergences and divergences between her and Picasso's masculinities.[181]

Thus, while 'If I Told Him' implies parallels between Stein and Picasso, it also calls their masculine homosociality into question and differentiates them from one another. As Glavey notes, by the time this portrait was written, Stein had 'come to question her identification with Picasso without abandoning it'.[182] 'If I Told Him' is therefore 'very much attuned to the costs and dangers of her resemblance to her friend', as well as to the threat of being taken for merely 'following' him.[183] This fear – bound up in Stein's transmasculinity and belief in her own genius – led her to guard '[h]er own identification with his masculine position' against 'the taint of the copy': against the 'homophobic association with imitation' to which heteronormative culture subjects queers.[184] Mobilising 'this association as a means to transform it', 'If I Told Him' is animated by amusement at both of their Napoleonic qualities.[185] This reverberates across the portrait as the 'master' falls to 'pieces' in playful rather than traumatic 'warping[s]'.[186]

Stein asks, 'Who comes first. Napoleon the first.', critiquing her subordinate relation to Picasso and substituting the past for the present tense to restage 'Napoleon' as the one 'Who *came* first.'[187] As Zox-Weaver observes, this highlights 'the diachronic nature of male authority' and the way 'history perpetuates' it by 'casting its power as innate and inevitable'.[188] Stein also implicates herself in the portrait's 'muscular assertion of control' by implicating 'herself' in 'the analogy between Picasso and Napoleon' and showing her 'dominance over those who claim a monopoly over knowing'.[189] Yet Blau notes that Stein's inclusion of 'Who comes too coming coming too' in the section on Napoleon also 'leaves open the questions of who comes too – Picasso and Napoleon, Napoleon and Stein, or all three'.[190] By raising these questions of priority, Stein not only calls attention to the potential for power conflicts within her and Picasso's bond but also proliferates viewpoints from which their masculinities' similarities and differences may be seen. A tone of affectionate questioning prevails throughout the portrait, challenging the notion that Stein's and Picasso's masculine homosocial alliance is unproblematic without destroying it entirely. The result is both 'disruption' and 'inventiveness' in their friendship and the poem's meanings.[191]

Whereas enthusiasm for Picasso eventually wanes in the earlier portrait, 'If I Told Him' leaves Stein the victor after a long struggle that challenges and reworks their friendship's power dynamics. The power and meaning of the pronoun 'he' is evacuated through giggling reiterations of 'He he he he and he and he.'[192] Although Thompson rightfully notes that this passage 'allows for a more pliable understanding of genius that is not necessarily tied to maleness' even if it repudiates femininity and the representational strategies of 'queens', she misses the subtle critique of Picasso through which Stein differentiates their masculinities.[193] Drawing on a distinctive feature of this phase of Stein's portraiture, which stresses 'phonological repetition', this passage points up and undermines the tautological aspects of Picasso's masculinity.[194] Sandwiching circular justifications for misogyny such as 'he is and as he is, and as he is and he is' between hilariously giggly iterations of 'He he he he and he and he' and 'he is and he and he and and he and he', the text's 'infectious humor . . . makes one wonder if Stein is laughing with glee at the possibilities available when entrenched patterns are unsettled and revised', as Thompson suggests.[195] Yet the poem's mockery also renders essentialist conceptions of gender and patriarchy laughable. Using the masculine pronoun 'he' to create the feminising and infantilising sound of giggling, Stein undercuts the law of the father.[196] Ultimately 'differentiating' and 'withdrawing' herself from Picasso, 'the king' grammatically identified with the position of the 'father' moves 'farther' from the portrait's attention, giving way to Stein's prominent 'I'.[197] This proliferates perspectives from which her and Picasso's masculinities may be seen, and in so doing, reveals the fractures – however affectionate – within their masculine homosocial bond.

The multiplicity of perspectives mobilised by fracturing masculine homosocial bonds is heightened in the concluding segment of the portrait, which builds to a final invocation: 'Let me recite what history teaches. History teaches.'[198] This ending refuses the closure suggested by the portrait's subtitle – 'A *Completed* Portrait of Picasso' – in favour of an ironic twist. If, at the beginning of the poem, Stein positions herself 'As a resemblance to' the Napoleonic Picasso, at the end of the poem she differentiates herself.[199] Poised to take up the role of paternalistic purveyor of didactic progress narratives that her textual practice works against, she declines to do so. The final buildup – 'One. / I land. Two. / I land. / Three / The land.' turns back upon itself, devolving from 'Three / The land.' to 'Two / I land. / Two. / I land.' to 'One / I land' and allowing the ground to slip out from under the speaker through subtle changes in punctuation.[200] Multiple recontextualisations of 'They cannot' set the stage for the speaker's recitation of 'what history teaches. History teaches.' – a lesson whose inconclusiveness undercuts language's apparent didacticism.[201] History's teachings overtake imperial masculinity's assertions, reminding us of Napoleon's failures and intimating that – whatever differences animated Stein's and Picasso's power struggles – their masculine homosocial bond was eventually subsumed into time's relentless rhythms.

The later portrait thereby proliferates opportunities for looking that allow masculinities to be viewed as other than 'imperial': as loving, playful, and – above all – provisional. By the end of this portrait, Stein has abdicated and destroyed Picasso's throne. Taking on the role of giggly 'king' while rejecting that of the 'father', her playful transmasculinity toys with the father's subject position while refusing to occupy it as an essential gender ontology. And while Stein's rise to prominence at the portrait's end is accompanied by its ostensible subject's disappearance into the background, that does not imply that she is decisively 'withdrawing' from and bidding 'farewell to Picasso', as Haselstein claims.[202] Instead, he remains in the portrait through Stein's ironic identification with his posture as 'king'. Toying with the position of the father while refusing to claim it as a stable identity, Stein – newly prominent in the role of 'king' – leaves masculinity open to destabilisation and resignification. This move mobilises yet undercuts Stein's and Picasso's masculine homosocial bond, furthering the cubist fragmentation of 'Picasso' and shifting the gaze that would valorise his hegemonic masculinity at the expense of her feminist transmasculinity.

Kolář's Picasso / Kolář's Stein

The transformations in perspective brought about through Stein's and Picasso's masculine homosocial bond are also central concerns of Kolář's collage. Whereas Lubar demonstrates that Picasso's misgivings about Stein's masculinity led him to mask her face in *Portrait of Gertrude Stein* – and to initiate his later paintings' cubist deployment of multiple perspectives – Kolář's work shifts the gaze at work in *Portrait of Gertrude Stein*. In a move whose plays on masking 'submit[s] the masculine position . . . to the level of discourse', Kolář's substitution of Picasso's self-portrait for Stein's head explicitly places the painter within the portrait, effacing the writing and breaking down the distinction between subject and object.[203] The viewer who recognises Picasso's portrayal of Stein's body recalls her masked face, however, and sees a palimpsest of the writer. Kolář's piece thus appears to align the writer's and the painter's looks, suggesting their similarity: both are avant-garde artists capable of powerful '"transvestite"' vision that shifts the gaze.[204] Yet Stein's and Picasso's masculinities were distinct. Through 'parallelling' and 'differentiating', these modernists reoriented the gaze through looks that often diverged even as they served as conduits for the writer's and the painter's masculine homosocial desires.[205]

Like Stein's 'If It Told Him', Kolář's image also undercuts the two modernists' claims to priority: if their heads are interchangeable, '[w]ho comes first'?[206] Kolář thus furthers Stein's teasing reiterations of 'Napoleon' and undercuts her and Picasso's claims to autonomous 'genius'.[207] Yet Kolář's collage destabilises the hegemonic gaze even more than Picasso's *Portrait of Gertrude Stein* by proliferating looks and questioning the origins of the visual trajectories animating the two modernists' portraits of one another. As Sayre writes, '[t]he transvestite look is . . . a sort of collage', and Kolář's replacement of Stein's head with Picasso's interrogates the painter's gender by placing his head on his own rendition of Stein's body, making explicit his implication in gender ambiguity.[208] The collage suggests that what was at stake in Stein's and Picasso's queer relationality and exchange of portraits was not only their egos and roles as emergent leaders of the avant-garde, but also the instability and malleability of gender itself. Offering a trace of the 'slantwise' desires through which these modernists and their admirers viewed one another, Kolář's collage shifts the gaze through which both Stein's and Picasso's masculinities are made available for view.[209]

Kolář's crumplage of Picasso's *Portrait of Gertrude Stein* similarly reflects not only the developments in cubism that were underway while Stein was writing her first portrait of Picasso but also a further fracturing of her masculine image and homosocial bond with the painter. Here, the 'incommensurate' character of Stein's and Picasso's bond across 'irreducible' differences is clearest.[210] Crumplage's 'warping' increases the size of Stein's body, making her hands more solid and prominent than in Picasso's version.[211] This enlargement enhances her phallic self-positioning and reverses Picasso's diminishment of her masculinity. At the same time, the piece's slicing of Stein's face skews her eyes and bisects her mouth. These 'twisting' and 'differentiating' movements reorient her look and challenge the viewer, furthering Picasso's assault on perspective and implicating viewers in their bond's queerness.[212]

However much Picasso's and Kolář's images attack dominant conceptions of pictorial space by thwarting established ways of looking and proliferating multiple angles of vision, they do not always challenge heterosexist modes of seeing or the gender constructs that inform them. For instance, Kolář's crumplage of Stein's face renders her mouth more clownlike and her eyes more menacing than Picasso's portrait. Simultaneously underscoring and undercutting her power, these features risk 'repelling' the viewer and prompting 'withdrawing' even as they evidence Stein's capacity for 'attracting' others.[213] The resultant 'warping' counters the more positive reorientations of the dominant gaze mobilised by Stein's poems and Kolář's collage, which downplay tensions and highlight her attractive qualities.[214] Taken as nodal points in a circuit of desire, these three artists' portraits – in all of their fracturings, occlusions and ocular reorientations – constitute a cubist picture of the fraught friendship between Stein and Picasso and the multivalent implications of viewers, readers and scholars in it. Serving as artefacts of a masculine homosocial bond that was both affectionate and fiercely rivalrous, these portraits register, renegotiate and recirculate apprehensions about and affirmations of Stein's transmasculinity that persist to this day.

Notes

1. Steiner, 'Postmodernist Portraits', p. 176.
2. Steiner, ibid., p. 176.
3. See Cope, *Passionate Collaborations*, for discussion of the implications of the concept of 'genius' for Stein's friendship with Picasso. See Drucker, *Theorizing Modernism*, pp. 112–19, for a critique of Picasso's self-positioning as the quintessential modernist 'artist/genius' (p. 114).

4. Ulla Haselstein, 'Gertrude Stein's Portraits of Matisse and Picasso', p. 732.
5. Cope, *Passionate Collaborations*, p. 15.
6. Drucker, *Theorizing Modernism*, p. 114.
7. Drucker, ibid., p. 116.
8. Drucker, ibid., p. 117.
9. Lubar, 'Unmasking Pablo's Gertrude', p. 59.
10. Cope, *Passionate Collaborations*, p. 59. See Gygax, 'The Portrait as Word and (A)Head', p. 218, for another argument that Stein's portraits of Picasso (as well as Hemingway) are inflected by their 'gender struggle'.
11. Sedgwick, *Between Men*.
12. Weiner and Young, 'Introduction: Queer Bonds', pp. 226–7.
13. Foucault, 'Friendship', p. 138; Cope, *Passionate Collaborations*, p. 59.
14. Lubar, 'Unmasking Pablo's Gertrude', p. 57.
15. Lubar, ibid., p. 57.
16. Lubar, ibid., p. 64. I distinguish between the gaze and the look to nuance Lubar's account of Lacan, which conflates them. In so doing, I follow Silverman's interpretation in *Threshold* of the multiple meanings of *le regard* in Lacan's theory of vision.
17. Garb, *The Painted Face*, p. 189.
18. Sedgwick, *Touching Feeling*, p. 8.
19. See note 15 to Chapter 4 on the limits of the analogy between cubist painting and Stein's writing.
20. See Hovey, *A Thousand Words*, p. 101, and Will, *Gertrude Stein*, for arguments that *The Autobiography* destabilises the concept of 'genius'.
21. Silverman, *Threshold*, p. 182, p. 223, p. 179.
22. Silverman, ibid., p. 179.
23. See Cope, *Passionate Collaborations*, and Lubar, 'Unmasking Pablo's Gertrude', for two different versions of this argument.
24. Lubar, 'Unmasking Pablo's Gertrude'. See Cope, *Passionate Collaborations*, pp. 39–41 and Richardson, *A Life of Picasso. Vol. I*, pp. 455–61, for information about additional sources for Picasso's masking of Stein.
25. Stein, 'Picasso', p. 142.
26. Richardson, *A Life of Picasso. Vol. I*, p. 400.
27. Richardson, ibid., p. 408.
28. Olivier, *Picasso and his Friends*, pp. 82–3.
29. Kahnweiler, 'Introduction', p. x.
30. Picasso and Stein, *Correspondence*, p. 81, p. 206. '[P]ard', short for 'pardner' from North American Westerns, was an 'in-name used by Apollinaire, Braque, and Picasso' (p. 206n5).
31. Picasso and Stein, ibid., p. 206n5.
32. Madeline, 'Preface', p. xxii.

33. Richardson, *A Life of Picasso. Vol. I*, p. 408.
34. See Wagner-Martin, *'Favored Strangers'*, for a correction of claims that Stein invested in men at women's expense.
35. Corn and Latimer, *Seeing Gertrude Stein*, p. 121.
36. Caramello, *Henry James, Gertrude Stein*, p. 155.
37. Garb, '"To Kill the Nineteenth Century"', p. 64; Daix, *Picasso*.
38. Sedgwick, *Between Men*.
39. Weiner and Young, 'Introduction: Queer Bonds', p. 225.
40. Sedgwick, *Touching Feeling*, p. 8.
41. Picasso and Stein, *Correspondence*, p. 115.
42. Kahnweiler, 'Introduction', pp. xiii–xiv; see Madeline, 'The Road to Belley', and the letters reproduced on pp. 287, pp. 292–3, p. 310, pp. 314–15 and pp. 317–20 of Picasso and Stein, *Correspondence*, for further discussion of Stein's proposed collaboration with the painter on the *Birthday Book*. See p. 320n6 of Picasso and Stein, *Correspondence*, for clarification that Stein finally gave up in 1929 (not 1925, as Kahnweiler claims) on obtaining Picasso's drawings.
43. Picasso quoted in Richardson, *A Life of Picasso. Vol. I*, p. 406. Richardson presents a hostile reading of Picasso's *Homage a Gertrude* that contrasts to Garb's and Corn and Latimer's more sympathetic assessments. Likening the image's figure bearing fruit to Toklas and the one blaring a horn to Stein, Richardson reads *Homage* as an 'ironical apotheosis' demonstrating the painter's view that she desired unmerited recognition for her writing (p. 407).

    Richardson's bias is apparent when he alleges that Annette Rosenshine, Toklas's cousin, first appeared in his studio while 'enslaved' to Stein (p. 464). Richardson does not clarify what this supposed enslavement entailed, but his charge resonates with the long history of misguided critiques of Stein as exploiting women. This represents a shocking double standard, as Richardson never criticises Picasso for the womanising he documents. Tellingly, in *'Favored Strangers'*, Wagner-Martin notes that Gertrude Stein and her sister-in-law Sally Stein accompanied the shy Rosenshine on her first visit to Picasso's studio because she had not understood his invitation's sexual subtext (pp. 83–4). While the contrast between Stein's confidence and Rosenshine's timidity must have been striking, Richardson unduly depicts the former as a power-hungry self-promoter whose ambitions exceeded her talents.
44. Richardson, *A Life of Picasso. Vol. I*, p. 407; Stein, YCAL MSS 76, Box 38, Folder 791 in Yale University's Beinecke Library.
45. Sedgwick, *Touching Feeling*, p. 8.
46. Caramello, *Henry James, Gertrude Stein*, pp. 119–68.
47. Cope, *Passionate Collaborations*, pp. 33–4.
48. Lubar, 'Unmasking Pablo's Gertrude'.

49. Cope, *Passionate Collaborations*, pp. 33–4.
50. Sedgwick, *Touching Feeling*, p. 8.
51. Sedgwick, ibid., p. 8.
52. Sayre, 'The Artist's Model', p. 31.
53. Sayre, ibid., p. 31.
54. Garb, *The Painted Face*, p. 201.
55. Lubar, 'Unmasking Pablo's Gertrude', p. 70–1n89.
56. Corn and Latimer, *Seeing Gertrude Stein*, p. 34; see Giroud, *Picasso and Gertrude Stein*, for further analysis of the portrait's sources.
57. Richardson, *A Life of Picasso. Vol. I*, p. 403.
58. Corn and Latimer, *Seeing Gertrude Stein*, p. 28.
59. Richardson, *A Life of Picasso. Vol. I*, p. 403.
60. Lubar, 'Unmasking Pablo's Gertrude', p. 61.
61. Lubar, ibid., p. 61.
62. Lubar, ibid., p. 60.
63. Lubar, ibid., p. 62.
64. Lubar, ibid., p. 59.
65. Sedgwick, *Touching Feeling*, p. 8.
66. See Pavloska, *Modern Primitives*, and Walker, *The Making of a Modernist*. See Harrison et al., *Primitivism, Cubism, Abstraction*, pp. 55–61, for an overview of primitivism in modern art.
67. Cheng, *Second Skin*, pp. 19–21.
68. Cheng, ibid., p. 21.
69. Cheng, ibid., p. 19.
70. Cheng, ibid., p. 19.
71. The phrase 'master in pieces, oh yes' appears in one of Stein's 1923 notebooks in the Beinecke Rare Book and Manuscript Library, Yale University, YCAL MSS 76, Box 92, Folder 1710.
72. Stein, YCAL MSS 76, Box 92, Folder 1710 in the Beinecke Rare Book and Manuscript Library, Yale University.
73. Sayre, 'The Artist's Model', pp. 31–2.
74. Sayre, ibid., p. 32.
75. Sayre, ibid., p. 31.
76. Cope, *Passionate Collaborations*, p. 94.
77. Cope, ibid., p. 94.
78. Corn and Latimer, *Seeing Gertrude Stein*, pp. 29–35.
79. Lubar, 'Unmasking Pablo's Gertrude'.
80. Cope, *Passionate Collaborations*, p. 58.
81. Sedgwick, *Touching Feeling*, p. 8.
82. Weiner and Young, 'Introduction: Queer Bonds', p. 225, p. 227.
83. Sedgwick, *Touching Feeling*, p. 8.
84. Corn and Latimer, *Seeing Gertrude Stein*, p. 23.
85. Stein, *Picasso*, p. 14.

86. Stein, ibid., pp. 21–2.
87. Garb, *The Painted Face*, p. 201.
88. Garb, ibid., p. 201.
89. Schmitz, *Of Huck and Alice*, pp. 206–7.
90. Corn and Latimer, *Seeing Gertrude Stein*, p. 51.
91. Stein, *The Autobiography*, p. 53. See Schmitz, *Of Huck and Alice*, pp. 200–40, for an extended analysis of Stein's response in *The Autobiography* to Picasso's *Gertrude Stein*.
92. Sayre, 'The Artist's Model', p. 32.
93. Glavey, *The Wallflower Avant-Garde*, p. 24.
94. Glavey, ibid., p. 28.
95. Haselstein, 'Gertrude Stein's Portraits of Matisse and Picasso', p. 730.
96. Lubar, 'Unmasking Pablo's Gertrude'.
97. Haselstein, 'Gertrude Stein's Portraits of Matisse and Picasso', p. 732.
98. Haselstein, ibid., p. 732.
99. Haselstein, ibid., p. 730.
100. Sedgwick, *Touching Feeling*, p. 8. For discussion of the limitations of the cubist analogy, see note 15 to Chapter 4.
101. Perloff, 'Poetry as Word-System', p. 75. In 'Out of Air', and *Modernism's Other Work*, Siraganian counters Perloff's argument that Stein's textual practice leads to indeterminate signification. However, Siraganian's case – which rests on the belief that Stein's first Picasso portrait tracks his production of 'a definite art object with a precise meaning' – is undermined by the portrait's reiterations, which undercut rather than stabilise words such as 'meaning' (Siraganian, 'Out of Air', p. 662).
102. Gertrude Stein, 'A Transatlantic Interview', p. 502; Norris, 'The "Wife" and the "Genius"', p. 85.
103. Weiner and Young, 'Introduction: Queer Bonds', p. 227.
104. See Picasso quoted in Richardson, *A Life of Picasso. Vol. I*, p. 406.
105. Walker, *The Making of a Modernist*, pp. 1–18.
106. Damon, 'Gertrude Stein's Jewishness', pp. 499–500.
107. Silverman, *Threshold*, p. 222.
108. Cheng, *Second Skin*, p. 21; Sedgwick, *Touching Feeling*, p. 8.
109. However, this textual practice does not forestall all hegemonic forms of looking. Stein's egalitarian textual practice sometimes has the disadvantage of failing to challenge heterosexist assumptions that enter reading. Texts such as 'As A Wife Has A Cow' and 'Lifting Belly' are often seen as inscriptions of butch/femme eroticism, but they can also be viewed through a heterosexist filter by readers unfamiliar with queer cultures.
110. Stein, 'A Transatlantic Interview', pp. 17–18.
111. Weiner and Young, 'Introduction: Queer Bonds', p. 225.
112. Weiner and Young, ibid., p. 225.

113. Stein, 'Picasso', p. 142.
114. Garb, *The Painted Face*, p. 189.
115. Garb, ibid., pp. 191–2. Garb's argument suggests that Stein's portrait influenced Picasso's painting rather than the other way around.
116. Garb, ibid., p. 191.
117. Garb, ibid., p. 193.
118. Foucault, 'Friendship', p. 138.
119. Walker, *The Making of a Modernist*, p. 79.
120. Walker, ibid., p. 79; Dydo, *Gertrude Stein*, p. 30, establishes that Stein composed 'Picasso' from 1909 to 1910.
121. Cope, *Passionate Collaborations*, p. 44. Walker, *The Making of a Modernist*, p. 7, notes that Stein's *Picasso* – and other writings showing her allegiance to Picasso and Cézanne – deploys the 'myth' of the 'innocent eye' with unmediated access to the object perceived.
122. Cope, *Passionate Collaborations*, p. 45.
123. Cope, ibid., p. 49.
124. Daniel, *Gertrude Stein*, p. 100.
125. Stein, 'Picasso', p. 142.
126. Stein, ibid., p. 142.
127. Stein, ibid., p. 142.
128. Haselstein, 'Gertrude Stein's Portraits of Matisse and Picasso', p. 736.
129. Haselstein, ibid., p. 732.
130. Sedgwick, *Touching Feeling*, p. 8.
131. Stein, 'Picasso', p. 142.
132. Stein, ibid., p. 142.
133. Stein, ibid., p. 142.
134. Garb, *The Painted Face*, p. 189.
135. Picasso paraphrased in Stein, *Picasso*, p. 14; Stein, 'Picasso', pp. 142–3.
136. Stein, *Picasso*, pp. 16–17. For a similar claim attributed to Picasso, see Stein, 'A Transatlantic Interview', p. 514.
137. Stein, *Picasso*, p. 21.
138. Sedgwick, *Touching Feeling*, p. 8; Stein, 'Picasso', p. 143; Sedgwick, ibid., p. 8.
139. Sedgwick, ibid., p. 8.
140. Stein, *Three Lives*, p. 117.
141. Cheng, *Second Skin*, p. 21.
142. Stein, 'Picasso', p. 143.
143. Stein, ibid., p. 143.
144. Stein, ibid., p. 143.
145. Stein, ibid., p. 142.
146. Stein, ibid., p. 143.
147. Stein, ibid., p. 142.
148. Sedgwick, *Touching Feeling*, p. 8.

149. Stein, 'Picasso', p. 143.
150. Weiner and Young, 'Introduction: Queer Bonds', p. 225.
151. See Madeline, 'The Road to Belley'; Richardson, *A Life of Picasso. Vol. III*, p. 171; Stein, *The Autobiography*, pp. 182–3; and Wagner-Martin, *'Favored Strangers'*, p. 148, on this stage of their friendship.
152. Murphy quoted in Wagner-Martin, *'Favored Strangers'*, p. 170.
153. Voris, *The Composition of Sense*, p. 159, p. 174.
154. Haselstein, 'Gertrude Stein's Portraits of Matisse and Picasso', p. 736.
155. Stein, 'If I Told Him', p. 464.
156. Thompson, 'Language and Democracy', p. 146.
157. Stein, 'If I Told Him', p. 464; Will, *Gertrude Stein*, p. 3.
158. Blau, 'The Artist in Word and Image', p. 134.
159. Will, *Gertrude Stein*, pp. 68–9.
160. Dydo, *A Stein Reader*, p. 453.
161. Dydo, ibid., p. 453.
162. Stein references 'Caesars' in 'Lifting Belly', and 'A Sonatina Followed by Another'. She references 'cows' in those texts as well as in 'As A Wife Has A Cow A Love Story'; *Baby Precious Always Shines*; and various unpublished *carnets* held in the Beinecke Library. See Engelbrecht, '"Lifting Belly Is a Language"', for discussions of 'Caesars'. See Chessman, *The Public is Invited to Dance*; Dydo, *Gertrude Stein*; Engelbrecht, ibid.; and Turner, 'This "Very Beautiful Form of Literature"', for discussions of 'cows'.
163. Will, *Gertrude Stein*, pp. 68–9. See Halberstam, *Female Masculinity*, on differences between male, female and transmasculinities.
164. Weiner and Young, 'Introduction: Queer Bonds', p. 225.
165. Stein, 'As A Wife Has A Cow A Love Story', pp. 460–1.
166. Richardson, *A Life of Picasso. Vol. I*, p. 463.
167. Dydo, *Gertrude Stein*, p. 70. See Steiner, *Exact Resemblance*, pp. 106–10, for an overview of stylistic similarities and differences between the 1912 and 1924 portraits.
168. Voris, '"Shutters shut and open"', p. 179.
169. Voris, ibid., p. 179.
170. Voris, ibid., p. 179.
171. Sedgwick, *Touching Feeling*, p. 8.
172. Stein, 'If I Told Him', p. 464.
173. Stein's 'Patriarchal Poetry' deploys and undercuts a variety of patriarchal poetic practices. See Benstock, *Women*; Chessman, *The Public is Invited to Dance*; Cole, 'Remaking Sense'; DeKoven, *A Different Language*; Engelbrecht, '"Lifting Belly Is a Language"'; and Ruddick, *Reading Gertrude Stein*, for analyses of Stein in relation to theories of patriarchal language and literature.
174. Stein, 'If I Told Him', p. 464.

175. Voris, '"Shutters shut and open"', p. 196.
176. Weiner and Young, 'Introduction: Queer Bonds', p. 225.
177. DeKoven, *A Different Language*, p. 111.
178. Thompson, 'Language and Democracy', p. 148.
179. Thompson, ibid., 149; Stein, 'If I Told Him', p. 176.
180. Work on butch masculinities frequently points to the orientation of masculine partners toward feminine partners' pleasure: see Case, 'Toward a Butch-Femme Aesthetic'; Munt, *Butch/Femme*; and Nestle, *The Persistent Desire*.
181. Sedgwick, *Touching Feeling*, p. 8.
182. Glavey, *The Wallflower Avant-Garde*, p. 46.
183. Glavey, ibid., pp. 46–7.
184. Glavey, ibid., p. 47, p. 7.
185. Glavey, ibid., p. 7.
186. Stein, 1923, YCAL MSS 76, Box 92, Folder 1710 in the Beinecke Rare Book and Manuscript Library, Yale University; Sedgwick, *Touching Feeling*, p. 8.
187. Stein, 'If I Told Him', p. 464; emphasis added.
188. Zox-Weaver, *Women Modernists and Fascism*, p. 90.
189. Zox-Weaver, ibid., pp. 90–1.
190. Stein, 'If I Told Him', p. 464; Blau, 'The Artist in Word and Image', p. 139.
191. Weiner and Young, 'Introduction: Queer Bonds', p. 225.
192. Stein, 'If I Told Him', p. 465.
193. Thompson, 'Language and Democracy', p. 150; Stein, 'If I Told Him', p. 464. Thompson's conflation of 'maleness' with 'masculinity' is also problematic (pp. 150–1).
194. Steiner, *Exact Resemblance*, p. 106.
195. Stein, 'If I Told Him', p. 465; Thompson, 'Language and Democracy', p. 151.
196. Stein, ibid., p. 465.
197. Sedgwick, *Touching Feeling*, 8; Stein, 'If I Told Him', p. 465.
198. Stein, ibid., p. 466.
199. Stein, ibid., p. 464; emphasis added.
200. Stein, ibid., p. 466.
201. Stein, ibid., p. 466.
202. Sedgwick, *Touching Feeling*, p. 8; Haselstein, 'Gertrude Stein's Portraits of Matisse and Picasso', p. 740.
203. Sayre, 'The Artist's Model', p. 32.
204. Sayre, ibid., p. 32.
205. Sedgwick, *Touching Feeling*, p. 8.
206. Stein, 'If I Told Him', p. 464.
207. Stein, ibid., p. 464.

208. Sayre, 'The Artist's Model', p. 32.
209. Foucault, 'Friendship', p. 138.
210. Weiner and Young, 'Introduction: Queer Bonds', pp. 226–7.
211. Sedgwick, *Touching Feeling*, p. 8.
212. Sedgwick, ibid., p. 8.
213. Sedgwick, ibid., p. 8.
214. Sedgwick, ibid., p. 8.

Chapter 6

'Torquere': Stein's and Hemingway's Queer Relationality

'Gertrude Stein and me are just like brothers'

Ernest Hemingway to Sherwood Anderson

'I liked her better before she cut her hair and that was a sort of turning point in all sorts of things. She used to talk to me about homosexuality and how it was fine in and for women and no good in men and I used to listen and learn and I always wanted to fuck her and she knew it and it was a good healthy feeling and made more sense than some of the talk.'

Ernest Hemingway to W. G. Rogers

'Hemingway was yellow, he is . . . But what a book . . . would be the real story of Hemingway, not those he writes but the confessions of the real Ernest Hemingway. It would be for another audience than the audience Hemingway now has but it would be very wonderful.'

Gertrude Stein, *The Autobiography of Alice B. Toklas*

In the years leading up to Hemingway's December 1921 arrival in Paris, Stein reinvented 'herself as the great undiscovered American writer', becoming 'the oracle' of expatriate modernism and regularly walking past George Sand's statue in the Jardin du Luxembourg for inspiration.[1] Sand's feminism and gender-bending practices – such as '[w]earing trousers and smoking in public' – resonated with Stein's challenges to the gender binary.[2] Sand was respected by her fellow writers for 'her work and what they saw as her masculinity'; Gustave Flaubert even called her a 'great man' at her funeral.[3] Part of the Pantheon of Great Men who were among Stein's lifelong fascinations, Sand provided a model for her professional persona.[4]

Plate 1 Oil painting by Pablo Picasso, *Portrait of Gertrude Stein* (1906).

Plate 2 Oil painting by Pablo Picasso, *Les Demoiselles d'Avignon* (1907).

Plate 3 Tempera painting by Pablo Picasso, *Homage a Gertrude* (1909, *sic*).

Plate 4 Oil painting by Pablo Picasso, *The Architect's Table* (1912).

Plate 5 Oil painting by Edouard Manet, *Le déjeuner sur l'herbe* (1863).

When Hemingway first met Stein in 1922, he was drawn to her lively personality and power within modernist networks. Shortly after they established a friendship, he declared to Sherwood Anderson that 'Gertrude Stein and me are just like brothers', prompting scholars to observe that 'Hemingway felt something very like a masculine bond' with her.[5] Stein admitted that she always had a 'weakness for Hemingway', and he acknowledged that 'I always wanted to fuck her and she knew it and it was a good healthy feeling.'[6] Their masculine homosociality would take some interesting turns, however. Once Hemingway learned from Stein and became her peer, he began to react negatively to her masculinity because it challenged the putative distinction between masculinity and femininity, heterosexuality and homosexuality that grounded his public image. The result was a fraught friendship whose vicissitudes troubled both writers.

Stein's masculinity threatened Hemingway as much as it attracted him. Her 'quick eye and sharp tongue' met his match and 'allowed him little room to posture'.[7] His third wife, Martha Gellhorn Hemingway, similarly defied hegemonic gender roles. Her success as a journalist and fiction writer initially enticed him but eventually incited his envy.[8] After he outmanoeuvred her for the role of 'chief war correspondent' for *Collier's*, she left him.[9] Like Martha's 'assertiveness and ambition', Stein's personality and professional activities provoked 'complex feelings of love, fear, dislike, and respect' in Hemingway because they placed her among his 'intellectual equals'.[10] Moreover, Stein resembled his mother, Grace Hall Hemingway, 'not only in age and appearance but also in self-confidence, artistic ambitions' and 'homosexual preferences', which elicited a 'complicated response'.[11] Stein differed from Martha and Grace, however, by living out her aspirations through a masculinity made visible in relation to Toklas.

Hemingway cultivated a hypermasculine persona to advance his career, retaliating in 'Oedipal fashion' against Stein and other precursors to establish his position.[12] Moreover, as Debra A. Moddelmog argues, Hemingway deliberately leveraged hegemonic masculinities for financial gain by flattening his drafts' complex treatment of gender and sexuality.[13] By selecting 'manly topics' for his fiction, he established himself as 'a male authority figure' and gained 'an advantage' over women writers whose growing prominence threatened to 'devalue' writing as 'effeminate'.[14] He also 'felt that the intense homosociality of his fiction demanded equally intense heterosexuality to deflect suspicions that either his male characters or he had homosexual tendencies'.[15]

Hemingway was among '[m]any . . . American visitors' to Stein's salon in the early 1920s who 'perplexed her' because they were deeply invested in 'gender differences'.[16] Anticipating David Wyatt's recent study of the ways Hemingway's fiction registers emotional suppression, Stein saw his 'truly sensitive capacity for emotion' but criticised his tendency to hide it behind hypermasculine personae.[17] She could tell that '[t]he individual she knew on her own terms was obviously not the one in the legend he had begun to generate in the personality-conscious' Parisian cafés.[18] Stein was aware that because Hemingway's masculinity was established through the circulation of 'signs' within varied 'theaters' of representation, it was 'subject to dramatic slippage and transformation', as Thomas Strychacz argues.[19]

The discrepancy between the private and public Hemingway so perturbed Stein that she made him 'emblematic of a national defect in the creative realization of gender'.[20] Calling him 'yellow' and a 'good pupil' in *The Autobiography*, she claims that his writings do not tell 'the real story of Hemingway' and asserts that 'the confessions of the real Ernest Hemingway' – which 'would be very wonderful' – 'would be for another audience than the audience Hemingway now has'.[21] Wyndham Lewis's misogynist assertion that the 'master' that wielded an 'overmastering influence' over Hemingway had actually been 'a *mistress*' deepened these blows, staging Stein's masculinity as emasculating.[22]

Cope posits that Hemingway's hostility also 'had its origins in his attraction to Stein', which left him deeply unsettled by the ontological instability of gender and sexuality.[23] The resulting 'crisis' caused turbulence at the level of desire.[24] As J. Gerald Kennedy and Kirk Curnutt note, Hemingway 'felt something very like a masculine bond' with Stein but 'also wanted to bed her, perhaps in his mind to feminize her'.[25] Dodging the implications of his attraction to Stein's masculinity, Hemingway disavowed their friendship's queerness, which threatened his self-understanding. Differences between the public and private Hemingway precipitated crises as he denied the possibility that his attraction may have been driven by something far queerer than the heteronormative logics governing his published works.

Lyle Larsen's *Stein and Hemingway* aptly identifies the instability of the two writers' bond and documents its biographical contexts, yet misses the opportunity to interrogate the role of gender and sexuality in their 'Turbulent Friendship'.[26] The hostile turnabouts through which they retaliated against one another recall Sedgwick's account of queerness as 'a continuing moment, movement, motive – recurrent, eddying, *troublant*'.[27] The word '*torquere*', which suggests torture, further stresses their queer relationality's turbulence.[28] Cope thus observes that Hemingway's correspondence gives 'full rein to the ambivalence that Stein inspired in him: feelings of desire, aggression, fondness, competition, confusion, and envy'; of 'attraction, identification, jealousy, and rejection'.[29] Hemingway's fear of gender instability has reverberated across his and Stein's exchanges from the middle of the 1920s to the present. Although *A Moveable Feast* obscures many of the reasons for Hemingway's split with Stein, the full range of Sedgwickian relational modes animated their thwarted friendship and the texts through which they engaged one another.

Hemingway mocked Stein in print as early as 1924 in a poem entitled 'The Soul of Spain with McAlmon and Bird the Publishers'.[30] After becoming 'outraged' that reviews of his debut short story collection, *In Our Time* (1925), noted Stein's and Anderson's 'influence', Hemingway parodied her in *The Torrents of Spring* (1926).[31] Stein, in turn, registered her growing misgivings about him in 'He and They, Hemingway' (1923: 1923), 'Evidence' (1929: 1930, 1993), 'Genuine Creative Ability' (1929–30: 1930), and 'Sentences and Paragraphs' (1929–30: 1931).[32] In the early 1930s, her 'Objects Lie on a Table' (1922: 1932) and *The Autobiography* (1932: 1933) infuriated Hemingway by placing him in the subordinate position of 'pupil', so he retaliated in *Green Hills of Africa* (1935) and *A Moveable Feast* (1964, 2009).[33]

As Weiner and Young argue, 'Queer bonds . . . occur not in spite of but *because* of some force of negation, in which it is precisely negativity that organizes scenes of togetherness.'[34] Yet these ties also 'reach beyond sexual self-recognition' and traverse 'positionings that will remain forever incommensurate'.[35] Stein's and Hemingway's queer bonds played out in this fashion, animating a variety of movements from 'desiring, identifying, representing, repelling, paralleling, differentiating' and 'rivaling' to 'leaning, twisting, mimicking, withdrawing, attracting, aggressing' and 'warping'.[36] These varied forms of relationality register in the texts they wrote about one another.

Stein and Hemingway: warping modernism's gaze

In 1947, Hemingway began writing *A Moveable Feast* – a memoir of his time in Paris from 1921 to 1926 – after reclaiming from the Paris

Ritz 'two small steamer trunks' filled with 'pages of typed fiction, notebooks . . ., books, newspaper clippings, and old clothes' he had left behind in 1928.[37] Like Stein's *The Autobiography*, Hemingway's book contains numerous inaccuracies and mischaracterisations; both texts are more interesting as evidence of the myths through which the authors constructed themselves than as factual documentation of their lives. Whereas *The Autobiography* deploys a queer gaze to foreground Stein's importance within modernist Paris and influence over Hemingway, *A Moveable Feast* uses a resolutely heteromasculine gaze to feminise her, devalue her transmasculinity and promote Hemingway's heteromasculine image.

As Hovey observes, even though *A Moveable Feast* attempts to stabilise gender by positioning Hemingway's presumably 'heterosexual masculinity . . . as the site of an authentic identity' over and against Stein's putative fraudulence, his memoir reveals the cracks in the mask of heteromasculinity he used to hide their affinities.[38] *A Moveable Feast* differs from Stein's deliberately decentred *Autobiography* because Hemingway strives 'to shore up his identity and his voice, even as it becomes more and more apparent that a hole is opening up in the fabric of that coherence'.[39] Although Hovey stresses the 'hole' exposing his 'regret' over his failed marriage to Hadley, I also see gaps in his portrayal of his friendship with Stein.[40] These fissures appear through a pretence to stylistic plainness that Scott St. Pierre wisely advises us to question. Commenting on Hemingway's disdain for textual '"ornament"', St. Pierre argues that his 'style' often 'only pretends to be straight in order to cover up the embarrassing fact of being bent': it 'uses a subtle form of strategic ambiguity that deceives us into seeing it as much more straightforward than it actually is. It performs or flaunts a mirage of straightness.'[41] These performances 'evidence what Hemingway would have *liked* to be secure about, but clearly was not'.[42]

The resulting 'hole' in Hemingway's subjectivity manifested through the 'bent' style he uses to characterise Stein in *A Moveable Feast*.[43] Abravanel observes that Hemingway 'does in fact borrow Stein's voice on his way to becoming a writer', although he claims otherwise; Hovey similarly notes that *A Moveable Feast* imitates the style of *The Autobiography* in 'a masquerade of Stein's masquerade'.[44] Presenting 'many' of her 'opinions as his own wisdom', Hemingway engages in what Cope calls 'a curious and backhanded sort of homage' through which he 'denounces Stein even as he confesses elsewhere, but not in name, to her centrality'.[45] Hemingway's 'mirage of straightness' works throughout *A Moveable Feast* to disavow his complex desires: his attraction to her transmasculinity and fear of his own transfemininity.[46]

As Valerie Rohy has established, while drafting *A Moveable Feast* Hemingway experienced transfeminine jouissance during gender-bending sexual play with his fourth wife, Mary Welsh Hemingway. Their marriage (1946–61) enabled him to explore more complex configurations of gender and desire than those foregrounded in much of his published fiction.[47] Mary's memoir, *How It Was* (1951), includes details suggesting that he 'chose to explore male femininity' during their 'sexual encounters'.[48] In a passage recording a 'fantasy' about 'sodomy', Hemingway will 'speak no further' about their sexual acts, but Mary's role is clear: she is 'a boy'.[49] Ernest's note after Mary's transcription of their 'fantasy' asserts that 'She loves me to be her girls, which I love to be' as well.[50]

How It Was deploys a gaze that validates forms of desire that are not structured by the opposition between masculinity and femininity. Rohy describes the Hemingways' sexuality as driven by 'an additive logic of gender, by which Mary can be a boy "without ever losing any femininity," and Ernest can be a girl without losing masculinity'.[51] Rohy argues that transfeminine 'jouissance' with Mary allowed Hemingway's desiring subjectivity to accommodate male femininity and female masculinity in more complex ways than a superficial reading of many of his fictional texts' gender politics would suggest.[52] This argument is salutary, critiquing the transphobia driving criticism pathologising Hemingway's interest in male femininity and going beyond Lacanian arguments that predicate desire on 'lack' rather than 'plenitude'.[53] Affirming gender's complexity, Ernest tells readers of Mary's diary that his wife 'has always wanted to be a boy and thinks as a boy without ever losing any femininity. If you should become confused on this you should retire.'[54] This statement owns his desire, characterising those who cannot understand it as old-fashioned and out of touch. He insists upon the viability of a gaze in which Mary's mixture of masculinity and femininity is attractive.

Rohy rightfully notes that Moddelmog 'tends to translate questions of (trans)gender into issues of (homo)sexuality', minimising the possibility that Hemingway's transfeminine self-positioning might concern gender rather than sexuality.[55] However, Hemingway's heteronormative rhetoric suggests that his gender identifications may be more difficult to disentangle from homophobia than Rohy suggests. Moddelmog observes that Hemingway repudiates claims that his and Mary's sexual practices were homosexual, aggressively disavowing the possibility that she had even 'one lesbian impulse' or that he enjoyed 'tactile contact with men except the normal Spanish *abrazo*'.[56] This language, which indirectly 'names the repressed desire that makes its way into consciousness only on the condition that it be negated', is Ernest Hemingway's own rather than evidence of Moddelmog's propensity to 'translate'.[57] Negating the prospect that he might, as a man, have enjoyed sex with Mary because of her boyishness, he 'normalizes his and Mary's desire' by reaffirming her femininity and his masculinity.[58] Although he calls Mary 'a boy' and acknowledges that he plays 'her girls', they do not undercut 'the binary of heterosexual and homosexual'.[59] Thus, as Richard Fantina observes, Hemingway 'celebrates sodomy on the man', but his 'relentlessly expressed homophobia precludes him from entertaining the idea of submitting to sodomy from a man'.[60] Drawing on Bersani's argument that homophobia stems from the belief that male sexual submission approximates '"the terrifying phenomenon of female sexuality"', Fantina suggests that Hemingway's 'awareness of his alternative sexuality led him to associate it with both female sexuality and with homosexuality and part of him shrank from this', revealing the limited scope of his transfeminine 'jouissance'.[61] Hemingway's observation that Mary 'has always wanted to be a boy and thinks like a boy without losing any femininity' does not express openness to all forms of transgender but rather an insistence that her masculinity is appealing only if it includes 'femininity'.

Stein was not as defensive about gender crossings. Instead, her transmasculinity included erotic play that radically rearticulated jouissance and gendered embodiment. Hemingway, by contrast, avoided the implications of his and Mary's sexual practices by situating them '"outside all tribal law"'.[62] This denial led him to target Stein, whose masculinity both attracted and repelled him. As Eric Haralson observes, Hemingway's *Torrents* asks 'What was at the bottom of' Stein's writing, mocking her desire to get to 'the "bottom nature" of all human types' in *The Making of Americans*.[63] This routes Hemingway's disavowed anality through Stein's novel, which sidesteps 'genital sexual difference in favor of' an 'indistinct notion of anal identity'.[64] Whereas this anality affords Stein Barthesian 'bliss', it is more tightly bound for Hemingway.[65] Its trajectory was only an undercurrent in the writings published during his lifetime.[66] This suggests that Hemingway's lingering homophobia curbed his desire to abandon hegemonic gender constructs, damaging his friendship with the transmasculine Stein.

Although Hemingway eventually derided Stein's transmasculinity, they initially bonded over his desire to cut Hadley's hair. She 'had been wearing her hair in a bob, and because her husband wanted it to be even shorter, she too wanted it that way'.[67] After Stein 'got out a pair of scissors and showed Ernest how to trim his wife's hair', he started to 'think of her as "family"'.[68] She, in turn, wrote to Anderson that 'the Hemingways you sent . . . are charming. He is a delightful fellow and I like his talk and I am teaching him to cut his wife's hair.'[69] Using a phallogocentric logic predicating desire on lack, Carl Eby takes this exchange as a strategy for avoiding castration: as evidence of Hemingway's 'fetishistic association' of Stein with his mother through the trope of short hair.[70] I see it instead as a vehicle for Stein's and Hemingway's masculine homosociality. Whereas Sedgwick's *Between Men* tracks the ties men establish by exchanging women, Stein and Hemingway bonded by masculinising Hadley. Hemingway further complicated the resulting 'family of choice' by interpreting it through rivalry with Picasso, whose son, Paulo, was already Stein's and Toklas's godchild when they agreed to be Bumby Hemingway's godparents.[71]

Hemingway's second wife, Pauline, also participated in Hadley's and her own masculinisation, using language suggesting that they explicitly eroticised masculine homosociality.[72] Whereas Mark Spilka reads Pauline's statements as evidence of the 'oddly androgynous terms' through which she construed their marriage, I read them as signs of Hemingway's sexual interest in masculine homosociality and her willing participation in it.[73] However, Hemingway's masculine homosocial desires for his wives circulated in heterosexual marriages. His erotic investments in Pauline and Hadley were distinct from his attraction to Stein, whose queerness implicated him yet ultimately prompted him to repudiate her. This volatility did not emerge from flaws in Hemingway's 'ego' and 'gender identity', but rather from the ways his privately enjoyed queer sexuality was at odds with the hegemonic masculinities that dominate his fiction.[74]

Spilka leaves the implications of these dynamics unexplored when he notes that Hemingway used *Torrents* to mock Stein and Anderson after leaving Hadley for Pauline.[75] Although *Torrents* primarily pillories Anderson, it also parodies Stein in a chapter called 'The Passing of a Great Race and the Making and Marring of Americans' – an attack on the novel whose influence Hemingway disavows.[76] *Torrents*' direct references to Stein miss her writings' resonances. Hemingway's character Yogi Johnson offhandedly asks, 'Where were her experiments in words leading her? What was at the bottom of it? All that in Paris. Ah, Paris. How far was it to Paris now. Paris in the morning. Paris in the evening. Paris at night. Paris in the morning again. Paris at noon, perhaps. Why not?'[77] Abravanel observes that 'this passage mocks Steinian repetition through its attention to place', conveying stuckness rather than highlighting reiteration's ability to unfix meaning and generate fresh significations.[78] Haralson hears echoes of *The Making of Americans*' anal preoccupations in *Torrents* and finds in Johnson the same attitude toward Stein that Hemingway displays in *A Moveable Feast*.[79] Asking 'Would it help him to want a woman?' and going on to declare 'Ah, there was a woman!', Johnson 'indirectly and ironically' hints at Stein's queerness, stressing her 'emphatic femininity' rather than the masculinity her crop made apparent.[80] This echoes Hemingway's mocking characterisation of Stein as 'a woman who isn't a woman'.[81]

Although *Torrents* tiptoes condescendingly around Stein's sexuality and gender, Hemingway is more direct and cutting in *Green Hills*, written in the wake of *The Autobiography*'s success. He asserts that:

> At a certain age the men writers change into Old Mother Hubbard. The women writers become Joan of Arc without the fighting. They become leaders. It doesn't matter who they lead. If they do not have followers they invent them. It is useless for those selected as followers to protest. They are accused of disloyalty.[82]

This passage uses negative characterisations of transgender crossings to present ageing writers as past their prime. Associating Stein with the cross-dressing medieval martyr Joan of Arc, *Green Hills* suggests that transmasculinity drives arrogant and authoritarian behaviours. Generalising his perceptions of Stein to all 'women writers', Hemingway alleges that their ambitions lead them to 'invent' and abuse disciples through delusional fantasies of success and influence.[83]

Green Hills' portrayal of Stein as an overweening martyr anticipates *A Moveable Feast*'s characterisation of her as overbearing and divisive. In the latter, Hemingway stages Stein and James Joyce as competing 'general[s]' and describes her short haircut as that of a 'Roman emperor'.[84] He wrote that '[i]f you brought up Joyce twice, you would not be invited back' to her salon: 'It was like mentioning one general favourably to another general. You learned not to do it the first time you made the mistake.'[85] Although Hemingway acknowledges Stein's intelligence and ambition by invoking her 'imperial' presence, he also underhandedly criticises the competitiveness and decisiveness he codes as masculine.[86] Expressing disdain for the new image created by her crop, Hemingway admitted that he 'liked her better before she cut her hair'.[87] His reaction is telling: by using masculine stylisation, Stein's short haircut drew on 'a communal system of gender representation' that signalled her equal standing with the men in her network and established her 'imperial' presence within modernist Paris.[88] Stein's stature, not just her hair, rankled him, and he used *A Moveable Feast* to undermine the masculine authority she claimed.

A Moveable Feast implies that Stein's new hairstyle caused Hemingway's change of heart because it excised the femininity that initially attracted him. After describing her 'quarrels' with her 'other men friends' and 'the new friends' that replaced them, Hemingway states that 'She got to look like a Roman emperor and that was fine if you liked your women to look like Roman emperors. But Picasso had painted her, and I could remember her, when she looked like a woman from Friuli.'[89] This characterisation recalls not Picasso's painting but Hemingway's description of her, earlier in *A Moveable Feast*, as an 'Italian peasant woman'.[90] Telling of his first visit to 27, rue de Fleurus, he describes Stein as:

> Very big but not tall and . . . heavily built like a peasant woman. She had beautiful eyes and a strong German-Jewish face that also could have been Friulano and she reminded me of a northern Italian peasant woman with her clothes, her mobile face and her lovely, thick, alive immigrant hair which she wore put up.[91]

Hemingway's attraction to Stein is apparent in this passage. Characterising her clothes in national terms, he stresses her plumpness and lively personality: her 'strong' and 'mobile face'; her 'lovely, thick, alive immigrant hair'.[92] Refusing to see anything other than this image, Hemingway does not register the subtle signs of 'mannishness' that neutralised Stein's 'femininity' and were legible even before her haircut in her 'androgynous' robes.[93] By feminising Stein, Hemingway reveals his attraction to her yet disavows that masculinity was part of her appeal.

Even after the 'Caesar' crop challenges Hemingway's view of Stein, prompting repressed signs of her 'mannishness' to return within his consciousness, he continues to insist on his own perspective's superiority. His complaint about Stein's new look is part of a broader charge that she has developed poor vision since their break: as 'the new friends moved in' to the salon and the hosts purchased their artworks, '[i]t was sad to see new worthless pictures hung in with the great pictures'.[94] The gaze governing Hemingway's 1920s contrasts dramatically with the one animating *The Autobiography*. Stein shows Anderson approving of the short haircut and aligning his look with hers in the wake of *Torrents*.[95] *The Autobiography* also features an initially perturbed Picasso adjusting to the new gaze implied by the crop. Whereas in Stein's version, the painter ultimately realises that despite the change, 'all the same it [his painting] is there' – as if his work has captured her unchangeable essence – from Hemingway's standpoint the haircut has altered something fundamental.[96] Although the writer acknowledges that there are multiple ways of looking at Stein's newfound guise – it is 'fine if you liked your women to look like Roman emperors' – he is dismissively snide.[97] Whereas the painter accepted signs of Stein's masculinity even when they threatened the gaze through which he saw her, Hemingway disavowed his attraction to her and devalued her appearance.

By trading on his and Picasso's celebrity and questionably presuming their looks to be aligned, Hemingway presents modernism's gaze as uniformly heteronormative, using it to diminish Stein's appearance and artistic judgement. His feminisation of her is important to this process. Conflating her Parisian persona with Picasso's representation and his own memory, Hemingway claims that the artist 'had painted her, and I could remember her, when she looked like a woman from Friuli'.[98] This formulation overrides details from Picasso's painting that register Stein's masculinity: her claim to the frame's entire 'pictorial space' and placement of her hands on her knees, for instance.[99] Feminising her anyway, Hemingway disavows her transmasculinity and attempts to maintain a heteronormative gaze.

Heteronormativity also drives other descriptions of Stein's attire in *A Moveable Feast*. Although Hemingway initially includes her 'clothes' in his portrayal of her as an 'Italian peasant woman', he sees her differently when following Hadley's look.[100] After hearing Stein complaining about the high cost of women's clothing and advising her visitors to '"either buy clothes or buy pictures"', Hemingway notes that 'I saw my wife trying not to look at the strange, steerage clothes that Miss Stein wore.'[101] This suggests that Hadley saw Stein through the lens of heteronormative femininity: not as a lively and attractive 'peasant' woman or breaker of gender norms but an unappealing example of sartorial sacrifice.[102] Feminising and marginalising her appearance, Hemingway deflects the possibility that he may have been drawn to her masculinity and mobilises a heteronormative gaze that refuses to register its appeal.

Hemingway's disapproval of the new gaze constituted by Stein's and Toklas's salon also extended to 'the new friends' whose growing presence threatened to displace him.[103] Although he does not say so explicitly in *A Moveable Feast*, he considered them 'a 4th rate lot of fairies'.[104] They comprised 'la seconde famille', the queer family of choice that dominated Stein's and Toklas's social life after their friendship with Hemingway crumbled.[105] Stein gravitated to these men hoping that their shared experience of '[s]exual nonconformity' would leave their friendships 'unperturbed by the frictions that had frayed her attachments with heterosexual men'.[106] Many of these artists were neoromantics; their art's openly 'emotional theatricality' differed markedly 'from Picasso's strain of modernism' and Hemingway's fictional style.[107] As Stein and Toklas acquired neoromantic paintings, the collection at 27, rue de Fleurus changed: what Hemingway claims were 'worthless pictures' appeared among 'the great pictures'.[108] He exaggerates the 'quarrels' that emerged in Stein's 'passionate' but 'unstable' new friendships while refusing to acknowledge his own quarrelsomeness or her longstanding ties with Anderson, Fäy and Van Vechten.[109] While the economic value of Stein's neoromantic acquisitions never approached that of her Cézannes, Matisses and Picassos, Hemingway objected to the work of her 'new friends' not only on economic but also on aesthetic and sexual grounds.[110] The influence of 'la seconde famille' shifted the gaze through which he saw Stein and the salon, causing him to devalue it and its visitors.[111]

Stein recognised that the growing prominence of 'fairies' at 27, rue de Fleurus was an especially sore point for Hemingway.[112] Even though he did not complain to Stein's face, she could sense his discomfort with her friends' femininity and publicly criticised his tendency to hide his sensitivity in the 1930s. Describing Hemingway in *The Autobiography* as too 'yellow' to reveal his 'real story', she declared that while his early work held promise, 'he was not really good after 1925'.[113] She later expressed disappointment with his obsession with 'sex and violent death' and use of masculinity as a 'shield'.[114] In 1939, she mocked his 'big man act' to Samuel Steward, who asserted that Hemingway's behaviour was 'compensation' for his very small 'size' and evidence of resentment over Stein's 'influence on him'.[115] Agreeing, she predicted what was to come in *A Moveable Feast*: 'one of these days when he sees fit he'll really attack all those he thinks had anything to do with his "greatness," Fitzgerald and Zelda and Alice and me and all the rest, just the way he attacked Sherwood'.[116] Anticipating recent studies of Hemingway's masculine performativity and emotional suppression, Stein could see the fragility of the hyperbolic acts through which he enacted hegemonic masculinity and the forms of disavowed vulnerability subtending his subjectivity.[117]

Moreover, Stein suspected that Hemingway was hiding queer desires behind hypermasculine performances. Although *A Moveable Feast* shows her asserting that 'the act male homosexuals commit is ugly and repugnant', breeding self-hatred, Cope finds the idea that she was homophobic hard to believe because she 'assiduously collected young gay men and their lovers'.[118] Stein also spoke positively about gay male sexuality before and after their friendship; she later claimed that her hostile characterisation of gay male sexuality was designed to provoke Hemingway.[119] 'We are surrounded by homosexuals', she told Steward; 'when I ran down the male ones to Hemingway it was because I thought he was a secret one'.[120]

Stein's comments about gay men thus may have been insincere, designed 'to seduce Hemingway . . . via his rather pronounced and obviously highly eroticized pathways of disgust', as Cope suggests.[121] Hemingway's response to Stein's praise of gay men supports Cope's theory. Robert McAlmon had been claiming that Hemingway and F. Scott Fitzgerald were gay; Stein, believing the rumour mill, told the former that she had learned he was gay, or at least 'unconsciously' homosexual, and tried to convince him that 'homosexuals of both genders possessed inherently greater creative sensibilities'.[122] Hemingway then railed to Janet Flanner that Stein 'told me she had heard an incident, some fag story, which proved me conclusively to be very queer indeed' until he challenged her into admitting the evidence was 'circumstantial'.[123] He left Paris for Key West shortly thereafter and put the entire Atlantic Ocean between them, suggesting that his own desire was at stake in their exchange.[124]

Furthering these gaps around sexuality, *A Moveable Feast* presents Stein's and Hemingway's exchange about homosexuality as structured by disavowals on both sides. At the same time as she is shown using homophobic assertions about gay men to provoke her interlocutor into disclosures that do not come, she also states that lesbians are 'happy' because '[t]hey do nothing that they are disgusted by and nothing that is repulsive'.[125] Much is omitted from this passage: although she does not name her relationship with Toklas, Hemingway's letters reveal that during this conversation, Stein explained 'the mechanics' of queer sexuality in detail.[126] *A Moveable Feast* also refers to Toklas only as Stein's 'friend' or 'companion' – words that, while common in the early twentieth century, suggest they are lovers while enabling heteronormative readers' disavowals.[127]

Hemingway's occlusions are hypocritical and underhanded inversions of his critique of Stein's view that literature should leave some things unsaid. Early in *A Moveable Feast*, he sharply criticises her statement that his story 'Up in Michigan' is '*inaccrochable*', suggesting that she prudishly disapproves of all sexual representation instead of considering that she might object on feminist grounds to the text's nonjudgemental treatment of rape.[128] Hemingway tells readers that Stein's comment made him reluctant to use the language the homosexual 'wolves used on the lake boats' to approach other men, and chose 'interfered with' as a euphemism for anal penetration.[129] Two sentences later, he shares the '*inaccrochable* phrase' in question – '"Oh gash may be fine but one eye for mine"' – and tells readers that 'I was always careful of my language with Miss Stein even when true phrases might have clarified or better expressed a prejudice.'[130] This statement is difficult to believe because 'Stein had an enormous curiosity about sexuality, and, at times, a real zeal to speak of it.'[131] Falsely suggesting that she objects to all direct representations of sexuality, Hemingway's comment elevates his professed preference for straight talk over Stein's indirection. Attempting to fend off the 'emasculating' pressure to cut 'passages that might prove offensive', this gesture masks Hemingway's stylistic bentness and props up his image as a masculine writer in command of his craft.[132] This 'mirage of straightness' works throughout the memoir to project Hemingway's refusal of sexual representation onto Stein.[133]

After *The Autobiography* exposed Hemingway's fear of feminisation, he retaliated, revealing and attempting to neutralise the threat posed by her comments about male homosexuality. In *A Moveable Feast*, as Stein builds up to her statement that 'the act male homosexuals commit is ugly and repugnant', he insists that he knows all about it:[134]

> I knew it was why you carried a knife and would use it when you were in the company of tramps when you were a boy in the days when wolves was not a slang term for men obsessed by the pursuit of women . . . Under questioning I tried to tell Miss Stein that when you were a boy and moved in the company of men, you had to be prepared to kill a man, know how to do it and really know that you would do it in order not to be interfered with . . . If you knew you would kill, other people sensed it very quickly and you were let alone.[135]

This passage's reiterations show Stein's stylistic influence and suggest that the prospect of being penetrated by a man was so traumatic that Hemingway would kill 'wolves' to prevent it. Moreover, in noting the historical variability of sexual connotations attached to the word 'wolves', he shows awareness of the social construction of gender and sexuality. Yet his narration works like a palimpsest, layering the two meanings of 'wolves' atop one another and showing that he views its earlier, homosexual significance through its more recent, heterosexual connotations. When he goes on to claim that 'I could have expressed myself more vividly by using an *inaccrochable* phrase that wolves used on the lake boats, "Oh gash may be fine but one eye for mine"', he draws on early twentieth-century 'sexual slang terms for vagina and anus, "gash" and "one eye"', to suggest a parallel between taking the submissive role in gay male sex and assuming the position of a penetrated woman in a heterosexual encounter.[136] This filters gay male sexuality through the later construction of 'wolves' as men who hound 'women', showing that Hemingway has 'a certain kind of feminine knowledge, the knowledge of what it is to be hounded by men', as Hovey puts it.[137] His willingness to engage in 'homophobic violence' to thwart them asserts and undercuts his claim to masculinity, revealing the disavowal of his own femininity animating his defensive claim to 'dislike tactile contact with men' despite the jouissance he enjoyed by playing Mary's 'girls'.[138]

A similar disavowal underpins the sketch from *A Moveable Feast* called 'A Strange Enough Ending', the most notorious example of Hemingway's retaliation for Stein's claim that he was 'yellow'.[139] In this chapter, Hemingway creates a void around his final visit to 27, rue de Fleurus by refusing to name Toklas, acknowledge her and Stein's lifelong relationship, or describe what he claims to have upset him. Stopping by one afternoon, he overhears a snatch of the couple's conversation and says that:

> I heard someone speaking to Miss Stein as I had never heard one person speak to another; never, anywhere, ever.
>
> Then Miss Stein's voice came pleading and begging, saying, 'Don't, pussy. Don't. Don't, please don't. I'll do anything, pussy, but please don't do it. Please don't. Please don't, pussy.'[140]

Hemingway's feigned shock is implausible and 'disingenuous' given his 'crush' on Stein and earlier revelation that they had 'frankly discussed homosexuality'.[141] Moreover, his use of one of the couple's terms of endearment – 'pussy' – has rightfully led scholars to identify this passage as a homophobic attack on their sexuality.[142] The supposed 'horrors' from which Hemingway flees could be little more than Toklas tickling Stein with 'a large brilliant peacock feather', as Steward wittily suggests in a parody of this scene.[143]

Although Hemingway begins 'A Strange Enough Ending' with the complaint that there is little 'future in men being friends with great women', especially 'truly ambitious women writers', at the chapter's centre is not – as one might expect – a scene in which a domineering Stein lords over the man she describes as a 'good pupil' who 'takes training' and acts on it 'without understanding'.[144] Instead, Hemingway shows Stein's submission to the unnamed Toklas. As Kenneth Lynn observes, this passage proposes 'a symbolic truth about the power relationship that obtained between Gertrude and Alice'.[145] However, in so doing it also launches what Benstock aptly calls a 'vicious attack' on Stein's 'role as the "male" lover to a wife who secretly controls and manipulates her'.[146] In 'exposing her lack of "manliness"', this depiction homophobically and transphobically targets Stein's and Toklas's gendered eroticism.[147]

Although he rightfully observes that Hemingway 'did not acknowledge the dimension of symbolic self-involvement in the love affair he was describing', Lynn unnecessarily pathologises him by bringing the scene at the rue de Fleurus back to Hemingway's childhood experience of having been dressed in girls' clothes.[148] Lynn rightfully suggests, however, that Hemingway's own attraction to Stein and desire for erotic surrender were at stake in his flight. By characterising Stein as an 'Italian peasant woman' and mocking her submission to Toklas, he avoids considering that her masculinity – which was flexible and open to erotic submission – might be a valuable alternative to his own.[149] In *A Moveable Feast*, the exchange between Stein and Toklas that elicits his condemnation highlights the mobility of the gendered power structure they enjoyed. Given the discrepancy between Hemingway's public persona and private reflections, he might have reacted so strongly to the sound of Stein 'pleading and begging' because it revealed a submissiveness he craved but felt the need to condemn publicly.[150] He thus feminised and devalued her, intimating that she was as 'yellow' as she claimed him to be.[151]

Hemingway's claim that '[t]here is not much future in men being friends with great women' similarly feminises Stein while backhandedly acknowledging her investment in the concept of the Great Man.[152] In a spectacular feat of projection, he insinuates that Stein was misogynist whereas he was not. In a passage Gerry Brenner mistakes as evidence that Hemingway was 'no chauvinist', he notes that Hadley conversed with her husband's colleagues: 'It wasn't like being a wife at Miss Stein's', she notes.[153] Hemingway's misogyny is apparent, however, when he attacks Stein in the introduction to bartender Jimmy Charters's memoir about Montparnasse. Hemingway jokes that when 'literary ladies' write memoirs, they

> usually prove that a lady's brain may still be between her thighs . . . and will treat you in her memoirs exactly as any girl around the Dôme or the Select would, imputing you this, denying you that, and only withholding the Billingsgate because it would fit illy in the pantheon to her own glory that every self-made legendary woman hopes to erect with her memoirs.[154]

This bizarre remark discredits Stein by heterosexualising her. Associating her with the denizens of Montparnasse's bars, Hemingway insinuates that she is a deceitful flirt who seeks celebrity at his expense. This construction reveals his inability to grapple with his attraction to Stein's queerness and shows that he feminises his rivals to discredit them.

As Rohy observes, *A Moveable Feast* similarly 'makes every effort to unman F. Scott Fitzgerald' by describing his face with feminising language before portraying him as manipulated by Zelda.[155] Hemingway's treatment of Stein works analogously. His opprobrious picture of her relationship with Toklas attacks Stein for her sexuality, gender and presumably flawed belief in her literary genius. Hemingway tells readers that he left because the couple's exchange was 'bad to hear and the answers were worse', but cagily acknowledges that 'it was really much more complicated than that'.[156] By transphobically shaming Stein, he disavows the complexity of his own gender and sexuality to further his heteromasculine self-portrait in *A Moveable Feast*.

The resulting distortions in Hemingway's portrayals of Stein thereby echo Sedgwick's account of the modes of 'desiring, identifying, representing, repelling, paralleling, differentiating, rivaling, leaning, twisting, mimicking, withdrawing, attracting, aggressing' and 'warping' that can characterise queer relationality.[157] *A Moveable Feast* reveals that Hemingway's reaction to Stein was inflected by his aversion to their masculine homosocial bond's queerness, fear of his own femininity, and disdain for the alternative masculinity she modelled with Toklas. Stein's alternatives to hegemonic constructs of gender, sexuality and literary form countered the norms underpinning Hemingway's public persona. These differences animate *A Moveable Feast* as it reveals the cracks in the hypermasculine self-image he so desperately promoted.

Queer relationality in Stein's and Hemingway's shorter texts

Stein, 'Objects Lie on a Table' (1922: 1932)

Before Stein called Hemingway a 'good pupil' in *The Autobiography*, she positioned him similarly in a play called 'Objects Lie On A Table', composed shortly after they met in 1922.[158] Although Hemingway is not named in 'Objects', its content and the timing of its composition reflect their 'early talks on writing'.[159] Although Dydo argues that this text 'suggests not the play it is but a still life', she misses its relationality.[160] As Bridgman observes, the first line – 'Nuns ask for them for recreation' – registers the pleasure nuns took in reading Stein's work, 'probably *Tender Buttons*, whose first section was "Objects"'.[161] This opening places the rest of the text in the dual contexts of the cloister and the domestic sphere, feminising the interactions that follow.

The piece's insistent references to the traditional subjects of 'still life' painting appear in the context of Stein's and Hemingway's 'master/student relationship' as he is 'asked to practice rendering objects'.[162] Phrases like 'Now then read for me to me what you can and will see. I see what there is to see' suggest the two parties' different levels of professional experience as well as the play of their looks.[163] Reading leads to seeing and to Stein's gentle admonition that 'You want to show more effort than that.'[164] Similarly, the lines 'What is the difference between houses and a table. What is the difference between objects on a table and furniture in houses' build to a pedantic question – 'Had you ever thought of that' – followed by an answer: 'Objects on a table make a standpoint of recompense and result, furniture in houses do decide matters.'[165] Although this passage recalls Ahmed's observation that 'orientations involve different ways of registering the proximity of objects and others', Stein's decisive tone uncharacteristically stabilises rather than queers orientation.[166] This distinguishes 'Objects' from many of her other experimental works, whose bent orientations and destabilised ontologies mobilise shifting forms of relationality.

In 'Objects', Stein and Hemingway are locked into 'master/student' roles.[167] Her admonishments to 'Study again and again and leave me to my wishes I wish that they could copy all of it as well as they do copy it' build to a conclusion that hints at the likelihood of Hemingway's ascendance, yet frames it as as uncertain as that of Matisse and Picasso.[168] Stein interrogates and supports Hemingway's vision for his professional future, asking 'the question I say have you succeeded, you succeed' only to destabilise it: 'Can you succeed and do you succeed. I succeed in recalling this to their mind. I do not fall behind.'[169] This language shifts attention to Stein and stresses her success as Hemingway's mentor, stoking his motivation and reminding him of his goal while noting that she continues to make progress: 'I do not fall behind.'[170] This final line is the sole way the text softens Stein's authoritative stance. While maintaining the 'master/student' distinction, this formulation implies not that Stein has succeeded as a writer but that she does 'not fall behind'.[171] 'Objects' thereby queers linear understandings of success, suggesting that Stein does not fit its constrictions. This proved prescient: Hemingway's emphasis on conventional constructions of 'the career, the career' motivated cutthroat behaviours that exacerbated his and Stein's differences, fuelling their attacks.[172]

Stein, 'He and They, Hemingway' (1923: 1923)

Although Stein did not directly attack Hemingway until *The Autobiography*, her other writings from the 1920s register her reservations about him. In August 1923, while she was still in Paris, she composed 'He and They, Hemingway', a poem about her new friend.[173] Written shortly before the burst of writing in the south of France that included 'As A Wife Has A Cow' and her second portraits of Picasso and Van Vechten, 'He and They' is less jubilant than the texts that follow. As Knapp observes, the fact that Stein wrote this portrait 'in a schoolchild's notebook bearing the title *The Educators of Youth* might indicate her' parental 'feelings for him'.[174] Whereas 'If I Told Him' affectionately teases Picasso, criticising his overbearing qualities while showing Stein's continued good will, 'He and They' pays tribute to its subject while suggesting that 'Stein had reservations not about Hemingway's gift but about how he used it.'[175] This portrait shows Stein's interest in Hemingway while communicating her doubts about him.

Stein's concerns about Hemingway are apparent in the negations opening the portrait; their sonorities playfully highlight the disavowals that drove his Left Bank manoeuvrings. Writing that he is 'Not Lucretia Borgia. / Not in or on a building. / Not a crime not in the time. / Not by this time. / Not in the way.', Stein introduces several ideas through negation.[176] These 'negative anaphoras', which recall the works by Victor Hugo on Stein's manuscript notebook, all concern 'murder' and hint at the cut-throat tactics masked by Hemingway's apparent innocence.[177] By stating 'not a crime not in the time' and claiming that Hemingway is 'Not Lucretia Borgia', Stein makes and disavows several comparisons: that he is a young, feminine beauty; that he is a Machiavellian manipulator; and that he is playing politics within Left Bank literary networks to advance his career. In so doing, Stein reveals her attraction to the young writer, feminising him – as he later feminises her in *A Moveable Feast* – to justify her desire. In *The Autobiography*, Stein discloses her 'weakness for Hemingway' and complains that he has withheld his 'real story' from public view to protect 'the career, the career'.[178] Even the portrait's title, which conflates 'He' and 'They' with 'Hemingway', folds him in with the Borgias to suggest analogies the text disavows.

The poem's wording both introduces and reveals the limitations of its comparison between Hemingway and Lucretia Borgia, suggesting that he is and is not like a conniving figure from the past. Through these disavowals, 'He and They' mobilises queer time's disjointedness. As Freeman argues, 'the double-time of the late nineteenth and early twentieth centuries' that led to queer subjects' emergence 'trafficked in signs of fractured time', as 'Freud's concept of the unconscious acknowledged' by shifting 'modernity's temporal splittings into the psyche's interior'.[179] 'He and They' uses negation to mobilise these redoublings, fragmenting time and invoking figures from the Renaissance to suggest its subject's queer potential. Even Stein's opening reference to Hemingway's youth – 'Among and then young. / Not ninety-three.' – cannot be taken at face value given her later observation that he 'looks like a modern' but 'smells of the museums'.[180]

Dydo argues that 'He and They' suggests that Hemingway 'lives in our time and his own way', rather than in the manner of the past; she points to echoes with *In Our Time*, an early version of which he had completed by the time Stein composed her poem.[181] Two stories from this collection – 'Mr. and Mrs. Elliott' and 'Soldier's Home' – regularly appear as examples of Stein's influence on Hemingway's style and create resonances across their work from the 1920s.[182] The 'strategic ambiguity' St. Pierre identifies in Hemingway's 'bent' style is evident in *In Our Time*, whose title reverberates across Hemingway's stories and Stein's portrait to unsettle conventional approaches to time in ways Dydo does not acknowledge.[183] Stein claims that Hemingway's narration 'has a false sense of time' because of 'his newspaper training', which geared him not for 'the time in which to write' but 'the time in which the newspaper' was to appear.[184] 'He and They' plays on his collection's title to dislocate rather than reinforce the notion that people are grounded in a singular time and place. The poem's temporal jumps also suggest that Hemingway was capable of writing that registers a far more radical temporality than Dydo admits.

Stein's departures from grammatical convention reinforce these temporal disjunctures. The lines 'Not a crime not in the time. / Not by this time' are ambiguous: to what do 'the time' and 'this time' refer?[185] We need not assume, as does Dydo, that 'this time' refers to that of the portrait's composition: the early twentieth century, whose polemicists were determined to distinguish themselves by 'making it new'.[186] Instead, the undecidability of Stein's diction – which offers no clear antecedents for 'the time' and 'this time' – suggests that time subsists within the portrait's resonant significations, unbound by grammatical structure.[187] By signifying outside of sequential time,

'He and They' looks 'backward to prior moments' to another mode 'of being and belonging'.[188] In so doing, the poem performs what Benjamin describes as the historian's task: to 'brush history against the grain' of Hemingway's own time and the ways he and Stein made their desires legible.[189]

Situating Hemingway's disavowed feminine sensitivity in the interstices of queer time, Stein's portrait reveals her attraction to him and suggests that he is implicated in a queer temporality whose promise he would never realise because of his investment in hegemonic masculinity's marketability. As Freeman argues, 'Queer temporalities . . . are points of resistance to' futurally oriented temporalities: ones 'that, in turn, propose other possibilities for living in relation to indeterminately past, present, and future others'.[190] Looking askance at her young friend through a simultaneously avant-garde and conservative queer eye, Stein could see that Hemingway was and was not both 'He and They': the ambitious modernist writer and conniving Renaissance beauty. 'He and They' thus shows its subject through a gaze whose temporal and ontological indeterminacies point to Stein's fear that his queer potential would never be realised.

The poem's temporal oscillations also mobilise geographical displacements to situate Hemingway outside of space and time. As Dydo observes, 'They' and 'Hemingway' rhyme with 'away', which kicks off a series of puns at the beginning of the portrait's longest stanza to invoke Ernest's and Hadley's imminent departure for Toronto.[191] Plays on 'a head' and references to 'extreme savagedom' follow.[192] These words invoke 'headhunters, savages, and primitive rituals' – all of which suggest that Hemingway 'himself is a cannibal' because he 'does not understand the avant-garde-techniques' he imitates.[193] In so doing, the portrait's primitivist turn points to pervasive characterisations of the European avant-garde as barbaric and echoes Picasso's and Stein's work from the first decade of the twentieth century: his *Portrait of Gertrude Stein* and *Demoiselles*; her *Three Lives*.[194] 'He and They' thereby hints that something about its subject recalls times and places other than post-war Paris: not only the Borgias' Renaissance but also Picasso's and Stein's turn-of-the-century modernism and Hemingway's fictions set on 'the African velt'.[195] The text thus suggests that Hemingway occupies the mythological time and place of their purportedly primitive precursors, problematically assumed to have lived in 'extreme savagedom'.[196] The poem inflects this idea through the claim that 'A head is what every one not in the north of Australia returns for', suggesting that the Hemingways are returning to their primitive roots.[197] Yet the location to which they would return is uncertain: is it Toronto? Paris? An unnamed place in the distant past? The portrait puts its subject in constant motion, unsettling time and space while calling the distinction between the 'civilised' and the 'primitive' into question.

Moreover, the text's primitivist language anticipates Hemingway's much later declaration that his and Mary's sexual play takes place '"outside all tribal law"'.[198] Suggesting that their erotic practices abandon all civilisation, his statement resonates with a line from 'He and They' that asks whether there is 'any memorial of the failure of civilization to cope with extreme and extremely well begun to cope with extreme savagedom'.[199] This wording blurs the line between the 'civilised' and the 'primitive', investigating the vicissitudes of 'civilisation' as it attempts to 'cope with extreme savagedom': a process that begins 'nearly finished', slides back into apparent 'failure', seems 'extremely well begun' near its finish and ultimately succeeds.[200] These temporal disjunctures convey uncertainty about both 'civilisation' and 'savagedom', but end by casting the latter in a positive light, as 'extreme' and 'extremely well begun'.[201] Although Stein could not have predicted Hemingway's later statements about his sexual practices, the portrait's wording suggests that during his young adulthood, she sensed his willingness to abandon social convention: that there might be another Hemingway whose story had yet to be told. Although scholars now know that Hemingway engaged in gender-bending sexual play, Stein was not privy to these details. In their absence, 'He and They' calls upon the language of the 'primitive' to push representation's limits and hint at desires transgressing dominant social norms.

The end of the portrait's longest stanza also associates Hemingway with primitivism. The phrase 'cope with extreme savagedom' opens to the next two lines, 'There and we know. / Hemingway', brief statements that are the portrait's moments of greatest certitude.[202] Temporarily halting oscillations between 'He' and 'They', these lines converge on 'Hemingway', who is 'There', and insist upon his association with 'extreme savagedom'.[203] The end of the poem unsettles the previous lines by moving between greetings and farewells: 'How do you do and good-bye. Good-bye and how do you do. Well and how do you do.'[204] These niceties send Hemingway off to Canada and 'in advance welcome him back' to Paris, as Dydo notes.[205]

By anticipating Hemingway's return before he has even left Paris, the portrait warps diachronic accounts of space and time to depart from conventional perspective.

The poem's queer oscillations also anticipate 'Van or Twenty Years After' (1923: 1924), which Stein wrote shortly after 'He and They'.[206] Both portraits' spatialising vectors recall Sedgwick's observation that '[t]he word "queer" itself means *across*' and connotes 'a continuing moment, movement, motive – recurrent, eddying, *troublant*'.[207] The uncertainty about Hemingway's departure for Toronto that mobilises the latter poem's conclusion also registers in its opening, which questions his careerism. Displacing its subject from the outset, the portrait's title demands that he share space with others: 'They'. The text's opening lines also suggest his struggle for professional space within modernist Paris. Sandwiched between five lines that enact temporal disavowals, the fourth stanza – consisting of the negation 'Not in or on a building' – precedes the assertion 'not in the way'.[208] We can read the latter claim in multiple ways. Does it stage Hemingway as somebody who is not in Stein's 'way'?[209] Does negation underhandedly suggest that he really is an obstacle for her? Does it hint that Stein is a barrier to Hemingway's success – or that she is not? The portrait's disavowals mobilise all of these possibilities, displacing both 'He and They'. By setting these temporal and spatial dislocations into motion, 'He and They' suggests that its subject was somehow out of place even as he established his reputation as an important modernist writer.

Hemingway, 'The Soul of Spain' (1924)

Hemingway responded to 'He and They' in a 1924 poem called 'The Soul of Spain with McAlmon and Bird the Publishers', which mocks Stein's style yet pays underhanded homage to her portraits.[210] Following Stein's example, he shows loyalty to friends and supporters: McAlmon, Bill Bird and especially Pound. Yet unlike Stein's texts, 'The Soul of Spain' does not focus on a single person but on a broad array of early twentieth-century icons. Ultimately rejecting lesser modernists and erecting 'a monument to Ezra', Hemingway's poem has a different goal than Stein's even though portraits and monuments both register a person's importance within their social context.[211] Writing of Stein's 'seconde famille', Corn and Latimer observe that 'portraiture' is well 'adapted to the exchange of artistic tributes that' bolster 'communal bonds'.[212] The informal relationality and focus on subjectivity lived out by gifting portraits differs significantly from the institutionalising impulse driving the building of monuments, which are works of public art. By declaring that by the end of his poem 'We have done a monument to Ezra', Hemingway repeats Stein's textual experiments with a difference.[213] Downplaying Pound's personality, a typical topic for portraiture, Hemingway stresses his influence on modernism.

Moreover, as Verna Kale points out, 'The Soul of Spain' 'borders on parody' of Stein.[214] Kale identifies similarities between Hemingway's reiterations of 'In the rain in the rain in the rain in the rain in Spain. / Does it rain in Spain?' and the line '"Little sales ladies little sales ladies little saddles of mutton"' from *Tender Buttons*.[215] Hemingway's poem also mimics Steinian 'insistence' without its sonorities, mischaracterising and diminishing her style by rendering reiteration banal.[216] Words such as 'In the rain in the rain in the rain in the rain in Spain' repeat with no difference, falling flat.[217] The phrase 'Does it rain in Spain? / Oh yes my dear on the contrary and there are no bull fights' is the only negation that echoes Stein's use of disavowal in 'He and They'.[218] Both affirming and condescendingly contradicting the beloved's voice, the speaker proclaims that there will be no bloody spectacles as he attacks early twentieth-century icons. Other reiterations convey even more juvenile forms of masculine aggression. 'Home is where the heart is' turns to 'home is where the fart is' before the speaker declares that '[t]here is no art in a fart' even though 'a fart may not be artless'.[219] These passages imitate Stein's writing to suggest that it is meaningless. This preoccupation with the anus and its products continues as the poem progresses and its masculine exhortations redouble.

This begins with a double-edged commentary on American political parties – 'Bill's father would never knowingly sit down at table with a Democrat. / Now Bill says Democracy must go. / Go on Democracy.'[220] The poem then modulates into a play on excrement in a list recalling the negations driving the first part of 'He and They'. Hemingway writes that

> Democracy is the shit.
> Relativity is the shit.
> Dictators are the shit.
> Menken is the shit.

Waldo Frank is the shit.
The Broom is the shit.
Dada is the shit.
Dempsey is the shit.
This is not a complete list.
They say Ezra is the shit.
But Ezra is nice.
Come let us build a monument to Ezra.[221]

Unlike Stein's use of the word 'cow' to invoke both orgasms and fecal matter, 'The Soul of Spain' offers far simpler repetitions of the word 'shit'.[222] To contemporary ears, the exclamation 'the shit' might suggest that Hemingway is praising 'Democracy', 'Relativity', 'Dictators' and the various men named in the poem, but only since 1987 has 'the shit' identified 'the acme of excellence'.[223] Earlier, the phrase's connotations were decidedly negative, and Hemingway's 1924 poem uses it to malign early twentieth-century icons.[224]

Displaying none of the uncertainties of 'He and They', 'The Soul of Spain' follows the line 'Dictators are the shit' with influential men's names.[225] The first, S. Stanwood Menken, was a 'right-wing' leader whose name rhymes with that of H. L. Mencken, a writer who rejected several of Hemingway's stories right before publishing an essay refuting the claim that 'young writers . . . could not find sympathetic publishers'.[226] Hemingway covertly retaliates against Mencken by targeting Menken. Similarly, Hemingway's identification of 'Dada' as 'the shit' simultaneously attacks Stein and the Dadaists.[227] Conflating their aim of eviscerating meaning with Stein's use of reiteration to resignify it, Hemingway's poem caricatures and discredits her work. Imitating Stein's style while acknowledging only its similarities to 'Dada', Hemingway uses condemnatory language that flattens the multiplicity mobilised by her writings' negations.

A disavowal finally introduces complexity into 'The Soul of Spain' after its series of shits. Hinging from the line 'They say Ezra is the shit' to the claim 'But Ezra is nice', the poem both conveys and rejects the widespread perception that Pound was a talented jerk. Hemingway then calls upon various followers to 'Come . . . build a monument to Ezra.'[228] The remainder of the poem imitates the more childlike aspects of Stein's dialogic practice by showing multiple people joining in to monumentalise Pound. The affirmation 'Good' follows the first 'monument' and reappears after the speaker, his interlocutor, and 'the little girl over there on the corner' deliver.[229] Telling the others that 'You have all been successful children', the speaker finally proclaims that 'We have done a monument to Ezra.' Following on the heels of the poem's rejection of other early twentieth-century icons, this comparison suggests that the efforts of Pound's followers have enabled him to supplant Marcel Proust in literary history.

As John Cohassey observes, this aspect of 'The Soul of Spain' reflects Hemingway's 'contempt' for the '"Monument to Proust"' published in *The Dial* by its editor, Scofield Thayer, who blocked Pound from receiving the Dial Award because of their mutual disdain.[230] Hemingway's poem elevates Pound over Proust, carefully manipulating tense to reverse the two writers' relationship to time. Proust, whose narratives excavate memory's non-linear temporalities, is the subject of a present monument: 'The Dial does a monument to Proust.'[231] By contrast, Pound, who insists that modern writers should 'make it new', is the subject of a past monument: 'We have done a monument to Ezra.'[232] Hemingway thus claims to have honoured Pound before *The Dial* did Proust. Affirming the value of the public recognition provided by monuments while also hinting at their primordial motives, the text harkens back to an earlier time. Prematurely monumentalising Pound, the poem's speaker proclaims his work to be 'done' before he moves to the text's conclusion.[233] Through these temporal plays, 'The Soul of Spain' employs 'the double-time of the late nineteenth and early twentieth centuries' to situate Pound as simultaneously reactionary and avant-garde – and to position the poem's author, Hemingway, as a man similarly out of time.[234]

'The Soul of Spain' thereby echoes and transforms the temporal manipulations of Stein's 'He and They'. His poem's closing lines – 'A monument is a monument. / After all it is the spirit of the thing that counts.' – imitates Steinese to posit that monuments convey an atemporal 'spirit'.[235] The first phrase's repetitions also suggest that some of Proust's and Pound's qualities elude representation. The phrase 'the spirit of the thing' points to monuments' role in representing the unrepresentable aspects of those they memorialise, and also harkens back to the poem's opening promise to address 'The Soul of Spain'.[236] Yet this purpose is quite different from that of Steinian reiteration, which undermines representation and its ontological claims. In proclaiming that 'A monument is a monument', Hemingway imitates Stein's style, demonstrating that he misunderstands her method even as he mocks it. Thus, as Stein realised, Hemingway 'does not understand the avant-garde techniques that he is able to assimilate'.[237] Instead, like the 'cannibals' of 'He and They', he leverages other modern writers' 'fame' without crediting the 'literary pioneers' that preceded him.[238] Yet 'The Soul of Spain' also suggests that in failing fully to understand the implications of Stein's experiments with language, Hemingway reworks them in a way that inadvertently prompts different innovations: ones that pertain not to language's materiality but to its temporality. Whereas temporal plays in 'He and They' shine a light into the cracks of diachronic time to reveal a potential for queerness the young writer would never realise, 'The Soul of Spain' rejects the time of the present to elevate Pound's notoriously sexist 'spirit' over Proust's queerly temporal narratives.[239]

'The Soul of Spain' also briefly warps time, but does so differently than Stein's poem: by contrasting *The Dial*'s present-tense memorialising of Proust with Hemingway's retroactively projected monumentalising of Pound. The resulting temporal disjunctures unexpectedly reverberate in the poem's closing lines, which use Steinian elements to enact in poetry the 'bent' style St. Pierre finds in Hemingway's prose.[240] At first glance, the poem's final sentences suggest with deceptive simplicity that monuments are alike in their ability to convey 'the spirit of the thing': after all, '[a] monument is a monument'.[241] Yet under closer scrutiny, these lines render ambiguous the identity of the 'thing' whose spirit is in question: is 'it' the monument?[242] The monumentalised? Spain? Can we equate 'spirit' with 'soul', as the poem's move from the latter to the former suggests?[243] Hemingway's diction leaves the reader uncertain, like Stein's when she releases time from the grammatical structures of 'He and They'. Far from unmooring meaning entirely, however, in 'The Soul of Spain' signification's undecidability folds Pound and Proust together with Spain as eternal monuments of magnificence. In so doing, Proust's queerness returns from beneath the text's surface despite the speaker's and his interlocutors' determination to erect a monument to Pound. This reveals the other sense in which 'a monument is a monument': unlike ideas and people who are 'the shit', Hemingway's 'monument to Ezra' and *The Dial*'s 'monument to Proust' stand on their own, reverberating across time in a temporality and style that have become Hemingway's own.[244]

A similar process of making repetition his own emerges within Hemingway's follow-up poems, 'Part Two of the Soul of Spain with McAlmon and Bird the Publishers' (1923: 1924) through 'Part Six A Serious and Vivid Account of a Dramatic Moment in the Cruel Sport' (1923: 1924). These pieces poorly imitate Steinian reiteration to mobilise forms of violence the first poem disavows. 'Part Two' opens with a banal rhyme – 'You come to Spain but do not remain' – and goes on to play on the bullfighting manoeuvre called the 'veronica'.[245] Listing a series of names – 'Anna Veronica, Marcial Veronica, Pablo Veronica, Gitanillo Veronica' – and stating that 'No they cannot Veronica because the wind blows', Hemingway associates bullfighting's violence with the anti-patriarchal heroine of H. G. Wells's *Ann Veronica* (1909).[246] In another set of rhymes – 'The wind blows and it does not snows look at the bull with his bloody nose' – Hemingway highlights bullfighting's violent consequences, setting up for 'Part Six'.[247]

Departing from the teasing suggestiveness of 'The Soul of Spain' and 'Part Two', 'Part Six' explicitly describes the sport:

> Estocada stuck well stuck. They run round in circles with the capes and the bull whirls round and round and then goes down and folds his knees under and his tongue sticks out and the sword sticks out dully the hilt and the banderillos stick out sharply at angles. Well stuck by the applauded diestro. Well stuck by the afamoused espada. They are going to kill him back of the horns with the short knife.[248]

Although this passage does not mobilise the sonorities of Steinian 'insistence', it shows Hemingway's ability to reinflect Stein's style into something quite his own. Not falling flat like the reiterations in the first five poems, this language effectively captures the swiftly paced and violently swirling bullfight, with all of its 'twisting', 'leaning', 'aggressing', 'repelling' and 'warping'.[249] Though the poem depicts the bullfight as 'a continuing moment, movement, motive – recurrent, eddying, *troublant*', thereby suggesting its torturous nature, 'Part Six' does not queer temporality in the manner of the first 'Soul of Spain' poem.[250] The line that follows the description of the bullfight – 'Short knives are thick short knives are quick short knives make a needed nick' – does not mobilise Steinian resonances but instead uses a new brand of iteration to invoke the fight's jolting acts of violence.[251] Here, Hemingway's poetic style begins to approximate that of his fiction. These lines' diachronic temporality contrasts to that of the first 'Soul of Spain' poem: they do not warp time as much as compress it. This conclusion shows that although the 'Soul of Spain' poems initially toy with queer temporality, they eventually straighten into motions approximating Hemingway's prose. Although St. Pierre rightfully reminds us that Hemingway's seemingly 'straight' style is more 'bent' than it appears, the writer's narrowing down of language's temporal vicissitudes contrasts with Stein's reiterations.[252]

Hemingway and 'La seconde famille': Stein's texts from 1929 to 1931

In September 1929, Stein composed a letter of recommendation for Bravig Imbs, a member of the 'seconde famille' who was applying for a Guggenheim fellowship.[253] The Guggenheim Foundation's request that her letter testify to the applicant's '"unusual and proved creative ability"' prompted several of Stein's texts from this period, from 'Evidence' (1929: 1930, 1993) and 'Genuine Creative Ability' (1929–30: 1930) to 'Sentences and Paragraphs' (1929–30: 1931).[254] Stein's reflections on creative ability echo between these texts, revealing her perceptions of men who frequented her salon in the late 1920s and early 1930s. Even though Stein received Hemingway warmly upon his return to Paris in the wake of the success of *A Farewell to Arms*, by the end of the year she used her writings about creativity to reconsider her artistic theories and feelings about her old friend.[255]

'Genuine Creative Ability' focuses on the nature of creativity and makes only elliptical reference to Hemingway.[256] Yet to those familiar with Stein's and Hemingway's friendship, he is clearly the man whose 'name' Stein refuses to 'mention'.[257] Ernest and Hadley Hemingway's friendship with Stein and Toklas first surfaces in the line 'He looks like a young man grown old', which Stein offers as an elegant sentence exemplifying genuine creativity.[258] Dydo traces these words to a 'a single leaf torn from a *carnet*' included along with a picture of Bumby in an 'undated Christmas card' the Hemingways sent Stein and Toklas.[259] Written in Stein's hand, this sentence – which may be hers or Hemingway's – reveals their early enmeshment, strong creative sympathies and familial relationship.[260] Though their alliance was institutionally sanctioned – Bumby was baptised in an Episcopalian church – it was also queerly relational.[261] Motivated by Stein's and Hemingway's masculine homosocial bond, their alliance dissipated as soon as it proved to be 'of no particular use'.[262] That Stein included the comment about Bumby in 'Genuine Creative Ability' suggests that at the end of 1929, she still felt an undercurrent of affection for Hemingway even though their friendship had faded.

'Genuine Creative Ability' is written in the past tense, suggesting that it was composed after Stein's and Hemingway's friendship had come to an 'end'.[263] However, he is referenced through negation in a stanza that plays with synchronous and diachronous temporalities while ruminating over her visits with fellow writers and artists. The speaker claims that 'If they had been one after the other it makes no difference, first I saw one well first I saw one. His name I will not mention. I was pleased, very flattered to be pleased.'[264] Here Stein dispenses with sequence and insists that Hemingway was the 'first' to occupy her vision.[265] Unlike Woolf, whose streams of consciousness track the mind's capacity to wander despite the clock, Stein uses 'insistence' to write synchronic time.[266] The phrase 'first I saw one well first I saw one' unfolds across the page, suggesting that her eyes immediately lock onto Hemingway and remain focused on him despite distractions.[267] She then admits that 'I was pleased, very flattered to be pleased' by his attentions: she was incited by and receptive to his approach.[268] This formulation riffs on yet complicates standard accounts of the young Hemingway's courtship of Stein by emphasising the great pleasure she took in being 'flattered'.[269] Her language escalates as she underscores her enjoyment of 'la seconde famille' and especially Hemingway's concentrated attention: 'I do not deny that I love to have them one at a time.'[270] This passage highlights her joy in all of her guests – 'them', not just the one she saw 'first' – and her delight in locking eyes and ears with her interlocutor.[271]

The conclusion to this stanza suggests that departures from Stein's preferred mode of interaction ultimately undermined her friendships. Whereas *A Moveable Feast* assigns responsibility for these breaks to her quarrelsome nature, 'Genuine Creative Ability' identifies other factors. After she does 'not deny that I love to have them one at a time', she concedes that 'if they are not one at a time then I see them all the time'.[272] This raises several possibilities. Perhaps when Stein's friends appeared in groups so frequently, she no longer enjoyed them; perhaps when the men visited together they broke her attention, causing her to 'see them all the time', fragmenting rather than concentrating her vision.[273] Regardless, once the men 'were of no particular use', it was 'the end'.[274]

Just as she refuses to name Hemingway, she also refuses to identify the other friends with whom she has come to 'the end'.[275] In the next stanza, though, she references 'Kristian Tonney', harkening back to the text's opening paragraph, which lists 'First Basket', 'then paragraphs, then Tonney' as 'subjects about which I can write'.[276] In 1930

Tonny painted Basket, showing Stein and her dog exchanging looks.[277] His picture suggests that she was 'formulating some of the reflections on dogs in general and Basket in particular that infiltrated her writings at this time'.[278] Although Tonny had not finished this painting when Stein was composing 'Genuine Creative Ability', these preoccupations are evident. After the statement 'That is Tonney he was made for Tonney Kristian and now he is Kristian Tonney', Stein begins the other paragraph's successor by switching to 'other subjects' such as 'Basket'.[279] Having caught Stein's eye and noticed her preoccupation with her poodle, Tonny stands as the text's sole named example of a person possessed of 'Genuine Creative Ability'. He has chosen his subject wisely by appreciating her interests, not just the ways she could help him.[280] Susceptible to his flattery, she noticed and rewarded his attentiveness. Revealing the fleeting nature of Stein's attraction to Hemingway, 'Genuine Creative Ability' refuses to name and ultimately dismisses him as a genuinely creative person.

Two iterations of Stein's 'Evidence' are in print. The first, abridged copy (1930) omits the direct references to Hemingway that appear in the 'manuscript and typescript'; the second, complete version appears in *A Stein Reader* (1993).[281] In staging unnamed people's interactions at a party, 'Evidence' exemplifies the qualities Sara Ford finds in Stein's experimental plays. It uses simultaneity to stress the 'relationality of selves in the world', showing that they cannot be 'reduced to their position in a temporal sequence or to their position in conventionally rigid language patterns'.[282] The resulting ambiguities register the troubled vicissitudes of Stein's and Hemingway's homosocial desire. As Dydo observes, Stein wrote 'Evidence' in late 1929, after she and Toklas hosted Fitzgerald, Ernest and Pauline Hemingway, and others at 27, rue de Fleurus.[283] The 1930 version's omissions defy Stein's typical refusal to destroy 'the unity of a piece by cutting'; she likely took the unusual measure of doing so because she was annoyed by Hemingway but afraid of offending a celebrity.[284] The full version constitutes 'a malicious, personal attack on' the writer whose success with *A Farewell to Arms* triggered her envy.[285] Channelling Stein's reaction to his career, the play asks 'bitter questions about success as evidence of creative ability'.[286]

The long version of 'Evidence' reiterates some passages from 'Sentences and Paragraphs' with a difference, backhandedly attacking Hemingway. In the latter, Stein insists upon the example of good writing she offered in 'Genuine Creative Ability' – 'He looks like a young man grown old' – and follows it with her opinion that 'That is a sentence that they could use.'[287] The rest of the text considers the merits of different types of sentences, one of which concerns Hemingway. Dydo calls attention to the line 'That is the cruelest thing I ever heard is the favourite phrase of Gilbert', which appears first in 'Sentences and Paragraphs' and then in the full version of 'Evidence', where 'That is the cruelest thing I ever heard' is first assigned to 'Herman'.[288] 'Sentences and Paragraphs' then offers a variation on this line: 'It is the cruelest thing I ever heard is the favourite phrase of Gilbert.'[289] This second formulation also reappears verbatim in 'Evidence', with Gilbert rather than Herman its fan.[290] Stein's attribution of the phrase to two different men creates an effect similar to that of 'He looks like a young man grown old' in 'Genuine Creative Ability': identity and origin become uncertain.[291] Further heightening this ambiguity, Dydo observes that the manuscript version of 'Sentences and Paragraphs' initially attributed the phrase 'That is the cruelest thing I ever heard' to Fitzgerald but replaced him with Gilbert.[292] Larsen nonetheless pegs Herman as Fitzgerald, who, in *The Autobiography*, similarly 'says that he thinks Gertrude Stein says these things just to annoy him by making him think that she means them . . . and her doing it is the cruellest thing I ever heard'.[293] Moreover, as Dydo notes, in *The Autobiography* Stein identifies Fitzgerald as 'the only one of the younger writers who wrote naturally in sentences', negating her intimation in 'Genuine Creative Ability' that Hemingway was the only one capable of writing – or at least recognising – effective sentences.[294] This move in *The Autobiography* publicly severs the ties of Stein's and Hemingway's affection that were already frayed in 'Genuine Creative Ability'. Aware of Stein's shifting taste, Hemingway wrote to Fitzgerald to reassure him that she had complimented rather than insulted him at the party that prompted 'Evidence': she 'wanted to organize a hare and tortoise race and picked me to tortoise and you to hare'.[295]

Whereas Stein's hints at her preference for Fitzgerald underhandedly undermine Hemingway, the passages originally excised from 'Evidence' attack him directly. As Dydo observes, lines such as 'He mingled with a way' suggest 'Hemingway' and echo the title of 'He and They', making the text's subject clear.[296] Targeting Hemingway's businesslike American mindset, Stein begins the full text's opening section with the statement 'American and strange', and continues by criticising his attitude that 'A man is a person if he has a reputation to fulfill.'[297] Later in the poem, she declares that 'Ernest is a judge. He is with it. / He says and means it', noting shortly thereafter that 'He has the money.'[298] Her emphasis on Hemingway's financial success echoes an earlier passage in which he and Fitzgerald 'waited without a chance to sing anything' at the rue de Fleurus, even though they are generally 'very well paid for singing' – that is, for writing – unlike Stein.[299]

Stein also points to Hemingway's unconventional behaviour in her home, stating that 'He has a chance to come away if they are waiting to seat him. He is sitting when they are coming. / He will all, add whenever he likes.'[300] These sentences bear out Dydo's argument that the piece concerns 'a meeting or dinner, with infractions against the proper order of precedence in seating or conversation'.[301] Attacking Hemingway's hobbies and diminishing his art by comparing it to the tall tales of 'seamen', Stein presents a scene in which 'He told a story. Two stories shorter. This is alright with seamen. Come to our right. / It is always a virtue to be our man.'[302] This mockery of masculine 'virtue' is followed by Stein's declaration that 'I could I could I could cough' at his hegemonic performance of masculine mediocrity.[303] She then asks 'How long can you listen with hearers. As long. As they are there.'[304] Breaking up her words with periods and showing her fatigue at his spectacle, Stein suggests that Hemingway has left her wanting to leave her own party.

The next section, 'Evidence II', focuses on two men, 'Herman and Ernest', who are disappointed with their wives; it begins with the statement that 'That is the cruelest thing I ever knew is the favourite phrase of Herman.'[305] Larsen identifies 'Ernest' as Hemingway and 'Herman' as Fitzgerald; Dydo notes that the passage plays with names that 'sound as if they were both one and not one'.[306] This calls attention to Hemingway's and Fitzgerald's similarities, especially their shifting views of 'their wives', whose gender they associate with their sense of 'disappointment'.[307] Stein writes:

> That is the cruelest thing I ever knew is the favorite phrase of Herman.
>
> Herman and Ernest were sitting where they were willing to be sitting. As they were waiting they met with disappointment all of a sudden. Their wives had been women. If their wives had been women they would not have been a disappointment or anything.
>
> After a bit there was nothing that would be sudden in a disappointment.[308]

This humourous passage mocks Fitzgerald's tendency to see things for the worst and suggests that the 'cruelest thing' about the men's situations is their wives' gender.[309] Yet Stein's wording also exploits the ambiguities afforded by her experimental drama, which uses the 'relationality' of 'performance' to foster the 'illusion of coherence and stability'.[310] Is 'Their wives had been women' an essentialist epiphany revealing that their wives had acted as women naturally would and shaming the men for misunderstanding them?[311] Does the line suggest that their wives once 'had been women', but no longer were?[312] Does the sentence disclose Herman's and Ernest's preference for wives who were something other than women: men, perhaps, given McAlmon's rumours?[313] Or does the men's disappointment suggest that their desires ranged beyond binary genders? Making it impossible to say, Stein's wording suggests that both desire and gender are illusory.

The sentence that follows – 'If their wives had been women they would not have been a disappointment or anything' – introduces further possibilities by undercutting its predecessor's premise.[314] Does the second sentence contradict the first and shame the men for not realising that their wives have not been living up to their roles as women – that if their wives had only been acting as they 'should' have been, they would not have been disappointed? Or does this apparent contradiction call gender's stability into question by resignifying the category 'women'?[315] The latter reading emphasises the speculative aspect of the word 'If'.[316] The statement that 'After a bit there was nothing that would be sudden in a disappointment' suggests that this state of affairs was not new, whatever it was: that even if Hemingway and Fitzgerald first realised at Stein's party that 'their wives had been women', that had been the case all along.[317]

Stein's shifting significations mobilise elusive trajectories of desire between Hemingway and Fitzgerald; the two men and their wives; and Stein and her fellow writers, especially Hemingway. Provoking the reader's frustration at being unable to pin down a single person or gender as 'object', this passage traces out and queers desire's vicissitudes. As the object of desire vanishes its gender becomes undecidable. At one point in the portrait – at the end of a long passage filled with 'Disappointment', 'Indifference' and 'disinterestedness' that was not included in the original and echoes the language of the section on 'Herman and Ernest' – the speaker observes that 'Gazing and looking without seeing is not the same thing.'[318] This remark goes beyond Lacan's split between the look and the gaze by suggesting that not all forms of vision result in 'seeing': that there can be 'looking without seeing'.[319] The resulting visual twists queer the gaze through which Stein, Hemingway and Fitzgerald are given to be seen.

After the first four sections, the full version of 'Evidence' seems to lose contact with Hemingway altogether, aside from the echoes of disappointment in the longest section. As Dydo argues, this portion of the text 'marks Stein's effort to counter discomfort and maintain calm by writing'.[320] It begins with the warning that 'We may be late' and ends with 'Gazing and looking', reflecting upon Stein's and Toklas's domestic arrangement and attitude toward guests.[321] Noting that 'we are a victim of impatient visiting', Stein observes that she and Toklas are 'patient' and might experience a 'delay' in their return home, not because of 'A disappointment' but because of 'the streets'.[322] She also admonishes, 'Do not disturb me while I write.'[323] This suggests that Stein guarded her writing time yet was more flexible while wandering Paris's Left Bank. Complaining about being 'a victim of impatient visiting' by those like Hemingway who employed a businesslike temporality, Stein points to the different ways they inhabited the 'double-time' of modernity.[324]

Thus, if Dydo is right that the 'sections not printed' in the 1930 version of 'Evidence' comprise 'Stein's second portrait of Hemingway', it is important to recognise that the full text presents him through the prism of his relations to others: to Stein and Toklas (the latter 'sitting and working at tapestry' as guests arrive); Fitzgerald; Imbs; and other of his contemporaries.[325] Although 'He and They' also stresses relationality, 'Evidence' broadens the network of modernists implicated in Stein's and Hemingway's tumultuous attraction. The text's final iteration of 'It is the cruelest thing I ever heard' is followed by a portrait of Toklas and then a 'Portrait of Bravig Imbs', the only named writer.[326] The disappearance of 'Herman' and 'Ernest' from the second half of the text suggests that Hemingway's importance to Stein is fading – that in the course of writing 'Evidence', 'Genuine Creative Ability', and 'Sentences and Paragraphs', her initial attraction had turned to anger and then to the 'Indifference' of which she speaks in the play's longest section.[327]

Notes

1. Wagner-Martin, *'Favored Strangers'*, pp. 162.
2. Wagner-Martin, ibid., p. 164.
3. Wagner-Martin, ibid., p. 164.
4. See Zox-Weaver, *Women Modernists and Fascism*, for more on Stein's fascination with Great Men.

5. Ernest Hemingway to Sherwood Anderson, 9 March 1922, *Ernest Hemingway: Selected Letters*, 62; Kennedy and Curnutt, 'Out of the Picture', p. 4.
6. Stein, *The Autobiography*, p. 204; Ernest Hemingway to W. G. Rogers, 29 July 1948, *Ernest Hemingway: Selected Letters,* p. 650. See Curnutt, '"In the Temps de Gertrude"', for further analysis of the erotic underpinnings of Hemingway's response to Stein.
7. Larsen, *Stein and Hemingway*, p. 70.
8. Larsen, ibid., pp. 138–52.
9. Larsen, ibid., pp. 150–2.
10. Larsen, ibid., p. 152.
11. Sanderson, 'Hemingway and Gender History', p. 174. See also Lynn, *Hemingway*, pp. 168–9; and Spilka, *Hemingway's Quarrel with Androgyny*, p. 298; and Eby, *Hemingway's Fetishism*, pp. 46–85. See Rohy, 'Hemingway, Literalism, and Transgender Reading', for an important critique of Lynn's and Eby's premises, and Fantina, *Ernest Hemingway*, p. 87 for details about Grace Hall Hemingway's lesbian relationships and their influence on Hemingway's fiction.
12. Abravanel, 'Anglophones in Paris', p. 99.
13. Moddelmog, *Reading Desire*. For arguments that Hemingway's writings reveal more complex approaches to gender and sexuality than those with which he is often credited, see Moddelmog as well as Comley and Scholes, *Hemingway's Genders*.
14. Sanderson, 'Hemingway and Gender History', pp. 182–3.
15. Moddelmog, *Reading Desire*, p. 92.
16. Wagner-Martin, *'Favored Strangers'*, p. 188.
17. Wyatt, *Hemingway, Style, and the Art of Emotion*; Stein quoted in Preston, 'A Conversation with Gertrude Stein', p. 159.
18. Brinnin, *The Third Rose*, p. 251.
19. Strychacz, *Hemingway's Theaters of Masculinity*, pp. 168–9.
20. Haralson, *Henry James and Queer Modernity*, p. 175.
21. Stein, *The Autobiography*, p. 204. Cope, *Passionate Collaborations*, p. 152, observes that Hemingway's letters tell that other 'story'.
22. Lewis, 'The "Dumb Ox"', pp. 17–41. Thanks to Len Gutkin for directing me to this piece. See Perloff, 'The Extra: "Ninety Percent Rotarian"', for analysis of Lewis's essay.
23. Cope, *Passionate Collaborations*, p. 143. See also Brinnin, *The Third Rose*, p. 4; Haralson, *Henry James and Queer Modernity*; Kennedy and Curnutt, 'Inside and Outside', p. 4; North, *Reading 1922*; and Sutherland, 'Alice and Gertrude and Others', p. 297.
24. Cope, *Passionate Collaborations*, p. 152.
25. Kennedy and Curnutt, 'Out of the Picture', p. 4.

26. Larsen, *Stein and Hemingway*. Larsen offers the most sustained examination of Stein's and Hemingway's friendship currently available, competently describing their intersecting lives but favouring his perspective. However, Larsen takes *The Autobiography* and *A Moveable Feast* at face value despite their distortions; see Tavernier-Courbin, *Ernest Hemingway's A Moveable Feast*, for analysis of factual versus mythological elements of the latter. Tavernier-Courbin is unusual among Hemingway scholars for placing her sympathies with Stein. See also Brenner, *A Comprehensive Companion*, Book 1 and Book 2, for detailed discussions of *A Moveable Feast*'s accuracy.

    Persistently referring to Toklas as Stein's 'companion' and validating Hemingway's misogynist theory that her attitude toward him was poisoned by menopause, *Stein and Hemingway* exemplifies Rohy's observation in 'Hemingway, Literalism, and Transgender Reading' that many mainstream Hemingway scholars have lagged behind other researchers in responding to several decades' worth of 'feminist and queer readings' of his work (pp. 149–50). Notably, Larsen engages memoirs, letters and literary texts but not recent scholarship.
27. Sedgwick, *Tendencies*, p. xii.
28. Sedgwick, ibid., p. xii. Thanks to Eileen Harney for pointing out that *torquere* connotes torture.
29. Cope, *Passionate Collaborations*, p. 157, p. 152.
30. Hemingway, 'The Soul of Spain', pp. 70–3.
31. Cohassey, *Hemingway and Pound*, p. 72; see also Lynn, *Hemingway*, p. 302.
32. The full version of 'Evidence' was not published until it appeared in *A Stein Reader* in 1993; an incomplete version appeared in 1930.
33. Stein, *The Autobiography*, p. 204. In addition to the published texts quoted in this chapter, the Ernest Hemingway Collection at the John F. Kennedy Library in Boston holds unpublished manuscripts that enact vengeance against Stein for *The Autobiography*. A manuscript fragment called 'Mr. Haywood Brown calls your correspondent a phony' (EHPP-MS54-037, folder #588) engages in retaliatory reverse discourse for Stein's depiction of Hemingway's subordination; a typescript entitled 'The Autobiography of Alice B. Hemingway' (EHPP-MS37-019, folder #265a) offers a bitter portrayal of their friendship and a hostile picture of her relationship with Toklas.
34. Weiner and Young, 'Introduction: Queer Bonds', p. 236.
35. Weiner and Young, ibid., p. 227.
36. Sedgwick, *Touching Feeling*, p. 8.
37. Séan Hemingway, 'Introduction', p. 1. A collaboration between Hemingway's sons Patrick and Séan, the 2009 Restored Edition shows

a slightly softer attitude toward Stein than the version Scribner's initially published in 1964, but it retains much of the earlier version's homophobia. It is impossible to ascertain 'how and to what extent the author himself would have changed and revised his own manuscripts had he been allowed the opportunity' (Larson, 'Bibliographical Essay', p. 217). In this book I cite from the Restored Edition because it is 'based on a typed manuscript with original notations in Hemingway's hand – the last draft of the book that he ever worked on' (Séan Hemingway, ibid., p. 3). See Tavernier-Courbin, *Ernest Hemingway's A Moveable Feast*, for a detailed assessment of the accuracy of the 1964 edition.

38. Hovey, *A Thousand Words*, pp. 110–11. See Halberstam, *Female Masculinity*, for critique of claims that female and transmasculinities are fraudulent and male masculinities authentic.
39. Hovey, ibid., p. 108.
40. Hovey, ibid., p. 108.
41. St. Pierre, 'Bent Hemingway', p. 371, p. 375. This observation also applies to many other aspects of Hemingway's life and writing.
42. St. Pierre, ibid., p. 375.
43. Hovey, *A Thousand Words*, p. 108; St. Pierre, 'Bent Hemingway', p. 371.
44. Abravanel, 'Anglophones in Paris', pp. 99–102; Hovey, ibid., pp. 110–11.
45. Cope, *Passionate Collaborations*, p. 144.
46. St. Pierre, 'Bent Hemingway', p. 375.
47. Hemingway's posthumously published *The Garden of Eden* (1986) is a notable exception that resonates with his and Mary's marriage.
48. Rohy, 'Hemingway, Literalism, and Transgender Reading', pp. 149.
49. Rohy, ibid., p. 170; Mary Welsh Hemingway, *The Way It Was*, pp. 368–9. The latter includes Mary's transcription of this fantasy, in which Ernest appears as a character.
50. Rohy, 'Hemingway, Literalism, and Transgender Reading', p. 170; Ernest Hemingway in Mary Hemingway, ibid., p. 369.
51. Rohy, ibid., p. 172.
52. Rohy, ibid., pp. 170–2. See Fantina, *Ernest Hemingway*, pp. 75–6 for another reading of Hemingway as transgender, and Rohy, ibid., pp. 173–4n7 for a critique of lingering transphobia in what is otherwise Fantina's trans-affirmative text.
53. Rohy, 'Hemingway, Literalism, and Transgender Reading', p. 173. Rohy offers a trenchant critique of prior scholarly discussion of this time in Hemingway's life. I concur with and am indebted to her argument that Eby, *Hemingway's Fetishism*, Lynn, *Hemingway* and Spilka, *Hemingway's Quarrel with Androgyny*, transphobically pathologise Hemingway's cross-gender identifications.

54. Ernest Hemingway in Mary Welsh Hemingway, *The Way It Was*, p. 369.
55. Rohy, 'Hemingway, Literalism, and Transgender Reading', p. 151.
56. Ernest Hemingway in Mary Welsh Hemingway, *The Way It Was*, p. 369.
57. Moddelmog, *Reading Desire*, p. 83; Rohy, 'Hemingway, Literalism, and Transgender Reading', p. 151.
58. Moddelmog, *Reading Desire*, p. 83.
59. Ernest Hemingway in Mary Welsh Hemingway, *The Way It Was*, p. 369; Cromwell, *Transmen & FTMs*, p. 130.
60. Fantina, *Ernest Hemingway*, p. 71.
61. Fantina, ibid., p. 72; Rohy, 'Hemingway, Literalism, and Transgender Reading', p. 172.
62. Ernest Hemingway in Mary Welsh Hemingway, *The Way It Was*, p. 370. See Moddelmog, *Reading Desire*, for an insightful discussion of the troubling implications of this statement's primitivist language.
63. Hemingway, *Torrents*, p. 75; Haralson, *Henry James and Queer Modernity*, p. 183.
64. Ruddick, *Reading Gertrude Stein*, p. 83. See Lorange, *How Reading Is Written*, pp. 199–203, for a critique of Ruddick's argument that Stein's anality is pre-Oedipal.
65. Lorange, *How Reading Is Written*, p. 201.
66. Hemingway's posthumously published *The Garden of Eden* (1986) begins to undermine gender dichotomy but still reinforces heteronormativity.
67. Lynn, *Hemingway*, p. 170.
68. Lynn, ibid., p. 170.
69. Gertrude Stein to Sherwood Anderson, March 1922, *Sherwood Anderson / Gertrude Stein*, p. 18. On Hadley's hair, see Lynn, *Hemingway*, p. 170, and Eby, *Hemingway's Fetishism*.
70. Eby, *Hemingway's Fetishism*, p. 48. As Silverman demonstrates, it is more important to understand lack's linguistic dimension than to insist that either the penis or the symbolic phallus is lost through castration ('The Lacanian Phallus'). See Ruti, 'Why There Is Always a Future in the Future'; 'The Fall of Fantasies'; and 'Life beyond Fantasy' for Lacanian accounts of existential lack.
71. I draw the phrase 'family of choice' from Weston's *Families We Choose*. See Wagner-Martin, *'Favored Strangers'*, p. 173, and Larsen, *Stein and Hemingway*, pp. 44–5, for two histories of Stein's and Toklas's agreement to be Bumby's godparents.
72. Spilka, *Hemingway's Quarrel with Androgyny*, p. 9.
73. Spilka, ibid., p. 9.
74. Eby, *Hemingway's Fetishism*, p. 142, claims that because 'The fetishist . . . never successfully negotiates separation-individuation', he 'fails to form an entirely stable ego or sense of gender identity.' He further

claims that 'It would be pretty to think that an extraordinarily talented, sensitive, and insightful writer like Hemingway was a gender hero who "transgressed the oppressive norms of patriarchal culture"; but unfortunately he was no such thing. His masculine and feminine selves were founded upon rigid, infantile gender stereotypes' (p. 239). These statements' transphobia is apparent when Eby reveals his horror at the prospect that Hemingway enjoyed 'a transvestic self-image': 'I can't imagine – nor do I *want* to imagine – Hemingway posing in front of the mirror wearing lipstick, high heels, and an evening gown' (p. 212). See Rohy for further critique of Eby.

75. Spilka, *Hemingway's Quarrel with Androgyny*, pp. 9–10.
76. Ernest Hemingway, *Torrents*, p. 73.
77. Hemingway, ibid., pp. 74–5. Hemingway later expressed regret for attacking Anderson; see 'The Art of the Short Story', p. 12.
78. Abravanel, 'Anglophones in Paris', p. 100. See also Pollack-Pelzner, 'Swiping Stein', for analysis of Hemingway's parodies of Stein.
79. Haralson, *Henry James and Queer Modernity*, pp. 176–94.
80. Hemingway, *Torrents*, pp. 74–5; Haralson, ibid., p. 184.
81. Hemingway, 'The Farm'.
82. Ernest Hemingway, *Green Hills*, p. 24.
83. Hemingway, ibid., p. 24.
84. Hemingway, *A Moveable Feast*, The Restored Edition, p. 60, p. 93.
85. Hemingway, ibid., p. 60. In 'The True Story of My Break with Gertrude Stein', p. 23, Hemingway similarly suggests that comparing Stein to Joyce may have caused her to terminate their friendship, and expresses regret over this 'great injustice'. However, he portrays her as petty by claiming that she dispatched her maid to flog him 'with a bicycle pump' to discourage further visits. This threat does not appear in an earlier draft in the Ernest Hemingway Collection at the John F. Kennedy Library in Boston, item EHPP-MS54-052, folder #593a. In earlier versions, Hemingway expresses more positive regard for Stein (folder #593a) and she shows more disdain for Joyce than in the published version (folder #593).

    Hemingway's claim that Stein forced writers to choose between her and Joyce is questionable: she enjoyed a lifelong friendship with Sherwood Anderson, who claimed both her and Joyce as influences (Jones, 'Introduction', 3). See also Hemingway, 'The Farm', and 'Introduction'. In *A Comprehensive Companion*, Book 1, p. 91, Brenner speculates that Hemingway overstates Stein's hatred of Joyce.
86. Corn and Latimer, *Seeing Gertrude Stein*, p. 58.
87. Ernest Hemingway to W. G. Rogers, 29 July 1948, *Ernest Hemingway: Selected Letters*, p. 650.
88. Strychacz, *Hemingway's Theaters of Masculinity*, p. 218, p. 168.

89. Hemingway, *A Moveable Feast*, The Restored Edition, p. 93. See Brenner, *A Comprehensive Companion*, Book 1, p. 361, for further discussion of this passage's portrayal of Stein as a 'masculinized Roman Emperor'; see Griffin, *Less Than a Treason*, p. 74 for another characterisation of Picasso as aligned with Hemingway against Stein.
90. Hemingway, *A Moveable Feast*, The Restored Edition, p. 24.
91. Hemingway, ibid., p. 24.
92. Hemingway, ibid., p. 24.
93. Corn and Latimer, *Seeing Gertrude Stein*, pp. 31–5.
94. Hemingway, *A Moveable Feast*, The Restored Edition, p. 93.
95. Stein, *The Autobiography*, p. 233.
96. Stein, ibid., p. 53.
97. Hemingway, *A Moveable Feast*, The Restored Edition, p. 93.
98. Hemingway, ibid., p. 93.
99. Corn and Latimer, *Seeing Gertrude Stein*, pp. 28–34.
100. Hemingway, *A Moveable Feast*, The Restored Edition, p. 24.
101. Hemingway, ibid., pp. 25–6.
102. Hadley would live out this advice despite her adverse reaction shown in *A Moveable Feast*: Reynolds writes that she 'always looked a bit dowdy in clothes that were out of tune with the cafés and boulevards' because Ernest 'insisted she spend no money on clothes' so they could buy art (*Hemingway: The Paris Years*, p. 52). The notoriously stingy Hemingway may have invented this 'convenient memory' to 'blame a woman as old as his mother for the way he dressed his wife' (p. 52).
103. Hemingway, *A Moveable Feast*, The Restored Edition, p. 93.
104. Hemingway to Max Perkins, 31 August 1933, in Bruccoli, ed., *The Only Thing That Counts*, p. 198. An unpublished typescript of *A Moveable Feast* replaces a homophobic slur with the language used in the Restored Edition; see EHPP-MS25-036, folder #163 in the Ernest Hemingway Collection at the John F. Kennedy Library in Boston. See Brenner, *A Comprehensive Companion*, Book 1, pp. 358–9, for more about Hemingway's disapproval of the 'new friends'' art.
105. Corn and Latimer, *Seeing Gertrude Stein*, pp. 139–51.
106. Corn and Latimer, ibid., p. 139.
107. Corn and Latimer, ibid., p. 140.
108. Hemingway, *A Moveable Feast*, The Restored Edition, p. 93.
109. Hemingway, ibid., p. 93; Corn and Latimer, *Seeing Gertrude Stein*, pp. 145–51; Although writers such as Larsen (*Stein and Hemingway*), Reynolds (*Hemingway in the 1930s*, p. 29), Simon (*The Biography of Alice B. Toklas*, pp. 116–24), Souhami (*Gertrude and Alice*, p. 152), and Wagner-Martin ('*Favored Strangers*') blame Toklas for ending many of Stein's friendships – including Hemingway's – Steward ('The

Memoir', p. 95) recalls that 'It is true . . . that there were quarrels and "Byzantine intrigues" between Gertrude and the others – but there was always a good reason for the complete break, and the cause usually lay on the other side, not Alice's.'

Scholars who suggest that Toklas's jealousy prompted Stein's distancing from Hemingway find support in his letters and other writings, such as his claim in 'Introduction' that Stein terminated their friendship 'by domestic compulsion' (p. 12). See Lynn, *Hemingway*, p. 172; Hoffman, *Gertrude Stein*, pp. 118–20; Souhami, *Gertrude and Alice*, pp. 152–3; and Sutherland, 'Alice and Gertrude and Others', pp. 297–8. Hemingway makes similar assertions in letters to Edmund Wilson, in *Ernest Hemingway: Selected Letters*, pp. 736–7, and Bernard Berenson, 17 February 1953, in *Ernest Hemingway: Selected Letters,* pp. 801–2. In the latter, Hemingway asserts that 'Gertrude I always loved in spite of everything, and she loved me too and that made Alice murderous jealous' (p. 802). Yet as Engelbrecht observes, 'phallogocentric observers' such as Hemingway may have overlooked the ways Stein's and Toklas's 'power dynamic was not hierarchical, but mutual' ('Lifting Belly Is a Language', p. 101). Although Engelbrecht misses that Stein and Toklas played with roles rather than evaded all hierarchy, she rightfully calls our attention to bias's influence on Hemingway's perceptions.

Hemingway eventually alienated all his friends but Ezra Pound; see Larsen, *Stein and Hemingway*, p. 70, and Cohassey, *Hemingway and Pound.*

110. Hemingway, *A Moveable Feast*, The Restored Edition, p. 93.
111. Corn and Latimer, *Seeing Gertrude Stein*, p. 139.
112. Larsen, *Stein and Hemingway*, p. 108.
113. Stein, *The Autobiography*, p. 204; Stein quoted in Preston, 'A Conversation with Gertrude Stein', p. 159.
114. Stein quoted in Preston, ibid., p. 159.
115. Steward, 'The Memoir', p. 65.
116. Steward, ibid., pp. 65–6. Hemingway told writer Morrill Cody that 'he would really get' back at Stein, and 'was particularly infuriated by her claim that she had "discovered" him and had helped him find a publisher. "It is we who tried like hell to find a publisher for *her*"', he declared (Cody, *The Women of Montparnasse*, p. 84). Cody also reports that 'by the mid-twenties Hemingway harbored some sort of resentment against many of the people of Montparnasse, both men and women'; in the wake of *The Autobiography* he told Cody that '"I'm going to get even with those bastards"' (p. 103).
117. See Strychacz, *Hemingway's Theaters of Masculinity*, and Wyatt, *Hemingway, Style, and the Art of Emotion.*

118. Cope, *Passionate Collaborations*, p. 145.
119. Hemingway, *A Moveable Feast*, The Restored Edition, p. 30; Steward, 'The Memoir', p. 56. Thanks to Jordana Greenblatt for calling my attention to Steward's text.
120. Stein quoted in Steward, 'The Memoir', p. 56.
121. Cope, *Passionate Collaborations*, p. 145.
122. Larsen, *Stein and Hemingway*, pp. 82–4. Larsen, p. 114, also reports that Hemingway later struck McAlmon in retaliation for the rumours. See Meyers, *Hemingway*, pp. 88–90, for further details about Hemingway's friendship and eventual fight with McAlmon.
123. Hemingway to Janet Flanner, 8 April 1933, in *Ernest Hemingway: Selected Letters*, pp. 386–9.
124. Larsen, *Stein and Hemingway*, p. 84.
125. Stein quoted in Hemingway, *A Moveable Feast*, The Restored Edition, p. 30.
126. Larsen, *Stein and Hemingway*, p. 29.
127. Hemingway, *A Moveable Feast*, The Restored Edition, pp. 23–4. As Fantina (*Ernest Hemingway*, p. 155) notes, Hemingway declined to name Toklas during her lifetime because he feared legal action.
128. Hemingway, ibid., p. 25. Given Liz's protests against her and Jim's walk leading to sex, Fantina is wrong to describe her as 'a willing virgin' (p. 94).
129. Hemingway, ibid., p. 28. See Hemingway, 'The Art of the Short Story', p. 2, for a condescending attack on an unnamed Stein for her suggestion that 'shit, or *merde* – a word which teacher will explain' – could be 'cut out of a book' even though 'the odor of it . . . remains perceptible'.
130. Hemingway, *A Moveable Feast*, The Restored Edition, p. 28.
131. Cope, *Passionate Collaborations*, p. 145.
132. Sanderson, 'Hemingway and Gender History', p. 183. Sanderson usefully historicises Hemingway's stress in the 1930s on his persona as a masculine writer, situating it as part of a larger cultural movement to restore the 'patriarchal bias' of 'American society' in response to challenges from the feminine culture of domesticity in the late nineteenth century and the New Woman in the early twentieth century (p. 183).
133. St. Pierre, 'Bent Hemingway', p. 375.
134. Hemingway, *A Moveable Feast*, The Restored Edition, p. 30.
135. Hemingway, ibid., p. 28.
136. Hemingway, ibid., p. 28; Brenner, *A Comprehensive Companion*, Book 1, p. 68.
137. Hovey, *A Thousand Words*, p. 109.

138. Hovey, ibid., p. 109. Ernest Hemingway in Mary Welsh Hemingway, pp. 369–70.
139. Stein, *The Autobiography*, p. 204.
140. Hemingway, *A Moveable Feast*, The Restored Edition, pp. 92–3.
141. Fantina, *Ernest Hemingway*, p. 155.
142. See Benstock, *Women*, pp. 170–3; Caramello, *Henry James, Gertrude Stein, and the Biographical Act*, p. 120; Cope, *Passionate Collaborations*, pp. 143–59; Haralson, *Henry James and Queer Modernity*, pp. 186–7; Hovey, *A Thousand Words*, pp. 109–11.
143. Steward, *Murder is Murder is Murder*, pp. 83–4. See Brenner, *A Comprehensive Companion*, Book 1, pp. 351–6 and pp. 362–5, for possible interpretations of omissions in 'A Strange Enough Ending'.
144. Hemingway, *A Moveable Feast*, The Restored Edition, p. 91; Stein, *The Autobiography*, p. 204.
145. Lynn, *Hemingway*, p. 322.
146. Benstock, *Women*, p. 170.
147. Mellow, *Charmed Circle*, p. 339.
148. Lynn, *Hemingway*, p. 322. See Rohy, 'Hemingway, Literalism, and Transgender Reading', for an insightful critique of Lynn. Similar characterisations of Stein's and Toklas's relationship appear in Hemingway's 'The Autobiography of Alice B. Hemingway', EHPP-MS37-019, folder #265a in the Ernest Hemingway Collection at the John F. Kennedy Library in Boston.
149. Hemingway, *A Moveable Feast*, The Restored Edition, p. 24.
150. Hemingway, ibid., p. 92.
151. Stein, *The Autobiography*, p. 204.
152. Hemingway, *A Moveable Feast*, The Restored Edition, p. 91.
153. Brenner, *Concealments*, p. 223; Hemingway, ibid., p. 46.
154. Hemingway, 'Introduction', p. 12.
155. Rohy, 'Hemingway, Literalism, and Transgender Reading', p. 153.
156. Hemingway, *A Moveable Feast*, The Restored Edition, pp. 92–3.
157. Sedgwick, *Touching Feeling*, p. 8.
158. Stein, *The Autobiography*, p. 204; Stein, 'Objects Lie on a Table', pp. 105–11.
159. Larsen, *Stein and Hemingway*, p. 37. See also Bridgman, *Gertrude Stein in Pieces*, pp. 165–6; and Daniel, *Gertrude Stein*, p. 131.
160. Dydo, *Gertrude Stein*, p. 12.
161. Stein, 'Objects', p. 105; Bridgman, *Gertrude Stein in Pieces*, p. 165.
162. Daniel, *Gertrude Stein*, p. 131; Bridgman, *Gertrude Stein in Pieces*, p. 166.
163. Stein, 'Objects', p. 105.
164. Stein, ibid., p. 105.

165. Stein, ibid., p. 108.
166. Ahmed, *Queer Phenomenology*, p. 3.
167. Daniel, *Gertrude Stein*, p. 131.
168. Stein, 'Objects', p. 110.
169. Stein, ibid., p. 111.
170. Stein, ibid., p. 111.
171. Daniel, *Gertrude Stein*, p. 131; Stein, 'Objects', p. 111.
172. Stein, *The Autobiography*, p. 204.
173. Stein, 'He and They, Hemingway', pp. 449–50.
174. Knapp, *Gertrude Stein*, p. 105.
175. Dydo, *Gertrude Stein*, p. 71.
176. Stein, 'He and They, Hemingway', p. 450. As Steiner (in *Exact Resemblance*, p. 113) and Dydo (in *A Stein Reader*, p. 449) observe, the portrait references texts by Victor Hugo that appear on the covers of the notebooks in which Stein composed 'He and They': *Quatre-vingt treize*, *Lucrèce Borgia*, and *Notre-Dame de Paris*. See Steiner, *Exact Resemblance*, for discussion of the 'emphasis on phonological repetition, rhyme, and rhythm' during this stage of Stein's portraiture (p. 106).
177. Knapp, *Gertrude Stein*, p. 105.
178. Stein, *The Autobiography*, p. 204.
179. Freeman, *Time Binds*, pp. 7–8.
180. Stein, 'He and They', p. 450; Stein, *The Autobiography*, p. 204.
181. Dydo, in *A Stein Reader*, p. 449; see also Knapp, *Gertrude Stein*, p. 105. For the publication history of *in our time* and *In Our Time*, see Cohassey, *Hemingway and Pound*, pp. 38–9, pp. 45–7, pp. 61–2, p. 72; Audre Hanneman, *Ernest Hemingway*; and Reynolds, *Hemingway: The Paris Years*.
182. See Abravanel, 'Anglophones in Paris'; Bridgman, *The Colloquial Style*; Lodge, *The Modes of Modern Writing*, pp. 154–9; Perloff, 'The Extra'; and Strychacz, *Hemingway's Theaters of Masculinity*, to name just a few, for analysis of Stein's and Hemingway's stylistic similarities and divergences.
183. St. Pierre, 'Bent Hemingway', p. 375, p. 371.
184. Stein, 'A Transatlantic Interview', pp. 505–6.
185. Stein, 'He and They', p. 450.
186. Stein, ibid., p. 450.
187. Stein, ibid., p. 450.
188. Freeman, *Time Binds*, p. xiii.
189. Benjamin, 'Theses', p. 257.
190. Freeman, *Time Binds*, p. xxii.
191. Dydo, *A Stein Reader*, p. 449.
192. Stein, 'He and They', p. 450.

193. Dydo, *A Stein Reader*, 449; Steiner, *Exact Resemblance*, p. 115.
194. Steiner, ibid., p. 115.
195. Voris, *The Composition of Sense*, p. 150.
196. Stein, 'He and They', p. 450.
197. Stein, ibid., p. 450.
198. Ernest Hemingway in Mary Welsh Hemingway, *The Way It Was*, p. 370. See Moddelmog, *Reading Desire*, for discussion of the troubling implications of this primitivist language.
199. Stein, 'He and They', p. 450.
200. Stein, ibid., p. 450.
201. Stein, ibid., p. 450.
202. Stein, ibid., p. 450.
203. Stein, ibid., p. 450.
204. Stein, ibid., p. 450.
205. Dydo, *A Stein Reader*, p. 449.
206. Stein, 'Van', pp. 462–3.
207. Sedgwick, *Tendencies*, p. xii.
208. Stein, 'He and They', p. 450.
209. Stein, ibid., p. 450.
210. There are multiple versions of this poem; I use the one called 'The Soul of Spain with McAlmon and Bird the Publishers'. For its publication history, see Hanneman, *Ernest Hemingway*, p. 68, pp. 143–4, and p. 266; and Hanneman, *Supplement to Ernest Hemingway*, p. 13.
211. Hemingway, 'The Soul of Spain', p. 71.
212. Corn and Latimer, *Seeing Gertrude Stein*, p. 140.
213. Hemingway, 'The Soul of Spain', p. 71.
214. Kale, 'Hemingway's Poetry', p. 71n4.
215. Hemingway, 'The Soul of Spain', 70; Kale, ibid., p. 71n4.
216. Hemingway, ibid., pp. 70–1.
217. Hemingway, ibid., p. 70.
218. Hemingway, ibid., p. 70.
219. Hemingway, ibid., p. 70.
220. Hemingway, ibid., p. 70.
221. Hemingway, ibid., pp. 70–1.
222. See Chapter 3 for discussion of references to faeces in Stein's and Toklas's love notes; Hemingway, 'The Soul of Spain', p. 70.
223. Hemingway, ibid., p. 70; 'shit, n. and adj.' *OED Online*. Oxford University Press, June 2016. Web. 23 August 2016.
224. 'shit, n. and adj.' *OED Online*, ibid. The *OED* lists E. Hemingway as a source in four different entries under 'shit', all of them negative. See Reynolds, *Hemingway: The Paris Years*, for an account of his negative views of the men named in this poem. Waldo Frank is among those

identified as Hemingway's 'enemies' in a complaint about the blurbs for the first printing of *In Our Time* (Ernest Hemingway to Barklie McKee Henry, 12 August 1925, *The Letters of Ernest Hemingway, 1923–1925*, pp. 370–1). *The Broom* (1921–4) was a modernist periodical published by Alfred Kreymborg and Harold Loeb, the latter of whom Hemingway portrayed as Robert Cohn in *The Sun Also Rises*. Loeb – Hemingway's friend when he wrote 'The Soul of Spain' – eventually became the victim of his anti-semitism. For an account of their friendship's 1925 turning point, see Reynolds, *Hemingway: The Paris Years*, pp. 300–6. Professional heavyweight boxer Jack Dempsey was at the peak of his career when his victory over underdog Luis Firpo caused Hemingway to lose a bet (p. 165). Despite the writer's claim that he would henceforth back the likeliest winners, Hemingway continued to bet against Dempsey whenever he could (p. 165).

225. Hemingway, 'The Soul of Spain', p. 70.
226. Hemingway, ibid., p. 70; Reynolds, *Hemingway: The Paris Years*, pp. 235–6, pp. 337–8.
227. Hemingway, ibid., p. 70.
228. Hemingway, ibid., pp. 70–1.
229. Hemingway, ibid., p. 71.
230. Cohassey, *Hemingway and Pound*, p. 72. Although Pound hated literary prizes, he eventually won The Dial Award in 1927, after Thayer's editorship ended (pp. 71–2).
231. Hemingway, 'The Soul of Spain', p. 71.
232. Hemingway, ibid., p. 71. Here I reference Pound's *Make It New*.
233. Hemingway, ibid., p. 71.
234. Freeman, *Time Binds*, p. 7.
235. Hemingway, 'The Soul of Spain', p. 71.
236. Hemingway, ibid., p. 71.
237. Steiner, *Exact Resemblance*, p. 115. Steiner finds support in 'He and They' and in Stein's observation in *The Autobiography* that Hemingway '"smells of the museums"' (pp. 114–15).
238. Steiner, ibid., pp. 114–15.
239. Hemingway, 'The Soul of Spain', p. 71.
240. St. Pierre, 'Bent Hemingway', p. 371.
241. Hemingway, 'The Soul of Spain', p. 71.
242. Hemingway, ibid., p. 71.
243. Hemingway, ibid., pp. 70–1.
244. Hemingway, ibid., pp. 70–1.
245. Hemingway, 'Part Two of the Soul of Spain', p. 72.
246. Hemingway, ibid., p. 72.
247. Hemingway, ibid., p. 72; Hemingway, 'Part Six', p. 73.

248. Hemingway, 'Part Six', p. 73.
249. Sedgwick, *Touching Feeling*, p. 8.
250. Sedgwick, *Tendencies*, p. xii.
251. Hemingway, 'Part Six', p. 73.
252. St. Pierre, 'Bent Hemingway', p. 371.
253. Corn and Latimer, *Seeing Gertrude Stein*, pp. 139–51.
254. The Guggenheim Foundation quoted in Dydo, *A Stein Reader*, p. 541.
255. Larsen, *Stein and Hemingway*, pp. 78–82.
256. Dydo, *Gertrude Stein*, p. 368.
257. Dydo, ibid., p. 370; Stein, 'Genuine Creative Ability', p. 104.
258. Stein, ibid., p. 104.
259. Dydo, *Gertrude Stein*, p. 370. Dydo identifies further iterations of this line in Hemingway's *A Farewell to Arms* and *Islands in the Stream*.
260. Dydo, ibid., p. 370.
261. Larsen, *Stein and Hemingway*, p. 44.
262. Stein, 'Genuine Creative Ability', p. 105.
263. Stein, ibid., p. 105.
264. Stein, ibid., pp. 104–5.
265. Stein, ibid., p. 104.
266. See especially Woolf's 1925 *Mrs. Dalloway* and 1927 *To the Lighthouse*.
267. Stein, 'Genuine Creative Ability', p. 104.
268. Stein, ibid., pp. 104–5.
269. Stein, ibid., p. 104.
270. Stein, ibid., p. 105.
271. Stein, ibid., pp. 104–5.
272. Stein, ibid., p. 105.
273. Stein, ibid., p. 105
274. Stein, ibid., p. 105. For accounts of the ends of these friendships, see Wagner-Martin, *Favored Strangers*, pp. 192–4, and Corn and Latimer, *Seeing Gertrude Stein*, pp. 139–59.
275. Stein, 'Genuine Creative Ability', p. 105.
276. Stein, ibid., pp. 104–5.
277. Corn and Latimer, *Seeing Gertrude Stein*, pp. 113–15.
278. Corn and Latimer, ibid., p. 113.
279. Stein, 'Genuine Creative Ability', p. 105.
280. Tonny's attention to Stein ultimately benefited his career: he received a commission to decorate the Wadsworth Atheneum, where Stein's *Four Saints in Three Acts* was first performed (Corn and Latimer, *Seeing Gertrude Stein*, pp. 192–3).
281. Dydo, *A Stein Reader*, p. 541.
282. Ford, *Gertrude Stein and Wallace Stevens*, pp. 16–21.

283. Dydo, *A Stein Reader*, p. 541. See Reynolds, *Hemingway: The 1930s*, pp. 29–31, for a narrative of the party referenced in 'Evidence' that places far less emphasis on its queer aspects than Stein's version.
284. Dydo, *A Stein Reader*, p. 542.
285. Dydo, *Gertrude Stein*, p. 382.
286. Dydo, ibid., p. 382.
287. Stein, 'Sentences and Paragraphs', p. 21.
288. Stein, ibid., p. 26; Stein, 'Evidence', in *A Stein Reader*, p. 543.
289. Stein, 'Sentences and Paragraphs', p. 27.
290. Stein, 'Evidence', in *A Stein Reader*, p. 544.
291. Stein, 'Sentences and Paragraphs', p. 21.
292. Dydo, *Gertrude Stein*, p. 379.
293. Larsen, *Stein and Hemingway*, p. 81; Stein, *The Autobiography*, p. 206.
294. Stein, ibid., p. 206; Dydo, *Gertrude Stein*, p. 379.
295. Ernest Hemingway to F. Scott Fitzgerald, 24 or 31 October 1929, in *Ernest Hemingway: Selected Letters*, p. 310.
296. Stein, 'Evidence', in *A Stein Reader*, p. 543; Dydo, *Gertrude Stein*, p. 384.
297. Stein, ibid., p. 543.
298. Stein, ibid., p. 543.
299. Stein, ibid., p. 543.
300. Stein, ibid., p. 543.
301. Dydo, *Gertrude Stein*, p. 382.
302. Stein, 'Evidence', in *A Stein Reader*, p. 543.
303. Stein, ibid., p. 543.
304. Stein, ibid., p. 543.
305. Stein, ibid., p. 543.
306. Larsen, *Stein and Hemingway*, p. 81; Dydo, *Gertrude Stein*, p. 383.
307. Stein, 'Evidence', in *A Stein Reader*, p. 543.
308. Stein, ibid., p. 543.
309. Stein, ibid., p. 543.
310. Ford, *Gertrude Stein and Wallace Stevens*, p. 16, p. 21.
311. Stein, 'Evidence', in *A Stein Reader*, p. 543.
312. Stein, ibid., p. 543.
313. See Larsen, *Stein and Hemingway*, pp. 82–4, concerning these rumours.
314. Stein, 'Evidence', in *A Stein Reader*, p. 543.
315. Stein, ibid., p. 543.
316. Stein, ibid., p. 543.
317. Stein, ibid., p. 543.
318. Stein, ibid., pp. 543–5.
319. Stein, ibid., p. 545.
320. Dydo, *Gertrude Stein*, p. 384.

321. Stein, 'Evidence', in *A Stein Reader*, p. 545.
322. Stein, ibid., p. 545.
323. Stein, ibid., p. 545.
324. Stein, ibid., p. 545; Freeman, *Time Binds*, p. 7.
325. Dydo, *Gertrude Stein*, p. 382; Stein, 'Evidence', in *A Stein Reader*, p. 544. Dydo also identifies the 'lady sitting and working at tapestry' as Toklas, p. 542.
326. Stein, ibid., p. 544.
327. Stein, ibid., p. 545.

Chapter 7

Stein, Van Vechten and Modernism's Queer Gaze

> 'The only thing that is different from one time to another is what is seen and what is seen depends upon how everybody is doing everything. This makes the thing we are looking at very different and this makes what those who describe it make of it, it makes a composition, it confuses, it shows, it is, it looks, it likes it as it is, and this makes what is seen as it is seen.'
>
> Gertrude Stein, 'Composition as Explanation'

As Edward White observes, Carl 'Van Vechten would not be the first or last young man to feel the force of' Stein's 'unconventional powers of seduction'.[1] Yet their flirtatious friendship stands out for supporting Stein's transmasculine embodiment, queering 'the binary of heterosexual and homosexual' in ways informing their modernist innovations.[2] Unlike her shakier ties to Picasso and Hemingway, her rapport with Van Vechten never waned. Instead, Stein's 'magnetism' exerted such a 'highly sexual' pull that he gregariously corresponded with her and Toklas throughout their lifetimes and remained Stein's loyal advocate even after her death.[3] Although Blackmer argues that Stein's and Van Vechten's alliance represents an 'unparalleled' example of 'mutual cooperation, support, and good will between a woman and man of letters', Stein's transmasculinity defies identity categories more profoundly than this formulation suggests.[4] As Cromwell observes, 'transsituated' subjectivities undermine the distinction between woman and man, 'heterosexual and homosexual'.[5] This produces even queerer bonds between Stein, Toklas and Van Vechten than Blackmer envisions.

Rather than deriding Stein's writing like Hemingway and Picasso, Van Vechten helped place her manuscripts, served as her literary executor, edited her *Selected Writings*, organised her 1934–5 lecture tour of the United States, and took photographs that furthered her celebrity image.[6] Stein continued this circuit of masculine homosocial desire by writing three verbal portraits of him and recounting their friendship in *The Autobiography* (1932: 1933). Their shared concern with challenging early twentieth-century culture's heterosexist norms shows in their artwork, which registers their masculine homosocial bonds and Stein's transmasculine embodiment. These works queer modernism's gaze, offering fresh ways of perceiving the movement and their roles within it.

Van Vechten's photographs of Stein in *Everybody's Autobiography* (1936: 1937) 'have served to crystallize her public image'; his other images register the affectionate ties of the 'Woojums' family they eventually formed with Toklas.[7] These representations constitute a counter-archive refuting perturbed portrayals of Stein.[8] Rather than expressing discomfort over her transmasculinity, Van Vechten produced, circulated and archived photographs that allow her gender to be viewed in a favourable light. In turn, Stein – who hints at this dynamic when she observes that 'what is seen depends upon how everybody is doing everything' – wrote word-portraits of Van Vechten that reveal her devotion to him and serve as additional conduits of their homosocial desire.[9] These poems show none of the teasing uncertainty of her writings about Picasso and Hemingway. Instead, Stein dwells lovingly on Van Vechten, affirming her affection for him.

These portraits facilitate the emergence of a queer gaze within modernism. The gazes at play in Van Vechten's images of Stein contrast to works such as Picasso's *Portrait of Gertrude Stein* (Plate 1), which uses masking and hollowed-out eyes to register her masculinity and the disturbance it produces within a heteronormative gaze. Van Vechten's photographs of Stein convey no such uneasiness. Instead, they deploy a queer gaze in which her masculinity registers as a source of strength. In so doing, Van Vechten's images mobilise 'the eye's transformative potentiality – its capacity for looking from a position which is not assigned in advance, and for affirming certain ostensibly marginal elements . . . at the expense of those that are culturally valorized'.[10] As Silverman argues, 'the screen' – the image constituted through the gaze – consists of '[t]he full range of representational coordinates which are culturally available at a particular moment in time'.[11] By selecting from those 'representational coordinates' those 'subcultural representations' that show their subjects' queerness in a favourable light, Van

Vechten's photos open up new ways of looking at Stein's writing and transmasculinity. Bringing the figure Agee depicted as 'a huge squat mountain on a distant border of the literary kingdom' in from the margins and placing her at the centre of American expatriate modernism, Van Vechten's images offer a fresh way of envisioning Stein's role in the movement.[12]

Stein and Van Vechten first met in Paris even though he resided in New York City, so the three friends were rarely present at the same location. They nonetheless sustained a lifelong friendship through correspondence whose tones ranged from affectionate to exuberant. Like Stein's famous statement that 'America is my country and Paris is my home town', her transatlantic ties with Van Vechten undercut the concept of national identity.[13] This transnational movement informed, in turn, the queerings of desire, gender and embodiment produced through Stein's and Van Vechten's bond. In the 1910s and 1920s, the geographical displacements animating their friendship registered in Stein's verbal portraits of Van Vechten in ways that destabilise nation. In the 1930s, however – as Van Vechten shepherded Stein and Toklas across the United States and fascist dictators rose to power across Europe – his photographs invoked nationalist tropes to promote the masculine Stein as an American icon. Even though Stein and Toklas were always identifiable as American expatriates in Paris, they made France's Bugey region their home during World War II despite the threat of the Final Solution. These Americans' embrace of France as their homeland complicate conventional understandings of national belonging.

These apparent contradictions are consistent with the anti-identitarian politics animating other aspects of Stein's and Van Vechten's lives. Stein cultivated friendships across genders and sexualities; Van Vechten socialised in ways that crossed sexual and racial lines. As Scott Herring argues, Van Vechten was not driven by the fantasy of a community based on common sexual or racial categorisation but by forms of queer relationality that defied deeply 'entrenched boundaries between homosexuality and heterosexuality', blackness and whiteness.[14] Herring stresses Van Vechten's friendships with African Americans, but his point may be extended to the photographer's queer bonds with Stein and Toklas. Their relationality scrambled gender and sexual identities, helping Stein's transmasculine embodiment emerge. Moreover, by facilitating the publication of Stein's writings and creating a counter-archive of iconic photographic images, Van Vechten placed her transmasculinity at the centre of American expatriate modernism. Their portraits of one another foreground the queerness of modernism's destabilisation of form, allowing us to envision the movement and its makers anew.

Stein, Van Vechten and the new: queering space, time and vision in *The Autobiography*

The queerness of Stein's and Van Vechten's modernism is evident in their accounts of their initial meeting. Blurring the line between fiction and non-fiction, Stein's 'bent' version of their friendship in *The Autobiography* queers the gaze through which modernism is given to be seen. The text stages Stein's, Toklas's and Van Vechten's first encounters in the couple's Parisian household and at the second night of the Ballets Russes's performance of Igor Stravinsky's *The Rite of Spring*. Recounting these events twice and reversing their order, Stein presents her and Van Vechten's friendship as formed by and decentred through the artistic innovations animating Modernist Paris. These parts of *The Autobiography* enhance Stein's image as a modernist. Van Vechten's narrative of his attendance at the Ballets Russes similarly uses factual distortions for self-promotion.[15] While their versions differ, both writers stress their importance to the modernist project of 'making it new'.

With its reiterations, jumps in time and plays with perception, *The Autobiography* uses cubist visual strategies to show Stein's and Van Vechten's friendship from multiple angles.[16] In keeping with its emphasis on Stein's and Toklas's involvement in Parisian networks of artists and writers, *The Autobiography* begins and ends its sections on their friendship with Van Vechten by revealing the connections that brought them together. This strategy has a decentring effect, stressing that they were not part of a closed but an open system that entailed many transatlantic crossings and displaced the idea that Paris was modernism's centre.

Arriving through Stein's networks in the course of a series of events *The Autobiography* presents out of sequence, Van Vechten initially appears as one of three 'young men' sent by Mabel Dodge, who had introduced him to Stein's experimental writing during the 1913 Armory Show.[17] *The Autobiography* teases the reader with the news that one of the few occasions Stein's and Toklas's cook, Hélène, 'cooked a very bad dinner' was the day 'Carl Van Vechten turned up', but then disclaims that 'that is later' and launches into an account of their dinner with his ex-wife.[18] Toklas stresses the physical attractiveness of Mrs Van Vechten (Anna Snyder), who had divorced her husband by the time she arrived in Paris. Describing her as 'a very tall woman' who 'was good looking', Toklas does not reveal that the Van Vechtens had already divorced or that Snyder's ex-husband was not straight.[19] Instead, Toklas presents them in heterosexual masquerade by referring to Snyder as 'Mrs. Van Vechten'.[20] In keeping with the text's treatment of homosexuality as an open secret, Toklas cagily states that 'Mrs. Van Vechten told the story of the tragedy of her married life' and observes that 'Gertrude Stein was not particularly interested' in Mrs Van Vechten's narrative of heterosexual tragedy.[21] Snyder's conversation falls outside the salon's regular pattern of Stein sitting with the 'geniuses' and Toklas with their 'wives'.[22] Even though *The Autobiography* stages these roles as destabilising 'impersonations' rather than fixed essences, its recounting of Snyder's story presents Stein as uninterested in moving outside her role and engaging in conversation with a fellow modernist's wife.[23]

The Autobiography does, however, present Stein as keen to engage Carl Van Vechten once he appears, even though it would be hard to describe him as a 'genius'. Though he eventually established himself as a writer of reviews and financially lucrative popular novels, Van Vechten is now best known for his role as one of modernism's great impressarios: as a party-thrower, white patron of the Harlem Renaissance, celebrity photographer and facilitator of others' careers. A queer sociability animated his and Stein's friendship, which began – so *The Autobiography* claims – when she 'began to tease' him over Hélène's failed meal 'by dropping a word here and there of intimate knowledge of his past life'.[24] Perhaps Stein was more interested in his former wife than 'Toklas' initially leads us to believe, or at least in what Snyder had to say about her ex-husband's sexual orientation. Identifying Van Vechten as 'the hero or villain of Mrs. Van Vechten's tragic tale', Toklas suggests that Anna may have deserved sympathy but also that there might be something admirable in Carl's refusal to cede on his sexual and literary desires.[25] Stein's sympathies, however, are presented as far less equivocal than Toklas's: the story of this 'curious evening' concludes with the statement that 'Gertrude Stein and he became dear friends'.[26]

This declaration is immediately followed by anecdotes showing Stein's and Van Vechten's artistic reciprocation: he helped her place the first piece of writing she ever saw 'printed in a little magazine'; he wrote an essay about her work; he printed her famous phrase 'a rose is a rose is a rose is a rose' inside one of his own books; she had a French potter make 'yellow clay' plates with 'a rose is a rose' as 'the border' and 'to Carl' at 'the centre'.[27] Shortly thereafter – in keeping with *The Autobiography*'s feminist emphasis on Toklas's agency at 27, rue de Fleurus – Toklas claims her importance to this exchange: 'it was I who found it in one of Gertrude Stein's manuscripts and insisted upon putting it as a device on the letter paper, on the table linen and anywhere that she would permit that I would put it'.[28] This calls attention to Toklas's active role in Stein's celebrity branding. *The Autobiography* then moves on from Van Vechten's introduction by praising his 'delightful habit of giving letters of introduction to people who he thought would amuse Gertrude Stein' – a successful practice introducing members of their network that form the narrative's subsequent subjects.[29]

This material is preceded, however, by the text's portrayal of Stein's and Toklas's encounter with Van Vechten at *The Rite of Spring*, an event the text presents out of sequence – as before rather than after the dinner that cemented their friendship. This temporal rupture and distortion of fact allows the narrator to play up the three friends' attendance at a ballet that quickly achieved notoriety for the 'terrible uproar' caused by its dissonant score.[30] *The Autobiography* presents the second performance as drowned out by the crowd as its 'outraged' detractors 'hiss' and its 'defenders . . . applaud'.[31] Because of this din, Toklas – who observes that the ballet's 'brilliantly coloured background' would not have been considered 'at all extraordinary' by the time *The Autobiography* was published in 1933 – was unable to 'hear any of the music'.[32] She and Stein were able to see that '[t]he dancing was very fine', though.[33]

They also noticed Van Vechten when – as Toklas tells it – he enters their box right before the performance. Acting as if the dinner at the rue de Fleurus had not yet happened, Toklas describes him as 'a tall well-built young man' who 'might have been a dutchman, a scandinavian or an American'.[34] Above all, Van Vechten's attire was striking: 'he wore a soft evening shirt with the tiniest pleats all over the front of it. It was impressive, we had never even heard that they were wearing evening shirts like that.'[35] This suggests that Van Vechten's appearance is as avant-garde as the performance that followed his arrival. Moreover, it reveals that Stein and Toklas were attracted to his physical presence in ways that defied identity categories and surfaced in praise of his sartorial aesthetics.

An arresting feature of Van Vechten's appearance – the 'tiniest pleats' on his shirt – later came to animate Stein's first portrait of him, 'One Carl Van Vechten' (1913: 1922), which *The Autobiography* cagily claims to concern the 'unknown' man at *The Rite of Spring*.[36] The pretence of not knowing Van Vechten's identity structures *The Autobiography*'s presentation of his arrival for dinner at the rue de Fleurus: 'He came and he was the young man of the soft much-pleated evening shirt and it was the same shirt.'[37] Of course it was – a fact of which Stein and Toklas were well aware. The text's equivocation adds a magical air to both events: a man who later came to be one of Stein's most loyal supporters suddenly appears to them as an alluring and mysterious feature of Paris's modernist spectacle, his newfangled shirt standing out as a herald of the new.

The vacillations suggested by Van Vechten's shirt mobilise uncertainty in ways that echo *The Autobiography*'s depiction of the insecurity Stein felt in their friendship. When Toklas recounts Van Vechten's much-anticipated return to Paris after World War I, she says that after years of maintaining 'a friendship and correspondence' across the Atlantic, '[n]ow that he was actually coming Gertrude Stein was a little worried. When he came they were better friends than ever. Gertrude Stein told him that she had been worried. I wasn't, said Carl.'[38] The two friends' divergent perceptions reveal their transatlantic friendship's decentring effects despite Van Vechten's show of certitude about his and Stein's bond. The book's placement of their ties within open-ended modernist networks, inventive treatment of facts and departures from linear time all further *The Autobiography*'s queering of the gaze. As Freeman observes, 'the manipulation of time' can be 'a way to produce' – and to queer – 'both bodies and relationalities (or even nonrelationality)'.[39] Temporal plays facilitated Stein's and Van Vechten's queer relationality and Stein's transmasculinity, queering the space of 'Modernist Paris' and our image of their roles within it.

Van Vechten by Stein

'One Carl Van Vechten' (1913: 1922): queering literary cubism

Whereas *The Autobiography* uses Stein's and Toklas's split subjectivity to re-envision modernism through a gaze that hides queerness in plain sight, Stein and Van Vechten extended and transformed that gaze through their portraits of one another. In the wake of their first encounters in Paris, Stein composed a portrait called 'One' that mobilises the sensory plenitude of Van Vechten's pleated shirt and their enticing experience at Stravinsky's ballet. Composed two years after Stein's more famous *Tender Buttons*, for which Van Vechten would find a publisher in 1914, 'One' similarly approximates strategies from the visual arts to register queer erotics.[40] The portrait juxtaposes different elements in a manner recalling the strategies of collage that – along with 'bright colour' and 'bold compositional shapes' – came to characterise synthetic cubism, a style Picasso and Juan Gris were beginning to develop when Stein met Van Vechten.[41] In 'One', different sensory elements – colours, textures, sounds and rhythms – invoke Stein's perception of Van Vechten's physical presence at Stravinsky's ballet. The portrait's mixture of textures with incongruous objects – such as 'An oil in a cup and a woolen coin, a woolen card and a best satin' – foreshadows Meret Oppenheim's 1936 fur-lined teacup.[42] The objects utilised in 'Van' are more pliable than Oppenheim's, however. What Walker calls Stein's 'artful reordering of the familiar world' through the syntactical manipulations of *Tender Buttons* also characterises the tenderness of 'One', whose departures from conventional grammar stretch at objects to render them anew.[43] This undercuts categories of gender and sexual identity, creating a sensory space for Stein's transmasculine embodiment to emerge through queer relationality with Van Vechten.

The portrait's juxtapositions also evoke the 'Deleuzian interest in planar relations' characterising the Sedgwickian '*beside*'.[44] Stressing spatiality, Sedgwick calls attention to the queer possibilities of showing 'extra alertness to the multisided interactions among people "beside" each other in a room'.[45] 'One' concerns Van Vechten's queer relation with his and Stein's shared box at *The Rite of Spring*. The first section of the portrait emphasises sight and touch, noting 'the ample checked fur in the back' and the 'next cloth . . . in the chest, in mean wind', made of 'the best most silk' as smooth as 'water'.[46] The wind's motion carries through the section – 'In the best might last and wind that. In the best might last and wind in the best might last.' – to the shiny spectacle of gold's arrival: 'In the gold presently, in the gold presently unsuddenly and decapsized and dewalking. In the gold coming in.'[47] Rather than depicting Van Vechten in literal terms, this sequence riffs on the textures of his pleated shirt and suggests the entrance of a fabulous queen decked out in gold lamé.

The portrait's next section further plays with vision and sensation to call perception into question: after the arrival of the 'One', we see 'None in stable, none at ghosts, none in the latter spot.'[48] Nothing may be seen or placed, whether in a concrete 'spot' or the ethereal realm of the 'ghosts'.[49] The material world grounding identity dissolves, allowing the new to emerge. By the third section, one may sense the smoothness of 'oil', as well as that of the 'can' and 'cup' that contain it.[50] A 'vial' and 'steel sofa', too, contribute cool smoothness that one also finds in the references to 'nickel' and 'glass' opening Stein's *Tender Buttons*.[51] The 'vial' has 'a thousand stems', taking its unnamed contents in multiple directions at irregular times and anticipating the juxtapositions that eventually emerge between '[a]n oil in a cup' and 'a woolen coin'.[52] These queer reorientations reveal new directions for desire.

'One' quickly juxtaposes the senses by warping space and time, much like the opening sections of *Tender Buttons*. *Tender Buttons* mixes references to objects' textures and colours with temporal displacements ('A kind in glass . . . a single hurt color'; 'Nickel, what is nickel, it is originally rid of a cover. / The change in that is that red weakens an hour') and spatial complications ('The difference is spreading').[53] 'One', too, queers space and time by enacting paradoxes. 'An oil in a cup and a woolen coin' contrast with 'a woolen card and a best satin'; 'A water house and a hut to speak' collapse through the sheer force of paradox and personification into 'a water house and entirely water, water and water'.[54]

This movement redoubles the senses in the portrait's next section, 'Two', which is similarly animated by textures and colours: 'Two. / A touching white shining sash and a touching white green undercoat and a touching white colored orange and a touching piece of elastic.'[55] This passage's play on physical and emotional touch stretches beyond the realistic. 'White' is both 'green' and 'colored orange' as its smooth textures 'hurry' along a 'ruddy' flush, much as the 'elastic suddenly' touches an unspecified object or person.[56] This 'touching research' into the space's mysterious queer relationality 'is an over show' that goes beyond what one can visually apprehend.[57] By contrast, touch – which requires proximity rather than distance – is a sensation that 'is in the best way', its rhythmic 'beat' forming 'an example of work' that leads to 'expartition' – reunion.[58]

This 'work', both spatial and temporal, initiates Van Vechten's friendship with Stein and Toklas. At *The Rite of Spring*, the three modernists sit in a 'touching box' that fosters queer relationality that moves toward stasis: 'A touching box is in a coach seat so that a touching box is on a coach seat so a touching box is on a coach seat, a touching box is on a coat seat, a touching box is on a coat seat.'[59] The word 'coat' suggests a sense of comforting enclosure that becomes even warmer in the next line, which states that 'A touching box is on the touching so helping held.'[60] Visual movement – 'Any left in the touch is a scene, a scene' – quickly unsettles the box's occupants, however: a pun on the word 'left' in the subsequent phrase, 'Any left in is left somehow', simultaneously invokes stasis and lateral movement to dislodge any sense of certitude.[61]

Spatial divisions and movement animate the portrait's closing section, 'Four', which opens with the phrase 'Four between, four between and hacking. Four between and hacking. / Five.'[62] The word 'hacking' and stress on recurrent separations invoke the violent rhythms of *The Rite of Spring* and its crowd. This recalls the poem's opening, in which a 'mean wind' provides the movement behind the edgy pleats on Van Vechten's shirt.[63] As 'One' spirals to its end, 'a saddle' bridges the text's spatial divisions and 'a kind of dim judge' recalls the earlier passages' blurring of vision.[64] With 'a great big so colored dog' bounding into its final line, the portrait stretches size and refuses to name colour.[65] This introduces an element of chaos befitting the raucous scene at Stravinsky's ballet and anticipates the Ballets Russes's performances of Erik Satie's *Parade* (1917), which featured Picasso's costumes and set designs.[66]

The performative aspects of 'One' are further underscored by its complication of temporal sequencing: linear conceptions of space and time run off the rails by the text's close. The poem's structuring iterations of 'One', 'One', 'Two' and 'Four' – section headings that reverberate within each textual division – mimic the irregular rhythms of Stravinsky's score and thereby queer temporality.[67] The manuscript version of this portrait was subtitled 'A kind of play', suggesting a drama presented by 'five characters' or in 'five acts'.[68] By combining dramatic, visual and musical innovations, 'One' stretches the boundaries of reality to stage Van Vechten as a flashy and appealing part of modernism's spectacle, as integral to the scene as the inflamed spectators at *The Rite of Spring*. His aesthetic innovation grips Stein and Toklas, setting in motion the queer desires and genders they will later live out as the 'Woojums' family.

'Van or Twenty Years After' (1923: 1924): queering relationality and queering the gaze

The rhythms of 'One' transform the pleats on Van Vechten's shirt into a spectacle and eventually modulate into the hesitant opening of 'Van', Stein's 'Second Portrait of Van Vechten'. She wrote this poem in fall of 1923 in Nice during a burst of writings following her visit to Picasso in Antibes.[69] By this time, she had not seen Van Vechten in years: she and Toklas were in France; he was in New York. Following 'As A Wife Has A Cow' in Stein's manuscript notebooks and written around the same time as her second portrait of Picasso, her second poem about Van Vechten is part of a trio of texts that echo earlier pieces about the same subjects.[70] Emerging from 'a single process in the mind', these texts all concern 'creation, mastery, identity' and 'engenderment'; they immerse 'the subject in the flux of transitive relations'.[71] In so doing, Stein's writings show a slippage between social and sexual bonds. Whereas 'As A Wife Has A Cow' is explicitly erotic, 'If I Told Him' vacillates between homosocial and homosexual desire. 'Van or Twenty Years After' registers these vicissitudes while openly affirming its subject.

The sixth paragraph of 'Van' stresses several key elements of Stein's and Van Vechten's ties by mobilising punning oscillations between the words 'tied', 'untied' and 'beside'. Reiterations of these and other words figure the movement of Stein's and Van Vechten's queer relationality. Physically separated for most of their friendship, Stein and Van Vechten repeatedly affirmed their bond through correspondence, with periods of waiting in between letters. 'Van' captures this dynamic of being '[t]ied and untied', made to 'wait' repeatedly in anticipation of the next letter – the next sign of their creative connection.[72]

However, sometimes – during Van Vechten's occasional visits to France; during Stein's and Toklas's lecture tour of the United States – they were able to be physically 'beside' one another.[73] These moments' sporadic nature is captured in punnings between the words 'beside', 'tied' and 'untied' occurring throughout the sixth paragraph: 'And as tied and as beside, and as beside and tied'; 'Tied and untied and beside and as beside and as untied and as tied and as untied and as beside', etc.[74] Yet this passage does not assert the text's 'self-sufficiency' in ways that 'disregard . . . her reader's response' and the social aspects of language, as Glavey claims.[75] Rather, these lines from 'Van' are relational. They do not mobilise the open-ended form of relationality that Glavey's book addresses but highlight the oscillatory movements of Stein's and Van Vechten's bond. Like 'beside', the words 'tied and untied' signal proximity and connection – emotional and physical ties that are insistently ruptured and re-established.

The word 'beside' – which also appears as the title of a section of 'As A Wife Has A Cow' – does not necessarily connote smooth relations.[76] It stresses immediate proximity but figures a form of relationality involving many vicissitudes. The poem's reiterations of 'tied and untied' register the movement of 'attracting', 'withdrawing' and 'differentiating'.[77] Through repeatedly deferred correspondence and occasional visits in person, Stein and Van Vechten 'reinstate the act of birth' – create – each time they re-establish their bond.[78] In this, their correspondence works like Stein's and Toklas's love notes. Stein's and Van Vechten's effusive friendship echoes and modulates her and Toklas's resignification of the metaphor that presents writing as akin to childbirth: as Dydo notes, Stein's texts – their 'babies' – are 'joint creations'.[79] 'Van' extends the queerly affectionate tone of 'As A Wife Has A Cow' without overtly reiterating its orgasmic language and rhythms. Both 'Van' and Stein's and Van Vechten's letters to one another also strongly accentuate positive affects such as desire and imitation.[80] While some words in 'Van' imply difference or departure, there is no overt hostility.

From the outset, 'Van' takes up the irregular timing of Stein's and Van Vechten's visits, creating what Freeman describes as 'moments when an established temporal order gets interrupted and new encounters consequently take place'.[81] The text amplifies the temporal oscillations of 'He and They, Hemingway', echoing and complicating the playfully queer temporality animating an unpublished portrait of Van Vechten Stein drafted in 1923.[82] In so doing, 'Van' distorts perspective in ways that hint at other forms of sociality and actively mobilise alternate modes of relating, orienting, looking, connecting and disconnecting. These forms of relationship inform Stein's and Van Vechten's queer friendship.

For Freeman, 'nonsequential forms of time' create openings for 'living aslant to dominant forms of object-choice, coupledom, family, marriage, sociability, and self-presentation and thus out of synch with state-sponsored narratives of belonging and becoming'.[83] Stein's portraits of Van Vechten play with time to reveal these possibilities. Opening by declaring itself 'a sequel to One', Stein's unpublished poem scrambles the sequential logic by which it would 'follow one' that came 'before'.[84] Whereas its movements collapse diachronic time into the synchronic expanses of reiterative 'moment[s]' and 'instance[s]', 'Van' oscillates between various temporal modes.[85] The latter text opens by noting that 'twenty years' have passed since Stein met and wrote her first portrait of Van Vechten. However, their first meeting – and Stein's composition of 'One' – took place only ten years before she wrote 'Van'. This inaccurate opening line initiates the first of the poem's interrogations of different 'ways of phrasing time', but the implications of the second portrait's title go well beyond the 'literary importance' with which Stein credits her subject by citing Alexandre Dumas's *Vingt ans après* and other texts.[86] Temporal manipulations drive the portrait's queering of Stein's and Van Vechten's friendship: the text reiterates 'twenty years' in contexts that first stress deferment ('Twenty years *after*'), then render time ambiguous ('as much as twenty years after'), and stretch it ('after twenty years and so on').[87] Stein builds anticipation with a hypothetical situation holding out the prospect of a happy future ('If it was to be a prize a surprise if it was to be a surprise to realize') and then calls it into question ('was it to be. What was it to be') before announcing its realisation ('And it was. So it was. As it was.')[88] Tense shifts as the speaker announces 'As it was. As it is', and calls the present, too, into question only to confirm it: 'Is it as it is. It is and as it is and as it is.'[89] Reassuring the reader that the present is like the past, Stein concludes this paragraph by declaring that 'And so and so as it was.'[90]

Or so we might think if we were not familiar with Stein's reiterative style and its tendency to undercut seemingly stable assertions. The next two lines orient and reorient the reader, initiating a concern with vision that is present in 'One' and even more dominant in 'Van'. They initially exhort her to 'Keep it in sight alright' and then insist that the line of sight should go 'Not to the future but to the fuchsia.'[91] This reorientation recalls the vibrant colours of 'One' and Fauvist paintings such as *La Femme au chapeau*, as well as the sights and smells activated by flowers. Queering space and time, this refuses what Lee Edelman calls 'reproductive futurism' and instead directs the reader to the aesthetic and erotic concerns animating Stein's and Toklas's bond with Van Vechten.[92] Van Vechten, the portrait suggests, prompts Stein to see things otherwise: to engage in what Freeman calls the 'unbinding' of 'time', looking through queer eyes to another possible world.[93]

This sequence's warped temporal pattern also sets into motion an imaginary scenario in which multiple people share the same look. This movement animates other portions of 'Van' as well. One sentence in the sixth paragraph – 'Weight, state, await, state, late state rate state, state await weight state, in state rate at any rate state weight state as stated' – builds up to a hypothetical situation in which 'six sat at the table' and 'all looked for those places together'.[94] At that point, 'each one in that direction look[s] down and see[s] the same as weight'.[95] While these looks are temporarily aligned and even set to the same measurement, their coincidence is only temporary.[96] 'As weight for weight as state to state as wait to wait' quickly turns to 'as not so', undermining the looks' parallelism.[97] This suggests that Stein's and Van Vechten's friendship enabled a fleeting sociality that mobilised multiple ways of looking.

Similarly, near the end of the poem, a paragraph that begins with iterations of the phrase 'Seating regard it as the very regard it as their very nearly or as the very regard it' initiates perspectival shifts that further undercut the uniformity of the looks deployed earlier in the portrait.[98] Spatial vacillations introduced several paragraphs earlier in iterations such as 'as they meant to be left and their center' reappear in the later paragraph to destabilise vision: 'seating and regard it, regard it as the very nearly center left and in the center'.[99] These lines' contradictions continue the earlier passages' work, mobilising and undercutting parallel looks. This visual regime offers up unpredictable 'moments when an established temporal order gets interrupted and new encounters consequently take place'.[100]

The portrait's final lines add to the earlier passages' reworking of vision by creating a cinematic fade-out. After the illusion of certainty induced by the speaker's pronouncement 'And so I say so' at the end of the paragraph that begins with 'Seating regard it', the poem ends with language that undermines certainty of vision: 'Now to fairly see it have, now to fairly see it have and now to fairly see it have.'[101] As if it were not enough to call sight into question, the word 'Naturally' – which ends the poem's reiterative permutations on 'Now to fairly see it have and to have' – recurs in ambiguous contexts at the text's close.[102] 'As naturally, naturally as, as naturally as' suggests comparison but refuses to provide a second term, leaving the reader hanging and calling into question the naturality the speaker claims. The text's final line – 'Now to fairly see it have as naturally.' – similarly stresses the indeterminacy of sight and what is seen.[103] Parallel looks that diverge, sight that fades, comparisons that are unclear, diachronic time that recurrently collapses into synchronic time in reiterations of the word 'now': the poem's plays with the visual all queer the gaze.[104] 'Van' thereby provides a novel way of viewing the portrait's subject and his role in modernism's social networks.

The text's scenario also foreshadows Van Vechten's later career as a photographer. This scene's plays with the visual queer modernism's gaze by mobilising looks that first appear to be paralleling or mimicking one another but ultimately diverge. Both of these forms of relationality are temporal in that they take place simultaneously. However, they emerge within a jerky passage that moves unpredictably between waiting and delayed stating. This play of looks enacts both relationality (in that the six act in unity) and nonrelationality (in that the situation is imaginary, staged '[o]nly as if' it had happened).[105] Because paralleling – like looking – is both temporal and spatial, these oscillations carry across time and space. By toying with both, the poem's gradual build-up to a tenaciously shared and ultimately untenable visual trajectory queers metaphysics by calling presence into question. Continually 'tied and untied', Stein's and Van Vechten's bond – and their efforts to reshape modernism – could have been undermined by absence but were maintained through writing: through open-ended linguistic reiteration.[106]

The poem's insistences create patterns of sound that further enhance and complicate these dynamics. Stressing 'phonological repetition, rhyme, and rhythm', the text's sonorities resonate within 'Van' and across the portraits that precede and follow it.[107] The 'auditory word modulations' driving 'Van' make its organisation 'spatial': 'hearing takes place in space, where words can be taken in free of reference as physical things that relate, resemble, rhyme, attract, and repel and do their sibling punching and punning by sound and volume'.[108] The poem's phonological patterns reinforce its semantic suggestions that attraction and withdrawal were at play in Stein's and Van Vechten's friendship, despite their letters' affectionate effusions.[109] Puns on the word 'by' – which rhymes with 'bye' – sonorously mobilise these dynamics, subtly echoing the uncertainty surrounding the speaker's opening anticipation of a 'surprise' reunion and the reiterations with which the two friends are '[t]ied and untied' through their arrivals and departures.[110]

These forms of attraction and withdrawal parallel the semantic and acoustical movements – 'And prepare and prepare so prepare to prepare'; 'Have it as having having it as happening'; 'my wife having a cow as now and having a cow as now . . . My wife has a cow.' – that 'As A Wife Has A Cow' uses to enact Stein's and Toklas's sexual relationship.[111] Although 'Van' concludes less definitively – and less orgasmically – than the portrait that immediately precedes it, the echoes between the two pieces suggest that eroticism subtended Stein's friendship with Van Vechten, even though it was likely not physically acted upon. A mixture of fondness and distancing also animates 'If I Told Him', the portrait Stein composed immediately after 'Van'. 'If I Told Him' uses teasing references to Picasso as 'Napoleon' to show her fondness for the painter while simultaneously taking ironic distance from him. 'Van' more subtly separates itself from its subject by mobilising the text as an acoustical space rather than a vehicle for depictions.[112]

In so doing, Stein suggests that her friendship with Van Vechten resonated across the Atlantic at unpredictable times. This dynamic points to another way their relationality was queer. Moving '*across genders, across sexualities, across genres*', and across the Atlantic Ocean, the queerness of 'Van' – and Stein's and Van Vechten's friendship – is 'multiply transitive'.[113] Relational and open to difference, this transitivity cannot be predicted in advance or confined by a single axis of identity.[114] Instead, Stein's and Van Vechten's friendship exemplifies the reasons for which Stryker, Currah and Moore prefer to speak of 'trans-' with a dash, as 'open-ended' in meaning, rather than conjoin it with the word 'gender'.[115] Resisting formulations that 'delimit and contain the relationship of "trans-" conceptual operations to "-gender" statuses and practices', the dash mobilises 'trans-'s' conjunctions with 'national' and 'Atlantic'.[116] These varied forms of transitivity inform the queerings of gender and desire in Stein's and Van Vechten's bond. Though this aspect of their connection is implicit rather than explicit, it is part of the portrait's context.

'Van' figures transatlantic exchanges most overtly in two paragraphs stressing shifts in location. The first of these intones, 'They meant to be left as they meant to be left, as they meant to be left left and their center, as they meant to be left and their center. So that in their and do, so that in their and to do.'[117] This passage's recurrent displacements between 'left' and 'center' figure, among other things, the geographic traversals that sustained Stein's and Van Vechten's friendship: his occasional visits to France; the letters and works they frequently exchanged; and the three (of eight) volumes of *The Making of Americans* whose passage across the Atlantic the portrait goes on to address.[118] Its directional reiterations – which also call to mind instructions for formatting manuscripts – are followed by the news that 'So suddenly and at his request. Get up and give it to him and so suddenly and at his request.'[119] The requested typescript's ontological status then comes into question through a series of reiterations of 'request' – 'Request to request in request, as request, for a request by request, requested, as requested as they requested' – that are followed by an undermining conclusion: 'or so have it to be nearly there'.[120] '[N]early there' but never quite placed, 'three' portions of the manuscript are left 'waiting' for publisher Alfred Knopf's return to the office.[121] As Stein waits for the typescript to appear as a book in its full 'One two three four five six seven' and eight volumes, she declares that she should 'regard it as the rapidly increased February' – the month in which Van Vechten asked her to send the first three volumes across the Atlantic.[122] Time and space compress simultaneously, moving the poem forward into another paragraph that stages the look and the gaze in tandem with displacements from 'left' to 'center'.[123]

Opening with an incantatory call to be 'Seating' and 'regard it as the very regard it as their very nearly regard', the fourth from final paragraph in the portrait moves from the sense of being 'very settled' to a series of unsettling spatial contradictions.[124] While the latter do not emerge until the paragraph's end, the stage for them is set from the start, as the seeming security of the seated and their looks is purely hypothetical. The reiterations of 'regard it' implore one to look and hint at the variability of the resultant perceptions. Phrases such as 'seating regard as their very nearly regard it as the very nice' suggest uncertainty and imprecision even as they lead the viewer toward specific value judgements.[125] After stating that 'the very nice' is 'known and seated', the portrait shifts into commands: 'seating regard it, seating and regard it'.[126] The viewer becomes the viewed and the viewer again in a Möbius strip of a sentence that unsettles the frame of reference and queers the gaze. From that point forward the poem decentres itself: 'seating and regard it, regard it as the very nearly center left and in the center, regard it as the very left and in the center'.[127] Spatial displacements figure the transatlantic crossings through which Stein and Van Vechten conducted their friendship and literary commerce. These movements recall, in turn, shiftings of the gaze mobilised in earlier passages. Although the text's plays with space recede as the poem concludes, Stein ends by stressing the ambiguity of perception: 'Now to fairly see it have as naturally.'[128]

Stein bends time and space by collapsing the distance created by traditional perspective. As Dydo observes, 'Van' – like other portraits from this stage – exemplifies Stein's desire to 'write her perception from inside, not to make pictures of it, tell stories about it, or explain it from outside. Being inside a wave is radically different from seeing, naming, and recognizing the wave from here or there.'[129] The sixth paragraph's puns on words such as 'wait', 'weight' and 'state' reflect metatextually on this project by suggesting that the temporality and spatiality of Stein's and Van Vechten's friendship is difficult to measure in linear terms. So are words' semantic meanings, which are endlessly undercut through reiteration in ways that move the portrait away from depiction.

Stein nonetheless asserts that Van Vechten can be 'seen' in the portrait. When asked in a 1934 interview to explain 'Van', she states that 'the words look like Carl Van Vechten, anyone can know that beside they mean Carl Van Vechten anybody can know that'.[130] Stein's remark that her words 'look like' her subject might lead her listeners to anticipate that 'Van' would manipulate the materiality of the signifier to create the kinds of patterns for which concrete poets would later become famous, but such a reading is unwarranted. While 'Van' can be described as a prose-poem consisting of paragraphs rather than stanzas, it does not otherwise exploit the page's visual qualities to provide a literal picture of its subject. The portrait's reiterations do, however, recall the rhythmic furls of Van Vechten's shirt that were mobilised ten years earlier in 'One', and the text does reference – without depicting – a variety of events that took place between them as they anticipated and exchanged letters, visits and manuscripts. As Dydo observes, Stein 'always wrote about real things', even when she bent facts.[131] In this sense, 'Van' captures Van Vechten's subjectivity in its varied enmeshments with Stein's, creating the likeness of its subject.

'Van' also mobilises the pleasures of her and Van Vechten's friendship and makes them available to readers. When Stein's interviewer asks her to explain her textual practice, incredulous that her lecture tour of the United States implies the existence of 'many people who will be able to comprehend' her work, she declares:

> Look here, being intelligible is not what it seems . . . You mean by understanding that you can talk about it in the way that you have a habit of talking . . . putting it in other words . . . but I mean by understanding enjoyment . . . If you enjoy it you understand it, and lots of people have enjoyed it so lots of people have understood it.[132]

The affective definition of understanding accounts for Stein's tendency to bend facts. Focusing on the subjective truth of the reader's engagement – on the pleasures he or she may take in her texts' sounds and significances – Stein stresses her writing's ability to recreate the experience of being with her subjects. Glavey thus rightfully stresses that this passage positions Stein's poetics as relational: as 'conceiving of a knowledge that is justified by joy rather than any form of discursive truth', and as drawing in others through her ability to be 'interesting' rather than convey factual meaning.[133]

In 'Portraits and Repetition', Stein further states that during this stage of her writing, 'I concentrated the internal melody of existence that I had learned in relation to things seen into the feeling I then had there in Saint Remy of light and air and moving and being still.'[134] This concentration of ambient emotions into 'melody' ultimately discomfited her: she follows her description of her goals for portraits such as 'Van' and 'If I Told Him' with the observation that they emerged at a time at which 'melody . . . rather got the better of me', making her feel 'rather drunk'.[135] This is a curious moment: Stein reveals discomfort with her own feelings and her ability to convey them in writing. But in the 1934 interview, she insists that these texts' enjoyable reiterations are the source of her growing audience in the United States – one whose swelling size she emphasises with a phrase, 'and how', that echoes the 'And now' with which she registers Toklas's multiple orgasms in 'As A Wife Has A Cow'.[136] These echoes complicate Glavey's suggestion that the interview valorises the 'more prosaic' state of 'enjoyment' over the ecstasies of jouissance.[137]

'And how' follows upon Stein's observation that increasing numbers of her contemporaries 'do see' the point of her writing.[138] Similarly, with the exclamation 'look here', she calls upon her interlocutor to change the way he views her writing and embrace pleasure as a mode of comprehension.[139] 'Van' – whose final four paragraphs are driven by reiterations of 'regard it' and 'see' – makes a comparable move.[140] By tracking her friendship with Van Vechten from within the pleasurable context of its movements, Stein invites the reader to enjoy looking at her subject from within her own perceptual field rather than from the distance entailed by conventional perspective. If desire is implicated in the field of vision, its subtle vicissitudes in 'Van' are enhanced by auditory echoes of the more openly erotic 'As A Wife Has A Cow'.[141] Like cubist paintings' perspectival distortions, this aspect of 'Van' shifts the gaze through which modernism and its makers are given to be seen. When her sceptical interviewer claims that what Stein sees in 'Van' is 'hard for us normal Americans to see', she asks 'What is a normal American' and then emphatically asserts that '[t]here are lots quite normal who do see. And how.'[142] Her statement supports the looks of her followers, offering an alternative to the assumptions about normalcy and common sense underlying her interviewer's comment. Insisting that modern art and writing are becoming increasingly 'normal', Stein destabilises and resignifies that word's meaning. She thereby suggests that by the middle of the 1930s, the gaze through which she, her colleagues, and modernism were presented for view was already beginning to shift.

Stein by Van Vechten

Seeing Stein's masculinity through Van Vechten's gaze

Van Vechten's photographs of Stein further queer the gaze by foregrounding the 'oppositional and subcultural representations' that are either left in the background or distorted in many other artists' images.[143] By casting a loving gaze on Stein's transmasculine embodiment, he and other gay male photographers countered perturbed responses to her gender by using iconography of her 'imperial' presence 'to interpret a powerful but simpatico woman whom they loved'.[144] His portraits show the short-haired Stein from behind, in profile, or directly facing the camera. In the illustrations for their chapter on 'Imperial Stein', Corn and Latimer include without individual comment two of Van Vechten's 1934 portraits of Stein: one showing her in profile against a dark backdrop (Figure 7.1); another depicting her from the rear (Figure 7.2). In both images, Stein faces the darkness in a pose that suggests seriousness and purpose, foregrounding and solidifying her transmasculinity. Yet there are significant differences between these two photographs – and their attitude towards Stein and other photographers' stances – that Corn and Latimer leave largely unremarked.

Stein's pose in the former shot echoes her position in a 1926 photograph by Man Ray (Figure 1.5). Observing that the latter image utilises 'the pictorial rhetoric of neoclassicism', Corn and Latimer note that Man Ray 'minimized her body and hands and lit her head and profile so that they read as solid and stony, in effect simulating Roman portrait busts of male figures of power'.[145] By the 1930s, this

Figure 7.1 Photograph by Carl Van Vechten, *Gertrude Stein* (1934).

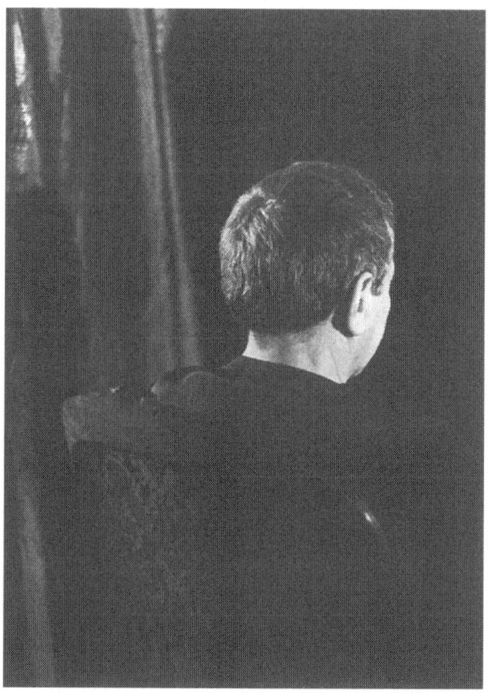

Figure 7.2 Photograph by Carl Van Vechten, *Gertrude Stein* (1934).

'had become an international style for representing the power and authority of strong personalities'.[146] Van Vechten's image of Stein in profile echoes Man Ray's by using light to stress the masculinity of her 'Caesar' crop and call attention to her signature brooch. However, Van Vechten's photograph differs from his peer's in ways Corn and Latimer do not notice. Instead of following Man Ray's pattern of using light to emphasise Stein's head and illuminate her entire torso, Van Vechten's photograph does not allow for such 'clarity of detail'.[147] His image of Stein in profile uses a starker play between light and dark than Man Ray's, illuminating her face's powerful profile and shrouding most of her clothing in darkness.

Whereas Man Ray uses stylisation to denaturalise Stein's gender and highlight its artificiality, Van Vechten paradoxically uses photographic style to suggest that her masculinity is natural. As Corn and Latimer observe, the former's 1926 photo emphasises 'performative' aspects of Stein's masculinity such as her 'slicked-back hair', suggesting that her 'sexual identity' is 'unfixed'.[148] Van Vechten's 1934 profile of Stein, by contrast, plays with light and dark to thicken her neck and face into a more masculine look than that conveyed by the even lighting in Man Ray's photograph, which illuminates feminine aspects of her angular jawline. Van Vechten's image also uses small shards of light to highlight aspects of her hairline – such as a rear cowlick pushing her hair forward – that make her 'Caesar' crop mannish.

Van Vechten's 1934 photograph of Stein from the rear further plays up the appearance of her masculinity's naturalness by illustrating her cowlick in detail and showing that it causes the back of her hair to fall into a masculine-patterned hairline. In this image, light falls intensely on Stein's sideburns, which are trimmed straight across. The photograph's lighting calls the viewer's attention to these signs of masculinity and hints at maleness. This effect is heightened by the photo's occlusion of facial details that would have been revealed had Stein been facing the camera. However, what Corn and Latimer fail to notice about these two photographers' very different stagings of Stein's 'imperial' presence is that Van Vechten stylises Stein as masculine by highlighting not her gender's 'instability' but its similarities to male masculinity.[149]

Both of Van Vechten's 1934 portraits of Stein feature copious dark space, cultivating an air of mystery and stressing her weighty intellect. The latter photograph sharply contrasts to two self-portraits showing

Van Vechten from behind. These images are medium shots emphasising his head and shoulders; they are more tightly focused than his rear-view image of her. They are also more typical of Van Vechten's 'signature portrait style' than his photographs of Stein.[150] Stringer observes that most of his portraits reflect

> a praxis of extreme artifice and resourceful improvisation, encompassing patterned backdrops (usually printed cloth or crinkled Mylar), a very compressed picture space, props, furniture, costumes and dramatic lighting, deliberate anachronisms and visual puns, and often a dynamic, animated sitter.[151]

The two self-portraits in question utilise this style. Unlike Stein, who faces the darkness, Van Vechten stares at abstractions. In one photograph (Figure 7.3), his messy hair suggests motion even as his head draws in viewers' vision and invites them to follow his look. His body askance and head positioned just left of centre, Van Vechten looks slightly upward and contemplates a set of concentric rectangles producing loopy distortions. The combination of the

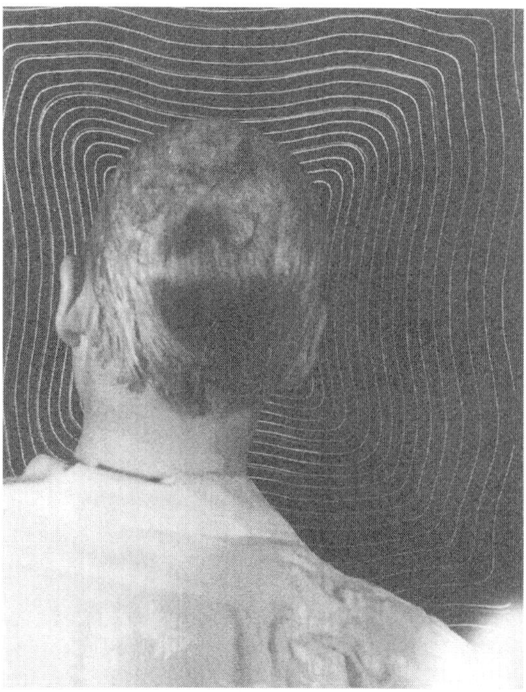

Figure 7.3 Photograph by Carl Van Vechten, *Carl Van Vechten* (1934).

image's backdrop with Van Vechten's self-positioning creates a sense of twisting that suggests his capacity for altering perceptions: that is, his creativity.

In another photograph (Figure 7.4), he sits in the same chair in which Stein is shown from the rear. Whereas Van Vechten places Stein's head in the top right-hand corner of the frame, his self-portrait shows his head only slightly off centre. Only the top of the chair appears along with his head and shoulders. Whereas the self-portrait stresses its subject, the image of Stein emphasises the chair in which she sits – and thus its symbolic power. The photograph of Van Vechten, by contrast, directs the viewer's attention to his head and the pattern at which he looks: lined triangles alternating with squares featuring a light, finely textured pattern. His body is positioned similarly to Stein's, but his pose is far more casual. His arms seem relaxed even though they lie outside of the frame. His hair is soft and voluminous, artfully flowing down the back of his neck and contrasting to the backdrop's sharp, direct lines. His head is tilted subtly upward and askance, whereas hers aims slightly downward. Although this self-portrait endows Van Vechten

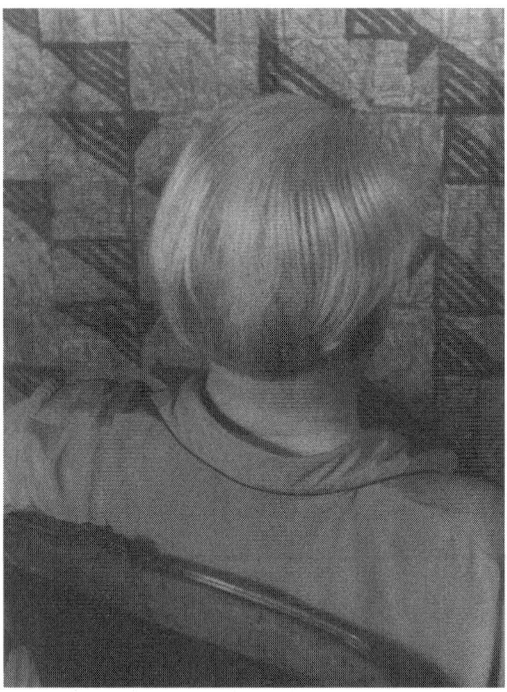

Figure 7.4 Photograph by Carl Van Vechten, *Carl Van Vechten* (1933).

with the same aura of seriousness attached to Stein, the two images have different emphases. This self-portrait plays between internal and external: he faces the geometrical patterns directly, as if engaged by their contrasts. His photograph of Stein, on the other hand, shows her looking slightly downward and uses the rear view to stress her capacity for contemplation.[152]

By emphasising Stein's intellect, Van Vechten points to the brilliant mind that animated her late nights of writing and calls attention to her commanding presence. In *The Autobiography*, Toklas recounts having repeatedly 'teased' Stein for her similarities to 'a civil war general', a word photographer Cecil Beaton also used to describe her.[153] Van Vechten's photograph deploys a similar trope. If in profile Stein appears as a general poised to launch an attack, from the rear she comes across as a leader in retreat, contemplating her next move. Both images stage Stein as a Great Man, an icon of masculine power. One of Stein's lifelong obsessions, this type informs the references to Caesar in her erotic writings, the fascination with Napoleon in 'If I Told Him', and her friendship with historian Fäy, with whom she bonded over discussion of these and other powerful historical figures.[154] Zox-Weaver points out that whereas Fäy wrote carefully researched historical studies of Great Men such as George Washington, Stein abstracted leaders and rendered them 'as icons embedded in myth rather than historical fact'.[155] Shrouding Stein in darkness, Van Vechten's photographs similarly detach her from her context and transform her into an icon of queer masculinity.

Man Ray's 1926 portrayal of Stein in the manner of 'Roman portrait busts' had also, by the 1930s, become a common technique for portraying fascist dictators.[156] In a 1935 piece for the right-wing journal *Je Suis Partout*, Fäy similarly uses fascist tropes to stage Stein's ascendance as 'a national and nationalist triumph'.[157] Although Stein's wartime political pronouncements are contradictory, Zox-Weaver points out that the ironic stance she sometimes took toward Nazism reveals her continued captivation by the very kinds of masculinities from which she distanced herself in *Everybody's Autobiography* by declaring that 'There is too much fathering going on.'[158] When the narrator of *The Autobiography* qualifies her statement that Stein is like a 'general' by specifying 'a civil war general of either or both sides', she hints at her conflicted investment in authoritarian personae.[159] By taking an impartial stance toward the parties in a conflict that ended slavery in the United States, this statement suggests – disturbingly – that ethical questions concerning the treatment of others were not important to Stein's attraction to powerful male leaders. At the same time, however, the vacillation at work in the phrase 'of either or both sides' mirrors Toklas's depiction of Van Vechten as 'the hero or villain of Mrs. Van Vechten's tragic tale' in *The Autobiography*.[160] Much as that text's narrator refuses to fix a stable ideological viewpoint by choosing between a narrative that validates Snyder's feelings of betrayal or one that affirms Van Vechten's need to embrace his queerness, so does its depiction of Stein as 'a civil war general of either or both sides' decline to choose.[161] The text thereby presents Stein's attraction to authoritarian masculinity as unbound by a singular political perspective and radically open to different – even appalling – viewpoints.[162] Similarly, Van Vechten's photographs of the 'Imperial Stein' demonstrate her attachment to authoritarian masculinity while undercutting simplistic accounts of her identification with it.[163] His lighting scheme leaves much of the portrait in darkness and refuses the 'clarity of detail' that characterised fascist imagery. Deploying and undermining visual language used to glorify leaders of fascist nations, Van Vechten's images suggest Stein's differences from the ideologies of 'great men' whose authoritative and 'controlling will' nonetheless attracted her imagination.[164]

'[C]larity of detail' may be absent from Van Vechten's photos of the 'imperial Stein', but it prevails in his photographs showing Stein directly facing the camera. One 1935 image (Figure 7.5) explicitly uses nationalist tropes to invoke her 'imperial' presence. His subject poses in front of the American flag, looking authoritatively at the camera and directly meeting the viewer's gaze. This shot is more artfully designed than many of Van Vechten's other photographs: Stein's body is positioned off centre in the midst of stars and stripes, her scarf at a diagonal adding to the movement created by the flag's furls. One of the most frequently reproduced and iconic of his images, this photograph associates Stein with the American flag, forming 'a symbolic bond between her and the country' that stages her as 'a female addition to Mount Rushmore'.[165] It thus serves one of the goals of his imagery of Stein: to present her 'as one of the country's greats'.[166]

This image's rhetoric is an early twentieth-century example of 'homonationalism'.[167] Analysing the contemporary War on Terror, Jasbir K. Puar defines 'homonationalism' as 'the dual movement in which certain homosexual constituencies have embraced U.S. nationalist agendas and have also been embraced by nationalist'

Figure 7.5 Photograph by Carl Van Vechten, *Gertrude Stein* (1935).

organisations such as the United States military.[168] Both geopolitically and sexually, Stein's historical moment was very different from our own.[169] Even though neither she nor Van Vechten publicly celebrated their queerness, he publicised Toklas's role as Stein's 'intimate companion' to boost Americans' interest in *The Autobiography*.[170] That cagey term for 'lover' would have been recognisable to at least some segments of the public, and therefore in play as the press covered their tour of the United States.[171] Stein's sexuality would have been on the minds of some of her readers, too, when they picked up *Lectures in America* and found Van Vechten's image of its author in front of the American flag as its 'frontispiece'.[172] In keeping with 1930s conventions, his visual strategies are more covert than those of the contemporary activists who have advocated for the right of LGBT Americans to serve in the armed forces. However, his image still places a queer writer at the centre of the United States' national project.

Stein and Toklas had been participating in the United States' nationalist project since World War I by supporting servicepeople in wartime: they served as ambulance drivers for the American Fund for the French Wounded and actively cultivated friendships with American soldiers during World War I.[173] After the Allies won World War II, American soldiers recruited Stein to do a live broadcast to the United States expressing her jubilance at France's liberation. She and Toklas also visited extensively with victorious American and French troops after the latter war.[174] Van Vechten – who had moved by the middle of the 1930s from an apolitical stance to an embrace of 'the vitality of American culture' and 'its founding commitment to the genius of the individual' – socialised with servicemen at New York's Stage Door Canteen, an entertainment venue established for their benefit.[175]

Van Vechten's photograph of Stein in front of the American flag aligns her with the United States body politic in the context of the lecture tour – prompted by her own 'insistence that she was a thoroughly American author' – that fuelled her rise to celebrity in her homeland.[176] This image situates her as an expatriate modernist and as an important American icon: as a figure whose centrality to the national project makes her appear far more monumental than the mysterious but influential mountain looming at the 'distant border' of Agee's prose.[177] This is not to say that Stein wholeheartedly subscribed to nationalist ideologies: research on her wartime writings suggests she was sceptical about nationalism and armed conflict.[178] Rather, it is to say that Van Vechten used nationalist visual rhetorics to present her as an appealing figure to the American public, associating patriotism with her transmasculinity.

Seeing the Woojums through Van Vechten's gaze

A different set of Van Vechten's images brings the queer affiliation of Stein, Toklas and Van Vechten out of marginality and into 'cultural prominence'.[179] Take, for example, a series of images from 1935. Held in the archives of the New York Public Library and at Yale University's Beinecke Library, these photographs (Figures 7.6, 7.7 and 7.8) are all medium shots featuring Stein, Toklas and Van Vechten. *Seeing Gertrude Stein* reproduces the first of these photos (Figure 7.6) at the beginning of the chapter on 'La seconde famille', which explores the families of choice Stein and Toklas established with gay male writers, artists and composers in the 1920s.[180] The varied configurations of Stein's, Toklas's and Van Vechten's bodies in these photographs reveal that their friendship took Stein's and Toklas's resignification of heterosexual gender roles several steps further than previous scholars understood.

Figure 7.6 Photograph by Carl Van Vechten, *Gertrude Stein, Carl Van Vechten, Alice B. Toklas* (1935).

Figure 7.7 Photograph by Carl Van Vechten, *Gertrude Stein, Carl Van Vechten and Alice B. Toklas* (1935).

Figure 7.8 Photograph by Carl Van Vechten, *Gertrude Stein, Carl Van Vechten, Alice B. Toklas* (1935).

During Stein's lecture tour of the United States, she, Van Vechten and Toklas came to describe themselves as the 'Woojums' family, enacting a queer twist on the language of heterosexual familial structure.[181] The 'Woojums' family helped constitute Stein's masculinity: as 'Baby Woojums', she was coddled and protected by 'Papa Woojums' (Van Vechten) and 'Mama Woojums' (Toklas).[182] This set-up triangulates Toklas's many references to Stein as 'baby' in their love notes with their flirtation with Van Vechten.[183] Much as Stein was masculinised in her and Toklas's love notes and erotic poetry, 'Baby Woojums' was 'sometimes referred to by the pronoun *he*'.[184] Within the 'Woojums' family, then, Stein was both masculinised and infantilised through a triple movement. She was situated as Toklas's 'baby' in accordance with the well-known pattern in which an adult man married to a woman continues to act like and be treated as a boy. At the same time, Toklas and Van Vechten positioned themselves as parents of the prodigious Stein and worked tirelessly to promote her writing. Finally, despite Stein's apparent infantilisation, she and Van Vechten were also professional colleagues who enjoyed an adult form of queer masculine homosociality, standing as equals on the modernist scene.

The series of photographs featuring Stein, Toklas and Van Vechten brings the 'Woojums' family into prominence and highlights the mobility of its roles. In one photo, all three of the Woojums face the camera. Van Vechten is at the centre, his arms encompassing Stein and Toklas. Although his body appears to create unity, their looks are askance and their bodies are not perfectly centred. The right side of the image fills one half of Toklas's face with light and shrouds the other in shadow. At first glance, her pose seems to be the most conventional of the portrait's three subjects: her visible eye looks directly at the camera and meets viewers' looks. This draws attention to her part of the frame while leaving viewers to wonder about her other eye. Thus, despite her look's apparent directness and conventionality, she skews the looks of the photo's viewers. With Van Vechten, too, a play between light and shadow tricks and confounds viewers' looks in a way that is only heightened by the visual crossings produced through the combination of his face's downward tilt with his eyes' upward and sideways glance. Stein is granted the most space, nearly crowding out the others. Her face is also the most consistently lit of the three, her head and eyes tilting upward and sideways. Like Van Vechten, she does not look directly at the image's viewers but rather aims for a space outside of the frame. The cumulative effect of the image's lighting and use of space – as well as the three subjects' variably positioned eyes and faces – is to mobilise looks that are 'askance', thwarting viewers who try to occupy a position 'assigned in advance'.[185] By forcing them to engage 'the eye's transformative potentiality', this photograph unfixes and queers the gaze.[186] In so doing, Van Vechten mobilises an alternative to modernism's dominantly heteronormative modes of visual representation by implying the existence of other scenes outside the portrait's frame.[187]

Two other photographs from this series highlight the mobility of roles afforded within this queer gaze. In one (Figure 7.7), Stein and Van Vechten are blocked together, their faces turned toward Toklas to meet her eyes in a manner contrasting with the divergent looks traversing the photo I just discussed. Stein is positioned as the most dominant figure, her face the best lit of the three. Her eye and Toklas's are on the same plane, although the latter's is partially obscured by shadow. Van Vechten's heavily lit forehead is angled slightly downward, conveying an air of submission toward Toklas even as he meets her look. Van Vechten's apparent subordination and the illumination of Stein's direct look suggest that both are paying close attention to Toklas. Even while shrouded and mysterious, Toklas is endowed with the power to attract Stein's and Van Vechten's eyes. All three of the subjects' expressions are direct and serious, as if they are discussing a weighty matter. Even so, the image seems off-kilter: the lighting directs attention to Stein's face and Van Vechten's forehead at the top left hand side of the photograph even as their looks focus on Toklas. Attention moves from Stein and Van Vechten to Toklas, yet shadows make a mirage of the latter's eye. The viewer thus vacillates between Toklas and the Stein – Van Vechten alliance, dramatising the shifting roles available within the 'Woojums' family.

Another photograph from this series (Figure 7.8) uses a different lighting scheme to show Stein and Van Vechten exchanging affectionate glances as Toklas looks on. This image presents Stein and Toklas in profile, highlighting stern facial features and reinflecting Sedgwick's classic homosocial scenario. Whereas Sedgwick exposes the way women circulate as objects of exchange between men to constitute and mediate 'male homosocial desire', Van Vechten's photo stresses what I call the flirtatious 'masculine homosocial' bond between 'Papa Woojums' and the masculinised 'Baby Woojums' as 'Mama Woojums' looks on.[188] In contrast to the photograph in which Stein and Van Vechten look at Toklas, in this image her profile and eye are evenly lit rather than shadowy. Moreover, Stein and

Van Vechten direct flirtatious glances at one another while Toklas looks gently at Stein. The photo's use of light and emphasis on Stein's and Van Vechten's visual exchange emphasise their affectionate ties. Although their looks make Toklas seem peripheral, she directs her eye at Stein in a way that involves her. The distribution of light in this photograph draws Toklas into the composition and creates a contrast with the earlier image, which uses a play between light and shadow to set Stein and Van Vechten apart from her even as she engages their attention.

This lighting highlights Toklas's role as a secondary figure echoing the woman in Édouard Manet's 1863 *Le déjeuner sur l'herbe* (Plate 5), the cover art for Sedgwick's *Between Men*. In Manet's painting, a nude woman sits with a man in a dark suit. Another suited man sits opposite them and reaches out in her partner's direction to draw him into conversation. But rather than look directly at the man who tries to engage him, the man seated with the woman looks askance. Aiming at the bottom right side of the painting, he seems to contemplate something outside of the frame. By contrast, the woman's eyes are directed at the painting's viewers, soliciting their looks. Although all three are frontlit, with no features left in shadow, the woman's naked body is the lightest element of the painting, which encourages viewers to look in her direction.[189] This play of looks pushes beyond Sedgwick's paradigms. Whereas she emphasises the various ways women are exchanged 'between men' whose homosocial desire is subtended by the disavowed possibility of homosexuality, Manet's painting does something quite different. The woman's direct look makes her an erotic object for viewers of all genders, yet neither male subject shows any interest. She is completely peripheral rather than an object of their exchange. Her male companion also declines to respond to the other man's invitation, looking sideways at a space other than that of the gaze constituted by the woman. He thereby sidesteps objectification and remains elusive. His refusal to engage undercuts the forms of connection the painting's other two subjects work to establish.

By contrast, in Van Vechten's photograph Toklas looks on as he and Stein connect. Reversing Manet's composition, which places the men opposite one another, Stein and Van Vechten are blocked together and exchange looks. Unlike the woman in the painting, Toklas looks at Stein. In contrast to the first photograph from Van Vechten's series, as well as *Le déjeuner sur l'herbe*, nobody solicits viewers' looks. The second of his photographs similarly emphasises its subjects' looks without directly addressing viewers. By refusing to interpellate viewers, the second and third images contrast to the first, which uses Toklas in the same way as Manet's painting uses the nude woman. Like Manet's woman, Toklas interpellates the viewer directly, even as she is placed on the opposite side of the frame as Manet's woman and is partially obscured by sidelighting. By contrast, the second and third photographs create an insular exchange of looks emphasising the three subjects' bonds. Whereas the first photograph in the series uses Toklas to draw viewers into its queer gaze's many trajectories, the second and third internally mobilise looks sustaining the 'Woojums' family. The latter two photographs also block Stein and Van Vechten together, setting them apart from Toklas even as they interact with her. This positioning emphasises Stein's and Van Vechten's masculine homosocial bond even as the series highlights role and power shifts within the 'Woojums' family.

As the flirtatious exchanges between the subjects of this series of photographs suggest, Stein's and Van Vechten's masculine homosociality differed from both the paranoid kinds of masculine homosociality Sedgwick exposes in *Between Men* and the fraught forms of masculinity that attended Stein's friendships with Picasso and Hemingway. Stein's and Van Vechten's homosocial bonding stands out among Stein's friendships with men because it affirmed rather than was fractured by their queer departures from heterosexuality and its normative expectations for masculinity and femininity. Their ties' queerness undermined the gender binary, providing a way for Stein's transmasculinity to emerge.

Van Vechten sometimes directed his self-portraits at Stein and used her look to queer the gaze through which they were seen. Dodge once described Van Vechten as 'really queer looking', construing his physical features as outside normative proportions for masculine attractiveness.[190] In one frequently reproduced photograph created for Stein (Figure 7.9), Van Vechten subverts these assumptions.[191] In this image, his look directly engages viewers. Whereas his eyes evince masculine directness, the rest of his self-presentation highlights his feminine features. Delicate bangs fall over his forehead as his lips gently purse in front of the photograph's most prominent feature, his arm adorned with multiple bracelets. His pose draws viewers into the queer gaze constituted by the portrait. His closeness to Stein helped establish this gaze, within which he donned 'his finest

Figure 7.9 Photograph by Carl Van Vechten, *Carl Van Vechten* (1934).

clothes and his best face' to please her eyes.[192] Although Corn and Latimer reproduce these norms by reading his self-positioning as an attempt to compensate for 'his outsize head' and high 'forehead', I read them as playing up prettiness that Stein – a good friend of many gay men – was well positioned to appreciate.[193] In flirtatiously sending Stein this self-portrait, Van Vechten employed her affirming look to counter Dodge's othering of his queeniness. Thus, as Stein's and Van Vechten's affectionate and collegial exchange worked to affirm the former's transmasculinity through a variety of flattering portraits, it also validated the latter's femininity and rearticulated the terms through which their homosocial bonding could occur.

Producing images that are frequently reproduced to this day, Van Vechten rendered Stein and a variety of other marginalised modernist figures iconic.[194] This is what Silverman means when she writes that the 'vicissitudes' of even a single look can depart from the visual trajectory encouraged by the culturally dominant gaze and operate 'in concert with enough other looks' to 'reterritorialize the screen' constituting the gaze.[195] By bringing Stein's masculinity and his own femininity 'into cultural prominence' over and against the forms of othering wrought by 'normative representation', Van Vechten's photography proliferated visual rhetorics that affirmed their queerness's value.[196] His work as a photographer and volunteer archivist provided scholars with rich caches of images through which to interpret modernism.[197] He thereby reconfigured 'the screen' through which we apprehend his and Stein's queering of modernism's gaze.[198] This gave Stein's transmasculinity to be seen in loving ways that have enabled contemporary interpretations of her gender.

Notes

1. White, *The Tastemaker*, p. 102.
2. Cromwell, *Transmen & FTMs*, p. 130.
3. Kellner, 'Baby Woojums in Iowa', p. 5. See also White, *The Tastemaker*, for an account of self-promotion in Van Vechten's and Stein's friendship.
4. Blackmer, 'Selling Taboo Subjects', p. 221.
5. Cromwell, *Transmen & FTMs*, p. 130.
6. Van Vechten found a publisher for *Tender Buttons* and attempted to place *The Making of Americans*. Of the former, see Appendix B to *The Letters of Gertrude Stein and Carl Van Vechten*, p. 861; of the latter, see Dydo, *A Stein Reader*, p. 453. Of both, see Van Vechten, 'Some "Literary Ladies" I Have Known'. In *Carl Van Vechten and the Irreverent Decades*, Kellner notes that Van Vechten did not volunteer for the role of Stein's executor and initially felt overwhelmed with the news that she had appointed him. This feeling subsided once presses became interested in her work (pp. 278–86). Thornton Wilder, not Van Vechten, secured a place for Stein's and Toklas's papers at Yale University's Beinecke

Library: see Burns and Dydo, 'Introduction', in *The Letters of Gertrude Stein and Thornton Wilder*, p. xxi.

For details about Van Vechten's roles during Stein's and Toklas's lecture tour of the United States, see Souhami, *Gertrude and Alice*, pp. 198–219; Wagner-Martin, *'Favored Strangers'*, pp. 206–20; and White, *The Tastemaker*, pp. 269–77. Souhami, pp. 198–202, reports that Stein's agent – William Bradley – was first to suggest the lecture tour of the United States, which she initially resisted; Fäy served as the test audience for Stein's lectures and recommended Baltimore curator Marvin Chauncey Ross to create the itinerary, for which Fäy and Van Vechten made additional recommendations. Though less visible than Van Vechten, Fäy also helped arrange the trip (Will, *Unlikely Collaboration*, p. 98), as did Elisabeth de Gramont, the Duchess of Clermont-Tonnerre (Van Pymbroeck, 'Triangular Politics', p. 89). Wagner-Martin, *'Favored Strangers'*, p. 206 states that Stein was encouraged to go on tour by Mike and Sally Stein as well as Fäy and Van Vechten; she and White detail the extensive work Van Vechten did during the tour to arrange social events for Stein and Toklas. Van Vechten ('Portraits of the Artists', p. 256) notes that he 'accompanied' Stein and Toklas for 'part of the tour and photographed her extensively in several cities of Virginia, and several times in New York'. See Wagner-Martin, *'Favored Strangers'*, pp. 206–20; and White, *The Tastemaker*, pp. 269–77. See note 83 to the Introduction for more about Stein's friendship with Fäy.

7. Blackmer, 'Selling Taboo Subjects', p. 246. The edition of *Everybody's Autobiography* that includes Van Vechten's photographs was published by Random House in 1937.
8. Stringer, *Not Even Past*, offers a detailed exposition of the counter-archival practices Van Vechten used in his photographs of African Americans; while her emphasis is different than mine, her analysis informs my arguments about Van Vechten's production and use of photographs. Unlike the racist photos Stringer analyses, however, Van Vechten's counterarchive of queer imagery responds to artworks that vary in their attitude toward Stein's queerness. Manuel's, Man Ray's and Picasso's depictions of Stein are more equivocal than Lynes's, for example. Moreover, images take on different valences depending on the context in which they are circulated. I stress the significance of Van Vechten's photographs of Stein in the middle of the 1930s as her status as a celebrity grew. See also Smith, *Photography on the Color Line*, for detailed analysis of photography as an archival and counter-archival practice.
9. Stein, 'Composition as Explanation', p. 513.
10. Silverman, *Threshold*, p. 182.

11. Silverman, ibid., p. 221.
12. Agee, 'Stein's Way', p. 57.
13. Stein, 'An American and France', p. 61.
14. Herring, *Queering the Underworld*, p. 145.
15. For Van Vechten's account of his first meeting with Stein, see 'Some "Literary Ladies" I Have Known'. For a careful comparison between Stein's and Van Vechten's versions of their first meeting and the facts revealed by their correspondence, see Appendix A to *The Letters of Gertrude Stein and Carl Van Vechten*, pp. 845–53. For Van Vechten's self-mythologising story of his appearance at what he inaccurately claims to be opening night of *The Rite of Spring*, see 'Igor Strawinsky'. As White, *The Tastemaker*, pp. 103–4 observes, Van Vechten's description of the event bends facts to situate its author as 'one of those privileged few who attended the infamous first night', even though his last-minute attempt to attend that performance was thwarted by its having 'sold out' well in advance.
16. See Chapter 4 for more detailed discussion of the cubist strategies at work in *The Autobiography*.
17. Stein, *The Autobiography*, p. 126; White, *The Tastemaker*, pp. 97–101.
18. Stein, ibid., p. 127.
19. Stein, ibid., p. 127. See White, *The Tastemaker*, pp. 43–119, for an account of the ways Carl Van Vechten's homosexual and heterosexual dalliances – and debts – contributed to the end of his and Synder's marriage.
20. Stein, *The Autobiography*, p. 127.
21. Stein, ibid., p. 127.
22. Stein, ibid., p. 81.
23. Hovey, *A Thousand Words*, p. 101.
24. Stein, *The Autobiography*, p. 129.
25. Stein, ibid., p. 129.
26. Stein, ibid., p. 129.
27. Stein, ibid., p. 129.
28. Stein, ibid., p. 130. The phrase 'a rose is a rose is a rose' originally appeared in Stein's 'Sacred Emily' (1913: 1922), and is attributed in *The Autobiography* to Stein's 'note-paper'.
29. Stein, *The Autobiography*, p. 130.
30. Stein, ibid., p. 127.
31. Stein, ibid., p. 129. Van Vechten offers a more detailed description of the audience's reaction: see 'Igor Strawinsky', p. 109.
32. Stein, *The Autobiography*, p. 129.
33. Stein, ibid., p. 129.
34. Stein, ibid., p. 128.
35. Stein, ibid., p. 128.

36. Stein, ibid., p. 128.
37. Stein, ibid., p. 129.
38. Stein, ibid., p. 224.
39. Freeman, 'Introduction: Queer Temporalities', p. 159.
40. See Schuster, 'The making of "Tender Buttons"', for a detailed history of the publication of *Tender Buttons*.
41. Cox, *Cubism*, p. 145. On the differences between 'analytic' (1908–12) and 'synthetic' cubism (1912–14), see pp. 145–6. I use words such as 'approximates' to describe the relationship between Stein's writings and cubist painting: structuralist and poststructuralist scholarship on Stein's texts and cubist paintings has used linguistic analysis to establish that the analogy between cubism in the literary and visual arts is not exact. See note 15 to Chapter 4 for a detailed discussion of debates about the limitations of this analogy.
42. Stein, 'One', p. 274. A reproduction of Oppenheim's teacup is available at http://www.moma.org/collection/works/80997 (last accessed 19 September 2017).
43. Walker, *The Making of a Modernist*, pp. 127–8. Walker points out differences between the 'obstinate concreteness' of Oppenheim's and other modernists' 'physical objects' and the more malleable aspects of Stein's *Tender Buttons*.
44. Sedgwick, *Touching Feeling*, p. 8.
45. Sedgwick, ibid., p. 9.
46. Stein, 'One', p. 274.
47. Stein, ibid., p. 274.
48. Stein, ibid., p. 274.
49. Stein, ibid., p. 274.
50. Stein, ibid., p. 274.
51. Stein, ibid., p. 274; Stein, *Tender Buttons*, p. 461.
52. Stein, 'One', p. 274.
53. Stein, *Tender Buttons*, p. 461.
54. Stein, 'One', p. 274.
55. Stein, ibid., p. 274.
56. Stein, ibid., p. 274.
57. Stein, ibid., p. 274.
58. Stein, ibid., p. 274.
59. Stein, ibid., p. 274.
60. Stein, ibid., p. 275.
61. Stein, ibid., p. 275.
62. Stein, ibid., p. 275.
63. Stein, ibid., p. 274.
64. Stein, ibid., p. 275.
65. Stein, ibid., p. 275.

66. Cox, *Cubism*, pp. 372–7.
67. Stein, 'One', pp. 274–5.
68. Dydo, *A Stein Reader*, p. 273.
69. Dydo, ibid., p. 451.
70. Dydo, ibid., p. 451.
71. Dydo, ibid., p. 451; Dydo, *Gertrude Stein*, p. 30; Voris, *The Composition of Sense*, p. 146.
72. Stein, 'Van', pp. 462–3.
73. Stein, ibid., p. 463.
74. Stein, ibid., p. 463.
75. Glavey, *The Wallflower Avant-Garde*, p. 23.
76. Stein, 'As A Wife Has A Cow', p. 456.
77. Stein, 'Van', p. 463; Sedgwick, *Touching Feeling*, p. 8.
78. Stein, ibid., p. 463.
79. Dydo, *Gertrude Stein*, p. 28.
80. *The Letters of Gertrude Stein and Carl Van Vechten*, ibid.
81. Freeman, *Time Binds*, p. xxii.
82. Stein, 'An Unpublished Portrait of Van Vechten', pp. 864–6.
83. Freeman, *Time Binds*, pp. xi–xv.
84. Stein, 'An Unpublished Portrait of Van Vechten', pp. 864–6.
85. Stein, ibid., pp. 864–6.
86. Dydo, *Gertrude Stein*, p. 75; Dydo, *A Stein Reader*, pp. 452–3.
87. Stein, 'Van', p. 462, emphasis added.
88. Stein, ibid., p. 462.
89. Stein, ibid., p. 462.
90. Stein, ibid., p. 462.
91. Stein, ibid., p. 462.
92. Edelman, *No Future*, p. 28.
93. Freeman, *Time Binds*, p. 172.
94. Stein, 'Van', p. 463.
95. Stein, ibid., p. 463.
96. Stein, ibid., p. 463.
97. Stein, ibid., p. 463.
98. Stein, ibid., p. 463.
99. Stein, ibid., p. 463.
100. Freeman, *Time Binds*, p. xxii.
101. Stein, 'Van', p. 463.
102. Stein, ibid., p. 463.
103. Stein, ibid., p. 463.
104. Stein, ibid., p. 463.
105. Stein, ibid., p. 463.
106. Stein, ibid., p. 463.
107. Steiner, *Exact Resemblance*, p. 106.

108. Dydo, *Gertrude Stein*, p. 75.
109. *The Letters of Gertrude Stein and Carl Van Vechten.*
110. Stein, 'Van', pp. 462–3.
111. Stein, 'As A Wife Has A Cow A Love Story', pp. 460–2.
112. Dydo, *Gertrude Stein*, p. 75.
113. Sedgwick, *Tendencies*, p. xii.
114. See Chapter 1 of Prosser, *Second Skins*, pp. 21–60, for a critique of the subordination of gender crossings to sexual crossings in Sedgwick's and Butler's inflections of queer theory. Since the publication of *Second Skins*, work in transgender studies has done much to expose and correct this tendency.
115. Stryker, Currah and Moore, 'Introduction', p. 11.
116. Stryker, Currah and Moore, ibid., p. 12.
117. Stein, 'Van', p. 463.
118. See Dydo, *A Stein Reader*, p. 453, who notes that this paragraph concerns Van Vechten's request for the manuscript of Stein's *The Making of Americans*. She sent only three volumes and left him waiting for the rest.
119. Stein, 'Van', p. 463.
120. Stein, ibid., p. 463.
121. Stein, ibid., p. 463. For more details about Van Vechten's and Stein's correspondence about arranging a publisher for *The Making of Americans*, see *The Letters of Gertrude Stein and Carl Van Vechten*, pp. 66–95; the 16 April 1923 letter from Van Vechten to Stein concerns the wait for Knopf's evaluation, which never came. See Gallup, 'The Making of *The Making of Americans*', pp. 173–214, for a detailed account of Stein's efforts to place *The Making of Americans*. It was first published in installments in *The Transatlantic* and subsequently in book form under Robert McAlmon's Contact Editions imprint.
122. Stein, 'Van', p. 463; *The Letters of Gertrude Stein and Carl Van Vechten*, pp. 66–7.
123. Stein, ibid., p. 463.
124. Stein, ibid., p. 463.
125. Stein, ibid., p. 463.
126. Stein, ibid., p. 463.
127. Stein, ibid., p. 463.
128. Stein, ibid., p. 463.
129. Dydo, *Gertrude Stein*, p. 75.
130. Stein, 'Gertrude Stein: A Radio Interview', p. 97. Also available as an audio file at https://media.sas.upenn.edu/pennsound/authors/Stein/Stein-Gertrude_Interview_1934.mp3 (last accessed 19 September 2017). At http://writing.upenn.edu/pennsound/x/Stein.html (last accessed 19 September 2017), Dydo notes that this conversation likely took place at the Algonquin Hotel in November 1934.

131. Dydo, *A Stein Reader*, p. 453.
132. Stein, 'Gertrude Stein: A Radio Interview', pp. 88–9.
133. Glavey, *The Wallflower Avant-Garde*, p. 39.
134. Stein, 'Portraits and Repetition', p. 197.
135. Stein, ibid., pp. 197–8.
136. Stein, 'Gertrude Stein: A Radio Interview', p. 97; Stein, 'As A Wife Has A Cow', p. 462.
137. Glavey, *The Wallflower Avant-Garde*, p. 38.
138. Available at https://media.sas.upenn.edu/pennsound/authors/Stein/Stein-Gertrude_Interview_1934.mp3 (last accessed 19 September 2017; transcription mine). A similar claim may be found in Stein, 'Gertrude Stein: A Radio Interview', p. 97.
139. Stein, 'Gertrude Stein: A Radio Interview', p. 89.
140. Stein, 'Van', p. 463.
141. See Lacan, *The Four Fundamental Concepts*, and Rose, *Sexuality*, as well as Chapter 1.
142. Stein, 'Gertrude Stein: A Radio Interview', p. 97.
143. Silverman, *Threshold*, p. 221, p. 179.
144. Corn and Latimer, *Seeing Gertrude Stein*, pp. 58–9.
145. Corn and Latimer, ibid., p. 54.
146. Corn and Latimer, ibid., p. 54.
147. Corn and Latimer, ibid., p. 54.
148. Corn and Latimer, ibid., pp. 53–4.
149. Corn and Latimer, ibid., p. 54.
150. Stringer, *Not Even Past*, p. 118.
151. Stringer, ibid., p. 118.
152. These photographs suggest a contrast in personalities that was not borne out in real life. Although Stein withdrew into her atelier nightly to write, she was also known as a gregarious interlocutor with wide networks of acquaintance.
153. Stein, *The Autobiography*, p. 15; this passage also recounts Stein's and Picasso's fondness for 'por[ing] over' her collection of 'photographs of the civil war'. See Souhami, *Gertrude and Alice*, p. 229 for Beaton's reference to Stein as 'the General'.
154. See Zox-Weaver, *Women Modernists and Fascism*, for an extended discussion of Stein's and Fäy's fascination with 'great men' and an analysis of its implications for fascism.
155. Zox-Weaver, ibid., p. 77.
156. Corn and Latimer, *Seeing Gertrude Stein*, p. 54.
157. Fäy quoted in Will, *Unlikely Collaboration*, p. 76.
158. Zox-Weaver, *Women Modernists and Fascism*, p. 67; Stein, *Everybody's Autobiography*, p. 137.
159. Stein, *The Autobiography*, p. 15.

160. Stein, ibid., p. 129.
161. Stein, ibid., p. 15.
162. See Van Pymbroeck, 'Triangular Politics', for a discussion of some of the friendships Stein sustained from across the political spectrum. The consequences of her openness to different political viewpoints – and her experimental writings' resistance to simplistic political reductions – have fuelled twenty years of scholarly debate: see note 83 to the Introduction.
163. Corn and Latimer, *Seeing Gertrude Stein*, p. 51.
164. Zox-Weaver, *Women Modernists and Fascism*, p. 79.
165. Corn and Latimer, *Seeing Gertrude Stein*, p. 233; White, *The Tastemaker*, p. 275.
166. Corn and Latimer, ibid., p. 233.
167. Puar, *Terrorist Assemblages*.
168. Puar, ibid., p. xxiv.
169. The differences between the contemporary War on Terror that Puar addresses in *Terrorist Assemblages* and the early twentieth-century rise of European fascism are too significant to address here. I am using Puar's concept of 'homonationalism' in its broadest sense and identifying a variation on it in which Stein and Van Vechten participated in the 1930s.
170. Corn and Latimer, *Seeing Gertrude Stein*, p. 215.
171. Corn and Latimer, ibid., p. 215.
172. Corn and Latimer, ibid., p. 233; note this placement of Van Vechten's photograph.
173. For more information about Stein's and Toklas's involvements with American soldiers during World War I, see Souhami, *Gertrude and Alice*, pp. 125–41.
174. Souhami, ibid., pp. 221–39.
175. White, *The Tastemaker*, pp. 286–7.
176. Wagner-Martin, *'Favored Strangers'*, p. 206.
177. Agee, 'Stein's Way', p. 57.
178. See Van Pymbroeck, 'Triangular Politics', pp. 96–8; Whittier-Ferguson, 'The Liberation'; and Whittier-Ferguson, 'Stein in Time', for arguments that suggest that Stein's writing and thinking ranged beyond the limits of narrowly defined political ideologies or nationalist rationales for war.
179. Silverman, *Threshold*, p. 223.
180. Corn and Latimer, *Seeing Gertrude Stein*, pp. 139–51.
181. 'Woojums' originated as a 'term of endearment' Van Vechten used with his inner circle (*The Letters of Gertrude Stein and Carl Van Vechten*, p. 255n2). The word first appears in his correspondence with Stein in a letter dated 26 April 1932; in the course of her lecture tour, it 'came to be used almost exclusively among Stein, Van Vechten, and Toklas'. On the few occasions that Van Vechten's second wife, Fania Marinoff, was

named as a member of the 'Woojums' family, she went by either 'the Empress' or 'Madame Woojums'. See also Wagner-Martin, *'Favored Strangers'*, p. 210, and White, *The Tastemaker*, p. 273.

182. Burns, 'Introduction', *The Letters of Gertrude Stein and Carl Van Vechten*, p. 3; Wagner-Martin, *'Favored Strangers'*, p. 210.
183. See Stein, *Baby Precious Always Shines*, and also the Stein/Toklas 'Papers' and 'Collection' housed in Yale University's Beinecke Library.
184. Burns, 'Introduction', *The Letters of Gertrude Stein and Carl Van Vechten*, p. 3.
185. Silverman, *Threshold*, p. 223.
186. Silverman, ibid., p. 223.
187. My use of the phrase 'other scenes' invokes de Lauretis's 'Queer Texts, Bad Habits' as well as my 'The Unpredictable Future'.
188. Sedgwick, *Between Men*, p. 1.
189. See Schwarz, *Reconfiguring Modernism*, pp. 58–60 for further analysis.
190. Dodge quoted in Corn and Latimer, *Seeing Gertrude Stein*, p. 149.
191. On Van Vechten's creation of this photograph, see Corn and Latimer, ibid., p. 149.
192. Corn and Latimer, ibid., p. 149.
193. Corn and Latimer, ibid., p. 149.
194. For analysis of Van Vechten's role in Stein's rise to celebrity in the 1930s, see Leick, *Gertrude Stein and the Making of an American Celebrity*; Curnutt, 'Inside and Outside'; and Weinberg, '"Boy Crazy"'. Van Vechten's photographs of African American modernists are also important images of modernist icons. They are beyond the scope of this chapter but are discussed at length in Smalls, *The Homoerotic Photography of Carl Van Vechten*; Stringer, *Not Even Past*; and Thaggart, *Images of Black Modernism*. See Rudolph P. Byrd (ed.), *Generations in Black and White*, for a sampling.
195. Silverman, *Threshold*, p. 223.
196. Silverman, ibid., p. 223.
197. For extended analysis of Van Vechten's participation in the construction of modernism's archives, see MacLeod, 'The "Librarian's Dream-Prince"'. See Stringer, *Not Even Past*, and Thaggart, *Images of Black Modernism*, for insightful discussions of those practices' implications for his portraits of African Americans.
198. See especially Smalls, *The Homoerotic Photography of Carl Van Vechten*, for analysis of ways Van Vechten's photographs of African Americans queered modernism's gaze.

Coda: Gertrude Stein Icon

By concluding *Gertrude Stein's Transmasculinity* with a chapter that traces Stein's felicitous friendship with Van Vechten, I stress the importance of the man who contributed more to her legacy than most of her other male friends. As her devoted champion and literary executor; as an organiser of her 1934–5 lecture tour of the United States; as the editor and author of the introduction to the *Selected Writings of Gertrude Stein*: Van Vechten's loving gaze upon Stein mobilised masculine homosocial desires that crystallised her status as a celebrity he considered equal to 'a moving picture star in Hollywood'.[1] If, in the last thirty years, Stein has emerged as a queer and modernist icon, her elevated status owes as much to 'Papa Woojums'' energetic publicity as to Stein's own decision to donate her materials to the Beinecke Library and Picasso's *Portrait of Gertrude Stein* to the Metropolitan Museum of Modern Art.

Although Van Vechten played a key role in establishing Stein's iconicity, their friendship was not without its problems. While their bond demonstrated her transmasculinity's capacity to queer sexuality and gendered embodiment, they nonetheless shared a fetishistic fascination with African American cultures that played out in both of their work. Moreover, despite the ways their ties destabilised concepts of nation, Stein and Van Vechten held patriotic attitudes toward the United States and American soldiers that beg for analysis as forms of 'homonationalism'.[2] Much remains to be said about the role these ideologies played in their masculine homosocial ties and the 'Woojums' family that facilitated them.

Stein's masculine homosocial bond with gay male Vichy collaborator Fäy was even more problematic than her ties to Van Vechten. Although Fäy's efforts on Stein's behalf were less visible to the public eye than Van Vechten's, the former was also an important agent in her rise to fame: he used 'behind-the-scenes brokerage' with his American colleagues to help arrange for her lecture tour, for example.[3] Stein's friendship with Fäy reveals that her transmasculinity was sometimes a conduit for outright reactionary politics. Will observes that a 'subtle, fluid, and complex' eroticism subtended Stein's friendship with Fäy, even though it was 'largely unconscious'; she offered him the example of a 'wholesome, desexualized' queerness that countered the stigmatising association between homosexuality and decadence promoted by the far right politicians he supported.[4] They also both held that France should return to its royalist past after what they believed to be its failed attempt at democratic governance.[5] These signs of Stein's conservatism hint at the problems that would emerge as her friendship with Fäy deepened and Europe headed towards World War II.

The two friends shared an admiration of Maréchal Pétain, who had beaten back the Germans in the Battle of Verdun and 'embodied resiliency and courage, honor and sobriety' – all masculine virtues – to those who believed that under his leadership, the Vichy regime would restore everyday tranquility to France.[6] Five years before Stein would translate Pétain's speeches into English while hiding in the Bugey under Fäy's protection, she would write in *Everybody's Autobiography* (1936: 1937) that when she and Toklas were sent corn by their friend Kiddie (W. G. Rogers), an American veteran of World War I, she responded to his admonishment not to 'give it to any fascists' with the question 'but why not if the fascists like it, and we liked the fascists', followed by the request to 'please send us unpolitical corn'.[7] This statement reveals Stein's alarming lack of concern about the dangers fascism presented to herself, Toklas and many others. It also represents a rejection of their American friend's antifascist masculinity that corresponds to her strengthened ties with Fäy.

Moreover, *Everybody's Autobiography* reveals that in the 1930s and 1940s, Stein did not oppose fascism specifically but patriarchal leadership styles generally. At one point, she bemoans the rise of authoritarianism on the world stage. She writes that:

> There is too much fathering going on just now and there is no doubt about it fathers are depressing. Everybody nowadays is a father, there is father Mussolini and father Hitler and father Roosevelt and father Stalin and father Lewis and father Blum and father Franco is just

> commencing now and there are ever so many more ready to be one. Fathers are depressing . . . The periods of the world's history that have always been most dismal ones are the ones where fathers were looming and filling up everything.[8]

This passage suggests a broad disidentification with authoritarian masculinity that is independent of ideology. In addition to fascist leaders Mussolini, Hitler and Franco, Stein's critique of 'fathering' extends to communist dictator Stalin and liberal democrat Roosevelt. As Will notes, Stein disapproved of Roosevelt because she believed that his New Deal programmes – which sought to mitigate the Great Depression by creating government jobs and strengthening the social safety net – were 'profligate and paternalistic', much like the policies of 'his French counterpart Léon Blum'.[9] *Everybody's Autobiography* articulates a politically conservative feminism that opposes paternalism but leaves gender's implication in other social justice issues unaddressed.

These limitations of Stein's feminism and the fact that two of her most enduring homosocial ties were with Van Vechten and Fäy recall Halberstam's observation that queers' politics can be 'contradictory and complicit' in ways we should acknowledge rather than minimise.[10] Moreover, Stein's example demonstrates that some modes of failure should not be valorised.[11] Throughout most of this book I have analysed the ways Stein's shifting transmasculinity moved 'horizontally between two established gendered spaces, "man" and "woman"'.[12] However, much more remains to be said about its troubling implication in what Stryker, Currah and Moore call transsubjectivity's 'vertical axis': how her transmasculinity became a 'resource for sovereign power' for both the United States and Vichy France before, during and after World War II.[13] Stein's desire for masculine homosocial bonding was a conduit for her and Van Vechten's nationalism and racial stereotyping, as well as for her and Fäy's support of the Vichy government. These vectors of her masculinity deserve more study.

Everybody's Autobiography stands as an example not only of the dangers of Stein's attraction to reactionary men such as Fäy but also of the pitfalls Halberstam identifies in queers' investments in normative narratives of productivity and success. As the 'Publisher's Note' to the 1993 Exact Change edition indicates, the book is 'a meditation on failure; almost a manifesto of failure' written in the wake of the 'writer's block' and period of professional 'doubt' following the success of *The Autobiography* and Stein's celebrity tour of the United States.[14] *Everybody's Autobiography*, itself a commercial 'failure', interrogates 'identity, success and failure' by reflecting on the way Stein's experience of having finally achieved long-sought public recognition shifted her view of herself – and therefore her subjectivity – in profoundly disorienting ways.[15] These themes also animate her genre-bending 'Identity A Poem' (1935: 1940) and lecture entitled 'What Are Masterpieces and Why Are There So Few of Them' (1936: 1940).[16]

Everybody's Autobiography echoes those texts' cadences on a larger scale, demonstrating that identity's inherent instability was compounded by the culture of celebrity through which Stein positioned *The Autobiography* and her lecture tour. Although recent scholarship rightfully emphasises Stein's active participation in the construction of her own iconicity, *Everybody's Autobiography* reveals her doubts about its consequences. The text not only points to the impossibility of the identity claims made by traditional autobiography but also bemoans the influence of the book industry's 'publicity' apparatus.[17] Stein claims that 'novels now cannot be written' because:

> In the old days when they wrote novels they made up the personality of the things that were the people as if they were a dream. But now well now how can you dream about a personality when it is always being created for you by a publicity, how can you believe what you make up when publicity makes them up to be so much realer than you can dream. And so autobiography is written which is in a way a way to say that publicity is right, they are as the public sees them.[18]

This passage indicates that part of Stein's difficulty with the 1930s literary world lies in the distortive effect its gaze has on fiction: the modern novelist must create characters that fit the advertising apparatus's representations rather than those that emerge from the imagination 'as if they were a dream'. This language intimates that one source of the sense of 'double time' by which Stein found herself torn in the 1930s was the conflict between the industry whose calculations made her an icon and the far more unpredictable psychical mechanisms that motivate creative work.[19] Although *The Autobiography* deliberately toys with the gaze constructed by celebrity culture to enhance Stein's reputation and explain her radically innovative writing to a mass audience, *Everybody's Autobiography* shows that this process's temporal disjointedness eventually undermined her ability to write.

Moreover, *Everybody's Autobiography* suggests that despite her use of Toklas's look to manipulate the gaze through which *The Autobiography* gives their modernist networks to be seen, being in the public eye disturbed Stein. After a series of reflections on names, Stein notes that it 'was upsetting' to see 'an electric sign moving around a building' with her name on it, Van Vechten's gushing description of her as 'a moving picture star' notwithstanding.[20] And upon landing in Los Angeles, she avoids representatives of Warner Brothers because she had been disturbed to see herself on a newsreel filmed in New York. She says that 'when I saw myself almost as large and moving around and talking I did not like it particularly the talking, it gave me a very funny feeling and I did not like that funny feeling'.[21] The gazes constituted by the camera and projector gave Stein to be seen from different vantages than before, prompting vertigo. Much like writing about herself, seeing herself through cinematic representation destabilised her identity and made her unable to write.

Although both *The Autobiography* and *Everybody's Autobiography* concern Stein's celebrity, the latter's open-endedness distinguishes it from the former. Whereas Stein's use of Toklas as narrator of *The Autobiography* manipulates readerly perspective by creating the illusion of clarity, playing with the look and the gaze to destabilise identity as she gives their participation in modernist networks to be seen, *Everybody's Autobiography* explicitly reflects upon the shifts in subjectivity its predecessor registers only implicitly. Stein emphasises that these concerns are bound up in autobiography's impossible demand for self-reflection. She writes that

> identity is funny being yourself is funny as you are never yourself to yourself except as you remember yourself and then of course you do not believe yourself. That is really the trouble with autobiography you do not of course you do not really believe yourself why should you, you know so well so very well that it is not yourself, it could not be yourself because you cannot remember right and if you do remember right it does not sound right and of course it does not sound right because it is not right. You are of course never yourself.[22]

This language anticipates Barthes's insight that 'the *I* that writes the text is never anything but a paper *I*': the subject is split by representation.[23]

Stein's sense that 'You are of course never yourself' in autobiographical narrative was surely heightened as she played with the genre's conventions in *The Autobiography*, which offers multiple versions of the same events through Toklas's rather than her own eyes to subvert the assumptions about the self-identical subject driving traditional autobiography.[24] Unlike *The Autobiography*, whose apparent accessibility can trick unsuspecting readers into believing in the stability of the image of Stein it ultimately undercuts, *Everybody's Autobiography* explicitly engages in metatextual reflections that force her readers, too, to confront the destabilisation of identity and splitting of subjectivity she privately encountered while composing her bestseller.

The impossibility of perfect memory, self-reflection and identity are all at stake in the personal crisis *Everybody's Autobiography* registers. Stein's and Toklas's dogs appear throughout the text as figures for the illusion of imaginary recognition. Basket's look appears early on in the memoir when Stein first explains that she was blocked because 'Nothing inside me needed to be written.'[25] After her sudden inability to write as fluidly as in the past caused her to 'worry about identity', her dog provides an affirming look that enables her temporarily to regain her 'I'.[26] Whereas in the past, she had 'always been I because I had words that had to be written inside me', now she is 'I because my little dog knows me' and has been 'I' all along.[27]

Although this claim serves as a temporary ballast during Stein's initial reflections on her crisis, she quickly abandons this account of the self-identical subject. Echoing Lacan's misgivings about the perils of imaginary (mis)recognition, she writes that '[t]he only thing that makes identity possible is no change but nevertheless there is no identity nobody really thinks they are the same as they remember'.[28] This language calls attention to the gap in the illusion of stable identity created by memory's unreliability, and insists that subjectivity is shifty. By contrast, Stein attributes an unchanging nature to her pets. After reflecting on how '[t]he minute you or anybody else knows what you are you are not it', she claims that '[d]ogs have not changed they have been dogs for a long time'.[29] By repudiating the idea that for humans, unlike dogs, there can be 'no change', Stein invokes transitivity to insist upon the open-ended character of her subjectivity and writing.[30]

Near the end of *Everybody's Autobiography*, when Stein recounts her return from the United States to France, she returns to the figure of the dog, reiterating that 'I am I because my little dog knows me' only to conclude 'that that only proved the dog was he and not that I was I'.[31] At this point, Stein no longer needs her pet's imaginary *méconnaissance* to stabilise her 'I'. And in 'Identity A Poem', a 'short play' with 'puppets' that reiterates lines from *Everybody's Autobiography* and *The Geographical History of America* (1935: 1936), Stein's reflections on her dog take an even more radical form.[32] Declaring that 'Not any dog can say not ever when he is at play. / And so dogs and human nature have no identity', she suggests that animals, too, are split subjects.[33] These and similar 'questions' about spurious 'identity constructions' foreground what Bernstein aptly calls 'identity's puppet show'.[34]

Having rejected the concept of identity earlier in *Everybody's Autobiography* and regained her ability to create, she notes that while writing *The Geographical History of America*:

> I meditated a good deal about how to yourself you were yourself at any moment that you were there to you inside you but that any moment back you could only remember yourself you could not feel yourself and I therefore began to think that insofar as you were yourself to yourself there was no feeling of time inside you you only had the sense of time when you remembered yourself.[35]

Here, Stein returns to the issues of memory and recognition that led to her initial insight that 'there is no identity'.[36] As Voris notes, 'Stein objected to the doubling practices of memory that are reproduced in representation', which requires 'comparison of one person to another or of one person at different times' and 'mixes time senses'.[37] Thus, in *Everybody's Autobiography*, Stein stresses that remembering foregrounds 'the sense of time' that reveals subjective splitting.[38] This also suggests that by contrast, the 'continuous present' evacuates time in ways that trick you into believing that 'to yourself you were yourself at any moment'.[39] Yet as McCallum argues, Stein's 'continuous present' also offers 'a propitious opportunity' to create alternatives to linear time that do not shore up momentary illusions of stable identity but subvert them.[40] *Everybody's Autobiography* suggests that Stein preferred the unruly temporality of the 'continuous present' to the linear understanding of time involved in reflecting on one's past.

Stein explicitly connects subjectivity's 'double time' to masculinity by following her reflections on time with the question, 'what is the use of being a little boy if you are to be a man'.[41] The suggestion that there may be some use in being a 'little boy' but not a 'man' implies a 'refusal of adulthood' that articulates her transmasculinity through a temporal mode Halberstam associates with 'forgetting', 'antidevelopment' and reiteration.[42] Stein explicitly connects both genius and the generative aspects of failure to masculinity, writing that '[m]ost of the great men in America had a long life of early failure and a long life of later failure'.[43] *Everybody's Autobiography* thereby suggests that genius lies in the willingness to fail, and therefore also in what I will call a queer disposition: a healthy degree of scepticism towards normative understandings of adult masculinity and the illusions of subjective stability they support.

Much as *Everybody's Autobiography* undercuts the concept of stable identity and reworks the construct of the masculine genius by reflecting on the effects of the celebrity Stein experienced late in life, so does the early twentieth century invite us to look at her iconic status from multiple vantages and see her transmasculinity as a shifting form of subjectivity. If *The Autobiography* presents Stein as an avant-garde innovator who played an important role in modernism's masculine homosocial networks, *Everybody's Autobiography* stresses that her transmasculinity was shifting, anti-identitarian and subject to 'change'.[44] Although the late twentieth century made Stein available for view in myriad ways – with poststructural, feminist and queer theories reversing earlier dismissals and providing lenses through which to see her as an influential queer participant in the early twentieth-century avant-garde – the early twenty-first century 'screen' still contains a wide variety of 'representational coordinates' that keep numerous looks upon Stein in play and her image constantly in motion.[45]

These vacillations in Stein's image should be read in the context of the shifts in the gaze through which her life and work have been given to be seen over the last hundred years. The 2011 Stein offerings in San Francisco demonstrate that the hegemonic gaze has changed so much since the early twentieth century that powerful champions within the city's literary, musical and art-historical establishments could present the public with an up-to-date scholarly assessment of her life, work and impact. *Seeing Gertrude Stein* and SFMOMA's contingent in the LGBT Pride Parade also deliberately directed the public's look at Stein's queerness, exploring its effect on her writing, art collecting and artistic collaborations as well as on others' representations of her.

These events showed queer scholarship's impact to such a degree that the distinction between 'dominant' and 'subcultural' representation blurs, demonstrating that a counterhegemonic look can indeed act 'in concert with enough other looks' to gain institutional power and 'reterritorialize the screen, bringing new elements into cultural prominence'.[46] One of those 'elements' was Stein's transmasculinity.

Despite the substantial institutional power that enabled the 2011 exhibits to present Stein in a largely flattering light, they were not fully able to shift the gaze through which she was given to be seen. Instead, Cotter and Kosman wielded the considerable institutional power of the *New York Times* and *San Francisco Chronicle* to remobilise early twentieth-century dismissals of her art collecting and writing, respectively. In offering the general public what are now non-dominant perspectives on her work, these two critics' reactionary angles of vision hardly constitute what Silverman calls 'oppositional and subcultural representations', if by that one means challenges to 'normative' and deeply entrenched biases.[47] Instead, these critics perpetuate outdated assumptions about aesthetics that contemporary scholarship has refuted. This shows that the Yerba Buena complex's up-to-date approach to Stein did not entirely erase those 'elements' that 'constitute normative representation' or normative histories of the arts.[48] Even though Cotter and Kosman do not explicitly malign Stein's gender or sexuality, their well-placed reviews negate contemporary scholarship instead of bringing it into the public eye. This suggests that some people may remain remarkably resilient to the effects of representations that shift the dominant look, screen and gaze to foreground Stein's positive contributions.

There is also an element of backlash at work in the popular press's attempts to use scholarship on Stein's Vichy collaboration to push her back into modernism's margins and diminish her contribution, despite the legitimacy of the questions raised about her and Toklas's wartime activities. Although evidence of Stein's 'contradictory and complicit' politics must remain in the frame, available for view, it should not lead to her banishment but to closer analysis. If *Gertrude Stein's Transmasculinity* has enabled Stein's iconic image to be seen from a new angle, one that gives her transmasculinity to be seen by those who might otherwise not be well positioned to see it, I hope that this book will also provide the means for others to continue to write the story of this literary 'character', masculine or otherwise.[49] These studies will surely call attention to the many meanings Stein's polyvocal texts can take on in contexts other than those I have surveyed here. I hope, however, that future work does not obscure those aspects of Stein's life that leave us 'unsettled', but rather engage in the kinds of thinking Halberstam finds at work in Heather Love's notion of 'feeling backward': those that engage the 'darker' elements 'of queer life without needing to redeem them'.[50] Such narratives need not choose simplistically between 'good' and 'bad' Steins, rendering her a stock hero or villain. Instead, my hope is that what John Keats calls the 'negative capability' – the capacity for 'being in uncertainties', sensitive to their complexities – will inform future studies of Stein.[51]

Notes

1. Van Vechten, 'Gertrude Stein', p. 63.
2. Puar, *Terrorist Assemblages*.
3. Will, *Unlikely Collaborations*, p. 98.
4. Will, ibid., p. 30. Will discusses Fäy's support of the right-wing l'Action Française and its 'spiritual leader', Charles Maurras, at length (p. 9), as well as Fäy's involvement with even more reactionary outfits (p. 26).
5. Will, *Unlikely Collaborations*, p. 26, p. 44, p. 66.
6. Will, ibid., p. 3, p. 6.
7. Stein, *Everybody's Autobiography*, pp. 318–19.
8. Stein, ibid., p. 137.
9. Will, *Unlikely Collaborations*, p. 9, p. 95.
10. Halberstam, *Queer Art*, p. 148.
11. Halberstam, ibid., p. 148.
12. Stryker, Currah and Moore, 'Introduction', p. 13.
13. Stryker, Currah and Moore, ibid., p. 14.
14. 'Publisher's Note', in Gertrude Stein, *Everybody's Autobiography*, p. viii.
15. 'Publisher's Note', ibid., p. viii.
16. Stein, 'Identity A Poem'; 'What Are Masterpieces'. These texts reiterate phrases from *Everybody's Autobiography* that I discuss in this Coda.
17. Stein, *Everybody's Autobiography*, p. 71.
18. Stein, ibid., p. 71.
19. Stein, 'How Writing Is Written', p. 490. Stein's language echoes Freud's 'Creative Writers and Day-Dreaming', which builds upon his account of the dreamwork in his 1899 *The Interpretation of Dreams*.
20. Stein, *Everybody's Autobiography*, p. 180; Van Vechten, 'Gertrude Stein', p. 63.

21. Stein, ibid., p. 288.
22. Stein, ibid., p. 70.
23. Barthes, 'From Work to Text', p. 62.
24. Stein, *Everybody's Autobiography*, p. 70.
25. Stein, ibid., p. 66.
26. Stein, ibid., p. 66.
27. Stein, ibid., p. 66.
28. Stein, ibid., p. 72.
29. Stein, ibid., p. 94.
30. Stein, ibid., p. 72.
31. Stein, ibid., p. 306.
32. Dydo, *A Stein Reader*, p. 588.
33. Stein, 'Identity A Poem', p. 590; Bernstein, 'Stein's Identity', p. 485.
34. Bernstein, ibid., p. 485.
35. Stein, *Everybody's Autobiography*, p. 307.
36. Stein, ibid., p. 72.
37. Voris, *The Composition of Sense*, p. xxxi.
38. Stein, *Everybody's Autobiography*, p. 307.
39. Stein, 'Composition as Explanation', pp. 517–18; Stein, *Everybody's Autobiography*, p. 307.
40. McCallum, 'Stein *und Zeit*', p. 240.
41. Stein, 'How Writing Is Written', p. 490; Stein, *Everybody's Autobiography*, p. 307.
42. Stein, *Everybody's Autobiography*, p. 307; Halberstam, *Queer Art*, p. 73.
43. Stein, *Everybody's Autobiography*, p. 88.
44. Stein, ibid., p. 72.
45. Silverman, *Threshold*, p. 221.
46. Silverman, ibid., p. 223.
47. Silverman, ibid., p. 179.
48. Silverman, ibid., p. 223.
49. Barthes, 'From Work to Text', p. 61.
50. Halberstam, *Queer Art*, p. 171, p. 99; Love, *Feeling Backward*.
51. In his back cover blurb, D. A. Miller praises the Keatsian 'negative capability' at work in Love's *Feeling Backward*; John Keats to George and Tom Keats, 21, 27 (?) December 1817, *Selected Letters of John Keats*, p. 59.

Bibliography

Abravanel, Genevieve, 'Anglophones in Paris', in Jean-Michel Rabaté (ed.), *1922: Literature, Culture, Politics* (Cambridge: Cambridge University Press, 2015), pp. 91–103.

Agee, James, 'Stein's Way', *Time* (11 September 1933), pp. 57–60.

Ahmed, Sara, *Queer Phenomenology* (Durham, NC: Duke University Press, 2006).

Andersen, Corinne, 'I Am Not Who "I" Pretend to Be: *The Autobiography of Alice B. Toklas* and its Photographic Frontispiece', *The Comparatist* 29 (2005), pp. 26–37.

Anderson, Sherwood, *Dark Laughter* [1925] (New York: Liveright, 1953).

—, 'Gertrude Stein', *The American Spectator* 2 (April 1934), n.p.

—, 'The Work of Gertrude Stein', in Stein, *Geography and Plays* [1922] (Madison: University of Wisconsin Press, 1993), pp. 5–8.

Anderson, Sherwood and Gertrude Stein, *Sherwood Anderson / Gertrude Stein: Correspondence and Personal Essays*, ed. Ray Elliott White (Chapel Hill: University of North Carolina Press, 1972).

Ashton, Jennifer, 'Our Bodies, Our Poems', *Modern Philology* 105:1 (August 2007), pp. 160–77.

Barnhart, Bruce, *Jazz in the Time of the Novel: The Temporal Politics of American Race and Culture* (Tuscaloosa: University of Alabama Press, 2013).

Barthes, Roland, 'The Death of the Author', in *The Rustle of Language*, trans. Richard Howard (Berkeley: University of California Press, 1989), pp. 49–55.

—, 'From Work to Text', in *The Rustle of Language*, trans. Richard Howard (Berkeley: University of California Press, 1989), pp. 56–64.

Battersby, Christine, *Gender and Genius: Towards a Feminist Aesthetic* (Bloomington: Indiana University Press, 1989).

Benjamin, Walter, 'Small History of Photography' [1931], in Esther Leslie (ed. and trans.), *On Photography* (London: Reaktion Books, 2015), pp. 53-105.

—, 'Theses on the Philosophy of History' [1950], in Hannah Arendt (ed.), *Illuminations* (New York: Harcourt Brace Jovanovich, 1968), pp. 253–64.

—, 'The Work of Art in the Age of Mechanical Reproduction' [1936], in Hannah Arendt (ed.), *Illuminations* (New York: Harcourt Brace Jovanovich, 1968), pp. 217–51.

Benstock, Shari, 'Paris Lesbianism and the Politics of Reaction', in Martin Duberman, Martha Vicinus and George Chauncey (eds), *Hidden from History: Reclaiming the Gay and Lesbian Past* (New York: NAL Books, 1989), pp. 332–46.

—, *Women of the Left Bank: Paris, 1900–1940* (Austin: University of Texas Press, 1986).

Bernstein, Charles, *Gertrude Stein's war years: Setting the record straight*, in *Jacket 2,* available at https://jacket2.org/feature/gertrude-steins-war-years-setting-record-straight (last accessed 19 September 2017).

—, 'Stein's Identity', *Modern Fiction Studies* 42:3 (1996), pp. 485–8.

Bersani, Leo, 'Is the Rectum a Grave?', *October* 43 (1987), pp. 197–222.

Blackmer, Corinne, 'African Masks and the Arts of Passing in Gertrude Stein's "Melanctha" and Nella Larsen's *Passing*', *Journal of the History of Sexuality* 4:2 (1993), pp. 230–63.

—, 'Lesbian Modernism in the Shorter Fiction of Virginia Woolf and Gertrude Stein', in Eileen Barrett (ed.), *Virginia Woolf: Lesbian Readings* (New York: New York University Press, 1997), pp. 78–94.

—, 'Selling Taboo Subjects: The Literary Commerce of Gertrude Stein and Carl Van Vechten', in Kevin J. H. Dettmar and Stephen Watt (eds), *Marketing Modernisms: Self-Promotion, Canonization, Rereading* (Ann Arbor: University of Michigan Press, 1996), pp. 221–52.

Blankley, Elyse, 'Beyond the "Talent of Knowing": Gertrude Stein and the New Woman', in Michael J. Hoffman (ed.), *Critical Essays on Gertrude Stein* (Boston: G. K. Hall, 1986), pp. 196–209.

Blau, Amy, 'The Artist in Word and Image in Gertrude Stein's *Dix Portraits*', *Mosaic: A Journal for the Interdisciplinary Study of Literature* 36:2 (2003), pp. 129–44.

Bloom, Harold, *The Anxiety of Influence: A Theory of Poetry* (New York: Oxford University Press, 1997).

Brenner, Gerry, *A Comprehensive Companion to Hemingway's 'A Moveable Feast'*, Book 1, (Lewiston: Edwin Mellen Press, 2000).

—, *A Comprehensive Companion to Hemingway's 'A Moveable Feast'*, Book 2 (Lewiston, NY: Edwin Mellen Press, 2000).

—, *Concealments in Hemingway's Works* (Columbus: Ohio State University Press, 1983).

Bridgman, Richard, *The Colloquial Style in America* (New York: Oxford University Press, 1966).

—, *Gertrude Stein in Pieces* (New York: Oxford University Press, 1970).

Brinnin, John Malcolm, *The Third Rose: Gertrude Stein and Her World* (New York: Addison-Wesley, 1987).

Brogan, Jacqueline Vaught, 'The "Founding Mother": Gertrude Stein and the Cubist Phenomenon', in Joyce W. Warren and Margaret Dickie (eds), *Challenging Boundaries: Gender and Periodization* (Athens: University of Georgia Press, 2000), pp. 248–66.

Brooke-Rose, Christine, 'Illiterations', in Ellen G. Friedman and Miriam Fuchs (eds), *Breaking the Sequence: Women's Experimental Fiction* (Princeton: Princeton University Press, 1989), pp. 55–71.

Brown, Elspeth H., 'Queering Glamour in Interwar Fashion Photography: The "Amorous Regard" of George Platt Lynes', *GLQ: A Journal of Lesbian and Gay Studies* 23:3 (2017), pp. 289–326.

Bruccoli, Matthew J. (ed.), *The Only Thing That Counts: The Ernest Hemingway / Maxwell Perkins Correspondence*, 1925–1947 (New York: Scribner, 1966).

Burns, Edward. 'Introduction', in *The Letters of Gertrude Stein and Carl Van Vechten* (New York: Columbia University Press, 2013), pp. 1–12.

Burns, Edward, and Ulla E. Dydo, 'Introduction', in *The Letters of Gertrude Stein and Thornton Wilder* (New Haven: Yale University Press, 1996), pp. xv–xxvi.

— (eds), *The Letters of Gertrude Stein and Thornton Wilder* (New Haven: Yale University Press, 1996).

Butler, Judith, *Bodies That Matter: On the Discursive Limits of 'Sex'* (New York: Routledge, 1993).

—, *Gender Trouble: Feminism and the Subversion of Identity* (New York: Routledge, 1990).

—, 'Imitation and Gender Insubordination', in Diana Fuss (ed.), *Inside/Out: Lesbian Theories, Gay Theories* (New York: Routledge, 1991), pp. 13–31.

Butler, Judith, and Athena Athanasiou, *Dispossession: The Performative in the Political* (Malden, MA: Polity Press, 2013).

Byrd, Rudolph P. (ed.), *Generations in Black and White: Photographs by Carl Van Vechten* (Athens: University of Georgia Press, 1993).

Caramello, Charles, *Henry James, Gertrude Stein, and the Biographical Act* (Chapel Hill: University of North Carolina Press, 1996).

Carlson, Shanna, 'Transgender Subjectivity and the Logic of Sexual Difference', *differences* 21:2 (2010), pp. 46–72.

Case, Sue-Ellen, 'Toward a Butch-Femme Aesthetic' in Henry Abelove, Michèle Aina Barale and David M. Halperin (eds), *The Lesbian and Gay Studies Reader* (New York: Routledge, 1993), pp. 294–306.

Caughie, Pamela, 'The Temporality of Modernist Life Writing in the Era of Transsexualism: Virginia Woolf's *Orlando* and Einar Wegener's *Man Into Woman*', *Modern Fiction Studies* 59:3 (2013), pp. 501–25.

Cheng, Anne, *Second Skin: Josephine Baker and the Modern Surface* (New York: Oxford University Press, 2011).

Chessman, Harriet Scott, *The Public is Invited to Dance: Representation, the Body, and Dialogue in Gertrude Stein* (Stanford: Stanford University Press, 1989).

Cixous, Hélène, *The Exile of James Joyce*, trans. Sally A. J. Purcell (New York: David Lewis, 1972).

—, 'The Laugh of the Medusa', in Robyn R. Warhol and Diane Price Herndl (eds), *Feminisms: An Anthology of Literary Theory and Criticism* (New Brunswick, NJ: Rutgers University Press, 1991), pp. 334–49.

Clark, T. J., *Picasso and Truth* (Princeton: Princeton University Press, 2013).

Cody, Morrill, *The Women of Montparnasse* (New York: Cornwall Books, 1984).

Coffman, Chris, *Insane Passions: Lesbianism and Psychosis in Literature and Film* (Middletown, CT: Wesleyan University Press, 2006).

—, 'Queering Žižek', *Postmodern Culture* 23:1 (2012).

—, 'The Unpredictable Future of Fantasy's Traversal', *Angelaki* 18:4 (2013), pp. 43–60.

—, 'Žižek's Antagonism and the Futures of Trans-Affirmative Lacanian Psychoanalysis', *TSQ: Transgender Studies Quarterly* 4:4 (2017), pp. 472–96.

Cohassey, John, *Hemingway and Pound: A Most Unlikely Friendship* (Jefferson, NC: McFarland, 2014).

Cole, Merrill, 'Remaking Sense: Gertrude Stein and the Names of the Father', *Women's Studies* 38:1 (2009), pp. 84–99.

Comley, Nancy R., and Robert Scholes, *Hemingway's Genders: Rereading the Hemingway Text* (New Haven: Yale University Press, 1994).

Cope, Karin, *Passionate Collaborations: Learning to Live with Gertrude Stein* (Victoria, BC: ELS Editions, 2005).

Corn, Wanda, and Tirza True Latimer, *Seeing Gertrude Stein: Five Stories* (Berkeley and London: University of California Press, 2011).

Cotter, Holland, 'Modern Is Modern Is . . .', *New York Times*, 2 June 2011, http://www.nytimes.com/2011/06/05/arts/design/gertrude-stein-in-two-san-francisco-exhibitions.html (last accessed 19 September 2017).

Cox, Neil, *Cubism* (London: Phaidon, 2000).

Cromwell, Jason, *Transmen & FTMs: Identities, Bodies, Genders & Sexualities* (Urbana and Chicago: University of Illinois Press, 1999).

Curnutt, Kirk, 'Inside and Outside: Gertrude Stein on Identity, Celebrity, and Authenticity', *Journal of Modern Literature* 23:2 (1999–2000), pp. 291–308.

—, '"In the Temps de Gertrude": Hemingway, Stein, and the Scene of Instruction at 27, rue de Fleurus', in J. Gerald Kennedy and Jackson R. Bryer (eds), *French Connections: Hemingway and Fitzgerald Abroad* (New York: St. Martin's Press, 1998), pp. 121–39.

Cvetkovich, Ann, *An Archive of Feelings: Trauma, Sexuality, and Lesbian Public Cultures* (Durham, NC and London: Duke University Press, 2003).

Daix, Pierre, *Picasso: Life and Art* (New York: HarperCollins, 1993).

Damon, Maria, 'Gertrude Stein's Jewishness, Jewish Social Scientists, and the "Jewish Question"', *Modern Fiction Studies* 42:3 (1996), pp. 489–506.

Daniel, Lucy, *Gertrude Stein* (London: Reaktion Books, 2009).

Davis, Phoebe Stein, '"Even Cake Gets to Have Another Meaning": History, Narrative, and "Daily Living" in Gertrude Stein's World War II Writings', *Modern Fiction Studies* 44:3 (1998), pp. 568–607.

—, 'Subjectivity and the Aesthetics of National Identity in Gertrude Stein's *The Autobiography of Alice B. Toklas*', *Twentieth-Century Literature* 45:1 (1999), pp. 18–45.

Dean, Tim, *Beyond Sexuality* (Chicago: University of Chicago Press, 2000).

DeKoven, Marianne, *A Different Language: Gertrude Stein's Experimental Writing* (Madison: University of Wisconsin Press, 1983).

—, 'Gertrude Stein and Modern Painting: Beyond Literary Cubism', *Contemporary Literature* 22:1 (1981), pp. 81–95.

—, *Rich and Strange: Gender, History, Modernism* (Princeton: Princeton University Press, 1991).

de Lauretis, Teresa, 'Queer Texts, Bad Habits, and the Issue of a Future', *GLQ: A Journal of Lesbian and Gay Studies* 17:2–3 (2011), pp. 243–63.

Derrida, Jacques, *Archive Fever: A Freudian Impression* (Chicago: University of Chicago Press, 1995).

—, *Dissemination* (Chicago: University of Chicago Press, 1981).

Detloff, Madelyn, *The Persistence of Modernism: Loss and Mourning in the Twentieth Century* (Cambridge: Cambridge University Press, 2009).

Dickie, Margaret, 'Recovering the Repression in Stein's Erotic Poetry', in Margaret Dickie and Thomas Travisano (eds), *Gendered Modernisms: American Poets and Their Readers* (Philadelphia: University of Pennsylvania Press, 1996), pp. 3–25.

Doan, Laura, *Fashioning Sapphism: The Origins of a Modern English Lesbian Culture* (New York: Columbia University Press, 2001).

Doan, Laura, and Jay Prosser (eds), *Palatable Poison: Critical Perspectives on* The Well of Loneliness (New York: Columbia University Press, 2001).

Doane, Janice L., *Silence and Narrative: The Early Novels of Gertrude Stein* (Westport: Greenwood Press, 1986).

Doyle, Laura, 'The Flat, the Round, and Gertrude Stein: Race and the Shape of Modern(ist) History', *Modernism/Modernity* 7:2 (2000), pp. 249–71.

Drucker, Johanna, *Theorizing Modernism: Visual Art and the Critical Tradition* (New York: Columbia University Press, 1994).

Dubnick, Randa, *The Structure of Obscurity: Gertrude Stein, Language, and Cubism* (Chicago and Urbana: University of Illinois Press, 1984).

—, 'Two Types of Obscurity in the Writings of Gertrude Stein' in Richard Kostelanetz (ed.), *Gertrude Stein Advanced: An Anthology of Criticism* (Jefferson, NC: McFarland and Company, 1990), pp. 63–84.

Dydo, Ulla, *Gertrude Stein: The Language That Rises. 1923–1934* (Evanston: Northwestern University Press, 2003).

— (ed.), *A Stein Reader* (Evanston: Northwestern University Press, 1993).

Eby, Carl P., *Hemingway's Fetishism: Psychoanalysis and the Mirror of Manhood* (Albany: SUNY Press, 1998).

Edelman, Lee, *No Future: Queer Theory and the Death Drive* (Durham, NC: Duke University Press, 2004).

Elfenbein, Andrew, *Romantic Genius: The Prehistory of a Homosexual Role* (New York: Columbia University Press, 1999).

Elliott, Bridget, and Jo-Ann Wallace, *Women Artists and Writers: Modernist (im)positionings* (New York: Routledge, 1994).

Elliot, Patricia, and Katrina Roen, 'Transgenderism and the Question of Embodiment: Promising Queer Politics?' *GLQ: A Journal of Lesbian and Gay Studies* 4:2 (1998), pp. 231–61.

Engelbrecht, Penelope, '"Lifting Belly Is a Language": The Postmodern Lesbian Subject', *Feminist Studies* 16:1 (1990), pp. 85–114.

Fantina, Richard, *Ernest Hemingway: Machismo and Masochism* (New York: Palgrave, 2005).

Fifer, Elizabeth, *Rescued Readings: A Reconstruction of Gertrude Stein's Difficult Texts* (Detroit: Wayne State University Press, 1992).

Folgarait, Leonard, *Painting 1909: Pablo Picasso, Gertrude Stein, Henri Bergson, Comics, Albert Einstein, and Anarchy* (New Haven: Yale University Press, 2017).

Ford, Sara, *Gertrude Stein and Wallace Stevens: The Performance of Modern Consciousness* (New York: Routledge, 2002).

Foucault, Michel, 'Friendship as a Way of Life', in Paul Rabinow (ed.), *Ethics: Subjectivity and Truth* (New York: New Press, 1997), pp. 135–40.

—, *The History of Sexuality, Vol. 1* (New York: Vintage Books, 1990).

—, 'The Social Triumph of the Sexual Will', in Paul Rabinow (ed.), *Ethics: Subjectivity and Truth* (New York: New Press, 1997), pp. 157–62.

—, 'What Is an Author?' in Donald F. Bouchard (ed.), *Language, Counter-memory, Practice* (Ithaca: Cornell University Press, 1977), pp. 113–38.

Freccero, Carla, *Queer / Early / Modern* (Durham, NC: Duke University Press, 2006).

—, 'Queer Times', in Janet Halley and Andrew Parker (eds), *After Sex? On Writing Since Queer Theory* (Durham, NC: Duke University Press, 2011), pp. 17–26.

Freeman, Elizabeth, 'Hopeless Cases: Queer Chronicities and Gertrude Stein's "Melanctha"', *Journal of Homosexuality* 63:3 (2016), pp. 329–48.

—, 'Introduction: Queer Temporalities', *GLQ: A Journal of Lesbian and Gay Studies* 13:2–3 (2007), pp. 159–76.

—, *Time Binds: Queer Temporalities, Queer Histories* (Durham, NC and London: Duke University Press, 2010).

Friedman, Ellen G. and Miriam Fuchs, 'Contexts and Continuities: An Introduction to Women's Experimental Fiction in English', in Ellen G. Friedman and Miriam Fuchs (eds), *Breaking the Sequence: Women's Experimental Fiction* (Princeton: Princeton University Press, 1989), pp. 3–51.

Friedman, Susan Stanford, 'Women's Autobiographical Selves: Theory and Practice', in Shari Benstock (ed.), *The Private Self: Theory and Practice of Women's Autobiographical Writings* (Chapel Hill: The University of North Carolina Press, 1988), pp. 34–62.

Freud, Sigmund, 'Creative Writers and Day-Dreaming', in Ethel Spector Person, Peter Fonagy, Sérvulo Augusto Figueira (eds), *On Freud's 'Creative Writers and Day-dreaming'* (London: Karnac, 2013), pp. 3–14.

—, *The Interpretation of Dreams* (New York: Avon Books, 1965).

Frost, Elisabeth, *The Feminist Avant-Garde in American Poetry* (Iowa City: University of Iowa Press, 2003).

Fuss, Diana, *Identification Papers* (London and New York: Routledge, 1995).

Gallup, Donald, 'The Making of *The Making of Americans*', in Gertrude Stein, *Fernhurst, Q.E.D., and Other Early Writings* (New York: Liveright, 1971), pp. 173–214.

Garb, Tamar, '"To Kill the Nineteenth Century": Sex and Spectatorship with Gertrude and Pablo', in Christopher Green (ed.), *Picasso's 'Les Demoiselles d'Avignon'* (Cambridge: Cambridge University Press, 2001), pp. 55–76.

—, *The Painted Face: Portraits of Women in France, 1814–1914* (New Haven and London: Yale University Press, 2007).

Garrity, Jane, and Tirza True Latimer, 'Queer Cross-gender Collaboration', in Hugh Stevens (ed.), *The Cambridge Companion to Gay and Lesbian Writing* (Cambridge: Cambridge University Press, 2011), pp. 185–201.

Gates, Jr, Henry Louis, 'Writing, "Race", and the Difference It Makes', in David H. Richter (ed.), *The Critical Tradition: Classic Texts and Contemporary Trends* (New York: Bedford/St. Martin's, 2007), pp. 1891–902.

Gherovici, Patricia, 'The Art of the Symptom: Body, Writing, and Sex Change', in Laura Marcus and Ankhi Mukherjee (eds), *A Concise Companion to Psychoanalysis, Literature, and Culture* (Hoboken, NJ: John Wiley & Sons, 2014), pp. 250–70.

—, 'The Transsexual Body Written: Writing as Sinthome', in *The Literary Lacan: From Literature to Lituraterre and Beyond* (London and New York: Seagull Books, 2012), pp. 259–90.

Gilbert, Sandra, and Susan Gubar, *No Man's Land: The Place of the Woman Writer in the Twentieth Century. Vol. 1: The War of the Words* (New Haven: Yale University Press, 1988).

—, *No Man's Land: The Place of the Woman Writer in the Twentieth Century. Vol. 2: Sexchanges* (New Haven: Yale University Press, 1989).

Gilmore, Leigh, 'A Signature of Lesbian Autobiography', in *Autobiographies: A Feminist Theory of Women's Self-Representation* (Ithaca: Cornell University Press, 1994), pp. 199–223.

Giroud, Vincent, *Picasso and Gertrude Stein* (New Haven and New York: Yale University Press and the Metropolitan Museum of Art, 2007).

Glass, Loren, *Authors Inc. Literary Celebrity in the Modern United States, 1880–1980* (New York: NYU Press, 2004).

Glavey, Brian, *The Wallflower Avant-Garde: Modernism, Sexuality, and Queer Ekphrasis* (Oxford: Oxford University Press, 2016).

Goldman, Jonathan, *Modernism is the Literature of Celebrity* (Austin: University of Texas Press, 2011).

Grahn, Judy, *Really Reading Gertrude Stein* (Freedom, CA: The Crossing Press, 1989).

Griffin, Peter, *Less Than a Treason: Hemingway in Paris* (New York: Oxford University Press, 1990).

Gygax, Franziska, 'The Portrait as Word and (A)Head: Gertrude Stein and the Staging of (Her)Self', in Beverly Maeder (ed.), *The Seeming and the Seen: Essays in Modern Visual and Literary Culture* (New York: Peter Lang, 2006), pp. 209–24.

Halberstam, J. Jack, *Female Masculinity* (Durham, NC: Duke University Press, 1998).

—, *In a Queer Time and Place* (New York: NYU Press, 2005).

—, *The Queer Art of Failure* (Durham, NC: Duke University Press, 2011).

Hall, Radclyffe, *The Well of Loneliness* [1928] (New York: Knopf, 1990).

Hall, Stuart, 'Notes on Deconstructing "the Popular"', in Imre Szeman and Timothy Kaposy (eds), *Cultural Theory: An Anthology* (West Sussex: Wiley-Blackwell, 2011), pp. 72–80.

Hanneman, Audre, *Ernest Hemingway: A Comprehensive Bibliography* (Princeton: Princeton University Press, 1967).

—, *Supplement to Ernest Hemingway: A Comprehensive Bibliography* (Princeton: Princeton University Press, 1975).

Hanson, Ellis (2016), 'Kink in Time', *b2o*, 6 October 2016, http://www.boundary2.org/2016/10/ellis-hanson-kink-in-time/ (last accessed 19 September 2017).

Haralson, Eric, *Henry James and Queer Modernity* (Cambridge: Cambridge University Press, 2003).

Harrison, Charles, Francis Frascina and Gill Perry, *Primitivism, Cubism, Abstraction: The Early Twentieth Century* (New Haven: Yale University Press / The Open University, 1993).

Haselstein, Ulla, 'Gertrude Stein's Portraits of Matisse and Picasso', *New Literary History* 34:4 (2003), pp. 723–43.

Heldrich, Philip, 'Connecting Surfaces: Gertrude Stein's *Three Lives*, Cubism, and the Metonymy of the Short Story Cycle', *Studies in Short Fiction* 34:4 (1997), pp. 427–39.

Hemingway, Ernest, 'The Art of the Short Story' in Jackson J. Benson (ed.), *New Critical Approaches to the Short Stories of Ernest Hemingway* (Durham, NC: Duke University Press, 1990), pp. 1–13.

—, *Ernest Hemingway: Selected Letters, 1917–1961*, ed. Carlos Baker (New York: Scribner's, 1981).

—, 'The Farm', *Cahiers d'art* 9 (1934), n.p.

—, *Green Hills of Africa* (New York: Scribner's, 1935).

—, *In Our Time* [1925], (New York: Scribner, 2003).

—, 'Introduction' to Jimmie Charters, *This Must Be the Place: Memoirs of Montparnasse* (London: Herbert Joseph, 1934), pp. 11–13.

—, *The Letters of Ernest Hemingway, 1923–1925*, ed. Sandra Spanier, Albert J. Defazio III, and Robert W. Trogdon (Cambridge: Cambridge University Press, 2013).

—, *A Moveable Feast*, The Restored Edition (New York: Scribner, 2009).

—, *A Moveable Feast* (New York: Scribner, 1964).

—, 'Part Six A Serious and Vivid Account of a Dramatic Moment in the Cruel Sport' [1924], in *88 Poems* (New York: Harcourt Brace Javanovich, 1979), pp. 73.

—, 'Part Two of the Soul of Spain with McAlmon and Bird the Publishers' [1924], in *88 Poems* (New York: Harcourt Brace Javanovich, 1979), pp. 72.

—, 'The Soul of Spain with McAlmon and Bird the Publishers' [1924], in *88 Poems* (New York: Harcourt Brace Javanovich, 1979), pp. 70–3.

—, *The Torrents of Spring* [1926], in Charles Poore (ed.), *A Hemingway Reader* (New York: Scribner's, 1953).

—, 'The True Story of My Break with Gertrude Stein', in 'My Own Life' in *The New Yorker* (12 February 1927), pp. 23–4.

Hemingway, Mary Welsh, *The Way It Was* (New York: Alfred A. Knopf, 1976).

Hemingway, Séan, 'Introduction' to Ernest Hemingway, *A Moveable Feast*, The Restored Edition (New York: Scribner, 2009), pp. 1–13.

Herring, Scott, *Queering the Underworld: Slumming, Literature, and the Undoing of Gay and Lesbian History* (Chicago and London: University of Chicago Press, 2007).

Hilder, Jamie, '"After all one must know more than one sees and one does not see a cube in its entirety": Gertrude Stein and Picasso and Cubism', *Critical Survey* 17:3 (2005), pp. 66–84.

Hoffman, Michael, *Gertrude Stein* (Boston: Twayne, 1976).

Holbrook, Susan, 'Lifting Bellies, Filling Petunias, and Making Meanings through the Trans-Poetic', *American Literature* 71:4 (1999), pp. 751–71.

Hovey, Jaime, 'Sapphic Primitivism in Gertrude Stein's *Q.E.D.*', *Modern Fiction Studies* 42:3 (1996), pp. 547–68.

—, *A Thousand Words: Portraiture, Style, and Queer Modernism* (Columbus: The Ohio State University Press, 2006).

Irigaray, Luce, *This Sex Which Is Not One* (Ithaca: Cornell University Press, 1985).

—, *Speculum of the Other Woman* (Ithaca: Cornell University Press, 1985).

Jaillant, Lise, '*Shucks, we've got glamour girls too!* Gertrude Stein, Bennett Cerf and the Culture of Celebrity', *Journal of Modern Literature* 39:1 (Fall 2015), pp. 149–69.

Johnston, Georgia, *The Formation of 20th-Century Queer Autobiography* (New York: Palgrave, 2007).

—, 'Narratologies of Pleasure: Gertrude Stein's *The Autobiography of Alice B. Toklas*', *Modern Fiction Studies* 42:3 (1996), pp. 590–606.

Jones, Howard Mumford, 'Introduction' to *Dark Laughter* by Anderson (New York: Liveright, 1953), pp. 1–7.

Kahnweiler, Daniel-Henry, 'Introduction', in Gertrude Stein, *The Yale Edition of the Unpublished Writings of Gertrude Stein*, Vol. 5 (Freeport, NY: Books for Libraries Press, 1969), pp. ix–xviii.

Kale, Verna, 'Hemingway's Poetry and the Paris Apprenticeship', *The Hemingway Review* 26:2 (2007), pp. 58–73.

Katz, Leon, 'Introduction', in Gertrude Stein, *Fernhurst, Q.E.D., and Other Early Writings* (New York and London: Liveright, 1973), pp. ix–xliii.

Keats, John, *Selected Letters of John Keats*, Revised Edition (Cambridge, MA: Harvard University Press, 2005).

Kellner, Bruce, 'Baby Woojums in Iowa', *Books at Iowa* 26 (April 1977), p. 5.

—, *Carl Van Vechten and the Irreverent Decades* (Norman: University of Oklahoma Press, 1968).

Kennedy, J. Gerald, and Kirk Curnutt, 'Out of the Picture: Mrs. Krebs, Mother Stein, and "Soldier's Home"', *The Hemingway Review* 12:1 (1992), pp. 1–11.

Kent, Kathryn, *Making Girls into Women: American Women's Writing and the Rise of Lesbian Identity* (Durham, NC: Duke University Press, 2003).

Knapp, Bettina, *Gertrude Stein* (New York: Continuum, 1990).

Kosman, Joshua, '"Four Saints in Three Acts" review: silly, naïve', *San Francisco Chronicle*, 23 August 2011, http://www.sfgate.com/performance/article/Four-Saints-in-Three-Acts-review-silly-naive-2334361.php (last accessed 20 September 2017).

Krauss, Rosalind, 'In the Name of Picasso', in *The Originality of the Avant-Garde and Other Modernist Myths* (Cambridge, MA: The MIT Press, 1985), pp. 23–41.

Kristeva, Julia, *Desire in Language: A Semiotic Approach to Literature and Art* (New York: Columbia University Press, 1980).

—, *Revolution in Poetic Language* (New York: Columbia University Press, 1984).

Lacan, Jacques, 'The agency of the letter in the unconscious, or reason since Freud', in *Écrits: A Selection*, trans. Alan Sheridan (New York: Norton, 1977), pp. 146–78.

—, 'The mirror stage as formative of the function of the I', in *Écrits: A Selection*, trans. Alan Sheridan (New York: Norton, 1977), pp. 1–7.

—, *The Four Fundamental Concepts of Psycho-Analysis*, trans. Alan Sheridan (New York: Norton, 1981).

—, *The Seminar of Jacques Lacan, Book III: The Psychoses 1955–56*, trans. Russell Grigg (New York: Norton, 1993).

—, *The Seminar of Jacques Lacan. Book XX: Encore, 1972–1973. On Feminine Sexuality, the Limits of Love and Knowledge*, trans. Bruce Fink (New York: W. W. Norton, 1998).

—, *The Seminar of Jacques Lacan, Book XXIII: The Sinthome 1975–1976*, trans. A. R. Price (Cambridge: Polity, 2016).

LaPlanche, Jean, and J. B. Pontalis, *The Language of Psycho-Analysis*, trans. Donald Nicholson-Smith (New York: W. W. Norton, 1973).

Larsen, Lyle, *Stein and Hemingway: The Story of a Turbulent Friendship* (Jefferson, NC: McFarland & Company, 2011).

Larson, Kelli A., 'Bibliographical Essay: Lies, Damned Lies, and Hemingway Criticism', in Linda Wagner-Martin (ed.), *A Historical Guide to Ernest Hemingway* (Oxford: Oxford University Press, 2000), pp. 213–34.

Lawrence, Karen R., 'Who Could Have Read the Signs? Politics and Prediction in Gertrude Stein's *Mrs. Reynolds* and Christine Brooke-Rose's *Amalgamemnon*', *The Western Humanities Review* 59:2 (2005), pp. 18–38.

Leick, Karen, *Gertrude Stein and the Making of an American Celebrity* (New York: Routledge, 2009).

Lesinska, Zofia, 'Gertrude Stein's War Autobiographies: Reception, History, and Dialogue', *Literature Interpretation Theory* 9:4 (1999), pp. 313–43.

Lewis, Wyndham. 'The "Dumb Ox"', 1934, in *Men Without Art* (New York: Russell & Russell, 1964), pp. 17–41.

Lodge, David, *The Modes of Modern Writing: Metaphor, Metonymy, and the Typology of Modern Literature* (Ithaca: Cornell University Press, 1977).

Lorange, Astrid, *How Reading Is Written: A Brief Index to Gertrude Stein* (Middletown, CT: Wesleyan University Press, 2014).

Love, Heather, *Feeling Backward: Loss and the Politics of Queer History* (Cambridge, MA: Harvard University Press, 2007).

Lubar, Robert, 'Unmasking Pablo's Gertrude: Queer Desire and the Subject of Portraiture', *The Art Bulletin* 79 (March 1997), pp. 57–84.

Lundén, Rolf, 'Men in Love? Male Friendship in Gertrude Stein's Early Portrait', *Modernism/Modernity* 18:2 (2011), pp. 335–54.

Lynn, Kenneth S., *Hemingway* (New York: Simon and Schuster, 1987).

McCabe, Susan, '"A Queer Lot" and the Lesbians of 1914: Amy Lowell, H.D., and Gertrude Stein', in Joyce W. Warren and Margaret Dickie (eds), *Challenging Boundaries: Gender and Periodization* (Athens: The University of Georgia Press, 2000), pp. 62–90.

McCallum, E. L., 'Stein *und Zeit*', in E. L. McCallum and Mikko Tuhkanen (eds), *Queer Times, Queer Becomings* (Albany: SUNY Press, 2011).

Mackey, Nathaniel, 'Other: From Noun to Verb', in *The Jazz Cadence of American Culture* (New York: Columbia University Press, 1998), pp. 513–32.

MacLeod, Kirsten, 'The "Librarian's Dream-Prince": Carl Van Vechten and America's Modernist Cultural Archives Industry', *Libraries and the Cultural Record* 46:4 (2011), pp. 360–87.

Madeline, Laurence, 'Preface' to Pablo Picasso and Gertrude Stein, *Correspondence* (New York: Seagull Books, 2008), pp. ix–xxiii.

—, 'The Road to Belley', in Pablo Picasso and Gertrude Stein, *Correspondence* (New York: Seagull Books, 2008), pp. 251–7.

Malcolm, Janet, *Two Lives: Gertrude and Alice* (New Haven: Yale University Press, 2008).

Mark, Rebecca, 'Introduction', in Gertrude Stein, *Lifting Belly* (Tallahassee: Naiad Press, 1989), pp. xi–xxxiv.

Martin, Biddy, *Femininity Played Straight: The Significance of Being Lesbian* (New York: Routledge, 1996).

Martin, Robert K., '*The Mother of Us All* and American History', in Shirely Neuman and Ira B. Nadel (eds), *Gertrude Stein and the Making of Literature*, pp. 210–22.

Meese, Elizabeth, 'Gertrude Stein and Me: A Revolution in the Letter', in *(Sem):Erotics: Theorizing Lesbian: Writing* (New York: New York University Press, 1992), pp. 63–83.

Mellow, James, *Charmed Circle: Gertrude Stein & Company* (New York: Avon, 1974).

Melnikova-Raich, Sonia, 'Exhibit leaves out how Gertrude Stein survived Holocaust', 9 June 2011, https://www.jweekly.com/2011/06/10/exhibit-leaves-out-how-gertrude-stein-survived-holocaust/ (last accessed 19 September 2017).

Merrill, Cynthia, 'Gertrude Stein and Autobiography', *Pacific Coast Philology* 20:1–2 (1985), pp. 11–17.

Meyers, Jeffrey, *Hemingway: A Biography* (New York: Da Capo Press, 1999).

Millot, Catherine, *Horsexe* (New York: Autonomedia, 1991).

Mills, Jean E, 'Gertrude Stein Took The War Like A Man', *The Gay and Lesbian Review* 10:2 (2003), pp. 16–18.

Mitrano, G. F., *Gertrude Stein: Woman without Qualities* (London: Ashgate, 2005).

Mix, Deborah, *A Vocabulary of Thinking: Gertrude Stein and Contemporary North American Women's Innovative Writing* (Iowa City: University of Iowa Press, 2007).

Moddelmog, Debra A., *Reading Desire: In Pursuit of Ernest Hemingway* (Ithaca: Cornell University Press, 1999).

Moon, Michael, 'Do You Smoke? Or, Is There Life? After Sex?', in Janet Halley and Andrew Parker (eds), *After Sex? On Writing Since Queer Theory* (Durham, NC: Duke University Press, 2011), pp. 55–65.

Mozgovaya, Natasha, 'Obama corrects controversial Jewish Heritage Month proclamation', *Haaretz*, 3 May 2012, http://www.haaretz.com/jewish/obama-corrects-controversial-jewish-heritage-month-proclamation-1.427880 (last accessed 20 September 2017).

Mulvey, Laura, 'Visual Pleasure and Narrative Cinema', in Vincent B. Leitch et al. (eds), *The Norton Anthology of Theory and Criticism* (New York: Norton, 2001), pp. 2179–92.

Munt, Sally (ed.), *Butch/Femme: Inside Lesbian Gender* (London: Cassell, 1998).

Nair, Sashi, *Secrecy and Sapphic Modernism: Reading 'Romans à Clef' between the Wars* (New York: Palgrave, 2012).

Nestle, Joan (ed.), *The Persistent Desire: A Femme-Butch Reader* (Boston: Alyson, 1992).

Neuman, Shirley, and Ira B. Nadel (eds), *Gertrude Stein and the Making of Literature* (Boston: Northeastern University Press, 1988).

Nevius, C. W., 'Guard cracks down on hand-holding at Stein exhibit', *The San Francisco Chronicle*, 19 July 2011, http://www.sfgate.com/bayarea/nevius/article/Guard-cracks-down-on-hand-holding-at-Stein-exhibit-2354117.php (last accessed 20 September 2017).

Norris, Margot, 'The "Wife" and the "Genius": Domesticating Modern Art in Stein's *Autobiography of Alice B. Toklas*', in Lisa Rado (ed.), *Modernism, Gender, and Culture: A Cultural Studies Approach* (New York: Garland, 1997), pp. 79–99.

North, Michael, 'Modernism's African Mask: The Stein-Picasso Collaboration', in *The Dialect of Modernism: Race, Language, and Twentieth-Century Literature* (Oxford: Oxford University Press, 1994), pp. 59–76.

—, *Reading 1922: A Return to the Scene of the Modern* (New York and Oxford: Oxford University Press, 1999).

Olivier, Fernande, *Picasso and his Friends* [1933], trans. Jane Miller (New York: Appleton-Century, 1965).

Olson, Liesl, 'Gertrude Stein, William James, and Habit in the Shadow of War', *Twentieth-Century Literature* 49:3 (2003), pp. 328–59.

Page, Barbara, 'Women Writers and the Restive Text: Feminism, Experimental Writing and Hypertext', *Postmodern Culture* 6:2 (1996).

Pavloska, Susanna, *Modern Primitives: Race and Language in Gertrude Stein, Ernest Hemingway, and Zora Neale Hurston* (New York and London: Garland, 2000).

Perloff, Marjorie, 'The Extra: "Ninety Percent Rotarian": Gertrude Stein's Hemingway', *American Literature* 62:4 (1990), pp. 668–83.

—, '"A Fine New Kind of Realism": Six Stein Styles in Search of a Reader', in *Poetic License: Essays on Modernist and Postmodernist Lyric* (Evanston: Northwestern University Press, 1990), pp. 145–59.

—, 'Poetry as Word-System', in *The Poetics of Indeterminacy: Rimbaud to Cage* (Evanston: Northwestern University Press, 1981), pp. 67–108.

Peterson, Carla, 'The Remaking of Americans: Gertrude Stein's "Melanctha" and African-American Musical Traditions', in Henry B. Wonham (ed.), *Criticism and the Color Line: Desegregating American Literary Studies* (New Brunswick, NJ: Rutgers University Press, 1996), pp. 140–57.

Picasso, Pablo, and Gertrude Stein, *Correspondence* (New York: Seagull Books, 2008).

Piper, Adrian, 'The Logic of Modernism', *Callaloo* 16:3 (1993), pp. 574–8.

Pollack-Pelzner, Daniel, 'Swiping Stein: The Ambivalence of Hemingway Parodies', *The Hemingway Review* 30.1 (2010), pp. 69–82.

Pound, Ezra, *Make It New: Essays by Ezra Pound* (New Haven: Yale University Press, 1935).

Preston, John Hyde, 'A Conversation with Gertrude Stein', in Linda Simon (ed.), *Gertrude Stein Remembered* (Lincoln: University of Nebraska Press, 1994), pp. 153–65.

Prosser, Jay. *Second Skins: The Body Narratives of Transsexuality* (New York: Columbia University Press, 1998).

Puar, Jasbir K., *Terrorist Assemblages: Homonationalism in Queer Times* (Durham, NC and London: Duke University Press, 2007).

Ragland, Ellie, *The Logic of Sexuation: From Aristotle to Lacan* (Albany: State University of New York Press, 2004).

Recker, Laurel, 'Pitting "Matisse" Against "Picasso": Gertrude Stein's Companion Portraits', *Arizona Quarterly* 72:4 (2016), pp. 27–52.

Rehling, Nicola, 'Taking Patriarchy out of Poetry: Eroticism and Subversion in Gertrude Stein's *Lifting Belly*', *Gramma: Journal of Theory and Criticism* 4 (1996), pp. 77–87.

Retallack, Joan, 'High Adventures in Indeterminacy', *Parnassus* 11:1 (1983), pp. 231–63.

Reynolds, Michael, *Hemingway in the 1930s* (New York: Norton, 1997).

—, *Hemingway: The Paris Years* (Oxford and Cambridge, MA: Blackwell, 1989).

Richardson, John, *A Life of Picasso. Vol. I: 1881–1906* (New York: Random House, 1991).

—, *A Life of Picasso. Vol. III: The Triumphant Years* (New York: Knopf, 2010).

Riggs, Damien W., 'Editorial: Trans Bodies, Lives and Representations', *Gay & Lesbian Issues and Psychology Review* 7:1 (2011), pp. 1–2.

Roberts, Mary Louise, 'Samson and Delilah Revisited: The Politics of Fashion in 1920s France', in Whitney Chadwick and Tirza True Latimer (eds), *The Modern Woman Revisited: Paris Between the Wars* (New Brunswick, NJ: Rutgers University Press, 2003), pp. 65–94.

Rohy, Valerie, 'Hemingway, Literalism, and Transgender Reading', *Twentieth-Century Literature* 57:2 (Summer 2011), pp. 148–79.

Roof, Judith, *What Gender Is, What Gender Does* (Minneapolis: University of Minnesota Press, 2016).

Rose, Jacqueline, *Sexuality in the Field of Vision* (London: Verso, 1986).

Rowe, John Carlos, 'Naming What Is Inside: Gertrude Stein's Use of Names in *Three Lives*', *Novel* 36:2 (Spring 2003), pp. 219–43.

Rubin, Gayle, 'Of Catamites and Kings: Reflections on Butch, Gender, and Boundaries', in Joan Nestle (ed.), *The Persistent Desire: A Femme-Butch Reader* (Boston: Alyson Publications, 1992), pp. 466–82.

Ruddick, Lisa, *Reading Gertrude Stein: Body, Text, Gnosis* (Ithaca: Cornell University Press, 1990).

Rule, Jane *Lesbian Images* (Trumansburg, NY: The Crossing Press, 1982).

Ruti, Mari, 'The Fall of Fantasies: A Lacanian Reading of Lack', *Journal of the American Psychoanalytic Association* 56:2 (2008), pp. 483–508.

—, 'Life beyond Fantasy: The Rewriting of Destiny in Lacanian Theory' *Culture, Theory, and Critique* 51:1 (2010), pp. 1–14.

—, 'Why There Is Always a Future in the Future', *Angelaki* 13:1 (2008), pp. 113–26.

Salamon, Gayle, *Assuming a Body: Transgender and Rhetorics of Materiality* (New York: Columbia University Press, 2010).

Sanderson, Rena, 'Hemingway and Gender History', in *The Cambridge Companion to Ernest Hemingway*, ed. Scott Donaldson (Cambridge: Cambridge University Press, 1996), pp. 170–96.

Sayre, Henry M., 'The Artist's Model: American Art and the Question of Looking like Gertrude Stein', in Shirely Neuman and Ira B. Nadel (eds), *Gertrude Stein and the Making of Literature* (Boston: Northeastern University Press, 1988), pp. 21–41.

Schmigel, Frank, 'Gertrude Stein Live!' (Public lecture delivered at the San Francisco Museum of Modern Art, San Francisco, California, 7 June 2011.)

Schmitz, Neil, *Of Huck and Alice: Humorous Writing in American Literature* (Minneapolis: University of Minnesota Press, 1983).

—, 'Portrait, Patriarchy, Mythos: The Revenge of Gertrude Stein', *Salmagundi* 40 (1978), pp. 69–91.

Schuster, Joshua, 'The making of "Tender Buttons": Gertrude Stein's subjects, objects, and the illegible', in *Jacket 2* at https://jacket2.org/article/making-tender-buttons (last accessed 19 September 2017).

Schwartz, Daniel R., *Reconfiguring Modernism: Explorations in the Relationship between Modern Art and Modern Literature* (New York: St. Martin's, 1997).

Scobie, Stephen, 'The Allure of Multiplicity: Metaphor and Metonymy in Cubism and Gertrude Stein', in Shirely Neuman and Ira B. Nadel (eds), *Gertrude Stein and the Making of Literature* (London: Macmillan, 1988), pp. 98–118.

—, *Earthquakes and Explorations: Language and Painting from Cubism to Concrete Poetry* (Toronto, Buffalo and London: University of Toronto Press, 1997).

Secor, Cynthia, 'Gertrude Stein: The Complex Force of her Femininity', in Kenneth W. Wheeler and Virginia Lee Lussier (eds), *Women, the Arts, and the 1920s in Paris and New York* (New Brunswick: Transaction Books, 1982), pp. 27–35.

Sedgwick, Eve Kosofsky, *Between Men: English Literature and Male Homosocial Desire* (New York: Columbia University Press, 1985).

—, 'Preface' to *Between Men: English Literature and Male Homosocial Desire* (New York: Columbia University Press, 1992).

—, *Tendencies* (Durham, NC: Duke University Press, 1993).

—, *Touching Feeling: Affect, Pedagogy, Performativity* (Durham, NC: Duke University Press, 2003).

Sengoopta, Chandak, *Otto Weininger: Sex, Science, and Self in Imperial Vienna* (Chicago: University of Chicago Press, 2000).

Shepherdson, Charles, 'The *Role* of Gender and the *Imperative* of Sex', in *Vital Signs: Nature, Culture, Psychoanalysis* (New York: Routledge, 2000), pp. 85–114.

Silver, Brenda, *Virginia Woolf Icon* (Chicago: University of Chicago Press, 1999).

Silverman, Kaja, 'The Lacanian Phallus,' *differences* 4:1 (1992), pp. 84–115.

—, *The Threshold of the Visible World* (New York: Routledge, 1996).

Simon, Linda, *The Biography of Alice B. Toklas* (Garden City: Doubleday, 1977).

Siraganian, Lisa, *Modernism's Other Work: The Art Object's Political Life* (Oxford: Oxford University Press, 2012).

—, 'Out of Air: Theorizing the Art Object in Gertrude Stein and Wyndham Lewis', *Modernism/Modernity* 10:4 (2003), pp. 657–76.

—, 'Speculating on an Art Movement: Gertrude Stein's *The Autobiography of Alice B. Toklas*', *Modern Fiction Studies* 59:3 (2013), pp. 591–609.

Skinner, B. F., 'Has Gertrude Stein a Secret?' *Atlantic Monthly* 153 (1934), pp. 50–7.

Smalls, James, *The Homoerotic Photography of Carl Van Vechten* (Philadelphia: Temple University Press, 2006).

Smith, Shawn Michelle, *Photography on the Color Line* (Durham, NC: Duke University Press, 2004).

Smith, Sidonie, *Subjectivity, Identity, and the Body: Women's Autobiographical Practices in the Twentieth Century* (Bloomington: Indiana University Press, 1993).

Souhami, Diana, *Gertrude and Alice* (London: Pandora, 1991).

Spilka, Mark, *Hemingway's Quarrel with Androgyny* (Lincoln and London: University of Nebraska Press, 1990).

St. Pierre, Scott, 'Bent Hemingway: Straightness, Sexuality, Style', *GLQ: A Journal of Lesbian and Gay Studies* 16:3 (2010), pp. 363–87.

Stein, Gertrude, 'Ada' [1922], in Ulla Dydo (ed.), *A Stein Reader* (Evanston: Northwestern University Press, 1993), pp. 100–3.

—, 'An American and France' [1936], in Robert Bartlett Haas (ed.), *What are Masterpieces* (New York: Pitman, 1970), pp. 61–70.

—, 'As A Wife Has A Cow A Love Story' [1926], in *A Book Concluding With As A Wife Has A Cow A Love Story*, in Ulla Dydo (ed.), *A Stein Reader* (Evanston: Northwestern University Press, 1993), pp. 451–66.

—, *The Autobiography of Alice B. Toklas* [1933], in Carl Van Vechten (ed.), *Selected Writings of Gertrude Stein* (New York: Vintage, 1990), pp. 1–237.

—, *Baby Precious Always Shines: Selected Love Notes Between Gertrude Stein and Alice B. Toklas*, Ed. Kay Turner (New York: St. Martin's Press, 1999).

—, 'Composition as Explanation' [1926], in Carl Van Vechten (ed.), *Selected Writings of Gertrude Stein* (New York: Vintage, 1990), pp. 511–24.

—, 'Every Afternoon' [1922], in *Geography and Plays* (Madison: University of Wisconsin Press, 1993), pp. 254–9.

—, *Everybody's Autobiography* [1937] (Cambridge: Exact Change, 1993).

—, 'Evidence' [1930], in *Reflection on the Atomic Bomb* (Los Angeles: Black Sparrow Press, 1973), pp. 153–4.

—, 'Evidence', in Ulla Dydo (ed.), *A Stein Reader* (Evanston: Northwestern University Press, 1993), pp. 541–6.

—, *Fernhurst, Q.E.D., and Other Writings* (New York: Liveright, 1971).

—, 'Genuine Creative Ability' [1930], in Robert Bartlett Haas (ed.), *A Primer for the Gradual Understanding of Gertrude Stein* (Los Angeles: Black Sparrow Press, 1973), pp. 104–5.

—, *The Geographical History of America or the Relation of Human Nature to the Human Mind* [1936] (New York: Vintage, 1973).

—, 'Gertrude Stein: A Radio Interview', *The Paris Review* 116 (Fall 1990).

—, 'He and They, Hemingway' [1923], in Ulla Dydo (ed.), *A Stein Reader* (Evanston: Northwestern University Press, 1993).

—, 'How Writing Is Written' [1938], in Bonnie Kime Scott (ed.), *The Gender of Modernism: A Critical Anthology* (Bloomington: Indiana University Press, 1990).

—, 'Identity A Poem' [1940], in Ulla Dydo (ed.), *A Stein Reader* (Evanston: Northwestern University Press, 1993), pp. 588–94.

—, 'If I Told Him A Completed Portrait of Picasso' [1924], in Ulla Dydo (ed.), *A Stein Reader* (Evanston: Northwestern University Press, 1993), pp. 464–6.

—, 'Lifting Belly' [1953], in *The Yale Gertrude Stein* (New Haven: Yale University Press, 1980), pp. 4–54.

—, *The Making of Americans* [1925] (Normal: Dalkey Archive Press, 1995).

—, 'Men' [1951], in *Two: Gertrude Stein and Her Brother and Other Early Portraits [1908–12]* (New Haven: Yale University Press, 1951), pp. 310–15.

—, 'Objects Lie on a Table' [1932], in *Operas & Plays* (Barrytown, NY: Station Hill Arts, 1998).

—, 'One Carl Van Vechten' [1922], in Ulla Dydo (ed.), *A Stein Reader* (Evanston: Northwestern University Press, 1993), pp. 273–5.

—, *Paris France* [1940] (New York and London: Liveright, 1970).

—, 'Patriarchal Poetry' [1953], in *The Yale Gertrude Stein* (New Haven: Yale University Press, 1980), pp. 106–46.

—, *Picasso* [1938], in *Gertrude Stein on Picasso* (New York: Liveright, 1970).

—, 'Picasso' [1912], in Ulla Dydo (ed.), *A Stein Reader* (Evanston: Northwestern University Press, 1993).

—, 'Poetry and Grammar' [1935], in *Lectures in America* (Boston: Beacon Press, 1985), pp. 209–46.

—, 'Portraits and Repetition' [1935], in *Lectures in America* (Boston: Beacon Press, 1985), pp. 165–208.

—, 'Sacred Emily' [1922], in *Geography and Plays* (Madison: University of Wisconsin Press, 1993), pp. 178–88.

—, 'Sentences and Paragraphs' [1931], in *How to Write* (Los Angeles: Sun & Moon Press, 1995), pp. 19–32.

—, 'A Sonatina Followed By Another' [1953], in *The Yale Gertrude Stein* (New Haven: Yale University Press, 1980), pp. 287–315.

—, *Tender Buttons* [1914], in Carl Van Vechten (ed.), *The Selected Writings of Gertrude Stein* (New York: Vintage, 1990), pp. 459–509.

—, *Three Lives* [1909] (New York: Vintage, 1936).

—, '*Three Lives* and *Q.E.D.*' (New York: W. W. Norton, 2006).

—, 'A Transatlantic Interview' [1962–4], in Bonnie Kime Scott (ed.), *The Gender of Modernism* (Bloomington: Indiana University Press, 1990), pp. 502–16.

—, 'An Unpublished Portrait of Van Vechten, 1923', in Edward Burns (ed.), *The Letters of Gertrude Stein and Carl Van Vechten, 1913–1946* (New York: Columbia University Press, 2013), pp. 864–6.

—, 'Van or Twenty Years After: A Second Portrait of Carl Van Vechten' [1924], in Ulla Dydo (ed.), *A Stein Reader* (Evanston: Northwestern University Press, 1993), pp. 462–3.

—, 'What Are Masterpieces and Why Are There So Few of Them' [1940], in Bonnie Kime Scott (ed.), *The Gender of Modernism: A Critical Anthology* (Bloomington: Indiana University Press, 1990), pp. 495–501.

Stein, Gertrude, and Carl Van Vechten, *The Letters of Gertrude Stein and Carl Van Vechten, 1913–1946*, ed. Edward Burns (New York: Columbia University Press, 2013).

Steiner, Wendy, *Exact Resemblance to Exact Resemblance: The Literary Portraiture of Gertrude Stein* (New Haven: Yale University Press, 1978).

—, 'Postmodernist Portraits', *Art Journal* 46:3 (1987), pp. 173–7.

Stendahl, Renate, 'Why the witch-hunt against Gertrude Stein?', in *Gertrude Stein's war years: Setting the record straight*, in *Jacket 2*, available at https://jacket2.org/feature/gertrude-steins-war-years-setting-record-straight (last accessed 19 September 2017).

Stephens, Paul, 'What Do We Mean by "Literary Experimentalism"?: Notes Toward a History of the Term', *Arizona Quarterly* 68:1 (2012), pp. 143–73.

Steward, Samuel, 'The Memoir', in *Dear Sammy: Letters from Gertrude Stein and Alice B. Toklas* (Boston: Houghton Mifflin, 1977), pp. 1–117.

—, *Murder is Murder is Murder* (Boston: Alyson Publications, 1985).

Stimpson, Catharine, 'Gertrice/Altrude: Stein, Toklas, and the Paradox of the Happy Marriage', in Ruth Perry and Martine Watson Brownley (eds), *Mothering the Mind: Twelve Studies of Writers and their Silent Partners* (New York: Holmes and Maier, 1984), pp. 122–39.

—, 'Gertrude Stein and the Lesbian Lie', in Kirk Curnutt (ed.), *The Critical Response to Gertrude Stein* (Westport, CT: Greenwood, 2000), pp. 309–24.

—, 'Gertrude Stein and the Transposition of Gender', in Nancy K. Miller (ed.), *The Poetics of Gender* (New York: Columbia University Press, 1986), pp. 1–18.

—, 'The Mind, the Body, and Gertrude Stein', in *Critical Inquiry* 3 (1977), pp. 489–506.

—, 'The Somagrams of Gertrude Stein', in Henry Abelove, Michèle Aina Barale and David M. Halperin (eds), *The Lesbian and Gay Studies Reader* (New York: Routledge, 1993), pp. 642–52.

Stimpson, Catharine et al., 'A Play to Be Performed: Excerpts from the Gertrude Stein Symposium at New York University', *Theater* 32:2 (2002), pp. 2–25.

Stockton, Kathryn Bond, 'Rhythm', in E. L. McCallum and Mikko Tuhkanen (eds), *Queer Times, Queer Becomings* (Albany: SUNY Press, 2011).

Stone, Sandy, 'The *Empire* Strikes Back: A Posttranssexual Manifesto', *Camera Obscura* 10:2 (1992), pp. 150–76.

Stringer, Dorothy, *Not Even Past: Race, Historical Trauma, and Subjectivity in Faulkner, Larsen, and Van Vechten* (New York: Fordham University Press, 2009).

Strychacz, Thomas, *Hemingway's Theaters of Masculinity* (Baton Rouge: Louisiana State University Press, 2003).

Stryker, Susan, *Transgender History* (Berkeley: Seal Press, 2008).

Stryker, Susan, and Aren Z. Aizura, 'Introduction: Transgender Studies 2.0', in Aren Aizura and Susan Stryker (eds), *The Transgender Studies Reader 2* (New York: Routledge, 2013), pp. 1–12.

Stryker, Susan, and Paisley Currah, 'Introduction', *TSQ: Transgender Studies Quarterly* 1:1–2 (2014), pp. 1–5.

Stryker, Susan, Paisley Currah and Lisa Jean Moore, 'Introduction: Trans-, Trans, or Transgender', in *WSQ: Women's Studies Quarterly* 36:3–4 (2008), pp. 11–22.

Sutherland, Donald, 'Alice and Gertrude and Others', *Prairie Schooner* 45:4 (1971–2), pp. 284–99.

—, *Gertrude Stein: A Biography of Her Work* (New Haven: Yale University Press, 1951).

Tavernier-Courbin, Jacqueline, *Ernest Hemingway's A Moveable Feast: The Making of a Myth* (Boston: Northeastern University Press, 1991).

Thaggart, Miriam, *Images of Black Modernism: Verbal and Visual Strategies of the Harlem Renaissance* (Amherst and Boston: University of Massachusetts Press, 2010).

Thomas, Kate, '"What Time We Kiss": Michael Field's Queer Temporalities"', *GLQ: A Journal of Lesbian and Gay Studies* 13:2–3 (2007), pp. 327–51.

Thompson, Aidan, 'Language and Democracy: Meaning Making as Existing in the Work of Gertrude Stein', *Arizona Quarterly* 69:3 (2013), pp. 129–55.

Toklas, Alice B., *The Alice B. Toklas Cookbook* [1954] (New York: Harper & Row, 1984).

—, *What Is Remembered* [1963] (New York: Holt, Rinehart and Winston, 1963).

Trask, Michael, *Cruising Modernism: Class and Sexuality in American Literature and Social Thought* (Ithaca: Cornell University Press, 2003).

Turner, Kay, 'This "Very Beautiful Form of Literature": An Introduction to the Love Notes Between Gertrude Stein and Alice B. Toklas', in Gertrude Stein, *Baby Precious Always Shines: Selected Love Notes Between Gertrude Stein and Alice B. Toklas* (New York: St. Martin's Press, 1999), pp. 1–37.

Van Dusen, Wanda, 'Portrait of a National Fetish: Gertrude Stein's "Introduction to the Speeches of Maréchal Pétain." 1942', *Modernism/Modernity* 3:3 (1996), pp. 69–92.

Van Pymbroeck, Birgit, 'Triangular Politics: Stein, Bernard Fäy, and Elisabeth de Gramont', in Sarah Posman and Laura Luise Schultz (eds), *Gertrude Stein in Europe: Reconfigurations Across Media, Disciplines, and Traditions* (London: Bloomsbury, 2015), pp. 85–103.

Van Vechten, Carl, 'Gertrude Stein', in *We Moderns* (New York: Gotham Book Mart, 1939), pp. 63.

—, 'Igor Strawinsky: A New Composer', in Paul Padgette (ed.), *The Dance Writings of Carl Van Vechten* (New York: Dance Horizons, 1980), pp. 107–16.

—, 'Portraits of the Artists', *Esquire*, December 1962, pp. 170–4, 256–8.

—, 'Some "Literary Ladies" I Have Known', in *Fragments from an Unwritten Biography* (New Haven: Yale University Press, 1955), pp. 19–64.

Voris, Linda, *The Composition of Sense in Gertrude Stein's Landscape Writing* (London: Palgrave, 2016).

—, 'Interpreting Cézanne: Immanence in Gertrude Stein's First Landscape Play, *Lend A Hand or Four Religions*', *Modernism/Modernity* 19:1 (2012), pp. 73–93.

—, '"Shutters shut and open": making sense of Gertrude Stein's second portrait of Picasso', *Studies in American Fiction* 39:2 (Fall 2012), pp. 175–205.

Wagner-Martin, Linda, *'Favored Strangers': Gertrude Stein and Her Family* (New Brunswick, NJ: Rutgers University Press, 1995).

Walker, Jayne, *The Making of a Modernist: Gertrude Stein from 'Three Lives' to 'Tender Buttons'* (Amherst: The University of Massachusetts Press, 1984).

Weinberg, Jonathan, '"Boy Crazy": Carl Van Vechten's Queer Collection', *The Yale Journal of Criticism* 7:2 (1994), pp. 25–49.

Weiner, Joshua J., and Damon Young, 'Introduction: Queer Bonds', *GLQ: A Journal of Lesbian and Gay Studies* 17:2–3 (2011), pp. 223–41.

Weininger, Otto, *Sex and Character: An Investigation of Fundamental Principles* [1903], (Bloomington: Indiana University Press, 2005).

Weiss, M. Lynn, '"Among Negroes": Gertrude Stein and African America', in Heather Hathaway, Josef Jarab and Jeffrey Melnick (eds), *Race and the Modern Artist* (Oxford: Oxford University Press, 2003), pp. 115–25.

Weston, Kath, *Families We Choose: Lesbians, Gays, Kinship*, Revised Edition (New York: Columbia University Press, 1991).

White, Edward, *The Tastemaker: Carl Van Vechten and the Birth of Modern Man* (New York: Farrar, Straus and Giroux, 2014).

Whittier-Ferguson, John, 'The Liberation of Gertrude Stein: War and Writing', *Modernism/Modernity* 8:3 (2001), pp. 405–28.

—, 'Stein in Time: History, Manuscripts, and Memory'. *Modernism/Modernity* 6:1 (1999), pp. 115–51.

Whittle, Stephen, 'Foreward', in Susan Stryker and Stephen Whittle (eds), *The Transgender Studies Reader* (New York and London: Routledge, 2006), pp. xi–xvi.

Will, Barbara, *Gertrude Stein, Modernism, and the Problem of "Genius"* (Edinburgh: Edinburgh University Press, 2000).

—, 'Lost in Translation: Stein's Vichy Collaboration', *Modernism/Modernity* 11:4 (2004), pp. 651–68.

—, *Unlikely Collaboration: Gertrude Stein, Bernard Fäy, and the Vichy Dilemma* (New York: Columbia University Press, 2011).

Wineapple, Brenda, 'Gertrude Stein and the Lost Ark', in Kirk Curnutt (ed.), *The Critical Response to Gertrude Stein* (Westport, CT: Greenwood, 2000), pp. 344–52.

—, 'The Politics of Politics; or, How the Atomic Bomb Didn't Interest Gertrude Stein and Emily Dickinson', *South Central Review* 23:3 (Fall 2006), pp. 37–45.

Woolf, Virginia, *Mrs. Dalloway* [1925] (New York: Harcourt, 2005).

—, *Orlando* [1928] (New York: Harcourt, 2006).

—, *To the Lighthouse* [1927] (New York: Harcourt, 2005).

Wyatt, David, *Hemingway, Style, and the Art of Emotion* (Cambridge: Cambridge University Press, 2015).

Zox-Weaver, Annalisa, *Women Modernists and Fascism* (Cambridge: Cambridge University Press, 2011).

Index